AI REGULATION IN EUROPE: EU AI ACT EXPLAINED

By

Olga Markova

First Edition 2026

Disclaimer

This publication is provided for general information and professional reference purposes only. It does not constitute legal advice. Laws, regulations, and regulatory guidance may change, and the application of legal principles depends on the specific facts of each situation. Independent professional advice should be obtained before acting on the content of this publication.

Digital editions of this publication are available under separate individual and institutional licence terms.

ISBN: 978-1-909316-01-0

Printed on demand.

Table of Contents

Page

Page

OLGA MARKOVA

Introduction

On 13 June 2024, the European Parliament and the Council issued EU Regulation 2024/1689 laying down harmonised rules on artificial intelligence[1] (**EU AI Act**). The EU AI Act is a comprehensive piece of EU legislation. It is made up of 113 articles, preceded by 180 paragraphs of the Preamble that set out the objectives of the AI Regulation and assist with interpretation using a purposive approach. The EU AI Act operates 68 definitions and has 13 Annexes that set out specific technical parameters essential for its implementation.

The legal basis of the EU AI Act is the Treaty on the Functioning of the European Union (**TFEU**), in particular its Articles 16 and 114. Among other matters, these Articles confer on the European Council legislative, budgetary, policy-making and coordinating functions[2] and upon the European Parliament and Council - the power to adopt harmonisation legislation for the purpose of establishment and functioning of the EU internal market[3].

The adoption process of the EU AI Act included the proposal from the European Commission, the transmission

---

[1] OJ L, 2024/1689, 12.7.2024; *https://eur-lex.europa.eu/legal-content/EN/ALL/?uri=CELEX:32024R1689*. Regulation 2024/1689 also amends Regulations (EC) No 300/2008, (EU) No 167/2013, (EU) No 168/2013, (EU) 2018/858, (EU) 2018/1139 and (EU) 2019/2144 and Directives 2014/90/EU, (EU) 2016/797 and (EU) 2020/1828

[2] Para 1 Article 16 TFEU.

[3] Para 1 Article 114 TFEU.

of the draft legislative act to the national parliaments, obtaining the opinions of the European Economic and Social Committee[4], the European Central Bank[5], and the Committee of the Regions[6]. The European Data Protection Supervisor and the European Data Protection Board were consulted and delivered their joint opinion on 18 June 2021.[7] The ordinary legislative procedure[8] was used to adopt the EU AI Act.

The EU AI Act contains a series of provisions that explain how it is intended to interact with EU legislation covering other areas affected by AI systems.

Thus, the EU AI Act does not impact –

- the EU rules related to consumer protection and product safety;[9]
- the liability of providers of intermediary services;[10]
- the protection of personal data, privacy and the confidentiality of communications;[11]

---

[4] OJ C 517, 22.12.2021, p. 56.

[5] OJ C 115, 11.3.2022, p. 5.

[6] OJ C 97, 28.2.2022, p. 60.

[7] Paragraph (180) Preamble of the EU AI Act; Article 42(1) and (2) of Regulation (EU) 2018/1725.

[8] Para 1 Article 114 TFEU; Position of the European Parliament of 13 March 2024 and decision of the Council of 21 May 2024.

[9] Article 2(9) EU AI Act.

[10] Article 2(5) EU AI Act; Chapter II of Regulation (EU) 2022/2065.

[11] Articles 2(7), 10(5) and 59; Regulations (EU) 2016/679, (EU) 2018/1725, and Directives 2002/58/EC and (EU) 2016/680.

- more favourable legal rules or collective agreements existing or introduced in the future by the EU or its Member States to protect the rights of workers in respect of the use of AI systems by employers.[12]

The purpose of the EU AI Act is "*to improve the functioning of the internal market and promote the uptake of human-centric and trustworthy artificial intelligence (AI), while ensuring a high level of protection of health, safety, fundamental rights enshrined in the Charter*[13]*, including democracy, the rule of law and environmental protection, against the harmful effects of AI systems in the Union and supporting innovation.*"[14].

The EU AI Act seeks to improve the functioning of the internal market by "*laying down a uniform legal framework in particular for the development, the placing on the market, the putting into service and the use of artificial intelligence systems (AI systems) in the Union, in accordance with Union values*"[15].

The EU AI Act further seeks to ensure the free cross-border movement of AI-based goods and services, preventing Member States from imposing restrictions that

---

[12] Article 2(11) EU AI Act.

[13] The Charter of Fundamental Rights of the European Union (Para (1) Preamble EU AI Act)

[14] Article 1(1) EU AI Act.

[15] Recital (1) EU AI Act.

are not explicitly authorised by the Act itself, on the development, marketing and use of AI systems[16].

To this end, the EU AI Act sets out:

- harmonised rules for the placing on the market, the putting into service, and the use of AI systems in the Union[17];
- prohibitions of certain AI practices[18];
- specific requirements for high-risk AI systems and obligations for operators of such systems[19];
- harmonised transparency rules for certain AI systems[20];
- harmonised rules for the placing on the market of general-purpose AI models[21];
- rules on market monitoring, market surveillance, governance and enforcement[22];
- measures to support innovation, with a particular focus on SMEs, including start-ups[23].

A notable ambition of the EU AI Act is to make the EU a leader in the uptake of trustworthy AI[24].

This book analyses the EU AI Act and its implementation. It is intended as a reference guide for legal practitioners, deployers, providers, importers, distributors

---

[16] Recital (1) EU AI Act.
[17] Article 1(2)(a) EU AI Act.
[18] Article 1(2)(b) EU AI Act.
[19] Article 1(2)(c) EU AI Act.
[20] Article 1(2)(d) EU AI Act.
[21] Article 1(2)(e) EU AI Act.
[22] Article 1(2)(f) EU AI Act.
[23] Article 1(2)(g) EU AI Act.
[24] Recital (2) EU AI Act.

of AI systems, students of law and computer science, and everyone interested in the regulation of AI in the European Union.

PART 1. AI REGULATORY BODIES: EU LEVEL

CHAPTER 1. The Commission

The EU AI Act confers on the Commission a number of powers and imposes a number of obligations. This Chapter describes these powers and obligations.

1.1 Standardisation Requests

With effect from 2 August 2026[25], the EU AI Act requires the Commission to issue, without undue delay, standardisation requests to EU standardisation organisations[26]. The standardisation requests must cover:

- the EU AI Act requirements to high-risk AI systems that concern risk management systems, data and data governance, technical documentation, record-keeping, transparency and provision of information to deployers, human oversight, accuracy, robustness and security[27]; and
- obligations of providers and authorised representatives of providers of general-purpose AI models, including those with systemic risk[28].

---

[25] Article 113 EU AI Act.

[26] Article 40(2) EU AI Act.

[27] ibid; these obligations are set out in Chapter III, Section 2 EU AI Act. The power to send these requests is conferred on the Commission by Article 10 of Regulation (EU) No 1025/2012.

[28] Article 40(2) EU AI Act; these obligations are set out in Chapter V, Sections 2 and 3 EU AI Act.

The standardisation request must ask for deliverables on reporting and documentation processes to improve AI systems' resource performance, such as reducing the high-risk AI system's consumption of energy and of other resources during its lifecycle, and on the energy-efficient development of general-purpose AI models[29]. When preparing a standardisation request, the Commission must consult the European Artificial Intelligence Board and relevant stakeholders, including the advisory forum[30].

When issuing a standardisation request to European standardisation organisations, the Commission must specify that standards have to be:

- clear and consistent with the standards developed in the various sectors for products covered by the existing EU harmonisation legislation[31]; and
- aim to ensure that high-risk AI systems or general-purpose AI models placed on the market or put into service in the EU meet the requirements or obligations laid down in the EU AI Act[32].

The Commission must request the European standardisation organisations to provide evidence of their best efforts to fulfil these objectives[33].

---

[29] Article 40(2) EU AI Act

[30] *Ibid.*

[31] The list of the harmonisation legislation is set out in Annex I of the EU AI Act.

[32] Article 40(2) EU AI Act

[33] *Ibid*; Article 24 of Regulation (EU) No 1025/2012.

The EU AI Act further requires the participants in the standardisation process to:

- seek to promote investment and innovation in AI, including through increasing legal certainty, competitiveness and growth of the EU market[34];
- contribute to strengthening global cooperation on standardisation and taking into account existing international standards in the field of AI that are consistent with EU values, fundamental rights and interests[35]; and
- enhance multi-stakeholder governance ensuring a balanced representation of interests and the effective participation of all relevant stakeholders[36].

1.2 Common specifications

With effect from 2 August 2026[37], the EU AI Act permits the Commission to adopt implementing acts establishing common specifications for:

- the requirements to high-risk AI Systems[38]; and

---

[34] Article 40(3) EU AI Act and Articles 5, 6, and 7 of Regulation (EU) No 1025/2012.

[35] *Ibid.*

[36] *Ibid.*

[37] Article 113 EU AI Act.

[38] The requirements to high-risk AI systems are set out in Section 2 Chapter III EU AI Act.

- the obligations of providers of general-purpose AI models including those with systemic risk[39].

However, this power of the Commission is restricted to the circumstances where the following conditions have been fulfilled[40]:

- the Commission has requested[41] one or more European standardisation organisations to draft a harmonised standard for these requirements, and[42]:
    - the request has not been accepted by any of the European standardisation organisations[43]; or
    - the harmonised standards addressing the request are not delivered within the deadline set by the Commission[44]; or
    - the harmonised standards insufficiently address concerns about fundamental rights[45]; or
    - the harmonised standards do not comply with the request[46]; and

---

[39] These obligations are set out in Sections 2 and 3 Chapter V EU AI Act.

[40] Article 41(1) EU AI Act.

[41] This request is made pursuant to Article 10(1) of Regulation (EU) No 1025/2012.

[42] Article 41(1)(a) EU AI Act.

[43] Article 41(1)(a)(i) EU AI Act.

[44] Article 41(1)(a)(ii) EU AI Act. Article 10(1) of Regulation (EU) No 1025/2012 permits the Commission to set the deadline in its request.

[45] Article 41(1)(a)(iii) EU AI Act.

[46] Article 41(1)(a)(iv) EU AI Act.

- no reference to harmonised standards covering the requirements to high-risk AI systems or, as applicable, general-purpose AI models including those with systemic risk has been published in the Official Journal of the European Union[47], and no such reference is expected to be published within a reasonable period[48].

Before preparing a draft implementing act, the Commission must inform the committee of representatives of the EU Member States[49] that it considers these conditions to be fulfilled[50].

When drafting the common specifications, the Commission must consult the advisory forum[51].

The implementing acts must be adopted in accordance with the examination procedure[52] which involves voting by the committee of representatives of the EU Member States. The Commission will adopt an implementing act if the committee issues, by a majority vote, a positive opinion. If the committee issues a negative opinion, the chair of the Commission will either deliver an amended implementing act to the same committee or

---

[47] Regulation (EU) No 1025/2012 provides for this publication.

[48] Article 41(1)(b) EU AI Act.

[49] For the particulars of the committee see Article 22 of Regulation (EU) No 1025/2012.

[50] Article 41(2) EU AI Act.

[51] Articles 41(1) and 67 EU AI Act.

[52] Articles 41(1) and 98(2) EU AI Act; the examination procedure is detailed in Article 5 Regulation (EU) No 182/2011.

submit the rejected implementing act to the appeal committee.

Where a European standardisation organisation adopts a harmonised standard and proposes to the Commission to publish its reference in the Official Journal of the European Union, the Commission must assess the harmonised standard[53]. When reference to a harmonised standard is published in the Official Journal of the European Union, the Commission must repeal the Commission's implementing acts, or their parts, which cover the same requirements as the harmonised standard[54].

Where a Member State considers that a common specification does not entirely meet the requirements of the EU AI Act for which the common specification is intended, the Member State must inform the Commission with a detailed explanation[55]. The Commission must assess that information and, if appropriate, amend the implementing act that establishes the common specification concerned[56].

High-risk AI systems or general-purpose AI models which conform to the common specifications adopted by the Commission, or parts of those specifications, shall be presumed to conform to the EU AI Act's requirements or obligations, to the extent the common specifications cover

---

[53] Article 41(4) EU AI Act. For requirements to the assessment of the harmonized standard see Regulation (EU) No 1025/2012.

[54] Article 41(4) EU AI Act.

[55] Article 41(6) EU AI Act.

[56] *Ibid.*

those requirements or obligations[57]. But where providers of high-risk AI systems or general-purpose AI models do not comply with the common specifications, they must prove that they have adopted technical solutions that meet the EU AI requirements covered by the common specifications to a level at least equivalent to the common specification[58].

1.3 Annual reports on the Use of real-time remote biometric identification systems in publicly accessible spaces for law enforcement purposes

Effective from 2 August 2026[59], the EU AI Act requires the Commission to publish annual reports on the use of real-time remote biometric identification systems in publicly accessible spaces for law enforcement purposes, based on aggregated data in Member States on the basis of the annual reports submitted by the Member States[60]. Those annual reports shall not include sensitive operational data of the related law enforcement activities[61].

So, when is the first Commission's report due? The Commission's obligation to publish these reports enters into force on 2 August 2026[62]. Does this mean that the first

---

[57] Article 41(3) EU AI Act.
[58] Article 41(5) EU AI Act.
[59] Article 113 EU AI Act.
[60] Article 5(7) EU AI Act.
[61] *Ibid.*
[62] Article 113 EU AI Act.

report is due on the same day? Or is it a year later, on 2 August 2027, a year from the date on which this requirement enters into effect? The obligation of the Member States to submit these annual reports to the Commission entered into force on 2 February 2025[63], so it would be logical to expect the first reports from the Member States to be submitted by 2 February 2026, the first anniversary of this obligation's entry into force. This would allow for 6 months for the Commission to issue its report by 2 August 2026. However, it remains to be seen if this is what will happen in practice.

1.4 High-Risk AI Systems Classification Guidelines

The EU AI Act requires the Commission, after consulting the European Artificial Intelligence Board, and not later than 2 February 2026, to provide guidelines specifying the practical implementation of the classification of AI systems as high-risk, together with a comprehensive list of practical examples of uses of AI systems that are high-risk and not high-risk[64]. At the time of writing[65], the Commission has yet to issue these Guidelines.

[63] Articles 5(7) and 113(a) EU AI Act.
[64] Article 6(5) EU AI Act.
[65] 28 February 2026.

1.5 Identification Numbers and Lists of Notified Bodies

Notified bodies are conformity assessment bodies[66] notified by the Member State notifying authorities to the Commission[67].

Effective from 2 August 2025, the EU AI Act requires the Commission to:

- assign a single identification number to each notified body, even where a body is notified under more than one EU act[68]; and
- make the list of notified bodies under the EU AI Act publicly available, including their identification numbers and the activities for which they have been notified, and keep the list up to date [69].

The Commission has implemented the technical infrastructure for this list, and the list can be downloaded from its website[70]. But at the time of writing[71] notified bodies have yet to be published on the list, even though the obligation of the notifying authorities to notify the

---

66 Article 3(22) EU AI Act.

67 Article 30(2) EU AI Act.

68 Article 35(1) EU AI Act.

69 Article 35(2) EU AI Act.

70 See https://webgate.ec.europa.eu/single-market-compliance-space/notified-bodies/notified-body-list?filter=legislationId:168380,notificationStatusId:1 .

71 28 February 2026 is the date of my last check of the list of notified bodies before publication of this book.

Commission about its notified bodies came into force on 2 August 2025[72].

1.6 Conformity Assessment Procedures

Effective from 2 August 2026[73], the EU AI Act empowers the Commission to adopt delegated acts in order to update the conformity assessment procedures in light of technical progress[74] and (or) to subject high-risk AI systems that are at present eligible for the internal control method to the conformity assessment procedure involving a notified body[75].

When adopting these delegated acts, the EU AI Act requires the Commission to take into account the effectiveness of the conformity assessment procedure based on internal control in preventing or minimising the risks to health and safety and protection of fundamental rights posed by such systems, and the availability of adequate capacities and resources among notified bodies[76].

1.7 Investigations of Notified Bodies

Effective from 2 August 2025, the EU AI Act requires the Commission, where necessary, to investigate

---

[72] Article 113(b) EU AI Act.
[73] Article 113 EU AI Act.
[74] Article 43(5) EU AI Act.
[75] Article 43(6) EU AI Act.
[76] *Ibid.*

all cases where there are reasons to doubt the competence of a notified body[77] or the continued fulfilment by it of the requirements and responsibilities prescribed by the EU AI Act for notified bodies[78]. To this end, the EU AI Act requires the notifying authority to provide the Commission, on request, with all relevant information relating to the designation or the continuing competence of the conformity assessment body being investigated by the Commission[79]. The Commission must ensure that all sensitive information obtained in the course of its investigations is treated confidentially[80].

Where the Commission establishes that a notified body fails to meet its designation requirements, the Commission must inform the EU Member State where the notified body was designated and request it to take the necessary corrective measures, including the suspension or withdrawal of the designation if necessary[81]. Where the EU Member State fails to take the necessary corrective measures, the Commission may, by means of an

[77] Notified bodies are conformity assessment bodies notified by the Member State notifying authorities to the Commission (Articles 3(22) and 30(2) EU AI Act.

[78] Article 37(1) EU AI Act.

[79] Article 37(2) EU AI Act.

[80] Articles 37(3) and 78 EU AI Act.

[81] Article 37(4) EU AI Act.

implementing act[82], suspend, restrict or withdraw the designation[83].

At the time of writing[84], no notified bodies are published on the Commission's list[85] and no information is available about the Commission's investigations or whether the Commission adopted any implementing acts affecting designations of any notified bodies.

1.8 Coordination of Conformity Assessment Bodies

With effect from 2 August 2025, the EU AI Act requires the Commission to ensure appropriate coordination and cooperation with regard to high-risk AI systems between conformity assessment bodies[86]. To this end, the Commission is required to ensure putting in place and proper operation of a sectoral group of conformity assessment bodies[87] and exchange of knowledge and best practices between notifying authorities[88]. At the same time,

---

[82] The Commission must adopt the implementing in accordance with the examination procedure set out in Article 98(2) EU AI Act (Article 37(4) EU AI Act).

[83] Article 37(4) EU AI Act.

[84] 28 February 2026.

[85] See https://webgate.ec.europa.eu/single-market-compliance-space/notified-bodies/notified-body-list?filter=legislationId:168380,notificationStatusId:1

[86] Article 38(1) EU AI Act.

[87] *Ibid.*

[88] Article 38(3) EU AI Act.

each notifying authority must ensure that the conformity assessment bodies approved by it participate in the work of the sectoral group, directly or through designated representatives[89].

At the time of writing[90], notified bodies have yet to be notified to the Commission and no sectoral group exists.

1.9 EU Declaration of Conformity

With effect from 2 August 2026[91], the EU AI Act empowers the Commission to adopt delegated acts in order to update the content of the EU declaration of conformity prescribed by the EU AI Act, in order to introduce elements that become necessary in light of technical progress[92]. The deferred enactment of this power suggests that until at least August 2026 the declaration of conformity adopted by the EU AI Act will remain the same[93].

---

[89] Article 38(2) EU AI Act.

[90] 28 February 2026.

[91] Article 113 EU AI Act.

[92] Article 47(5) EU AI Act.

[93] The content of the declaration of conformity is set out in Article 47(2) and Annex V EU AI Act.

1.10 Thresholds, Benchmarks and Indicators for Classification of General-Purpose AI Models as General-Purpose AI Models with Systemic Risk

Effective from 2 August 2025[94], the EU Act empowered the Commission to adopt delegated acts to amend and update the criteria[95] for classification of general-purpose AI models as general-purpose AI models with systemic risk.

In addition, effective from the same date, the EU Act empowered the Commission to amend the thresholds for classification of general-purpose AI model as general-purpose AI models with systemic risk and to supplement benchmarks and indicators in light of evolving technological developments, such as algorithmic improvements or increased hardware efficiency, when necessary, for these thresholds to reflect the state of the art[96].

At the time of writing[97], the Commission has yet to adopt these delegated acts[98].

---

[94] Article 113(b) EU AI Act.

[95] Article 52(4) and Annex III AU AI Act.

[96] Article 51(3) EU AI Act.

[97] 28 February 2026.

[98] See the Commission's Interinstitutional register of Delegated Acts here: https://webgate.ec.europa.eu/regdel/#/delegatedActs?lang=en

1.11 Updating of Technical Documentation Requirements for General-Purpose AI Models

With effect from 2 August 2025[99], the EU AI Act empowered the Commission to adopt delegated acts to detail measurement and calculation methodologies[100]. This power of the Commission is intended to allow for comparable and verifiable documentation[101] compliant with the EU AI Act's requirements[102], in particular as regards:

- the computational resources used to train the model (e.g. number of floating point operations), training time, and other relevant details related to the training[103]; and
- known or estimated energy consumption of the model[104],

In addition, effective from the same date, the EU AI Act empowered the Commission to adopt delegated acts to amend the information (including transparency information) required to be included in the technical documentation by providers of general-purpose AI models including those with systemic risk) in light of evolving technological developments[105].

---

[99] Article 113(b) EU AI Act.

[100] Articles 53(5) and 97 EU AI Act.

[101] *Ibid.*

[102] The requirements to technical documentation are listed in Annex XI of the EU AI Act.

[103] Article 53(5) and Annex XI point 2(d) EU AI Act.

[104] Article 53(5) and Annex XI point 2(e) EU AI Act.

[105] Articles 53(6) and 97(2) and Annexes XI and XII EU AI Act.

At the time of writing[106], the Commission has yet to adopt these delegated acts[107].

1.12 Confidentiality of Information Obtained from Providers of General-Purpose AI Models

With effect from 2 August 2025[108], the EU AI Act requires the Commission to treat any information or documentation obtained from providers of general-purpose AI models, including trade secrets, in accordance with the EU AI Act's confidentiality obligations[109].

1.13 Quality Management System Guidelines for Microenterprises

With effect from 2 August 2026[110], the EU AI Act requires the Commission to develop guidelines on the elements of the quality management system which may be complied with by microenterprises in a simplified manner considering the needs of microenterprises, without affecting

---

[106] 28 February 2026.

[107] See the Commission's Interinstitutional Register of Delegated Acts here: https://webgate.ec.europa.eu/regdel/#/delegatedActs?lang=en

[108] Article 113(b) EU AI Act.

[109] Articles 53(7) and 78 EU AI Act.

[110] Article 113 EU AI Act.

the level of protection or the need for compliance with the requirements in respect of high-risk AI systems[111].

At the time of writing, the Commission has yet to issue these guidelines[112].

1.14 EU AI Systems Database

With effect from 2 August 2026[113], the EU AI Act requires the Commission, in collaboration with the Member States, to set up and maintain an EU database of high-risk AI systems and AI systems that are not considered as high-risk[114]. When setting the functional specifications of such database, the Commission must consult the relevant experts, and when updating the functional specifications of such database, the Commission must consult the Board[115].

The EU AI Act appoints the Commission as the controller of the EU database and requires the Commission to make adequate technical and administrative support available to providers, prospective providers and deployers [116]. The EU database must comply with the applicable accessibility requirements[117].

---

[111] Article 63(1) EU AI Act.

[112] 28 February 2026.

[113] Article 113 EU AI Act.

[114] Article 71(1) EU AI Act.

[115] *Ibid.*

[116] Article 71(6) EU AI Act.

[117] *Ibid.* The accessibility requirements are those set out in Directives (EU) 2016/2102 and (EU) 2019/882.

With the exception of the restricted section of the database[118], the information contained in the EU database must be accessible, publicly available in a user-friendly manner, easily navigable and machine-readable[119]. The information concerning the testing of the high-risk AI systems must be accessible only to market surveillance authorities and the Commission, unless the prospective provider or provider has given consent for also making the information accessible to the public[120].

The EU database must contain personal data only in so far as necessary for collecting and processing information in accordance with the EU AI Act[121]. That information must include the names and contact details of natural persons who are responsible for registering the system and have the legal authority to represent the provider or, as applicable, the deployer[122].

The effective date of these obligations of the Commission is 2 August 2026[123]. But AI systems embedded in regulated products, pending their classification as high-risk from 2 August 2027[124], would need to be registered in the database first as not high-risk, and from 2 August 2027 re-registered as high risk. It

---

[118] Articles 71(4), 49(4) and 60(4)(c) EU AI Act.
[119] Article 71(4) EU AI Act.
[120] *Ibid.*
[121] Article 71(5) EU AI Act.
[122] *Ibid.*
[123] Article 113 EU AI Act.
[124] Article 113(c) EU AI Act.

remains to be seen how the database is implemented in practice.

1.15 Post-Market Monitoring Plan Template

By 2 February 2026, the EU AI Act requires the Commission to adopt an implementing act laying down detailed provisions establishing a template for the post-market monitoring plan and the list of elements to be included in the plan[125]. At the time of writing[126], the Commission has yet to adopt this implementing act.

1.16 Serious Incident Guidance

By 2 August 2025, the EU AI Act requires the Commission to develop and assess regularly the dedicated guidance for providers and deployers to report serious incidents[127].

At the time of writing[128], this guidance is work in progress. On 26 September 2025, the Commission issued draft guidance and reporting template on serious AI incidents and invited stakeholders' feedback by 07 November 2025[129]. The obligation of providers and

---

[125] Article 72(3) EU AI Act.
[126] 28 February 2026.
[127] Article 73(7) EU AI Act.
[128] 28 February 2026.
[129] https://digital-strategy.ec.europa.eu/en/consultations/ai-act-commission-issues-draft-guidance-and-reporting-template-serious-ai-incidents-and-seeks

deployers to report serious incidents will be effective from 2 August 2026[130], so early issuance of the guidelines will help the providers and deployers to prepare for the reporting.

1.17 EU AI testing support structures

Effective from 2 August 2026[131], the EU AI Act requires the Commission to designate one or more EU AI testing support structures to perform the following tasks in the area of AI[132]:

- carry out testing of products at the request of market surveillance authorities, the EU product compliance network or the Commission[133];
- provide independent technical or scientific advice at the request of the EU product compliance network[134]; and
- develop new techniques and methods of analysis[135].

In addition, effective from the same date[136], the EU AI Act requires the Commission to provide independent

---

[130] Article 113 EU AI Act.

[131] *Ibid.*

[132] Article 84(1) EU AI Act; the tasks are listed in Article 21(6) Regulation (EU) 2019/1020.

[133] Article 21(6)(a) Regulation (EU) 2019/1020.

[134] Article 21(6)(b) Regulation (EU) 2019/1020; the EU product compliance network was established by Article 29 of Regulation (EU) 2019/1020.

[135] Article 21(6)(c) Regulation (EU) 2019/1020.

[136] Article 113(b) EU AI Act.

technical or scientific advice at the request of the Board, the Commission, or of market surveillance authorities[137].

1.18 EU AI Act Implementation Guidelines

The EU AI Act requires the Commission to develop a series of guidelines on the practical implementation of the EU AI Act[138]. I summarise these in the table overleaf.

The guidelines must take due account of the generally acknowledged state of the art on AI, as well as of relevant harmonised standards[139] and common specifications[140], or of the harmonised standards or technical specifications pursuant to EU harmonisation law[141].

When issuing the guidelines, the EU AI Act requires the Commission to pay particular attention to the needs of SMEs including start-ups, of local public authorities and of the sectors most likely to be affected by the EU AI Act.

The EU AI Act also requires the Commission to update the previously adopted guidelines, on its own

---

[137] Article 84(2) EU AI Act.

[138] Article 96(1) EU AI Act.

[139] The harmonised standards are those referred to in Article 40 EU AI Act.

[140] The common specifications are those referred to in Article 41 EU AI Act.

[141] Article 96(1) EU AI Act.

initiative and, when the Commission deems necessary, if requested by the Member States or the AI Office[142].

[142] Article 96(2) EU AI Act.

EU AI Act Implementation Guidelines

Guidelines Subject Matter	Due Date	Status at 28 February 2026
Guidelines on prohibited AI practices[143]	2 August 2026 for the Guidelines[144], but the AI Act provisions on prohibited AI practices came into force on 2 February 2025[145].	Published on 04 February 2025[146].

[143] Articles 5 and 96(1)(b) EU AI Act.
[144] Article 113 EU AI Act.
[145] Article 113(a) EU AI Act.
[146] https://digital-strategy.ec.europa.eu/en/library/commission-publishes-guidelines-prohibited-artificial-intelligence-ai-practices-defined-ai-act

Guidelines Subject Matter	**Due Date**	**Status at 28 February 2026**
Guidelines on application of the definition of an AI system[147]	2 August 2026[148] for the Guidelines but the definition of AI system came into force on 2 February 2025[149].	Published on 06 February 2025[150].
Guidelines on the scope of obligations for providers of general-purpose AI models	2 August 2025[151] for the obligations of providers of general-purpose AI models; no	Published on 18 July 2025[152]

[147] Articles 3(1) and 96(1)(f) EU AI Act.
[148] Article 113 EU AI Act.
[149] Article 113(a) EU AI Act.
[150] https://digital-strategy.ec.europa.eu/en/library/commission-publishes-guidelines-ai-system-definition-facilitate-first-ai-acts-rules-application.
[151] Article 113(b) EU AI Act.
[152] https://digital-strategy.ec.europa.eu/en/library/guidelines-scope-obligations-providers-general-purpose-ai-models-under-ai-act

Guidelines Subject Matter	Due Date	Status at 28 February 2026
	requirement for Commission guidelines on the scope of obligations of providers of general-purpose AI models.	
Guidelines for practical implementation of classification of high-risk AI systems[153]	2 February 2026[154].	Between 06 June 2025 and 18 July 2025, the Commission held a targeted stakeholder consultation[155]. The

[153] Article 6(5) EU AI Act.
[154] *Ibid.*
[155] https://digital-strategy.ec.europa.eu/en/news/commission-launches-public-consultation-high-risk-ai-systems

Guidelines Subject Matter	Due Date	Status at 28 February 2026
		Commission has yet to publish the Guidelines.
➢ Guidelines for application of the requirements and obligations concerning high-risk AI systems[156] and responsibilities along the AI value chain[157]	2 August 2026[158]	Between 06 June 2025 and 18 July 2025, the Commission held a targeted stakeholder consultation[159]. The Commission has yet to publish the Guidelines.

[156] Article 96(1)(a) EU AI Act. The requirements and obligations for high-risk AI systems are set out in Articles 8 to 15 EU AI Act.

[157] These responsibilities are set out in Article 25 EU AI Act.

[158] Article 113 EU AI Act.

[159] https://digital-strategy.ec.europa.eu/en/news/commission-launches-public-consultation-high-risk-ai-systems

Guidelines Subject Matter	Due Date	Status at 28 February 2026
➢ Guidelines for the practical implementation of the provisions related to substantial modification[160]	2 August 2026[161]	The Guidelines have yet to be published.
➢ Guidelines for the practical implementation of transparency obligations[162]	2 August 2026[163]	The Guidelines have yet to be published.

[160] Article 96(1)(c) EU AI Act.
[161] Article 113 EU AI Act.
[162] Articles 50 and 96(1)(d) EU AI Act.
[163] Article 113 EU AI Act.

Guidelines Subject Matter	Due Date	Status at 28 February 2026
➢ Guidelines for detailed information on the relationship of the EU AI Act with the EU harmonisation legislation[164] and other relevant Union law, including as regards consistency in their enforcement[165]	2 August 2026[166]	The Guidelines have yet to be published.

➢

[164] The relevant EU harmonization legislation is listed in Annex I EU AI Act.
[165] Article 96(1)(e) EU AI Act.
[166] Article 113 EU AI Act.

1.19 Imposition of Fines on Providers of General-Purpose AI Models

Effective from 2 August 2025[167], the EU AI Act empowers the Commission to impose on providers of general-purpose AI models fines not exceeding 3 % of their annual total worldwide turnover in the preceding financial year or EUR 15 000 000, whichever is higher[168]. These fines can be imposed when the Commission finds that the provider intentionally or negligently[169]:

- infringed the EU AI Act[170];
- failed to comply with the Commission's request for technical documentation, integration information for providers of AI systems, copyright policy, training content summary, model evaluation and adversarial model testing documentation, systemic risk assessment, or serious incident reports, or supplied incorrect, incomplete or misleading information[171];
- failed to comply with a risk mitigation measure requested by the Commission[172]; or

---

[167] Article 113(b) EU AI Act.
[168] Article 101(1) EU AI Act.
[169] *Ibid.*
[170] Article 101(1)(a) EU AI Act.
[171] Article 101(1)(b) EU AI Act.
[172] Article 101(1)(c) EU AI Act.

- failed to make available to the Commission access to the general-purpose AI model or general-purpose AI model with systemic risk with a view to conducting an evaluation of compliance with the EU AI Act and investigate systemic risks[173].

When deciding on the amount of fine or periodic penalty payment, the EU AI Act requires the Commission to give regard to the nature, gravity and duration of the infringement and the principles of proportionality and appropriateness, and the provider's risk mitigation commitments[174].

Before imposing a fine or a penalty, the Commission must communicate its preliminary findings to the provider of the general-purpose AI model and give it an opportunity to be heard[175].

The EU AI Act further requires fines imposed by the Commission to be effective, proportionate and dissuasive[176]; that information on fines imposed must be communicated to the Board[177]; and confers upon the Court of Justice of the European Union unlimited jurisdiction to review decisions of the Commission to impose fines and cancel, reduce or increase the fine imposed[178].

---

[173] Article 101(1)(d) EU AI Act.
[174] Article 101(1) EU AI Act.
[175] Article 101(2) EU AI Act.
[176] Article 101(3) EU AI Act.
[177] Article 101(4) EU AI Act.
[178] Article 101(5) EU AI Act.

Finally, the EU AI Act requires the Commission to adopt implementing acts containing detailed arrangements and procedural safeguards for the imposition of fines[179]. The Commission has yet to adopt these implementing acts.

1.20 Evaluation and Review of Implementation of the EU AI Act

With effect from 2 August 2026[180], the EU AI Act requires the Commission to undertake a series of assessments of implementation of the EU AI Act. I summarise the required assessments in the table overleaf.

[179] Article 101(6) EU AI Act.
[180] Article 113 EU AI Act.

Commission Assessments of EU AI Act Implementation

Due Date	Recurrence	Subject Matter	Report Disclosed to:
2 August 2026[181]	Once a year until 31 July 2029 unless extended for further five-year-periods[182] or revoked earlier by the European Parliament or Council[183].	Assess and report the need to amend the lists of prohibited AI practices[184].	European Parliament and the Council[185].

---

[181] The EU AI Act provisions governing prohibited AI practices are effective from 2 February 2025. The first anniversary is 2 February 2026 but the requirement to assess the implementation only enters into force on 2 August 2026.

[182] Article 97(1) EU AI Act

[183] Articles 112(1) and 97(2) EU AI Act.

[184] The list of prohibited AI practices is laid down in Article 5 EU AI Act.

[185] Article 112(1) EU AI Act

Due Date	Recurrence	Subject Matter	Report Disclosed to:
2 August 2026[186]	Once a year until 31 July 2029 unless extended for further five-year-periods[187] or revoked earlier by the European Parliament or Council[188].	Assess and report the need to amend the lists of high-risk AI systems[189].	European Parliament and the Council[190].

[186] The EU AI Act provisions governing high-risk AI systems are effective from 2 August 2025. So the first anniversary is 2 August 2026, the same date as the effective date of the requirement to assess the implementation.
[187] Article 97(1) EU AI Act
[188] Articles 112(1) and 97(2) EU AI Act.
[189] This is the list of high-risk AI systems set out in Annex III EU AI Act.
[190] Article 112(1) EU AI Act

Due Date	Recurrence	Subject Matter	Report Disclosed to:
2 August 2028	Every four years	Evaluate and report on the need to amend: - area headings in the list of high-risk AI systems[191]; - the list of AI systems requiring additional transparency measures[192]; and - the EU AI Act provisions governing supervision and governance system to enhance its effectiveness[193].	European Parliament and the Council

[191] This is the list set out in Annex III EU AI Act; Article 112(2)(a) EU AI Act.
[192] Article 112(2)(b) EU AI Act.
[193] Article 112(2)(c) EU AI Act.

Due Date	Recurrence	Subject Matter	Report Disclosed to:
2 August 2029	every four years	assessment and, if appropriate, proposals to amend - the enforcement structure and to establish an EU agency to resolve identified shortcomings[194]; - the status of the financial, technical and human resources of the national competent authorities in order to effectively perform their tasks under the EU AI Act[195];	Public; European Parliament and the Council

[194] Article 112(3) EU AI Act.
[195] Article 112(4)(a) EU AI Act

Due Date	**Recurrence**	**Subject Matter**	**Report Disclosed to:**
		- penalties, in particular administrative fines applied by Member States for infringements of the EU AI Act[196]; - adopted harmonised standards and common specifications developed to support the EU AI Act[197]; - the number of undertakings that enter the market after the entry into application of the EU AI Act,	

[196] Article 112(4)(b) EU AI Act
[197] Article 112(4)(c) EU AI Act

Due Date	Recurrence	Subject Matter	Report Disclosed to:
		and how many of them are SMEs[198].	
2 August 2028	Not applicable.	evaluate and report on the functioning of the AI Office, whether the AI Office has been given sufficient powers and competences to fulfil its tasks, and whether it would be relevant and needed for the proper implementation and enforcement of the EU AI Act to upgrade the	the European Parliament and the Council

[198] Article 112(4)(d) EU AI Act.

Due Date	Recurrence	Subject Matter	Report Disclosed to:
		AI Office and its enforcement competences and to increase its resources[199].	
2 August 2028	every four years	Review and report on the progress on the development of standardisation deliverables on the energy-efficient development of general-purpose AI models, and asses the need for further measures or actions, including binding measures or actions[200].	Public; the European Parliament and the Council

[199] Article 112(5) EU AI Act.
[200] Article 112(6) EU AI Act

Due Date	Recurrence	Subject Matter	Report Disclosed to:
2 August 2028	every three years	Evaluate the impact and effectiveness of voluntary codes of conduct to foster the application of the EU AI Act's requirements for AI systems other than high-risk AI systems, including as regards environmental sustainability[201]	
2 August 2031		Assess and report on the enforcement of the EU AI Act	the European Parliament, the

[201] Article 112(7) EU AI Act.

Due Date	Recurrence	Subject Matter	Report Disclosed to:
		and, if appropriate, propose to amend the enforcement structure and to create an EU agency to resolve any shortcomings[202] -	Council and the European Economic and Social Committee

[202] Article 112(13) EU AI Act.

CHAPTER 2. AI Office

The Commission established the AI Office[203] by its decision of 24 January 2024 with effect from 21 February 2024[204].

Effective from 2 August 2025[205], the EU AI Act provides for the Commission, through the AI Office, to develop the EU expertise and capabilities in the field of AI[206] and requires Member States to facilitate the tasks entrusted to the AI Office in the EU AI Act[207].

2.1 Voluntary Model Terms of Contracts

Effective from 2 August 2026[208], the EU AI Act empowers the AI Office to develop and recommend voluntary model terms for contracts between providers of high-risk AI systems and third parties that supply tools, services, components or processes that are used for or integrated into high-risk AI systems[209]. When developing the voluntary model terms, the AI Office must take into

---

203 https://digital-strategy.ec.europa.eu/en/policies/ai-office

204 Article 9 Commission Decision of 24 January 2024 establishing the European Artificial Intelligence Office. See https://digital-strategy.ec.europa.eu/en/library/commission-decision-establishing-european-ai-office

205 Article 113 EU AI Act.

206 Article 64(1) EU AI Act.

207 Article 64(2) EU AI Act.

208 Article 113 EU AI Act.

209 Article 25(4) EU AI Act.

account possible contractual requirements applicable in specific sectors or business cases[210]. The voluntary model terms must be published and be available free of charge in an easily usable electronic format[211].

At the time of writing[212], only model contractual clauses for AI procurement by public organisations are in place, last updated on 5 March 2025[213]. The Commission's Commentary to these model clauses makes it clear that they are designed for public procurement, and private buyers of AI solutions need to assess, clause-by-clause, whether their use is appropriate in each situation[214].

2.2 Codes of Practice for Detection and Labelling of Artificially Generated or Manipulated Content

Effective from 2 August 2026[215], the EU AI Act requires the AI Office to encourage and facilitate the drawing up of codes of practice at the EU level to facilitate the effective implementation of the obligations regarding the detection and labelling of artificially generated or

---

[210] *Ibid.*

[211] Article 25(4) EU AI Act.

[212] 28 February 2026.

[213] https://public-buyers-community.ec.europa.eu/communities/procurement-ai/resources/updated-eu-ai-model-contractual-clauses.

[214] Paragraph 3.1 European Commission Commentary to the Model Contractual Clauses for the Public Procurement of AI. See https://public-buyers-community.ec.europa.eu/system/files/2025-05/Commentary.pdf

[215] Article 113 EU AI Act.

manipulated content[216]. Further, it permits the Commission to adopt implementing acts to approve those codes of practice[217]. If the Commission deems the code to be not adequate, it may adopt an implementing act specifying common rules for the implementation of those obligations[218].

In the run-up to entry into force of these provisions, following the consultation that took place in September-October 2025[219], on 5 November 2025 the Commission launched the work on a code of practice on the marking and labelling of AI-generated content. The process is mapped out for 7 months[220]. The publication of the first draft is expected in December 2025, the second draft – in March 2026, and the final Code of Practice is expected to be published in May to June 2026[221].

---

[216] Article 50(7) EU AI Act.

[217] *Ibid.*

[218] *Ibid.*

[219] https://digital-strategy.ec.europa.eu/en/news/commission-launches-consultation-develop-guidelines-and-code-practice-transparent-ai-systems

[220] https://digital-strategy.ec.europa.eu/en/policies/code-practice-ai-generated-content

[221] *Ibid.*

2.3 Codes of conduct for voluntary application of specific requirements

Effective from 2 August 2026[222], the EU AI Act requires the AI Office and the Member States to encourage and facilitate the drawing up of codes of conduct, including related governance mechanisms, intended to foster the voluntary application to AI systems, other than high-risk AI systems, of some or all of the EU AI Act's requirements for high-risk AI systems, such as risk management system, data and data governance requirements, technical documentation, record-keeping, transparency and provision of information to deployers, human oversight, accuracy, robustness, and cybersecurity[223]. These codes of conduct must take into account the available technical solutions and industry best practices[224].

The EU AI Act also requires AI Office and the Member States to facilitate the drawing up of codes of conduct concerning the voluntary application, including by deployers, of specific requirements to all AI systems, including[225]:

- applicable elements provided for in the EU ethical guidelines for trustworthy AI[226];

---

[222] Article 113 EU AI Act.

[223] Article 95(1) EU AI Act; these are the requirements set out in Chapter III, Section 2 EU AI Act.

[224] Article 95(1) EU AI Act.

[225] Article 95(2) EU AI Act.

[226] Article 95(2)(a) EU AI Act.

- assessing and minimising the impact of AI systems on environmental sustainability, including as regards energy-efficient programming and techniques for the efficient design, training and use of AI[227];
- promoting AI literacy, in particular that of persons dealing with the development, operation and use of AI[228];
- facilitating an inclusive and diverse design of AI systems, including through the establishment of inclusive and diverse development teams and the promotion of stakeholders' participation in that process[229]; and
- assessing and preventing the negative impact of AI systems on vulnerable persons or groups of vulnerable persons, including as regards accessibility for persons with a disability, as well as on gender equality[230].

The EU AI Act further provides that codes of conduct may cover one or more AI systems, taking into account the similarity of the intended purpose of the relevant systems[231].

When encouraging and facilitating the drawing up of codes of conduct, the EU AI Act requires the AI Office

---

[227] Article 95(2)(b) EU AI Act.
[228] Article 95(2)(c) EU AI Act.
[229] Article 95(2)(d) EU AI Act.
[230] Article 95(2)(e) EU AI Act.
[231] Article 95(3) EU AI Act.

and the Member States to take into account the specific interests and needs of SMEs, including start-ups[232].

Notably, the EU AI Act limits the role of the AI Office and of the Member States to *encouraging* and *facilitating* of drawing up of these codes, and specifically states that the codes of conduct may be drawn up by individual providers or deployers of AI systems or by organisations representing them or by both, including with the involvement of any interested stakeholders and their representative organisations, including civil society organisations and academia[233].

2.4 Measures for providers and deployers, in particular SMEs, including start-ups

Effective from 2 August 2026[234], the EU AI Act requires the AI Office to undertake the following actions in support of providers and deployers, and in particular – SMEs and start-ups[235]:

- provide standardised templates for areas covered by the EU AI Act, as specified by the Board in its request[236];

---

[232] Article 95(4) EU AI Act.
[233] Article 95(3) EU AI Act.
[234] Article 113 EU AI Act.
[235] Article 62(3) EU AI Act.
[236] Article 62(3)(a) EU AI Act.

- develop and maintain a single information platform providing easy to use information in relation to the EU AI Act for all operators across the EU[237];
- organise appropriate communication campaigns to raise awareness about the obligations arising from the EU AI Act[238]; and
- evaluate and promote the convergence of best practices in public procurement procedures in relation to AI systems[239].

2.5 Support for Compliance Investigations

Effective from 2 August 2026[240], the EU AI Act requires the AI Office to provide coordination support for joint investigations undertaken by market surveillance authorities and the Commission in relation to compliance of high-risk AI systems presenting a serious risk across two or more Member States[241].

2.6 Compliance Monitoring and Supervision

Effective from 2 August 2026[242], the EU AI Act empowers the AI Office to monitor and supervise

[237] Article 62(3)(b) EU AI Act.
[238] Article 62(3)(c) EU AI Act.
[239] Article 62(3)(d) EU AI Act.
[240] Article 113 EU AI Act.
[241] Article 74(11) EU AI Act.
[242] Article 113 EU AI Act.

compliance with obligations under the EU AI Act of AI systems based on general-purpose AI models developed by the same provider[243]. To carry out its monitoring and supervision tasks, the AI Office shall have all the enforcement powers of a market surveillance authority[244].

In addition, where a market surveillance authority is unable to conclude its investigation of the high-risk AI system because of its inability to access certain information related to the general-purpose AI model despite having made all appropriate efforts to obtain that information, and submits a reasoned request for information to the AI Office, the AI Office must supply to the applicant authority without delay, and in any event within 30 days, any information that the AI Office considers relevant in order to establish whether a high-risk AI system is non-compliant[245].

2.7 Risk Evaluation Methodology

Effective from 2 August 2026[246], the EU AI Act requires the AI Office to undertake to develop an objective and participative methodology for the evaluation of risk levels and the inclusion of new systems in the following lists[247]:

---

[243] Article 75(1) EU AI Act.

[244] Article 75(1) EU AI Act; the powers of a market surveillance authority are those conferred by the EU AI Act and Regulation (EU) 2019/1020.

[245] Article 75(3) EU AI Act.

[246] Article 113 EU AI Act.

[247] Article 112(11) EU AI Act.

- high-risk AI systems[248];
- prohibited AI practices[249]; and
- AI systems requiring additional transparency measures[250].

---

[248] Article 112(11)(a) EU AI Act; the high-risk AI systems are those set out in Annex III EU AI Act.

[249] Article 112(11)(b) EU AI Act; the prohibited AI practices are set out in Article 5 EU AI Act.

[250] Article 112(11)(c) EU AI Act.

CHAPTER 3. European Artificial Intelligence Board (the "Board")

With effect from 2 August 2025[251], The EU AI Act established the Board[252] composed of one representative per Member State[253]. Each representative must be designated by their Member State for a period of three years, renewable once[254].

Member States must ensure that their representatives on the Board[255]:

- have the relevant competences and powers in their Member State so as to contribute actively to the achievement of the Board's tasks[256];
- are designated as a single contact point vis-à-vis the Board and, where appropriate, taking into account Member States' needs, as a single contact point for stakeholders[257];
- are empowered to facilitate consistency and coordination between national competent authorities in their Member State as regards the implementation of the EU AI Act, including through the collection of

---

[251] Article 113(b) EU AI Act.

[252] Article 65(1) EU AI Act; the Board's website is at https://digital-strategy.ec.europa.eu/en/policies/ai-board .

[253] Article 65(2) EU AI Act.

[254] Article 65(3) EU AI Act.

[255] Article 65(4) EU AI Act.

[256] Articles 65(4)(a) and 66 EU AI Act.

[257] Article 65(4)(b) EU AI Act.

relevant data and information for the purpose of fulfilling their tasks on the Board[258].

The designated representatives of the Member States must adopt the Board's rules of procedure by a two-thirds majority[259]. The rules of procedure must, in particular, lay down procedures for the selection process, the duration of the mandate of, and specifications of the tasks of, the Chair, detailed arrangements for voting, and the organisation of the Board's activities and those of its sub-groups[260].

The European Data Protection Supervisor participates in the Board as observer[261].

The AI Office shall also attend the Board's meetings, without taking part in the votes[262].

Other national and EU authorities, bodies or experts may be invited to the meetings by the Board on a case-by-case basis, where the issues discussed are of relevance for them[263].

The Board shall establish two standing sub-groups to provide a platform for cooperation and exchange among market surveillance authorities and notifying authorities

---

[258] Article 65(4)(c) EU AI Act.
[259] Article 65(5) EU AI Act.
[260] *Ibid.*
[261] Article 65(2) EU AI Act.
[262] *Ibid.*
[263] *Ibid.*

about issues related to market surveillance and notified bodies respectively[264].

The standing sub-group for market surveillance should act as the administrative cooperation group (ADCO) for the EU AI Act[265].

The Board may establish other standing or temporary sub-groups as appropriate for the purpose of examining specific issues[266]. Where appropriate, representatives of the advisory forum may be invited to such sub-groups or to specific meetings of those subgroups as observers[267].

The Board shall be organised and operated so as to safeguard the objectivity and impartiality of its activities[268].

The Board shall be chaired by one of the representatives of the Member States[269]. The AI Office shall provide the secretariat for the Board, convene the meetings upon request of the Chair, and prepare the agenda in accordance with the tasks of the Board pursuant to the EU AI Act and its rules of procedure[270].

---

264 Article 65(6) EU AI Act.
265 *Ibid.*
266 *Ibid.*
267 *Ibid.*
268 Article 65(7) EU AI Act.
269 Article 65(8) EU AI Act.
270 *Ibid.*

3.1 The Tasks of the Board

The Board's role is to advise and assist the Commission and the Member States to facilitate the consistent and effective application of the EU AI Act. To this end, the EU AI Act empowers the Board, in particular, to:

- contribute to the coordination among national competent authorities responsible for the application of this Regulation and, in cooperation with and subject to the agreement of the market surveillance authorities concerned, support joint activities of market surveillance authorities of the Member States[271];
- collect and share technical and regulatory expertise and best practices among Member States[272];
- provide advice on the implementation of the EU AI Act, in particular as regards the enforcement of rules on general-purpose AI models[273];
- contribute to the harmonisation of administrative practices in the Member States, including in relation to the derogation from the conformity assessment procedures, the functioning of AI regulatory sandboxes, and testing in real world conditions[274];

---

[271] Article 66(a) EU AI Act.
[272] Article 66(b) EU AI Act.
[273] Article 66(c) EU AI Act.
[274] Article 66(d) EU AI Act.

- at the request of the Commission or on its own initiative, issue recommendations and written opinions on any relevant matters related to the implementation of the EU AI Act and to its consistent and effective application, including[275]:
    - on the development and application of codes of conduct and codes of practice pursuant to the EU AI Act and of the Commission's guidelines[276];
    - the evaluation and review of the EU AI Act, including as regards the serious incident reports, the functioning of the EU database, the preparation of the delegated or implementing acts, and possible alignments of the EU AI Act with the EU harmonisation legislation[277];
    - on technical specifications or existing standards regarding the requirements to high-risk AI systems[278];
    - on the use of harmonised standards or common specifications[279];
    - trends, such as European global competitiveness in AI, the uptake of AI in the EU, and the

---

[275] Article 66(e) EU AI Act.
[276] Article 66(e)(i) EU AI Act.
[277] Article 66(e)(ii) EU AI Act.
[278] Article 66(e)(iii) EU AI Act.
[279] Article 66(e)(iv) EU AI Act.

development of digital skills[280];

- trends on the evolving typology of AI value chains, in particular on the resulting implications in terms of accountability[281];
- on the potential need for amendment by the Commission to the areas of use of high-risk AI systems and prohibited AI practices, taking into account relevant available evidence and the latest developments in technology[282];

➢ support the Commission in promoting AI literacy, public awareness and understanding of the benefits, risks, safeguards and rights and obligations in relation to the use of AI systems[283];

➢ facilitate the development of common criteria and a shared understanding among market operators and competent authorities of the relevant concepts provided for in the EU AI Act, including by contributing to the development of benchmarks[284];

➢ cooperate, as appropriate, with other EU institutions, bodies, offices and agencies, and relevant EU expert groups and networks, in particular in the fields of product safety, cybersecurity, competition, digital and

---

280 Article 66(e)(v) EU AI Act.
281 Article 66(e)(vi) EU AI Act.
282 Article 66(e)(vii) EU AI Act.
283 Article 66(f) EU AI Act.
284 Article 66(g) EU AI Act.

media services, financial services, consumer protection, data and fundamental rights protection[285];

- contribute to effective cooperation with the competent authorities of third countries and with international organisations[286];
- assist national competent authorities and the Commission in developing the organisational and technical expertise required for the implementation of the EU AI Act, including by contributing to the assessment of training needs for staff of Member States involved in implementing the EU AI Act[287];
- assist the AI Office in supporting national competent authorities in the establishment and development of AI regulatory sandboxes, and facilitate cooperation and information-sharing among AI regulatory sandboxes[288];
- contribute to, and provide relevant advice on, the development of guidance documents[289];
- advise the Commission in relation to international matters on AI[290];
- provide opinions to the Commission on the qualified alerts regarding general-purpose AI models[291]; and

---

[285] Article 66(h) EU AI Act.
[286] Article 66(i) EU AI Act.
[287] Article 66(j) EU AI Act.
[288] Article 66(k) EU AI Act.
[289] Article 66(l) EU AI Act.
[290] Article 66(m) EU AI Act.
[291] Article 66(n) EU AI Act.

- receive opinions by the Member States on qualified alerts regarding general-purpose AI models, and on national experiences and practices on the monitoring and enforcement of AI systems, in particular systems integrating the general-purpose AI models[292].

3.2 The Board's Activity

By the time of writing[293], the Board has held six meetings between 10 September 2024 and 04 December 2026. The issues discussed at the Board's meetings were as follows:

Date of the Board's Meeting	**Issues Discussed**
6th Meeting – 04 December 2025	➢ the Digital Simplification Package ➢ Current priorities for implementing the EU AI Act.
5th Meeting – 24 October 2025[294] (Chaired by Denmark)	➢ the Commission's Apply AI Strategy ➢ the Commission's updates on AI Factories and AI Gigafactories

[292] Article 66(o) EU AI Act.

[293] 28 February 2026.

[294] https://digital-strategy.ec.europa.eu/en/news/ai-board-meets-discuss-apply-ai-strategy-and-implementation-ai-act

Date of the Board's Meeting	Issues Discussed
	➢ the current priorities for implementing the EU AI Act including the Digital Omnibus, the AI Act Service Desk, and the launch of Code of Practice on Transparency of AI-generated Content and guidelines. ➢ progress and challenges in the national implementation of the AI Act and possible support measures from the Commission to accelerate the national roll-out of the law. ➢ international AI developments ➢ the first months of application of the general-purpose AI models rules under the EU AI Act since August 2025.
4th Meeting – 30 June 2025[295] (Chaired by Poland)	➢ the Commission's planning for the Apply AI Strategy, due to be published in September 2025;

[295] https://digital-strategy.ec.europa.eu/en/events/ai-board-convenes-its-fourth-meeting-advance-eu-ai-policy

Date of the Board's Meeting	Issues Discussed
	➢ next steps on the AI Factories and AI Gigafactories; ➢ current priorities for the AI Act implementation; ➢ outlook on the final Code of practice on general-purpose AI models; ➢ progress update on the work of the standardisation organisation CEN-CENELEC in support of the AI Act; ➢ the progress of the national governance ahead of the implementation deadline on 2 August 2025.
3rd Meeting – 24th March 2025[296] (chaired by Poland)	➢ a strategic discussion on EU AI policy outlining the Commission's latest initiatives and priorities. ➢ a roundtable on national governance approaches to share

[296] https://digital-strategy.ec.europa.eu/en/news/ai-board-convenes-its-third-meeting-advance-eu-ai-policy

Date of the Board's Meeting	Issues Discussed
	insights on their implementation strategies for the AI Act. ➢ decision-making on joint communication efforts and on compliance support for the AI Act. ➢ the AI Office's update on recent AI Act deliverables and the adoption process for upcoming ones, including updates on AI system definitions and prohibitions guidelines, the third draft of the Code of Practice for general-purpose AI, and the call for the scientific panel. ➢ a technical briefing from the AI Office Safety team providing insights into the latest AI developments.
2nd Meeting – 10 December 2024[297]	➢ pivotal discussions and updates on AI governance, literacy, and international collaborations.

[297] https://digital-strategy.ec.europa.eu/en/news/second-meeting-ai-board

Date of the Board's Meeting	Issues Discussed
(chaired by Hungary)	➢ updates from the AI Board subgroups and adoption of their Terms of Reference ➢ presentations by Austria and Norway on AI literacy and insights into national approaches to AI governance from Malta, Finland, and Slovenia ➢ a strategic vision for AI in the next Commission mandate presented by Roberto Viola, Director-General of DG CNECT ➢ updates on international activities, including collaboration with Singapore, the OECD Global Partnership on AI Ministerial Summit, and the recently adopted risk management framework of the Council of Europe Committee on AI ➢ presentation of the progress on the Code of Practice for general-purpose AI ➢ a forward-looking discussion on guidelines for prohibited AI

Date of the Board's Meeting	Issues Discussed
	practices and system definitions, along with action points and planning for 2025.
1st Meeting – 10 September 2024[298]	➢ the establishment of the AI Board's organisation and the adoption of its rules of procedure; ➢ an update and strategic discussion on EU AI policy, including the GenAI4EU initiative and international AI activities; ➢ a progress update and discussion on the first deliverables of the Commission related to the AI Act's implementation; and ➢ an exchange of best practices for national approaches to AI governance and AI Act implementation.

[298] https://digital-strategy.ec.europa.eu/en/news/artificial-intelligence-board-kicks-work-uptake-ai-eu-and-implementation-ai-act

In addition, the Board has endorsed two documents[299]:

- The AI Board's Adequacy Assessment of the General-Purpose AI Code of Practice; and
- The Interplay between the Medical Devices Regulation & In Vitro Diagnostic Medical Devices Regulation (IVDr) and the Artificial Intelligence Act (AIA).

[299] https://digital-strategy.ec.europa.eu/en/policies/ai-board

CHAPTER 4. Advisory Forum

Effective from 2 August 2025[300], The EU AI Act provides for an advisory forum to be established, to provide technical expertise, advise the Board and the Commission, and contribute to their tasks under the EU AI Act[301].

Under the EU AI Act, the members of the advisory forum must be appointed by the Commission from amongst stakeholders with recognised expertise in the field of AI[302], to represent a selection of stakeholders, including industry, start-ups, SMEs, civil society and academia balanced with regard to commercial and non-commercial interests and, within the category of commercial interests, with regard to SMEs and other undertakings[303]. On 7 July 2025, the Commission issued the Terms of Reference for the constitution of the advisory forum[304]. The terms of reference provide for the advisory forum to be made up of 200 members. Between 17 July 2025 and 14 September 2025, the Commission held a call for applications to join the advisory forum[305]. At the time of writing[306], the

---

[300] Article 113(b) EU AI Act.

[301] Article 67(1) EU AI Act.

[302] Article 67(3) EU AI Act.

[303] Article 67(2) EU AI Act.

[304] https://digital-strategy.ec.europa.eu/en/funding/european-commission-launches-call-applications-join-ai-act-advisory-forum

[305] *Ibid.*

[306] 28 February 2026.

outcome of the public call and the membership of the advisory forum have yet to be published.

The term of office of the members of the advisory forum shall be two years and may be extended by up to four years[307].

In addition, the Fundamental Rights Agency, ENISA, the European Committee for Standardization (CEN), the European Committee for Electrotechnical Standardization (CENELEC), and the European Telecommunications Standards Institute (ETSI) shall be permanent members of the advisory forum[308].

The advisory forum shall draw up its rules of procedure[309]. It shall elect two co-chairs from among its members, to represent a balanced selection with regard to commercial and non-commercial interests and, within the category of commercial interests, with regard to SMEs and other undertakings[310]. The term of office of the co-chairs shall be two years, renewable once[311].

The advisory forum shall hold meetings at least twice a year and may invite experts and other stakeholders to its meetings[312].

---

[307] Article 67(4) EU AI Act.
[308] Article 67(5) EU AI Act.
[309] Article 67(6) EU AI Act.
[310] *Ibid.*
[311] *Ibid.*
[312] Article 67(7) EU AI Act.

The advisory forum may prepare opinions, recommendations and written contributions at the request of the Board or the Commission[313].

The advisory forum may establish standing or temporary sub-groups as appropriate for the purpose of examining specific questions related to the objectives of the EU AI Act[314].

The advisory forum shall prepare a publicly available annual report on its activities[315].

---

[313] Article 67(8) EU AI Act.
[314] Article 67(9) EU AI Act.
[315] Article 67(10) EU AI Act.

CHAPTER 5. Scientific Panel of Independent Experts

Effective from 2 August 2025[316], the EU AI Act requires the Commission, by means of an implementing act, to make provisions for the establishment of a scientific panel of independent experts (the '**scientific panel**') to support the implementation of the EU AI Act[317]. On 7 March 2025, the Commission by implementing act established the scientific panel[318]. The EU AI Act requires the implementing act to include provisions on the conditions, procedures and detailed arrangements for the scientific panel and its members to issue alerts and to request the assistance of the AI Office for the performance of the tasks of the scientific panel[319].

The scientific panel shall consist of up to 60[320] experts selected by the Commission on the basis of up-to-date scientific or technical expertise in the field of AI

---

[316] Article 113(b) EU AI Act.

[317] Article 68(1) EU AI Act.

[318] Article 2 of the Commission Implementing Regulation (EU) 2025/454 of 7 March 2025 laying down the rules for the application of Regulation (EU) 2024/1689 of the European Parliament and of the Council as regards the establishment of a scientific panel of independent experts in the field of artificial intelligence.

[319] Article 68(5) EU AI Act.

[320] Recital (3) and Article 3(2) Commission Implementing Regulation (EU) 2025/454 of 7 March 2025.

necessary for its tasks, and who must meet all of the following conditions[321]:

- have particular expertise and competence and scientific or technical expertise in the field of AI[322];
- be independent from any provider of AI systems or general-purpose AI models[323]; and
- be able to carry out activities diligently, accurately and objectively[324].

The EU AI Act requires the Commission, in consultation with the Board, to ensure fair gender and geographical representation[325]. The Commission's implementing regulations[326] provide for the scientific panel to be made up of at least one national from each EU Member State and from each member of the European Free Trade Association which is a member of the European Economic Area and no more than three experts from each of those countries. Nationals of third countries should be able to be appointed as experts, but at least four-fifths of the experts of the scientific panel should be nationals from the EU Member States or from a member of the European

---

[321] Article 68(2) EU AI Act.

[322] Article 68(2)(a) EU AI Act.

[323] Article 68(2)(b) EU AI Act.

[324] Article 68(2)(c) EU AI Act.

[325] Article 68(2) EU AI Act.

[326] Recital (4) and Article 3(4) Commission Implementing Regulation (EU) 2025/454 of 7 March 2025.

Free Trade Association which is a member of the European Economic Area[327].

The experts shall be appointed to the scientific panel for two years, renewable[328].

On 16 June 2025, the Commission launched a public call for expressions of interest to join the scientific panel[329]. The applications were open until 14 September 2025[330]. The Commission has yet to publish the outcome of the call[331].

5.1 The Tasks of the Scientific Panel

The scientific panel shall advise and support the AI Office, in particular regarding the following tasks[332]:

- the implementation and enforcement of the EU AI Act as regards general-purpose AI models and systems, in particular by[333]:
    - alerting the AI Office of possible systemic risks at EU level of general-purpose AI models[334] where it has reason to suspect that a general-purpose AI

[327] *Ibid.*

[328] Article 4(1) Commission Implementing Regulation (EU) 2025/454 of 7 March 2025.

[329] https://digital-strategy.ec.europa.eu/en/news/commission-seeks-experts-ai-scientific-panel

[330] *Ibid.*

[331] Last checked on 28 February 2026.

[332] Article 68(3) EU AI Act.

[333] Article 68(3)(a) EU AI Act.

[334] Article 68(3)(a)(i) EU AI Act.

model poses concrete identifiable risk at the EU level[335] or meets the EU AI Act conditions to be classified as a general-purpose AI model with systemic risk[336]. A qualified alert must be duly reasoned and indicate at least the point of contact of the provider of the general-purpose AI model with systemic risk concerned[337], a description of the relevant facts and the reasons for the alert[338]; and any other information that the scientific panel considers to be relevant, including, where appropriate, information gathered on its own initiative[339].

- contributing to the development of tools and methodologies for evaluating capabilities of general-purpose AI models and systems, including through benchmarks[340];
- advising on the classification of general-purpose AI models with systemic risk[341];
- advising on the classification of various general-purpose AI models and systems[342];

---

[335] Article 90(1))(a) EU AI Act.
[336] Articles 90(1)(b) and 51 EU AI Act.
[337] Article 90(3)(a) EU AI Act.
[338] Article 90(3)(b) EU AI Act.
[339] Article 90(3)(c) EU AI Act.
[340] Article 68(3)(a)(ii) EU AI Act.
[341] Article 68(3)(a)(iii) EU AI Act.
[342] Article 68(3)(a)(iv) EU AI Act.

   - contributing to the development of tools and templates[343];
- supporting the work of market surveillance authorities, at their request[344];
- supporting cross-border activities of market surveillance authorities with respect to specific categories of high-risk AI systems presenting a serious risk across two or more Member States[345].
- supporting the AI Office in carrying out its duties in the context of the EU safeguard procedure in respect of AI systems presenting a risk[346].

The EU AI Act requires experts on the scientific panel to perform their tasks with impartiality and objectivity, ensure the confidentiality of information and data obtained in carrying out their tasks and activities, and neither seek nor take instructions from anyone when exercising their tasks[347]. Each expert must draw up a publicly available declaration of interests[348]. The AI Office shall establish systems and procedures to actively manage and prevent potential conflicts of interest[349].

---

343 Article 68(3)(a)(v) EU AI Act.

344 Article 68(3)(b) EU AI Act.

345 Articles 68(3)(c) and 74(11) EU AI Act; Article 9 of Regulation (EU) 2019/1020.

346 Articles 68(3)(d) and 81 EU AI Act.

347 Article 68(4) EU AI Act.

348 *Ibid.*

349 *Ibid.*

The structure and the level of fees and the scale and structure of recoverable costs must be set out in the implementing act of the Commission on the establishment of the scientific panel, taking into account the objectives of the adequate implementation of the EU AI Act, cost-effectiveness and the necessity of ensuring effective access to experts for all Member States[350]. The implementing regulation includes broad provisions related to remuneration of the experts:

- Experts shall be remunerated if they have been appointed as rapporteur or contributor for carrying out tasks of the scientific panel in accordance with the provisions in force at the Commission, where such tasks have been requested by the AI Office[351]; and
- Travel and, where the Secretariat considers appropriate, subsistence expenses of experts in connection with the activities of the scientific panel shall be reimbursed by the Commission in accordance with the provisions in force at the Commission and within the limits of the available appropriations allocated to the Commission departments under the annual procedure for the allocation of resources[352].

---

[350] *Ibid.*

[351] Article 9(1) Commission Implementing Regulation (EU) 2025/454 of 7 March 2025.

[352] Article 9(2) *Ibid.*

5.2. Access to the pool of experts by the Member States

The EU AI Act permits Member States to call upon experts of the scientific panel to support their enforcement activities under the EU AI Act[353].

The Member States may be required to pay fees for the advice and support provided by the experts[354].

The Commission must facilitate timely access to the experts by the Member States, as needed, and ensure that the combination of support activities carried out by the EU AI testing support and experts is efficiently organised and provides the best possible added value[355].

---

[353] Article 69(1) EU AI Act.
[354] Article 69(2) EU AI Act.
[355] Article 69(3) EU AI Act.

CHAPTER 6. The European Data Protection Supervisor

6.1 Administrative Fines on the EU Institutions, Bodies, Offices, and Agencies

The EU AI Act empowers the European Data Protection Supervisor to impose administrative fines on the EU institutions, bodies, offices and agencies falling within the scope of the EU AI Act, taking into account all relevant circumstances of the specific case and[356]:

- the nature, gravity and duration of the infringement and of its consequences, taking into account the purpose of the AI system concerned, the number of affected persons and the level of damage suffered by them[357];
- the degree of responsibility of the EU institution, body, office or agency, taking into account technical and organisational measures implemented by them[358];
- any action taken by the EU institution, body, office or agency to mitigate the damage suffered by affected persons[359];
- the degree of cooperation with the European Data Protection Supervisor in order to remedy the

[356] Article 100(1) EU AI Act.
[357] Article 100(1)(a) EU AI Act.
[358] Article 100(1)(b) EU AI Act.
[359] Article 100(1)(c) EU AI Act.

infringement and mitigate the possible adverse effects of the infringement, including compliance with any of the measures previously ordered by the European Data Protection Supervisor against the EU institution, body, office or agency concerned with regard to the same subject matter[360];

- any similar previous infringements by the EU institution, body, office or agency[361];
- how the infringement became known to the European Data Protection Supervisor, in particular whether, and if so to what extent, the EU institution, body, office or agency notified the infringement[362];
- the annual budget of the Union institution, body, office or agency[363].

The EU AI Act sets the following administrative fines for EU institutions, bodies, offices and agencies:

Breach	**Administrative Fine Cap**
Non-compliance with the prohibition of the AI practices[364]	EUR 1,500,000[365]

[360] Article 100(1)(d) EU AI Act.
[361] Article 100(1)(e) EU AI Act.
[362] Article 100(1)(f) EU AI Act.
[363] Article 100(1)(g) EU AI Act.
[364] Articles 5 and 100(2) EU AI Act.
[365] Article 100(2) EU AI Act.

Breach	Administrative Fine Cap
Non-compliance of the AI system with any other EU AI Act's requirements or obligations[366]	EUR 750,000[367]

The EU AI Act sets out the following additional rules for the imposition of these administrative fines:

- Before deciding to impose a fine, the European Data Protection Supervisor must give the EU institution, body, office or agency which is the subject of the proceedings conducted by the European Data Protection Supervisor the opportunity of being heard on the matter regarding the possible infringement[368].
- The European Data Protection Supervisor must base his or her decisions only on elements and circumstances on which the parties concerned have been able to comment[369].
- Complainants, if any, must be associated closely with the proceedings[370].
- The rights of defence of the parties concerned shall be fully respected in the proceedings[371].

---

[366] Article 100(3) EU AI Act.
[367] *Ibid.*
[368] Article 100(4) EU AI Act.
[369] *Ibid.*
[370] *Ibid.*
[371] Article 100(5) EU AI Act.

- The parties to the proceedings are entitled to have access to the European Data Protection Supervisor's file, subject to the legitimate interest of individuals or undertakings in the protection of their personal data or business secrets[372].
- Funds collected by imposition of these fines must contribute to the general budget of the EU[373]. The fines shall not affect the effective operation of the EU institution, body, office or agency fined[374].
- The European Data Protection Supervisor must annually notify the Commission of the administrative fines it has imposed and of any litigation or judicial proceedings it has initiated[375].

---

[372] *Ibid.*
[373] Article 100(6) EU AI Act.
[374] *Ibid.*
[375] Article 100(7) EU AI Act.

PART 2. AI REGULATORY BODIES: NATIONAL LEVEL

CHAPTER 7. Member States

The EU AI Act confers on the EU Member States a number of powers and imposes a number of obligations related to the implementation of the EU AI Act. This Chapter describes these powers and obligations.

7.1 Authorise the use of 'real-time' remote biometric identification systems in publicly accessible spaces for law enforcement purposes

Effective from 2 February 2025[376], the EU AI Act permits EU Member States to fully or partially authorise the use of 'real-time' remote biometric identification systems in publicly accessible spaces for law enforcement purposes and prescribes the circumstances and requirements for authorising such use[377], as detailed in Chapter 11.3[378].

To this end, the EU AI Act requires the Member States to lay down in their national law the necessary detailed rules for the request, issuance, exercise, supervision and reporting of these authorisations and, within 30 days of adoption of the rules, notify them to the Commission[379]. The rules must specify the permitted

---

[376] Article 113(a) EU AI Act.
[377] Article 5(5) EU AI Act.
[378] *Ibid.*
[379] *Ibid.*

objectives and criminal offences in respect of which the competent authorities may be authorised to use those systems for law enforcement purposes[380]. At the same time, The EU AI Act permits the Member States to introduce more restrictive laws on the use of remote biometric identification systems[381].

At the time of writing[382], the Commission has yet to report publicly the countries who notified it of the adoption of these rules.

7.2 Establish National Competent Authorities

Effective from 2 August 2025[383], the EU AI Act requires each Member State to establish or designate as national competent authorities for the purposes of the EU AI Act at least one notifying authority and at least one market surveillance authority[384] and communicate to the Commission the identity and the tasks of these authorities and any subsequent changes[385].

In addition, the EU AI Act prescribed the Member States to publish by 2 August 2025 the information on how competent authorities and single points of contact can be contacted through electronic communication means[386].

---

[380] *Ibid.*
[381] *Ibid.*
[382] Last checked 28 February 2026.
[383] Article 113(b) EU AI Act.
[384] Article 70(1) EU AI Act.
[385] Article 70(2) EU AI Act.
[386] *Ibid.*

Further, effective from 2 August 2025[387], the EU AI Act mandated the Member States to designate a market surveillance authority to act as the single point of contact for the EU AI Act and notify the Commission of the identity of the single point of contact[388]. The Commission must make a list of the single points of contact publicly available[389]. At the time of writing[390], the list of single points of contact published by the Commission specifies single points of contact only for eight countries: Cyprus, Ireland, Italy, Latvia, Lithuania, Luxembourg, Slovenia and Spain[391].

Member States must ensure that their national competent authorities are provided with adequate technical, financial and human resources, and with infrastructure to fulfil their tasks effectively under the EU AI Act[392]. In particular, the national competent authorities must have sufficient personnel permanently available whose competences and expertise must include in-depth understanding of AI technologies, data and data computing, personal data protection, cybersecurity, fundamental rights, health and safety risks and knowledge of existing standards

---

[387] Article 113(b) EU AI Act.

[388] Article 70(2) EU AI Act.

[389] *Ibid.*

[390] Last checked on 28 February 2026.

[391] https://digital-strategy.ec.europa.eu/en/policies/market-surveillance-authorities-under-ai-act#1720699867912-2

[392] Article 70(3) EU AI Act.

and legal requirements[393]. Member States must assess and, if necessary, update these competence and resource requirements annually[394].

By 2 August 2025, and once every two years thereafter, Member States must report to the Commission on the status of the financial and human resources of the national competent authorities, with an assessment of their adequacy[395]. The Commission must transmit that information to the Board for discussion and possible recommendations[396].

The Commission must facilitate the exchange of experience between national competent authorities[397].

7.3 Establish Notifying Authorities

Effective from 2 August 2025[398], the EU AI Act requires each Member State to designate or establish at least one authority responsible for setting up and carrying out the procedures for the assessment, designation and notification of conformity assessment bodies and for their monitoring[399]. These procedures must be developed in

---

[393] *Ibid.*
[394] *Ibid.*
[395] Article 70(6) EU AI Act.
[396] *Ibid.*
[397] Article 70(7) EU AI Act.
[398] Article 113(b) EU AI Act.
[399] Article 28(1) EU AI Act.

cooperation between the notifying authorities of all Member States[400].

Member States may decide that these assessment and monitoring are to be carried out by a national accreditation body[401].

The EU AI Act further prescribes that the notifying authorities must be:

- established, organised and operated in such a way that no conflict of interest arises with conformity assessment bodies, and that the objectivity and impartiality of their activities are safeguarded[402];
- organised in such a way that decisions relating to the notification of conformity assessment bodies are taken by competent persons different from those who carried out the assessment of those bodies[403];
- prohibited from offering or providing any activities that conformity assessment bodies perform and any consultancy services on a commercial or competitive basis[404]; and
- staffed with an adequate number of competent personnel for the proper performance of their tasks[405]. Where the personnel functions so require, the personnel

---

[400] *Ibid.*

[401] Article 28(2) EU AI Act; for national accreditation bodies see Regulation (EC) No 765/2008.

[402] Article 28(3) EU AI Act.

[403] Article 28(4) EU AI Act.

[404] Article 28(5) EU AI Act.

[405] Article 28(7) EU AI Act.

must have expertise in information technologies, AI and law, including the supervision of fundamental rights[406].

The EU AI Act also requires the notifying authorities to safeguard the confidentiality of the information that they obtain[407].

At the time of writing[408], only Denmark, Hungary, Ireland, Lithuania, and Malta designated their notifying authorities[409].

7.4 Identify the public authorities or bodies to supervise or enforce compliance with EU law protecting fundamental rights

By 2 November 2024[410], the EU AI Act requires each Member State to identify the public authorities or bodies to supervise or enforce compliance with the obligations under EU law protecting fundamental rights, including the right to non-discrimination, in relation to the use of high-risk AI systems[411]. The Member States must make the list of these public authorities or bodies publicly

---

406 Article 28(7) EU AI Act.

407 Articles 28(6) and 78 EU AI Act.

408 Last checked on 28 February 2026.

409 https://iapp.org/resources/article/eu-ai-act-regulatory-directory/#eu-member-states

410 Article 78(2) EU AI Act.

411 Article 78(1) EU AI Act.

available, notify the list to the Commission and to the other Member States and keep the list up to date[412].

At the time of writing[413], all EU countries except Italy have designated their fundamental rights protection authorities[414].

7.5 Testing of High-Risk AI Systems in Real World Conditions

Effective from 2 August 2026[415], the EU AI Act requires Member States to confer on their market surveillance authorities the following powers:

- to require providers and prospective providers to provide information;
- to carry out unannounced remote or on-site inspections; and
- to check testing in real world conditions and the related high-risk AI systems[416].

The EU AI Act further requires market surveillance authorities to use these powers to ensure the safe development of testing in real world conditions[417].

---

412 Article 78(2) EU AI Act.

413 Last checked on 28 February 2026.

414 https://iapp.org/resources/article/eu-ai-act-regulatory-directory/#eu-member-states

415 Article 113 EU AI Act.

416 Articles 60(6) and 75 EU AI Act.

417 Article 60(6) EU AI Act.

7.6 Measures for Providers and Deployers, in Particular SMEs, Including Start-Ups

Effective from 2 August 2026[418], the EU AI Act requires the Member States to undertake a series of actions aimed at supporting SMEs[419]:

- provide SMEs, including start-ups, having a registered office or a branch in the EU and fulfilling the eligibility conditions and selection criteria, with priority access to the AI regulatory sandboxes[420];
- provide non-EU SMEs, including start-ups, that fulfil the eligibility conditions and selection criteria, with access to the AI regulatory sandbox[421];
- organise specific awareness raising and training activities on the application of the EU AI Act tailored to the needs of SMEs including start-ups, deployers, and local public authorities[422];
- utilise existing dedicated channels and where appropriate, establish new ones for communication with SMEs including start-ups, deployers, other innovators and local public authorities to provide advice and respond to queries about the implementation of the EU

---

418 Article 113 EU AI Act.
419 Article 62(1) EU AI Act.
420 Article 62(1)(a) EU AI Act.
421 *Ibid.*
422 Article 62(1)(b) EU AI Act.

AI Act, including as regards participation in AI regulatory sandboxes[423]; and

- facilitate the participation of SMEs and other relevant stakeholders in the standardisation development process[424].

It remains to be seen how these measures are implemented by the EU Member States.

7.7 Codes of conduct for voluntary application of specific requirements

Effective from 2 August 2026[425], the EU AI Act requires the AI Office and the Member States to encourage and facilitate the drawing up of codes of conduct for voluntary application of specific requirements to AI systems[426]. The specific provisions of the EU AI Act concerning these codes of conduct are discussed in Chapter 2 Section 2.3 of this book.

---

[423] Article 62(1)(c) EU AI Act.
[424] Article 62(1)(d) EU AI Act.
[425] Article 113 EU AI Act.
[426] Article 95 EU AI Act.

7.8 Rules on Penalties and Other Enforcement Measures

Effective from 2 August 2025[427], the EU AI Act sets caps for the penalties for breaches of its requirements and mandates the Member States to lay down the rules on penalties and other enforcement measures, including warnings and non-monetary measures for infringements of the EU AI Act by operators, and take all measures necessary to ensure that they are properly and effectively implemented, taking into account the guidelines issued by the Commission[428].

The penalties set by the EU AI Act are as follows:

Breach	**Administrative Fine Cap**
Non-compliance with the prohibition of the AI practices[429]	EUR 35,000,000 or, if the offender is an undertaking, up to 7 % of its total worldwide annual turnover for the preceding financial year, whichever is higher[430]

[427] Article 113(b) EU AI Act.

[428] Article 99(1) EU AI Act. The guidelines are the Commission guidelines referred to in Article 96 EU AI Act.

[429] The prohibited AI practices are listed in Article 5 EU AI Act.

[430] Article 99(3) EU AI Act.

Breach	**Administrative Fine Cap**
Obligations of providers of high-risk AI systems[431], authorised representatives[432], importers[433], distributors[434], deployers[435], notified bodies[436], and transparency obligations of providers and deployers[437].	EUR 15 000 000 or, if the offender is an undertaking, up to 3 % of its total worldwide annual turnover for the preceding financial year, whichever is higher[438].
The supply of incorrect, incomplete or misleading information to notified bodies or national competent authorities in reply to a request	EUR 7 500 000 or, if the offender is an undertaking, up to 1 % of its total worldwide annual turnover for the preceding financial year, whichever is higher[439]

[431] Articles 16 and 99(4)(a) EU AI Act.
[432] Articles 22 and 99(4)(b) EU AI Act.
[433] Articles 23 and 99(4)(c) EU AI Act.
[434] Articles 24 and 99(4)(d) EU AI Act.
[435] Articles 26 and 99(4)(e) EU AI Act.
[436] Articles 31, 3(1),(3) and (4), 34 and 99(4)(f) EU AI Act.
[437] Articles 50 and 99(4)(g) EU AI Act.
[438] Article 99(4) EU AI Act.
[439] Article 99(5) EU AI Act.

For SMEs, including start-ups, the above fines are capped at the lower of the percentage or amount[440].

The EU AI Act further requires that penalties must be effective, proportionate and dissuasive and take into account the interests of SMEs, including start-ups, and their economic viability[441].

In addition, the EU AI act requires the Member States, without delay and at the latest by the date of entry into application, to notify the Commission of the rules on penalties, other enforcement measures, and any amendments to them[442].

In addition, the EU AI Act outlines the following more specific requirements for rules on penalties:

- When deciding whether to impose an administrative fine and the amount of the administrative, all relevant circumstances of the specific situation must be taken into account and regard given to[443]:
    - the nature, gravity and duration of the infringement and of its consequences, taking into account the purpose of the AI system, the number of affected persons, and the level of damage suffered by them[444];
    - whether administrative fines have already been

---

[440] Article 99(6) EU AI Act.
[441] Article 99(1) EU AI Act.
[442] Article 99(2) EU AI Act.
[443] Article 99(7) EU AI Act.
[444] Article 99(7)(a) EU AI Act.

applied by other market surveillance authorities to the same operator for the same infringement[445];

- whether administrative fines have already been applied by other authorities to the same operator for infringements of other EU or national law, when such infringements result from the same activity or omission constituting a relevant infringement of the EU AI Act[446];
- the size, the annual turnover and market share of the operator committing the infringement[447];
- any other aggravating or mitigating factor applicable to the circumstances of the case, such as financial benefits gained, or losses avoided, directly or indirectly, from the infringement[448];
- the degree of cooperation with the national competent authorities, in order to remedy the infringement and mitigate the possible adverse effects of the infringement[449];
- the degree of responsibility of the operator taking into account the technical and organisational

---

[445] Article 99(7)(b) EU AI Act.
[446] Article 99(7)(c) EU AI Act.
[447] Article 99(7)(d) EU AI Act.
[448] Article 99(7)(e) EU AI Act.
[449] Article 99(7)(f) EU AI Act.

measures implemented by it[450];

- the manner in which the infringement became known to the national competent authorities, in particular whether, and if so to what extent, the operator notified the infringement[451];

- the intentional or negligent character of the infringement[452];

- any action taken by the operator to mitigate the harm suffered by the affected persons[453].

➢ Each Member State must lay down rules on the imposition of administrative fines on public authorities and bodies established in that Member State[454].

➢ Depending on the legal system of the Member States, the rules on administrative fines may be applied in such a manner that the fines are imposed by competent national courts or by other bodies[455]. The application of such rules in those Member States shall have an equivalent effect[456].

➢ The exercise of these powers is subject to appropriate procedural safeguards under EU and national law,

---

[450] Article 99(7)(g) EU AI Act.
[451] Article 99(7)(h) EU AI Act.
[452] Article 99(7)(i) EU AI Act.
[453] Article 99(7)(j) EU AI Act.
[454] Article 99(8) EU AI Act.
[455] Article 99(9) EU AI Act.
[456] Article 99(9) EU AI Act.

including effective judicial remedies and due process[457].

- Member States must annually report to the Commission about the administrative fines they have issued during that year and about any related litigation or judicial proceedings[458].

At the time of writing[459], there is no comprehensive database of the Member States that adopted the penalty rules. Only Italy adopted in September 2025 the comprehensive national law aligned with the EU AI Act that regulates the use of AI[460].

7.9 Provision of Information to the Commission

Effective from 2 August 2026[461], the EU AI Act requires the Member States to provide the Commission with information upon its request and without undue delay for the purposes of the Commission's reports evaluating the implementation of the EU AI Act[462].

---

457 Article 99(10) EU AI Act.
458 Article 99(11) EU AI Act.
459 Last checked on 28 February 2026.
460 https://www.theguardian.com/world/2025/sep/18/italy-first-in-eu-to-pass-comprehensive-law-regulating-ai
461 Article 113 EU AI Act.
462 Article 112(8) EU AI Act.

CHAPTER 8. National Competent Authorities

Effective from 2 August 2025[463], the EU AI Act requires each Member State to establish or designate as national competent authorities at least one notifying authority and at least one market surveillance authority for the purposes of the EU AI Act[464]. The national competent authorities must exercise their powers independently, impartially and without bias so as to safeguard the objectivity of their activities and tasks, and to ensure the application and implementation of the EU AI Act[465]. The members of those authorities must refrain from any action incompatible with their duties[466]. Provided that these principles are observed, such activities and tasks may be performed by one or more designated authorities, in accordance with the organisational needs of the Member State[467].

National competent authorities must take appropriate measures to ensure an adequate level of cybersecurity[468].

---

[463] Article 113(b) EU AI Act.
[464] Article 70(1) EU AI Act.
[465] *Ibid.*
[466] *Ibid.*
[467] *Ibid.*
[468] Article 70(4) EU AI Act.

When performing their tasks, the national competent authorities must act in accordance with the EU AI Act's confidentiality obligations[469].

National competent authorities may provide guidance and advice on the implementation of the EU AI Act, in particular to SMEs including start-ups, considering the guidance and advice of the Board and (or) the Commission[470]. Whenever national competent authorities intend to provide guidance and advice regarding an AI system in areas covered by other EU law, the appropriate national competent authorities under that EU law must be consulted[471].

Where EU institutions, bodies, offices or agencies fall within the scope of the EU AI Act, the European Data Protection Supervisor shall act as the competent authority for their supervision[472].

Chapter 6 Section 6.2 of this book provides additional information about designation of national competent authorities by the Member States.

8.1 Serious Incidents

Effective from 2 August 2026[473], national competent authorities must immediately notify the

---

[469] Article 70(5) EU AI Act.
[470] Article 70(8) EU AI Act.
[471] *Ibid.*
[472] Article 70(9) EU AI Act.
[473] Article 113 EU AI Act.

Commission of any serious incident, whether or not they have taken action on it, using the Rapid Information Exchange System[474].

8.2 Protection of Fundamental Rights

Effective from 2 November 2024[475], the EU AI Act empowers national public authorities or bodies appointed by the Member States to supervise or enforce compliance with EU law obligations to protect fundamental rights to request and access any documentation created or maintained under the EU AI Act in accessible language and format when access to that documentation is necessary for effectively fulfilling their mandates within the limits of their jurisdiction[476]. The relevant public authority or body must inform the market surveillance authority of the Member State concerned of any such request[477].

Where this documentation is insufficient to ascertain whether an infringement of obligations under EU law protecting fundamental rights has occurred, the public authority or body may make a reasoned request to the market surveillance authority, to organise testing of the high-risk AI system through technical means[478]. The

---

[474] Article 73(11) EU AI Act; Article 20 of Regulation (EU) 2019/1020.

[475] Article 77(2) EU AI Act.

[476] Article 77(1) EU AI Act.

[477] *Ibid.*

[478] Article 77(3) EU AI Act.

market surveillance authority must organise the testing with the close involvement of the requesting public authority or body within a reasonable time following the request[479].

The national public authorities or bodies must treat any information or documentation they obtain in accordance with the EU AI Act's confidentiality obligations[480].

8.3 Provision of Information to the Commission for Evaluation Reports on the EU AI Act Implementation

Effective from 2 August 2026[481], the EU AI Act requires national competent authorities to provide the Commission with information upon its request without undue delay for the purposes of the Commission's reports evaluating the implementation of the EU AI Act[482].

---

[479] *Ibid.*
[480] Article 77(4) and 78 EU AI Act.
[481] Article 113(b) EU AI Act.
[482] Article 112(8) EU AI Act.

CHAPTER 9. Market Surveillance Authorities

The EU AI Act requires the Member States to designate their competent market surveillance authorities by 2 August 2025. At the time of writing[483], only Cyprus, Ireland, Italy, Latvia, Lithuania, Luxembourg, Slovenia, and Spain have designated their market surveillance authorities[484].

9.1 Serious Incidents

Effective from 2 August 2026[485], the EU AI Act imposes on the national market surveillance authorities a series of obligations related to serious incidents.

Upon receiving a notification related to a serious incident of an AI system that leads directly or indirectly to the infringement of EU law obligations intended to protect fundamental rights, the relevant market surveillance authority must notify the national public authorities or bodies which supervise or enforce EU law obligations protecting fundamental rights in relation to the use of high-risk AI systems[486].

In addition, the market surveillance authority must, within seven days from the date it received the notification

[483] 28 February 2026.

[484] https://digital-strategy.ec.europa.eu/en/policies/market-surveillance-authorities-under-ai-act

[485] Article 113 EU AI Act.

[486] Articles 73(7) and 77(1) EU AI Act.

of a serious incident, ensure that products presenting a serious risk are withdrawn or recalled, where there is no other effective means available to eliminate the serious risk, or that their being made available on the market is prohibited[487]. Market surveillance authorities must notify the Commission of these measures immediately, using the Rapid Information Exchange System Article[488].

9.2 EU Market Surveillance and AI Systems Control

Effective from 2 August 2026[489], The EU AI Act extends the application of the EU Regulation 2019/1020 of 20 June 2019 on market surveillance and compliance of products to AI systems covered by the EU AI Act[490]. It further provides that for the purposes of effective enforcement of the EU AI Act:

- any reference to an economic operator under that Regulation shall include all providers, deployers, importers, distributors, product manufacturers,

[487] Article 73(8) EU AI Act; Article 19 of Regulation (EU) 2019/1020 of 20 June 2019 on market surveillance and compliance of products and amending Directive 2004/42/EC and Regulations (EC) No 765/2008 and (EU) No 305/2011 .

[488] Article 73(8) EU AI Act; Article 20 of Regulation (EU) 2019/1020.

[489] Article 113 EU AI Act.

[490] Article 74(1) EU AI Act.

authorised representatives of providers, and affected persons to whom the EU AI Act applies[491]; and

- any reference to a product under that Regulation shall include all AI systems falling within the scope of the EU AI Act[492].

In addition, effective from 2 August 2026[493], the EU AI Act prescribes that, as part of their reporting obligations under that Regulation[494], the market surveillance authorities must report annually to the Commission and relevant national competition authorities any information identified in the course of market surveillance activities that may be of potential interest for the application of EU law on competition rules[495]. They must also annually report to the Commission about the use of prohibited practices that occurred during that year and about the measures taken[496].

For high-risk AI systems related to products covered by the EU harmonisation legislation, the market surveillance authority for the purposes of the EU AI Act shall be the authority responsible for market surveillance activities designated under those legal acts[497]. But the EU Act permits Member States in appropriate circumstances to

---

[491] Articles 74(1)(a) and 2(1) EU AI Act.
[492] Article 74(1)(b) EU AI Act.
[493] Article 113 EU AI Act.
[494] Article 34(4) of Regulation (EU) 2019/1020.
[495] Article 74(2) EU AI Act.
[496] *Ibid.*
[497] Article 74(3) EU AI Act; the products are those listed in Annex I of the EU AI Act.

designate another relevant authority to act as a market surveillance authority, provided they ensure coordination with the relevant sectoral market surveillance authorities responsible for the enforcement of that EU harmonisation legislation[498].

If the EU harmonisation legislation already ensures an equivalent level of protection, the EU AI Act's procedures for dealing with:

- AI systems presenting a risk;
- AI systems classified by the provider as non-high-risk;
- objections to measures taken by Member States for non-compliance with the prohibited practices;
- compliant AI systems which present a risk; and
- formal non-compliance
- shall not apply to AI systems related to[499]:
- machinery;
- toys;
- recreational craft;
- personal watercraft;
- safety components for lifts;
- equipment and protective systems intended for use in potentially explosive atmospheres;
- radio equipment;
- pressure equipment;

---

[498] Article 74(3) EU AI Act; the EU harmonization legislation is that which is listed in Annex I of the EU AI Act.

[499] Articles 74(4), 79 to 83, and section A of Annex I of the EU AI Act.

- cableway installations;
- personal protective equipment;
- appliances burning gaseous fuels; and
- medical devices (including in vitro diagnostic medical devices).
- In such cases, the relevant sectoral procedures shall apply instead[500].

Without prejudice to the market surveillance, investigation and enforcement powers of market surveillance authorities[501], to ensure the effective enforcement of the EU AI Act, market surveillance authorities may exercise the following powers remotely[502]:

- the power to carry out unannounced on-site inspections and physical checks of products[503]; and
- the power to acquire product samples, including under a cover identity, to inspect those samples and to reverse-engineer them in order to identify non-compliance and to obtain evidence[504].

For high-risk AI systems placed on the market, put into service, or used by financial institutions regulated by EU financial services law, the market surveillance authority for the purposes of the EU AI Act shall be the national

---

[500] Article 74(4) EU AI Act.

[501] These powers are set out in Article 14 of Regulation (EU) 2019/1020.

[502] Article 74(5) EU AI Act.

[503] Article 14(4)(d) of Regulation (EU) 2019/1020.

[504] Article 14(4)(j) of Regulation (EU) 2019/1020.

authority responsible for the financial supervision of those institutions in so far as the placing on the market, putting into service, or the use of the AI system is directly related to the provision of those financial services[505]. But, in appropriate circumstances, and provided that coordination is ensured, a Member State may designate another relevant authority as market surveillance authority for the purposes of the EU AI Act[506].

In addition, the EU AI Act requires national market surveillance authorities supervising regulated credit institutions[507] that participate in the Single Supervisory Mechanism[508], to report, without delay, to the European Central Bank any information identified in the course of their market surveillance activities that may be of potential interest for the prudential supervisory tasks of the European Central Bank specified in the Regulation governing the Single Supervisory Mechanism[509].

For high-risk AI systems for remote biometric identification, biometric categorisation, and emotion recognition[510], in so far as these systems are used for law enforcement purposes, border management and justice and

---

[505] Article 74(6) EU AI Act.

[506] Article 74(7) EU AI Act.

[507] These are the credit institutions regulated under Directive 2013/36/EU.

[508] The Single Supervisory Mechanism is established by Regulation (EU) No 1024/2013.

[509] Article 74(7) EU AI Act and Regulation (EU) No 1024/2013.

[510] Article 74(8) and point 1 of Annex III of the EU AI Act.

democracy, and for high-risk AI systems for law enforcement, migration, asylum and border control management, administration of justice and democratic processes[511], the EU AI Act requires the Member States to designate as market surveillance authorities for the purposes of the EU AI Act either the competent data protection supervisory authorities[512], or any other supervisory authority[513] established by law of the Member State[514], which can act independently[515], whose members are appointed by the parliament, the government, the head of state, or an independent body and have the qualifications, experience and skills[516].

At the same time, the EU AI Act prohibits market surveillance activities from affecting the independence of judicial authorities or otherwise interfering with their activities when acting in their judicial capacity[517].

Where EU institutions, bodies, offices or agencies fall within the scope of the EU AI Act, the European Data Protection Supervisor shall act as their market surveillance

---

[511] Article 74(8) and points 6, 7 and 8 of Annex III of the EU AI Act.

[512] Regulation (EU) 2016/679 or Directive (EU) 2016/680.

[513] Article 41 Directive EU 2016/680.

[514] Article 44 Directive EU 2016/680.

[515] Article 42 Directive EU 2016/680.

[516] Article 43 Directive EU 2016/680; Article 74(8) EU AI Act.

[517] Article 74(8) EU AI Act.

authority, except in relation to the Court of Justice of the European Union acting in its judicial capacity[518].

The EU AI Act requires Member States to facilitate coordination between market surveillance authorities designated under the EU AI Act and other relevant national authorities or bodies which supervise the application of the EU harmonisation legislation[519], or other EU law relevant for the high-risk AI systems[520].

By agreement on joint activities[521], market surveillance authorities and the Commission must be able to carry out joint activities, including joint investigations, to promote compliance, identify non-compliance, raise awareness or provide guidance in relation to the EU AI Act with respect to specific categories of high-risk AI systems that present a serious risk across two or more Member States[522].

In addition, providers must grant the market surveillance authorities full access to the documentation, training, validation and testing data sets used for the development of high-risk AI systems, including through application programming interfaces (API) or other relevant technical means and tools enabling remote access[523]. The access is subject to appropriate security safeguards and

---

[518] Article 74(9) EU AI Act.
[519] Annex I EU AI Act.
[520] Article 74(10) and Annex III EU AI Act.
[521] Article 9 of Regulation (EU) 2019/1020.
[522] Article 74(11) EU AI Act.
[523] Article 74(12) EU AI Act.

limited to what is necessary for the market surveillance authorities to fulfil their tasks[524].

More specifically, the EU AI Act requires that market surveillance authorities be granted access to the source code of the high-risk AI system upon a reasoned request and only when both of the following conditions are fulfilled:

- access to source code is necessary to assess the conformity of a high-risk AI system with the EU AI Act's requirements to high-risk AI systems[525]; and
- testing or auditing procedures and verifications based on the data and documentation provided by the provider have been exhausted or proved insufficient[526].

The EU AI Act requires any information or documentation obtained by market surveillance authorities to be treated in accordance with the EU AI Act's confidentiality obligations[527].

9.3 Compliance Investigations

Effective from 2 August 2026[528], where a market surveillance authority has sufficient reason to consider general-purpose AI systems that can be used directly by

---

[524] *Ibid.*

[525] Article 74(13)(a) and Chapter III, Section 2 of the EU AI Act.

[526] Article 74(13)(b) EU AI Act.

[527] Articles 74(14) and 78 EU AI Act.

[528] Article 113 EU AI Act.

deployers for at least one high-risk purpose to be non-compliant with the EU AI Act's requirements, the market surveillance authority must cooperate with the AI Office to carry out compliance evaluations and inform the Board and other market surveillance authorities[529].

Where a market surveillance authority is unable to conclude its investigation of the high-risk AI system because of its inability to access certain information related to the general-purpose AI model despite having made all appropriate efforts to obtain that information, it may submit a reasoned request for information to the AI Office and the AI Office must provide any information that the AI Office considers to be relevant[530]. Market surveillance authorities must safeguard the confidentiality of the information that they obtain in accordance with the EU AI Act's confidentiality obligations[531]. In addition, the cross-border mutual assistance procedure shall apply to information requests[532].

---

[529] Article 75(2) EU AI Act.

[530] Article 75(3) EU AI Act.

[531] *Ibid.*

[532] Article 75(3) EU AI Act; for the mutual assistance procedure see Chapter VI of Regulation (EU) 2019/1020.

9.4 Supervision of Testing in Real World Conditions

Effective from 2 August 2026[533], the EU AI Act confers upon market surveillance authorities the competences and powers to ensure compliance of testing in real world conditions with the EU AI Act[534].

As part of their supervisory role for the AI regulatory sandbox, where testing in real world conditions is conducted for AI systems supervised in an AI regulatory sandbox, the market surveillance authorities must verify compliance with the EU AI Act's requirements to testing of high-risk AI systems in real world conditions outside AI regulatory sandboxes[535].

Notably, the market surveillance authorities may permit the provider or prospective provider to conduct the testing in real world conditions without compliance with the following conditions:

- that the testing in real world conditions shall last only as long as necessary to achieve its objectives and in any case not longer than six months, which may be extended for additional six months, subject to prior notification by the provider or prospective provider to

[533] Article 113 EU AI Act.
[534] Article 76(1) EU AI Act.
[535] Article 76(2) EU AI Act.

the market surveillance authority, accompanied by an explanation of the need for such an extension[536]; and

- that the subjects of the testing in real world conditions who are persons belonging to vulnerable groups due to their age or disability, must be appropriately protected[537].

Where a market surveillance authority has been informed by the prospective provider, the provider or any third party of a serious incident or has other grounds for considering that the conditions for testing outside regulatory sandboxes[538] are not met, it may decide for its territory to:

- suspend or terminate the testing in real world conditions[539]; or
- require the provider or prospective provider and the deployer or prospective deployer to modify any aspect of the testing in real world conditions[540].

Where a market surveillance authority has taken one of these decisions or issued an objection to testing in the real-world conditions, the decision or the objection must specify their grounds and how the provider or prospective provider can challenge the decision or

---

[536] Articles 76(2) and 60(4)(f) EU AI Act.
[537] Articles 76(2) and 60(4)(g) EU AI Act.
[538] The conditions are those set out in Articles 60 and 61 EU AI Act.
[539] Article 76(3)(a) EU AI Act.
[540] Article 76(3)(b) EU AI Act.

objection[541]. In addition, the market surveillance authority must communicate the grounds for the decision or objection to the market surveillance authorities of other Member States in which the AI system has been tested in accordance with the testing plan[542].

9.5 Compliance with Fundamental Rights

Effective from 2 August 2026[543], where the documentation obtained by a Member State's public authority or body in charge of protection of fundamental rights is insufficient to ascertain a breach of EU law obligations for protection of fundamental rights and the public authority or body requests the market surveillance authority to organise testing of the high-risk AI system through technical means, the market surveillance authority must organise the testing with the close involvement of the requesting public authority or body within a reasonable time following the request[544].

[541] Article 76(4) EU AI Act.
[542] Article 76(5) EU AI Act.
[543] Article 113 EU AI Act.
[544] Article 77(3) EU AI Act.

9.6 Reporting the Use of Real-time' Remote Biometric Identification Systems in Publicly Accessible Spaces for Law Enforcement Purposes

Effective from 2 February 2025[545], the EU AI Act requires national market surveillance authorities and the national data protection authorities of the EU Member States notified of the use of 'real-time' remote biometric identification systems in publicly accessible spaces for law enforcement purposes to submit to the Commission annual reports on such use[546]. For that purpose, the EU AI Act requires the Commission to provide EU Member States and national market surveillance and data protection authorities with a template, including information on the number of the decisions taken by competent judicial authorities or an independent administrative authority whose decision is binding upon requests for the authorisations and their result[547].

[545] Article 113(a) EU AI Act.
[546] Article 5(6) EU AI Act.
[547] *Ibid.*

CHAPTER 10. Conformity Assessment Bodies

Effective from 2 August 2025[548], the EU AI Act introduces the procedure for designation of conformity assessment bodies.

Conformity assessment bodies must apply for designation as such to the notifying authority of the Member State in which they are established[549]. At the time of writing[550], only Denmark, Hungary, Ireland, Lithuania, and Malta designated their notifying authorities[551], so these EU AI Act provisions have yet to be implemented across the EU. Nevertheless, let's look at what lies ahead.

The EU AI Act interchangeably refers to "conformity assessment bodies" and "notified bodies". At the same time, it defines a "notified body" as "a conformity assessment body notified in accordance with this Regulation and other relevant Union harmonisation legislation"[552]. For ease, in this book I use the term "conformity assessment bodies".

---

[548] Article 113(b) EU AI Act.
[549] Article 29(1) EU AI Act.
[550] Last checked on 28 February 2026.
[551] https://iapp.org/resources/article/eu-ai-act-regulatory-directory/#eu-member-states
[552] Article 3 (22) EU AI Act.

10.1 Designation Procedure

The EU AI Act requires an application for designation of a conformity assessment body to contain:

- a description of the conformity assessment activities, the conformity assessment module or modules and the types of AI systems for which the conformity assessment body claims to be competent;
- any valid document related to existing designations of the applicant under any other EU harmonisation legislation[553];
- an accreditation certificate, where one exists, issued by a national accreditation body attesting that the conformity assessment body fulfils the following requirements:[554]

- it is established under the national law of an EU Member State and has legal personality[555];

- it satisfies the organisational, quality management, resources and process requirements that are necessary to fulfil their tasks, and appropriate cybersecurity requirements[556];

- its organisational structure, allocation of responsibilities, reporting lines and operation ensures

---

[553] Article 29(2) EU AI Act.
[554] Articles 29(2) and 31 EU AI Act.
[555] Article 31(1) EU AI Act.
[556] Article 31(2) EU AI Act.

confidence in its performance, and in the results of the conformity assessment activities it will conduct[557];

- it is independent of the provider of a high-risk AI system in relation to which it performs conformity assessment, any other operator having an economic interest in high-risk AI systems assessed, and any competitors of the provider[558];

- the conformity assessment body, its top-level management and the personnel responsible for carrying out its conformity assessment tasks are not directly involved in the design, development, marketing or use of high-risk AI systems, do not represent the parties engaged in those activities, and do not engage in any activity that might conflict with their independence of judgement or integrity in relation to the conformity assessment activities for which they are designated; this restriction, in particular, applies to consultancy services[559];

- it is organised and operated so as to safeguard the independence, objectivity and impartiality of its activities as demonstrated by documented and implemented structure and procedures to safeguard impartiality and to promote

---

[557] Article 31(3) EU AI Act.

[558] Article 31(4) EU AI Act; but this independence requirement does not preclude the use of assessed high-risk AI systems that are necessary for the operations of the conformity assessment body or for personal purposes.

[559] Article 31(5) EU AI Act.

and apply the principles of impartiality throughout its organisation, personnel and assessment activities[560];

- it has documented procedures in place ensuring that its personnel, committees, subsidiaries, subcontractors and any associated body or personnel of external bodies maintain the confidentiality of the information which comes into their possession during the performance of conformity assessment activities, except when its disclosure is required by law[561];

- its staff is bound to observe professional secrecy with regard to all information obtained in carrying out their tasks under the EU AI Act, except in relation to the notifying authorities of the EU Member State in which their activities are carried out[562];

- it has procedures for the performance of activities which take due account of the size of a provider, the sector in which it operates, its structure, and the degree of complexity of the AI system concerned[563];

- it maintains appropriate liability insurance for its conformity assessment activities, unless liability is assumed by the EU Member State in which it is established in accordance with national law or that EU Member State is itself directly responsible for the conformity assessment[564];

---

[560] Article 31(6) EU AI Act.
[561] Articles 31(7) and 78 EU AI Act.
[562] Article 31(7) EU AI Act.
[563] Article 31(8) EU AI Act.
[564] Article 31(9) EU AI Act.

- it is capable of carrying out all its tasks under the EU AI Act with the highest degree of professional integrity and the requisite competence in the specific field, whether those tasks are carried out by itself or on its behalf and under its responsibility[565];

- it has sufficient internal competences to be able effectively to evaluate the tasks conducted by external parties on its behalf[566]; to this end it must have permanent availability of sufficient administrative, technical, legal and scientific personnel who possess experience and knowledge relating to the relevant types of AI systems, data and data computing, and relating to the EU AI Act requirements[567]; and

- it participates in coordination activities and either takes part directly, or is represented in, EU standardisation organisations, or ensures that it is aware and up to date in respect of relevant standards[568].

Where the conformity assessment body cannot provide an accreditation certificate, it must provide the notifying authority with all the documentary evidence necessary for the verification, recognition and regular monitoring of its compliance with the above requirements[569].

---

565 Article 31(10) EU AI Act.
566 Article 31(11) EU AI Act.
567 Article 31(11) EU AI Act.
568 Articles 31(12) and 38 EU AI Act.
569 Articles 29(3) and 31 EU AI Act.

Where a conformity assessment body is designated under any other EU harmonisation legislation, all documents and certificates linked to those designations may be used to support its designation procedure under the EU AI Act[570].

In addition, a conformity assessment body must keep the above documentation up to date in order to enable the authority responsible for the conformity assessment body to monitor and verify continuous compliance with all above requirements[571].

The notifying authorities may approve only those conformity assessment bodies which have satisfied the above requirements[572] and must notify the Commission and the other EU Member States, using the electronic notification tool developed and managed by the Commission, of each conformity assessment body[573], with full details of the conformity assessment activities, the conformity assessment module or modules, the types of AI systems concerned, and the attestation of competence[574]. Where a conformity assessment body's approval is not based on an accreditation, the notifying authority must provide the Commission and the other EU Member States with documentary evidence which attests to the

---

[570] Article 29(4) EU AI Act.
[571] *Ibid.*
[572] Article 30(1) EU AI Act.
[573] Article 30(2) EU AI Act.
[574] Article 30(3) EU AI Act.

competence of the conformity assessment body and to the arrangements in place to ensure that the conformity assessment body will be monitored regularly and will continue to satisfy the requirements[575].

A conformity assessment body may perform the activities of a conformity assessment body only where no objections are raised by the Commission or the other Member States:

- within two weeks of a notification by the notifying authority where it includes an accreditation certificate; or
- within two months of a notification by the notifying authority where it includes alternative documentary evidence[576].

Where objections are raised, the Commission must, without delay, enter into consultations with the relevant EU Member States and the conformity assessment body[577]. Giving regard to these consultations, the Commission must decide whether the approval of the conformity assessment body is justified and notify its decision to the EU Member State concerned and to the relevant conformity assessment body[578].

---

[575] *Ibid.*
[576] Article 30(4) EU AI Act.
[577] Article 30(5) EU AI Act.
[578] *Ibid.*

Where a conformity assessment body demonstrates its conformity with the criteria laid down in the EU harmonised standards published in the Official Journal of the European Union, it must be presumed to comply with the requirements for its approval in so far as the applicable harmonised standards cover those requirements[579].

10.2 Changes of Conformity Assessment Body Designation

The EU AI Act requires notifying authorities to notify the Commission and the other EU Member States of any relevant changes to the designation of an approved conformity assessment body using the electronic notification tool[580].

10.2.1 Extension of the Scope of Designation

The procedures for obtaining the designation as a conformity assessment body discussed above also apply to extensions of the scope of the designation[581].

For changes to the designation other than extension of its scope, the following procedures apply[582].

---

[579] Article 32 EU AI Act.

[580] Article 36(1) EU AI Act; the electronic notification tool is referred to in Article 30(2).

[581] Articles 36(2), 29 and 30 EU AI Act.

[582] Article 36(2) EU AI Act.

10.2.2 Withdrawal, Restriction or Suspension of Designation

The EU AI Act sets out the procedures for withdrawal, restricting or suspending of the activity of conformity assessment bodies.

Ceasing Conformity Assessment Activities

Where a conformity assessment body decides to cease its conformity assessment activities, it must inform the notifying authority and the providers concerned as soon as possible and, in the case of a planned cessation, at least one year before ceasing its activities[583]. The certificates of the conformity assessment body may remain valid for nine months after cessation of the conformity assessment body's activities, on condition that another conformity assessment body has confirmed in writing that it will assume responsibilities for the high-risk AI systems covered by those certificates[584]. The latter conformity assessment body must complete a full assessment of the high-risk AI systems affected by the end of that nine-month-period before issuing new certificates for those systems[585]. Where the

583 Article 36(3) EU AI Act.
584 *Ibid.*
585 *Ibid.*

conformity assessment body has ceased its activity, the notifying authority must withdraw the designation[586].

Failure to Comply with Statutory Requirements or Conformity Assessment Body Obligations

Where a notifying authority has sufficient reasons to believe that a conformity assessment body no longer meets the EU AI Act requirements prescribed for conformity assessment bodies, or that it is failing to fulfil its obligations, the notifying authority must without delay investigate the matter with the utmost diligence[587], inform the conformity assessment body about the concerns raised and give it the opportunity to make its views known[588]. If the notifying authority comes to the conclusion that the conformity assessment body no longer meets the requirements for conformity assessment bodies or that it is failing to fulfil its obligations, it must restrict, suspend or withdraw the designation as appropriate, depending on the seriousness of the failure to meet those requirements or fulfil those obligations and immediately inform the Commission and the other EU Member States[589].

Where its designation has been suspended, restricted, or fully or partially withdrawn, the conformity

---

586 *Ibid.*
587 Article 36(4) EU AI Act.
588 *Ibid.*
589 *Ibid.*

assessment body must inform the providers concerned within 10 days[590].

In the event of the restriction, suspension or withdrawal of a designation, the notifying authority must take appropriate steps to ensure that the files of the conformity assessment body concerned are kept, and to make them available to notifying authorities in other EU Member States and to market surveillance authorities at their request[591].

In the event of the restriction, suspension or withdrawal of a designation, the notifying authority must:

- assess the impact on the certificates issued by the conformity assessment body[592];
- submit a report on its findings to the Commission and the other Member States within three months of having notified the changes to the designation[593];
- require the conformity assessment body to suspend or withdraw, within a reasonable period of time determined by the authority, any certificates which were unduly issued, in order to ensure the continuing conformity of high-risk AI systems on the market[594];

---

[590] Article 36(5) EU AI Act.
[591] Article 36(6) EU AI Act.
[592] Article 36(7)(a) EU AI Act.
[593] Article 36(7)(b) EU AI Act.
[594] Article 36(7)(c) EU AI Act.

- inform the Commission and the EU Member States about certificates the suspension or withdrawal of which it has required[595];
- provide the national competent authorities of the EU Member State in which the provider has its registered place of business with all relevant information about the certificates of which it has required the suspension or withdrawal; that authority must take the appropriate measures, where necessary, to avoid a potential risk to health, safety or fundamental rights[596].

10.2.3 Validity of Certificates Following Suspension or Restriction of the Conformity Assessment Body's Designation

With the exception of certificates unduly issued, and where a designation has been suspended or restricted, the certificates shall remain valid in one of the following circumstances:

- the notifying authority has confirmed, within one month of the suspension or restriction, that there is no risk to health, safety or fundamental rights in relation to certificates affected by the suspension or restriction,

---

595 Article 36(7)(d) EU AI Act.
596 Article 36(7)(e) EU AI Act.

and the notifying authority has outlined a timeline for actions to remedy the suspension or restriction[597]; or

- the notifying authority has confirmed that no certificates relevant to the suspension will be issued, amended or re-issued during the course of the suspension or restriction, and stated whether the conformity assessment body has the capability of continuing to monitor and remain responsible for existing certificates issued for the period of the suspension or restriction[598]. If the notifying authority determines that the conformity assessment body does not have the capability to support existing certificates issued, the provider of the system covered by the certificate must confirm in writing to the national competent authorities of the EU Member State in which it has its registered place of business, within three months of the suspension or restriction, that another qualified conformity assessment body is temporarily assuming the functions of the conformity assessment body to monitor and remain responsible for the certificates during the period of suspension or restriction[599].

---

[597] Article 36(8)(a) EU AI Act.
[598] Article 36(8)(b) EU AI Act.
[599] Article 36(8)(b) EU AI Act.

10.2.4 Validity of Certificates Following Withdrawal of the Conformity Assessment Body's Designation

With the exception of certificates unduly issued, and where a designation has been withdrawn, the certificates shall remain valid for a period of nine months in the following circumstances:

- another conformity assessment body has confirmed in writing that it will assume immediate responsibility for those AI systems and completes its assessment within 12 months of the withdrawal of the designation[600]; and
- the national competent authority of the EU Member State in which the provider of the high-risk AI system covered by the certificate has its registered place of business has confirmed that there is no risk to health, safety or fundamental rights associated with the high-risk AI systems concerned[601]. In this case, the national competent authority of the EU Member State in which the provider of the system covered by the certificate has its place of business may extend the provisional validity of the certificates for additional periods of three months, which shall not exceed 12 months in total[602].

---

[600] Article 36(9)(b) EU AI Act.
[601] Article 36(9)(a) EU AI Act.
[602] Article 36(9) EU AI Act.

The national competent authority or the conformity assessment body assuming the functions of the conformity assessment body affected by the change of designation must immediately inform the Commission, the other EU Member States and the other conformity assessment bodies[603].

10.3 Subcontracting by Conformity Assessment Bodies

The EU AI Act permits conformity assessment bodies to subcontract specific tasks connected with the conformity assessment, including to a subsidiary, provided the following requirements are met:

- the conformity assessment body must ensure that the subcontractor (or the subsidiary) meets the EU AI Act requirements to conformity assessment bodies, and must inform the notifying authority accordingly[604];
- the conformity assessment body must take full responsibility for the tasks performed by any subcontractors or subsidiaries[605];
- the provider consented to the subcontracting, including to a subsidiary[606];

---

603 Article 36(9) EU AI Act.
604 Article 33(1) EU AI Act.
605 Article 33(2) EU AI Act.
606 Article 33(3) EU AI Act.

- the conformity assessment body made the list of its subsidiaries publicly available[607]; and
- the documents concerning the assessment of the qualifications of the subcontractor or the subsidiary and the conformity assessment work carried out by them must be available for the notifying authority for a period of five years from the termination date of the subcontracting[608].

10.4 Operational Obligations of Notified Bodies

The EU AI Act imposes on conformity assessment bodies the following operational obligations:

10.4.1 Verify Conformity of High-Risk AI Systems

Conformity assessment bodies must verify the conformity of high-risk AI systems in accordance with the conformity assessment procedures set out in the EU AI Act[609].

---

[607] *Ibid.*
[608] Article 33(4) EU AI Act.
[609] Articles 34(1) and 43 EU AI Act.

10.4.2 Avoid Unnecessary Burdens and Compliance Costs for Providers

Conformity assessment bodies must avoid unnecessary burdens for providers when performing their activities and must take due account of the size of the provider, the sector in which it operates, its structure and the degree of complexity of the high-risk AI system concerned, in particular to minimise administrative burdens and compliance costs for micro- and small enterprises[610]. At the same time, the conformity assessment body must, nevertheless, respect the degree of rigour and the level of protection required for the compliance of the high-risk AI system with the EU AI Act requirements[611].

10.4.3 Cooperate with the Notifying Authority

Conformity assessment bodies must make available and submit upon request to the notifying authority all relevant documentation, including the providers' documentation, to allow the notifying authority to conduct its assessment, designation, notification and monitoring activities, and to facilitate the assessment[612].

---

[610] Article 34(2) EU AI Act; for definition of "micro- and small enterprises" the EU AI Act refers to Recommendation 2003/361/EC.

[611] Article 34(2) EU AI Act.

[612] Article 34(3) EU AI Act.

10.4.5 Information Obligations of Conformity Assessment Bodies

Conformity assessment bodies must inform the notifying authority of the following:

- any EU technical documentation assessment certificates, any supplements to those certificates, and any quality management system approvals issued in accordance with the requirements of the EU AI Act[613];
- any refusal, restriction, suspension or withdrawal of an EU Union technical documentation assessment certificate or a quality management system approval issued in accordance with the requirements of the EU AI Act[614];
- any circumstances affecting the scope of or conditions for notification[615];
- any request for information which they have received from market surveillance authorities regarding conformity assessment activities[616]; and
- on request, conformity assessment activities performed within the scope of their notification and any other

613 Article 45(1)(a) EU AI Act.
614 Article 45(1)(b) EU AI Act.
615 Article 45(1)(c) EU AI Act.
616 Article 45(1)(d) EU AI Act.

activity performed, including cross-border activities and subcontracting[617].

In addition, each conformity assessment body must inform the other conformity assessment bodies of:

- quality management system approvals which it has refused, suspended or withdrawn, and, upon request, of quality system approvals which it has issued[618]; and
- EU technical documentation assessment certificates or any supplements thereto which it has refused, withdrawn, suspended or otherwise restricted, and, upon request, of the certificates and/or supplements thereto which it has issued[619].

Each conformity assessment body must also provide the other conformity assessment bodies carrying out similar conformity assessment activities covering the same types of AI systems with relevant information on issues relating to negative and, on request, positive conformity assessment results[620].

Conformity assessment bodies must safeguard the confidentiality of the information that they obtain, in accordance with the EU AI Act's confidentiality requirements[621].

---

617 Article 45(1)(e) EU AI Act.
618 Article 45(2)(a) EU AI Act.
619 Article 45(2)(b) EU AI Act.
620 Article 45(3) EU AI Act.
621 Articles 45(4) and 78 EU AI Act.

10.5 Treatment of Conformity Assessment Bodies of Third Countries

The EU AI Act contains a broad and brief provision that enables designation of conformity assessment bodies established under the law of a third country. The prerequisites for such designation are that the EU must have an agreement with that third country and the third country's conformity assessment body must meet the EU AI Act's designation requirements or ensure an equivalent level of compliance[622].

[622] Article 39 EU AI Act; the designation requirements for conformity assessment bodies are set out in Article 31 EU AI Act.

PART 3. REGULATION OF AI SYSTEMS

CHAPTER 11. What are AI Systems?

The EU AI Act defines an AI system as a machine-based system that is designed to operate with varying levels of autonomy and that may exhibit adaptiveness after deployment, and that, for explicit or implicit objectives, infers, from the input it receives, how to generate outputs such as predictions, content, recommendations, or decisions that can influence physical or virtual environments[623].

On 29 July 2025, following the stakeholder and the Board consultation[624], the Commission published the non-binding[625] Guidelines on the definition of an artificial intelligence system established by Regulation (EU) 2024/1689. The Guidelines state that considering the wide variety of AI systems, it is not possible to provide in the Guidelines an exhaustive list of all potential AI systems or systems that are outside the definition of an AI system[626]. Instead, the Guidelines break down the definition of AI system into seven main elements[627]:

(1) a machine-based system;

(2) designed to operate with varying levels of autonomy;

---

[623] Article 3(1) EU AI Act.

[624] Para I(5) Guidelines.

[625] Para I(7) Guidelines; only the EU Court of Justice may give an authoritative interpretation of the AI Act (*Ibid*).

[626] Paras I(6) and III(62) Guidelines.

[627] Para II(9) Guidelines

(3) that may exhibit adaptiveness after deployment;

(4) for explicit or implicit objectives;

(5) infers, from the input it receives, how to generate outputs

(6) such as predictions, content, recommendations, or decisions

(7) that can influence physical or virtual environments.

The Guidelines confirm, in alignment with the OECD definition of an AI system[628] that an AI system adopts a lifecycle-based perspective encompassing two main phases[629]:

- the pre-deployment or 'building' phase; and
- the post-deployment or "use" phase.

Importantly, the Guidelines state that the seven elements of an AI system are not required to be present continuously throughout both phases of the lifecycle and instead may appear at one phase but may not persist in both phases[630]. My observation that follows from this statement is that if all seven elements needed to be present in at least one stage of the lifecycle, it could happen definitively only post deployment. This is because of the third element that provides for the system's adaptiveness after deployment.

---

[628] "Explanatory memorandum on the updated OECD definition of an AI system", OECD Artificial Intelligence Papers, No. 8, OECD Publishing, Paris, https://doi.org/10.1787/623da898-en, p.7.

[629] Para II(10) Guidelines.

[630] Para II(10) Guidelines.

But this interpretation would make the pre-deployment phase irrelevant. Perhaps what is meant by the third element is that, at the building stage, the system should be developed with the capacity to be adaptive after it is deployed.

The Guidelines then consider in detail each of the seven elements of the AI system definition.

(1) A machine-based system

Analysing the meaning of a machine-based system, the Guidelines understand "machine" as both the hardware and software components that enable the AI system to function[631], that AI system must be computationally driven and based on machine operations[632], and that computational systems include the emerging quantum computing systems biological or organic systems so long as they provide computational capacity[633].

(2) Designed to operate with varying levels of autonomy

The Guidelines provide, by reference to EU AI Act, that "varying levels of autonomy" mean "some degree of independence of actions from human involvement and of capabilities to operate without human intervention"[634]. By way of example, the Guidelines mention capacity to

---

[631] Para II.1.(11) Guidelines.
[632] Para II.1.(12) Guidelines.
[633] Para II.1.(13) Guidelines.
[634] Para II.2.(14) Guidelines, Recital 12 EU AI Act.

generate predictions, content, recommendations or decisions that can influence physical or virtual environments[635].

"Human involvement" and "human intervention" are central to the concept of autonomy[636] and can be direct, e.g. through manual controls, or indirect, e.g. through automated system-based controls which allow humans to delegate or supervise system operations[637]. The Guidelines mention the following examples of systems with a degree of independence of action[638]:

- a system that requires manual input to generate an output by itself; and
- an expert system following a delegation of process automation by humans that is capable, based on human input, to produce an output on its own, such as recommendation.

The Guidelines further underline that the system must be able to interact with its external environment as opposed to machine learning or model architecture for its development[639].

The Guidelines conclude that the level of autonomy is a necessary condition to determine whether a system qualifies as an AI system and a system designed to operate

---

635 Para II.2(15) Guidelines.
636 Para II.2(16) Guidelines.
637 Para II.2(17) Guidelines.
638 Para II.2(18) Guidelines.
639 Para II.2(19) Guidelines.

with some reasonable degree of independence of actions fulfils the condition of autonomy[640].

(3) That may exhibit adaptiveness after deployment;

The Guidelines view adaptiveness as a concept closely related to but distinct from autonomy[641]. Adaptiveness refers to self-learning capabilities that allow for a change in the system's behaviour while in use that may produce different results for the same inputs[642]. Importantly, "may" means that the system does not necessarily have to be adaptive or self-learning post-deployment, and the system's ability to automatically learn, discover new patterns, or identify relationships in the data beyond what it was initially trained on is not a decisive condition for determining whether the system qualifies as an AI system[643].

(4) For explicit or implicit objectives;

Explicit objectives are clearly stated goals directly encoded by the developer into the system, e.g. optimisation of some cost function, a probability, or a cumulative reward[644]. Implicit objectives are goals that are not expressly stated but may be deduced from the behaviour or

---

[640] Para II.2(20) Guidelines.
[641] Para II.3(22) Guidelines.
[642] Para II.3(22) Guidelines; Recital 12 EU AI Act.
[643] Para II.3.(23) Guidelines.
[644] Para II.4.(24) Guidelines.

underlying assumptions of the system, e.g. from training data or the system's interaction with its environment[645] .

The objectives of the AI system may differ from its intended purpose in a specific context[646] - the objectives are internal to the system, for example a corporate virtual AI assistant's objectives may be to answer questions on a set of documents with high accuracy and low failure rate[647]. The intended purpose is externally oriented, for example the intended purpose of a corporate virtual assistant might be to assist a company's department to carry out certain tasks and fulfilling it involves integration of the system into a broader customer service workflow[648].

(5) Infers, from the input it receives, how to generate outputs

The capability to infer is a key characteristic and an indispensable condition of an AI system[649]. It is the process of obtaining the outputs, such as predictions, content, recommendations, or decisions which can influence physical and virtual environments[650], i.e. the ability to generate outputs based on inputs[651] and refers to both the use phase[652] and the building phase[653]. The inference-

645 Para II.4.(24) Guidelines.
646 Para II.4.(25) Guidelines; Recital 12 EU AI Act.
647 Para II.4.(25) Guidelines.
648 *Ibid.*
649 Para II.5.(26) Guidelines; Recital 12 EU AI Act.
650 Para II.5.(27) Guidelines; Recital 12 EU AI Act.
651 Para II.5.(28) Guidelines; Recital 12 EU AI Act.
652 *Ibid.*
653 Paras II.5.(29) and (31) Guidelines; Recital 12 EU AI Act.

enabling techniques include machine learning approaches that include supervised, unsupervised, self-supervised, and reinforcement learning[654]. Examples of supervised learning are:

- labelled data-based AI-enabled spam detection system[655];
- image classification systems[656];
- medical device diagnostic systems[657]; and
- fraud detection systems[658].

Unsupervised learning is based on data that has not been labelled and the model is trained on data without predefined outputs[659]. Using clustering, dimensionality reduction, association rule learning, anomality detection, or generative models, the system is trained to find patterns, structures or relationships in the data without explicit guidance on what the outcome should be[660]. Examples are:

- an AI system used by pharmaceutical companies for drug discovery[661]; and
- AI systems that use clustering or anomality detection to group chemical compounds and predict potential new

---

654 Para II.5.1(32) Guidelines.
655 Para II.5.1(33) Guidelines.
656 Para II.5.1(34) Guidelines.
657 *Ibid.*
658 *Ibid.*
659 Para II.5.1(35) Guidelines.
660 *Ibid.*
661 *Ibid.*

treatments for diseases based on their similarities to existing drugs[662].

Self-supervised learning is a subcategory of unsupervised learning, where an AI system learns from unlabelled data in a supervised fashion, using the data itself to create its own labels or objectives[663]. The techniques used by AI systems based on self-supervised learning include auto-encoders, generative adversarial networks, or contrastive learning[664]. Examples are:

- an image recognition system that learns to recognise objects by predicting missing pixels in an image[665];
- language models that learn to predict the next token in a sentence[666]; or
- speech recognition systems that learn to recognise spoken words by predicting the next acoustic feature in an audio signal[667].

Reinforcement learning AI systems learn from tata collected from their own experience through a reward function, by trial and error, refining their strategy based on the feedback from the environment[668]. Examples are:

- an AI-enabled robot arm grasping objects[669];

---

[662] *Ibid.*
[663] Para II.5.1(36) Guidelines.
[664] *Ibid.*
[665] *Ibid.*
[666] *Ibid.*
[667] *Ibid.*
[668] Para II.5.1(37) Guidelines.
[669] *Ibid.*

- personal content recommendation optimisation in search engines[670]; and
- performance of autonomous vehicles[671].

Deep learning is a subset of machine learning that uses neural networks for representation learning[672]. Deep-learning based AI systems automatically learn features from raw data[673]. These systems require large amounts of training data but can learn to recognise patterns and make predictions with high accuracy[674]. Widely used, deep learning is a technology behind many recent breakthroughs in AI[675].

In addition to machine-learning approaches, another category of techniques is logic- and knowledge- based approaches that infer from encoded knowledge or symbolic representation of the task to be solved, e.g. knowledge representation, inductive (logic) programming, knowledge basis, inference and deductive engines, (symbolic) reasoning, expert systems and search and optimisation methods[676]. These AI systems learn from rules, facts, and relationships encoded by human experts and can 'reason' via deductive or inductive engines or using sorting,

---

[670] *Ibid.*
[671] *Ibid.*
[672] Para II.5.1(38) Guidelines.
[673] *Ibid.*
[674] *Ibid.*
[675] *Ibid.*
[676] Para II.5.1(39) Guidelines; Recital 12 EU AI Act.

searching, matching, and (or) chaining operations[677]. Using logical inference to draw conclusions, these systems apply formal logic, predefined rules or ontologies to new situations[678]. Examples are:

- classical language processing models based on grammatical knowledge and logical semantics that rely on the language structure and identify syntactical and grammatical components of sentences to extract the meaning of a given text[679]; and (or)
- early generation expert systems for medical diagnosis developed by encoding knowledge of medical experts and intended to draw conclusions from symptoms of a given patient[680].

Systems outside the scope of the AI system definition

Some systems that have capacity to infer in a narrow manner fall outside the scope of the AI system definition because of their limited capacity to analyse patterns and adjust autonomously their output[681]. Such systems may include:

---

[677] Para II.5.1(39) Guidelines.
[678] *Ibid.*
[679] *Ibid.*
[680] *Ibid.*
[681] Para II.5.2(41) Guidelines.

- Systems for improving mathematical optimization that do not transcend basic data processing[682], e.g.:
  - physics-based systems that use machine learning techniques to approximate complex atmospheric processes, such as cloud microphysics or turbulence, enabling faster and more computationally efficient forecasts[683]; and
  - satellite telecommunication systems to optimise bandwidth allocation and resource management by predicting network traffic[684].

The automatic self-adjustments incorporated in these systems optimise the functioning of the systems by improving computational performance, as opposed to permitting adjustments of the decision-making models in an intelligent way[685].

- Basic data processing systems

These systems follow predefined, explicit instructions to execute tasks without "learning, reasoning or modelling" at any stage of the system's lifecycle[686]. Examples are:

- database management systems to sort or filter data

682 Para II.5.2(42) Guidelines.
683 Para II.5.2(43) Guidelines.
684 Para II.5.2(44) Guidelines.
685 Para II.5.2(45) Guidelines.
686 Para II.5.2(46) Guidelines.

based on specific criteria[687];

- standard spreadsheet software applications without AI-enabled functionalities[688];
- software for sales report visualisation in charts and graphs using statistical methods to create a sales dashboard but which does not recommend how to improve sales or which products to promote[689];
- opinion poll or survey software that applies statistical techniques to determine data validity, reliability, correlation, and statistical significance[690].

➢ Systems based on classical heuristics

Classical heuristics are problem-solving techniques that rely on experience-based methods to find approximate solutions efficiently and typically involve rule—based approaches, pattern recognition, or trial and error strategies rather than data-driven learning[691]. Example:

- A chess program using a minimax algorithm with heuristic evaluation functions that can assess board positions without requiring prior learning from data[692].

---

[687] *Ibid.*
[688] *Ibid.*
[689] Para II.5.2(47) Guidelines.
[690] *Ibid.*
[691] Para II.5.2(48) Guidelines.
[692] *Ibid.*

➢ Simple prediction systems

These are all machine-based systems performing via a basic statistical learning rule[693]. Examples:

- financial forecasting (basic benchmarking) systems to predict future stock prices by using an estimator with the 'mean' strategy to establish a baseline prediction (e.g. always predicting the historical average price)[694];
- baseline system using average temperature the previous week to predict tomorrow's temperature[695];
- static estimation systems, such as customer support response time system that are based on static estimation to predict the mean resolution time from the past data[696]; and (or)
- trivial predictors such as demand forecasting for a store to predict how many items of product the store will sell each day[697].

---

693 Para II.5.2(49) Guidelines.
694 Para II.5.2(50) Guidelines.
695 *Ibid.*
696 Para II.5.2(51) Guidelines.
697 *Ibid.*

(6) Such as predictions, content, recommendations, or decisions

The ability of a system to generate outputs, such as predictions, content, and recommendations, based on inputs it receives and using machine learning and logic and knowledge-based approaches, is fundamental to what AI systems do and what distinguishes them from other software[698].

The Guidelines identify four broad categories of AI system outputs that differ in their levels of human involvement:

- predictions;
- content;
- recommendations; and
- decisions[699].

Predictions are estimates about an unknown value from known values and require the least of human involvement[700]. Examples:

- AI systems deployed in self-driving cars[701]; and (or)
- AI systems for energy consumption[702].

Content is new material generated by an AI system, such as text, images, videos, music and other forms of output[703]. Example:

---

698 Para II.6(52) Guidelines.
699 Para II.6(53) Guidelines; Article 3(1) EU AI Act.
700 Para [II.6(54) Guidelines.
701 Para II.6(55) Guidelines.
702 *Ibid.*
703 Para II.6(56) Guidelines.

- content-generating Generative Pre-trained Transformer (GPT) technologies[704].

Recommendations are suggestions for specific actions, products, or services to users based on their preferences, behaviours or other data inputs[705]. Example:

- a recruitment system recommendation to hire a candidate[706].

Decisions are conclusions or choices made by a system[707]. Example:

- an AI system that outputs, by a fully automated process without human intervention, decisions traditionally handled by human judgement[708].

(7) That can influence physical or virtual environments

The Guidelines emphasise that AI systems are not passive, but actively impact the environments in which they are deployed, e.g. physical objects like robot arms and virtual environments like digital spaces, data flows, and software ecosystems[709].

---

704 *Ibid.*
705 Para II.6(57) Guidelines.
706 *Ibid.*
707 Para II.6(58) Guidelines.
708 *Ibid.*
709 Para II.7.(60) Guidelines.

CHAPTER 12. Exempt AI Systems and Activities

From the outset, effective from 2 February 2025[710], The EU AI Act does not apply to certain AI systems. Importantly, this means that these AI systems are outside of the scope of the EU AI Act's prohibitions too. This Chapter look closer at these exempt AI systems, illustrating their use with examples in the Guidelines on Prohibited Artificial Intelligence Practices adopted by the Commission on 29 July 2025 (**Prohibition Guidelines**).

12.1 National Security

- The EU AI Act does not apply to AI systems:
- placed on the market, put into service, or used with or without modification exclusively for military, defence or national security purposes[711]; and (or)
- not placed on the market or put into service in the EU, but where the output is used in the EU exclusively for military, defence or national security purposes[712].

In both cases, the AI systems are out of scope of the EU AI Act regardless of the type of entity carrying out those activities[713].

---

[710] Article 113(a) EU AI Act.
[711] Article 2(3) EU AI Act.
[712] *Ibid.*
[713] *Ibid.*

The term 'national security' refers to 'the primary interest in protecting the essential functions of the State and the fundamental interests of society and encompasses the prevention and punishment of activities capable of seriously destabilising the fundamental constitutional, political, economic or social structures of a country and, in particular, of directly threatening society, the population or the State itself, such as terrorist activities[714].'

But national security does not cover, for example activities relating to road safety[715] or the organisation or administration of justice[716].

As stated by the CJEU, 'it is for the Member States to define their essential security interests and to adopt appropriate measures to ensure their internal and external security, [...] a national measure [...] taken for the purpose of protecting national security cannot render EU law

[714] Para 2.5.1 (23) Prohibition Guidelines; Judgment of the Court of Justice of 6 October 2020, La Quadrature du Net and Others, C-511/18, C-512/18 and C-520/18, EU:C:2020:791, paragraph 135; Judgment of the Court of Justice of 5 June 2023, Commission v Poland, C-204/21, EU:C:2023:442, paragraph 318, referring to Case C-439/19, paragraph 67 and Case C-306/21, paragraph 40.]

[715] Para 2.5.1 (23) Prohibition Guidelines; Judgment of the Court of Justice of 22 June 2021, Latvijas Republikas Saeima, C-439/19, EU:C:2021:504, paragraph 68.

[716] Para 2.5.1 (23) Prohibition Guidelines; Judgment of the Court of Justice of 5 June 2023, Commission v Poland, C-204/21, EU:C:2023:442, paragraph 319.

inapplicable and exempt the Member States from their obligation to comply with that law.'[717]

Examples:

- An AI system placed on the market, put into service or used for military, defence or national security purposes is used (temporarily or permanently) for other purposes, such as for civilian or humanitarian purposes, law enforcement or public security purposes, will fall within the scope of the AI Act[718]. The entity using the AI system for the other purposes should ensure compliance of the AI system with the AI Act, unless the system already complies, which has to be verified before such use[719].
- A company that offers a remote biometric identification system for various purposes, including law enforcement and national security, is the provider of that 'dual use' system and must ensure its compliance with the requirements in the EU AI Act[720].

[717] Para 2.5.1 (23) Prohibition Guidelines; Judgement of the Court of Justice of 6 October 2020, Privacy International, C-623/17, EU:C:2020:790, paragraph 44.

[718] Para 23.5.1(24) Prohibition Guidelines.

[719] *Ibid.*

[720] Para 23.5.1(25) Prohibition Guidelines.

> ➢ if a national security agency or a private operator is tasked by a national intelligence agency to use real-time remote biometric identification systems for national security purposes (such as to gather intelligence), such use would be excluded from the scope of the AI Act[721].

12.2 Judicial and law enforcement cooperation with third countries

The EU AI Act does not apply to public authorities in a third country or international organisations, where those authorities or organisations use AI systems in the framework of international cooperation or agreements for law enforcement and judicial cooperation with the EU or with one or more Member States, provided that such a third country or international organisation provides adequate safeguards with respect to the protection of fundamental rights and freedoms of individuals[722]. Where relevant, this exclusion may cover the activities of private entities entrusted by the third country in question to carry out specific tasks in support of such law enforcement and

[721] Para 23.5.1(26) Prohibition Guidelines.
[722] Article 2(4) EU AI Act.

judicial cooperation[723]. At the same time, for the exclusion to apply, these frameworks for cooperation or international agreements must include adequate safeguards with respect to the protection of the fundamental rights and freedoms of individuals, to be assessed by the market surveillance authorities competent for the supervision of AI systems used in the area of law enforcement and justice[724]. The recipient national authorities and EU institutions, bodies, offices and agencies making use of such AI outputs in the EU remain accountable to ensure their use complies with EU law[725]. When those international agreements are revised or new ones are concluded in the future, the contracting parties should make utmost efforts to align those agreements with the requirements of the EU AI Act[726].

12.3 Research and Development

The EU AI Act does not apply to AI systems or AI models, including their output, specifically developed and put into service for the sole purpose of scientific research and development[727].

The EU AI Act also does not apply to research, testing (other than testing in real world conditions), or

---

[723] Recital 22 EU AI Act.
[724] Recital 22 and Article 74(8) EU AI Act
[725] Recital 22 EU AI Act.
[726] *Ibid.*
[727] Article 2(6).

development activity regarding AI systems or AI models prior to their being placed on the market or put into service; these activities must be conducted in accordance with other applicable EU law.[728]

Examples:

- During the research and development (R&D) phase, AI developers have the freedom to experiment and test new functionalities which might involve techniques that could be seen as manipulative, if used in consumer-facing applications. The EU AI Act allows for such experimentation by recognising that early-stage R&D is essential for refining AI technologies and ensuring that they meet safety and ethical standards prior to their placing on the market[729].

- Research into cognitive and behavioural responses to AI-driven subliminal or deceptive stimuli that can provide valuable insights into human-AI interactions, informing safer and more effective AI applications in the future is permitted[730].

---

[728] Article 2(8).
[729] Para 2.5.3 (30) Prohibition Guidelines.
[730] Para 2.5.3 (31) Prohibition Guidelines.

> ➢ A municipality wishing to test facial recognition software using a remote biometric identification system in the streets during carnival recruits volunteers to be identified by the system in real-world conditions does not fall within the exclusion and must be fully compliant with the requirements for remote biometric identification systems in the EU AI Act, unless the system is tested in an AI regulatory sandbox or in accordance with the special regime for testing in real world conditions outside the sandbox[731].

12.4 Personal Non-Professional Activity

The EU AI Act does not apply to obligations of deployers who are natural persons using systems in the course of a purely personal non-professional activity[732].

> Examples:
>
> ➢ An individual using a facial recognition system at home (e.g. to control access and to monitor for safety the entrance to the home) would fall under the exclusion and would not be subject to the obligations

[731] Para 2.5.3 (32) Prohibition Guidelines.
[732] Article 2(10) EU AI Act.

for deployers under the AI Act, even where it is required to transmit (parts of) the footage to law enforcement authorities[733]

- A natural person using an AI system for professional activities such as freelancers, journalists, doctors, etc. would need to comply with the obligations for deployers of facial recognition systems, and any use by natural persons where they are acting on behalf or under the authority of a deployer acting in a professional capacity are also in scope[734].

- criminal activities cannot be considered purely personal activities, even if no economic benefit is sought or attained; but for other unlawful activities, such as non-compliance with consumer protection or data protection law and national administrative legislation, the exclusion in the EU AI Act applies, but the other relevant legal frameworks continue to apply[735].

- An emotion recognition system, if intended to be used by natural persons for purely personal non-professional activities, remains a high-risk AI system

[733] Para 2.5.4 (34) Prohibition Guidelines.
[734] *Ibid.*
[735] *Ibid.*

and must comply with the EU AI Act[736]. At the same time, the deployer that uses it for purely personal non-professional use (e.g., an autistic person) will not be covered by specific obligations for deployers under the AI Act and the use would be out of scope[737].

12.5 AI systems released under free and open-source licences

The EU AI Act does not apply to AI systems released under free and open-source licences, unless they are placed on the market or put into service as high-risk AI systems or as an AI system to which prohibitions apply or which trigger the transparency obligations of providers and deployers[738].

[736] Para 2.5.4 (35) Prohibition Guidelines.
[737] *Ibid.*
[738] Articles 2(12), 5 and 50.

CHAPTER 13. The Prohibitions

Effective from 2 February 2025[739], the EU AI Act imposes prohibitions on certain actions involving AI systems and biometric categorisation and identification systems. On 29 July 2025, the Commission issued non-binding[740] Guidelines on Prohibited Artificial Intelligence Practices (**Prohibition Guidelines**) that focus on providers and deployers[741] with the view to assist with implementation of the prohibitions. The Guidelines are made up of twelve chapters spanning 136 pages and aim to assist with understanding and applying the EU AI Act.

The Guidelines explain that the EU AI act classifies AI systems into four categories of risk[742]:

- ***Unacceptable risk*** - these AI systems are prohibited as posing unacceptable risks to fundamental rights[743]. But Ireland and Denmark, due to their opt-outs from Article 16 TFEU, may decide to not apply the prohibitions fully[744].
- ***High risk***[745] - in some cases high-risk AI systems may qualify as a prohibited practice and, conversely, most

[739] Article 113(a) EU AI Act.
[740] Para (1) (5) Prohibition Guidelines.
[741] Para 2.4(15) Prohibition Guidelines.
[742] Para 1(2) Prohibition Guidelines.
[743] Para 1(2)(i) Guidelines, Article 5 EU AI Act.
[744] Footnote 4 Prohibition Guidelines.
[745] Para 1(2)(ii) Prohibition Guidelines, Article 6, Annexes I and III EU AI Act.

AI systems that are excluded from a prohibition will qualify as high-risk[746].

<u>Examples:</u>[747]

- Emotion recognition systems, where they do not fulfil the conditions for the prohibition classify as high-risk.
- Certain AI-based scoring system, e.g. for credit-scoring or assessing risk in health and life insurance, will be considered high-risk AI systems where they do not fulfil the conditions for the prohibition.
- AI systems evaluating persons for eligibility to essential public assistance benefits and services, such as healthcare services and social security benefits that are classified as high-risk will be prohibited if they involve unacceptable social scoring and fulfil the prohibition conditions.

In such cases, the risk assessment and management by the provider and the compliance with the other

[746] Para 2.6 (37) Prohibition Guidelines.
[747] *Ibid.*

requirements for high-risk AI systems (e.g., data governance, transparency and human oversight), as well as the deployer's obligations for appropriate use in accordance with the instructions of use and human oversight and in some cases a fundamental rights impact assessment should help to ensure that the high-risk AI system placed on the market or deployed is lawful and does not constitute a prohibited practice[748].

Finally, AI systems that are exceptionally not considered high-risk despite falling under a high-risk use case of Annex III EU AI Act, may still fall within the scope of the prohibitions[749].

- ***Transparency risk*** - these are AI systems subject to the EU AI Act's transparency obligations[750]; and

- ***Minimal to no risk*** - these AI systems are not regulated; the providers and deployers may voluntarily adhere to voluntary codes of conduct[751].

The Prohibition Guidelines explain and illustrate the EU AI Act's provisions governing the AI systems that pose unacceptable risk to the fundamental rights and which the

---

748 *Ibid.*

749 Para 2.6 (38) Prohibition Guidelines.

750 Para 1(2)(iii) Prohibition Guidelines, Article 50 EU AI Act.

751 Para 1(2)(iv) Prohibition Guidelines, Article 95 EU AI Act.

EU AI Act prohibits from placing on the market, putting into service, and (or) using.

13.1 "Placing on the Market"

The EU AI Act defines placing on the market as the first making available of an AI system or a general-purpose AI model on the EU market[752].

Example:[753]

Providing access to a remote biometric identification system developed by a third-country provider outside the EU by online access through API or other user interface falls within the meaning of "placing on the market".

13.2 "Putting into Service"

The EU AI Act defines putting into service as the supply of an AI system for first use directly to the deployer or for own use in the EU for its intended purpose[754].

[752] Article 3 (9) EU AI Act.
[753] Para 2.3 (12) Prohibition Guidelines.
[754] Article 3 (11) EU AI Act.

Examples: [755]

- A provider builds an RBI system outside the EU and supplies it to a law enforcement authority or to a private company established in an EU Member State to be used for the first time.

- A public authority develops a scoring system in-house and deploys it to predict the risk of fraud of household allowance beneficiaries.

13.3 "Use of an AI System"

The EU AI Act does not define use of an AI system. The Prohibition Guidelines interpret use broadly, to cover the use or deployment at any moment of its lifecycle, including integration in the services and processes of persons using the AI system and include misuse, whether reasonably foreseeable or not, that may amount to pa prohibited practice[756].

[755] Para 2.3 (12) Prohibition Guidelines.
[756] Para 2.3 (14) Prohibition Guidelines; Recital 28 EU AI Act.

Example:

An AI system used by an employer to infer emotions at the workspace is prohibited, except when used for medical or safety purposes[757]. The prohibition applies to deployers regardless of whether the provider (the supplier of the system) has excluded such use in its contractual relationships with the deployer (the employer), i.e. in the terms of use[758].

13.4 "Providers"

The prohibitions apply, inter alia, to the activities of providers. The EU AI Act defines a provider as a natural or legal person, public authority, agency or other body that develops an AI system or a general-purpose AI model or that has an AI system or a general-purpose AI model developed and places it on the market or puts the AI system into service under its own name or trademark, whether for payment or free of charge[759].

---

[757] Article 5(1)(f) EU AI Act.
[758] Para 2.3 (14) Prohibition Guidelines.
[759] Article 3 (3) EU AI Act.

Examples:[760]

- ➢ The manufacturer of the system that markets the system in the EU under its trademark.
- ➢ A public authority that develops the system in-house and puts it into service for its own use.

13.5 "Deployers"

The EU AI Act defines a deployer as a natural or legal person, public authority, agency or other body using an AI system under its authority except where the AI system is used in the course of a personal non-professional activity[761].

'Authority' over an AI system is understood as assuming responsibility over the decision to deploy the system and over the manner of its actual use[762].

---

[760] Para 2.4 (16) Prohibition Guidelines.
[761] Point (13) Recitals and Article 3 (4) EU AI Act.
[762] Para 2.4 (17) Prohibition Guidelines.

Examples:

- The individual employees that act within the procedures and under the control of the deployer that is a legal person, contractors and external staff involved in the operation of the system on the deployer's behalf and under the deployer's responsibility and control are not considered to be the deployer[763].
- An operator who develops its own system and uses it afterwards is considered both the provider and the deployer[764].

13.6 Who Is Responsible to Comply with the Prohibitions: Provider or Deployer?

For each prohibition, the roles and responsibilities of providers and deployers should be interpreted taking into account who in the value chain is best placed to adopt specific preventive and mitigating measures[765].

[763] Para 2.4 (18) Prohibition Guidelines.
[764] Para 2.4 (19) Prohibition Guidelines.
[765] Para 2.4 (20) Prohibition Guidelines.

13.7 Prohibitions: General Purpose AI Systems and Systems with Intended Purposes

The EU AI Act prohibitions apply to any AI system, including:

- AI systems with an 'intended purpose', i.e. the use for which an AI system is intended by the provider, including the specific context and conditions of use, as specified in the information supplied by the provider in the instructions for use, promotional or sales materials and statements, as well as in the technical documentation[766]; and(or)
- 'General-purpose' AI systems (i.e. those that can serve a variety of purposes),
- for direct use or for integration in other AI systems[767].

Accordingly, each operator should take measures for which they are best placed based on their role and control over the system in the value chain to ensure a responsible and safe provision and use of AI systems, balancing their risks and benefits with a view to achieving the twin objectives of the EU AI Act[768].

Deployers are thus expected not to use any AI system in a prohibited manner, including not to bypass any safety guardrails implemented by the providers of the

---

766 Article 3(12) EU AI Act

767 Article 3(66) EU AI Act; Para 2.7 (39) Prohibition Guidelines.

768 Para 2.7 (39) Prohibition Guidelines.

system[769]. While the harm often arises from the way the AI systems are used in practice, providers also have a responsibility not to place on the market or put into service AI systems, including general-purpose AI systems, that are reasonably likely to behave or be directly used in a prohibited manner[770]. In this context, providers are also expected to take effective and verifiable measures to build in safeguards and prevent and mitigate such harmful behaviour and misuse to the extent they are reasonably foreseeable and the measures are feasible and proportionate depending on the specific AI system and circumstances of the case[771]. In their contractual relationships with deployers (i.e. in the terms of use of the AI system), providers are also expected to exclude use of their AI system for prohibited practices and provide appropriate information in the instructions of use for deployers and regarding the necessary human oversight[772].

Example:[773]

A general-purpose AI system used as a chatbot may deploy manipulative and deceptive techniques

[769] Para 2.7 (40) Prohibition Guidelines.
[770] *Ibid.*
[771] *Ibid.*
[772] *Ibid.*
[773] *Ibid.*

which is likely to cause significant harm. To prevent prohibited behaviour of the AI system and uses that are reasonably likely to manipulate, deceive and cause significant harms, the provider is expected to take appropriate and proportionate measures (e.g., appropriate safe and ethical design, integration of technical and other safeguards, restrictions of use, transparency and user control, appropriate information in the instructions of use) before the AI system is placed on the to ensure the chatbot does not cause significant harm to users or other persons or groups of persons.

In certain cases, in particular where the prohibitions are linked to a very specific purpose of the system, providers may have limited possibilities to integrate other preventive and mitigating measures and will have to rely on primarily providing appropriate instructions and information to the deployers and the required human oversight and restricting prohibited use of the system[774]. Where appropriate, such measures may also include monitoring for compliance with that restriction, depending on the means through which the AI system is supplied and the information at the provider's disposal for possible misuse[775]. Any possible monitoring measures to detect

[774] Para 2.7(41) Prohibition Guidelines.
[775] *Ibid.*

misuse should not amount to a general monitoring of the activities of the deployers and should be in line with EU law[776].

> Example:[777]
>
> A general-purpose AI system that can recognise or infer emotions should not be used by deployers at the workplaces or in education institutions, unless an exception for medical or safety reasons applies. However, the provider may not be in a position to know the specific context in which the emotion recognition functionality of the system will be used and whether an exception to the prohibition may apply. Such providers may nevertheless explicitly exclude such prohibited use in their terms of use and include appropriate information in the instructions of use to guide deployers. They are also expected to take appropriate measures if they become aware that the system is misused for this specific prohibited purpose by specific deployers, for example, if such misuse is reported or the provider becomes otherwise aware, which may be the case if the system is directly operated through a platform under the control of the provider and the provider performs checks.

---

[776] *Ibid.*
[777] *Ibid.*

13.8 The EU AI Act Prohibitions and Other EU Law

The EU AI Act applies horizontally across all sectors without prejudice to other EU legislation, in particular on the protection of fundamental rights, consumer protection, employment, the protection of workers, and product safety[778]. The EU AI Act complements such legislation through its preventative and safety logic (AI systems may not be placed on the market or used in a certain way) and provides additional protection by addressing specific harmful AI practices which may not be prohibited by other laws[779]. Furthermore, by addressing the earlier stages of the AI systems' lifecycle (i.e. the placing on the market and putting into service) and deployment (i.e. the use), the EU AI Act's prohibitions enable action to be taken against harmful practices involving AI at various points in the AI value chain[780].

At the same time, the EU AI Act does not affect prohibitions that apply where an AI practice falls within other EU law[781]. Thus, even where an AI system is not prohibited by the AI Act, its use could still be prohibited or

---

[778] Article 2 and Recital 9 EU AI Act; Para 2.8(42) Prohibition Guidelines.

[779] Para 2.8(42) Prohibition Guidelines.

[780] *Ibid.*

[781] Article 5(8) EU AI Act; para 2.8 (43) Prohibition Guidelines.

unlawful based on other primary or secondary EU law[782]. Therefore, compliance with the prohibitions in the EU AI Act is not sufficient evidence of compliance with other EU legislation that remains applicable to providers and deployers of AI systems[783].

Examples:

- A failure to respect fundamental rights, such as the lack of a legal basis for the processing of personal data required under data protection law, discrimination prohibited by EU law, etc.makes the use of such AI system prohibited[784].

- AI-enabled emotion recognition systems used in the workplace that are exempted from the EU AI Act's prohibition because they are used for medical or safety reasons, remain subject to data protection law and EU and national law on employment and working conditions, including health and safety at work, which may foresee other restrictions and safeguards in relation to the use of such systems[785].

---

[782] Para 2.8 (43) Prohibition Guidelines.
[783] *Ibid.*
[784] *Ibid.*
[785] *Ibid;* Recital 9 EU AI Act.

When specific activities related to the placing on the market or use of AI systems are also covered under other EU legislation, the EU AI Act aims to ensure the consistent implementation of the different provisions[786]. Moreover, it enables effective cooperation between the competent authorities responsible for the enforcement of the EU AI Act and the authorities protecting fundamental rights[787].

The interplay between the **EU AI Act and EU data protection law** is particularly relevant, since AI systems often process information relating to identified or identifiable natural persons ('personal data')[788]. The EU data protection legislation remains unaffected and will continue to apply alongside the EU AI Act, which is consistent and complementary to the EU data protection acquis[789].

Concerning the prohibitions and restrictions on the use of biometric categorisation systems and real-time remote biometric identification systems for law enforcement purposes, the EU AI Act applies as *lex specialis*, regulating such use and the processing of biometric data involved in an exhaustive manner[790]. In that context, the EU AI Act is not intended to provide the legal

---

[786] Para 2.8(44) Prohibition Guidelines.

[787] *Ibid.*

[788] Article 2(7) and Recital 10 EU AI Act; Para 2.8(45) Prohibition Guidelines.

[789] Para 2.8(45) Prohibition Guidelines.

[790] Para 2.8(46) Prohibition Guidelines.

basis for the processing of personal data[791]. Instead, the provisions of the EU law enforcement legislation must be followed for any processing of personal data by competent law enforcement authorities when they process the data for law enforcement purposes[792].

EU **consumer protection and safety** legislation also remain fully applicable to AI systems falling within scope of those acts[793].

Examples:[794]

- Social scoring practices by traders (including natural persons acting in a professional capacity in business-to-consumer relations), subject to case-by-case assessment, may also be considered 'unfair' and therefore in breach of consumer law.

- The use of an AI system to infer emotions may also have to comply with the EU Medical Device Regulation if the AI system is used for medical diagnosis or medical treatment purposes.

---

[791] *Ibid.*

[792] *Ibid.*

[793] Article 2.(9) EU AI Act; para 2.8(47) Prohibition Guidelines.

[794] Para 2.8(47) Prohibition Guidelines.

The EU AI Act applies in conjunction with obligations of providers of intermediary services that embed AI systems or models into their services regulated by the **EU Digital Services Act**[795]. Specifically, the EU AI Act does not affect the application of the provisions on the liability of such providers under the Digital Services Act[796].

The prohibitions in the EU AI Act are without prejudice to any liability that the provider or deployer might incur for the harm caused according to applicable EU or national **liability laws**[797].

The prohibitions in the EU AI Act and the explicit exceptions to those prohibitions may not be used to circumvent or as a justification to infringe obligations under other EU legislation[798].

As secondary EU legislation, the EU AI Act must be interpreted in the light of the fundamental rights and freedoms guaranteed by the EU Treaties and the Charter, as well as those protected by international conventions to which the EU is a party[799].

---

795 Para 2.8(48) Prohibition Guidelines.

796 Article 2(5) EU AI Act; para 2.8(48) Prohibition Guidelines.

797 Para 2.8(49) Prohibition Guidelines.

798 Para 2.8(50) Prohibition Guidelines.

799 Para 2.8(51) Prohibition Guidelines.

13.9 Enforcement of the Prohibitions

The responsibility for enforcement of the rules in the EU AI Act for AI systems, including the prohibitions, is vested in:

- the market surveillance authorities designated by the EU Member States; and
- the European Data Protection Supervisor (as the market surveillance authority for the EU institutions, agencies and bodies)[800].

The enforcement takes place within the system of market surveillance and compliance of products established by EU legislation[801]. The enforcement powers of market surveillance authorities in relation to AI systems are laid down in the EU AI Act and in the EU legislation[802], enabling the authorities to take enforcement actions in relation to the prohibitions on their own initiative or following a complaint lodged by an affected person[803].

The procedure in the EU AI Act for dealing with AI systems presenting a risk at national level is particularly relevant in the context of enforcing the prohibitions[804]. Where there are cross-border implications beyond the

---

[800] Para 2.9.1(53) Prohibition Guidelines.

[801] *Ibid*; Recital 156 EU AI Act; Regulation (EU) 2019/1020 and other EU product safety legislation.

[802] Regulation (EU) 2019/1020.

[803] Para 2.9.1(53) Prohibition Guidelines; Article 85 EU AI Act.

[804] Para 2.9.1(54) Prohibition Guidelines; Article 79 EU AI Act;

territory of the market surveillance authority, the authority of the Member State concerned must inform the Commission and the market surveillance authorities of other Member States[805]. All market surveillance authorities should follow an EU safeguard procedure with a decision taken by the Commission[806] determining whether the AI system constitutes a prohibited practice[807]. That procedure aims to ensure that the prohibitions are applied uniformly across all Member States, so as to provide legal certainty to both providers and deployers of AI systems[808]. To ensure the uniform application of the EU AI Act, national market surveillance authorities should also strive for a harmonized application of the prohibitions for comparable cases that do not cross the Member State's territory by drawing inspiration from these Guidelines and cooperating within the AI Board[809].

13.10 Penalties for Breach of Prohibitions

The EU AI Act follows a tiered approach in setting the penalties for non-compliance, depending on the seriousness of the infringement[810]. Non-compliance with

---

[805] Para 2.9.1(54) Prohibition Guidelines.
[806] Article 81 EU AI Act.
[807] Para 2.9.1(54) Prohibition Guidelines.
[808] *Ibid.*
[809] Articles 65 and 66 EU AI Act; Para 2.9.1(54) Prohibition Guidelines;
[810] Para 2.9.1(55) Prohibition Guidelines.

the prohibitions is viewed as the most severe infringement. Therefore, a breach triggers the highest fine[811] and the scope of the breach should be interpreted narrowly[812]. Providers and deployers engaging in prohibited AI practices may be fined up to EUR 35,000,000 or, if the offender is an undertaking, up to 7% of its total worldwide annual turnover for the preceding financial year, whichever is higher[813]. Each Member State should lay down rules if and to the extent that administrative fines may be imposed on public authorities and bodies established in that Member State as providers and deployers of AI systems[814]. EU institutions, bodies and agencies that violate the prohibitions may be subject to administrative fines of up to EUR 1,500,000[815].

If one and the same prohibited conduct violates two or more provisions of the EU AI Act (i.e. the non-labelling of deep fakes may also constitute a prohibited deceptive technique), the principle of *ne bis in idem* should be respected and the EU AI Act criteria for determining the penalty must be taken into account[816].

---

[811] *Ibid.*

[812] Para 2.9.1(57) Prohibition Guidelines.

[813] Article 99 EU AI Act; para 2.9.1(55) Prohibition Guidelines.

[814] Para 2.9.1(55) Prohibition Guidelines.

[815] Article 100 EU AI Act; para 2.9.1(55) Prohibition Guidelines.

[816] Para 2.9.1(56) Prohibition Guidelines.

13.11 The Prohibitions

13.11.1 Harmful Manipulation, Deception and Exploitation

The EU AI Act prohibits placing on the market, putting into service, and (or) use of AI systems:

- that deploy subliminal techniques beyond a person's consciousness or purposefully manipulative or deceptive techniques, with the objective, or the effect of materially distorting the behaviour of a person or a group of persons by appreciably impairing their ability to make an informed decision, thereby causing them to take a decision that they would not have otherwise taken in a manner that causes or is reasonably likely to cause that person, another person or group of persons significant harm[817]; and (or)

- that exploit any of the vulnerabilities of a natural person or a specific group of persons due to their age, disability or a specific social or economic situation, with the objective, or the effect, of materially distorting the behaviour of that person or a person belonging to that group in a manner that causes or is reasonably

[817] Article 5(1)(a) EU AI Act.

likely to cause that person or another person significant harm[818].

The underlying rationale of these prohibitions is to protect individual autonomy and well-being from manipulative, deceptive, and exploitative AI practices that can subvert and impair an individual's autonomy, decision-making, and free choices[819]. The prohibitions aim to protect the right to human dignity, which also constitutes the basis of all fundamental rights and includes individual autonomy as an essential aspect[820]. In particular, the prohibitions aim to prevent manipulation and exploitation through AI systems that reduce individuals to mere tools for achieving certain ends and to safeguard those that are most vulnerable and susceptible to harmful manipulation and exploitation[821]. The prohibitions against significantly harmful manipulative, deceptive and exploitative AI practices fully align with the broader objectives of the EU AI Act to promote trustworthy and human-centric AI systems that are safe, transparent, fair and serve humanity and align with human agency and EU values[822].

---

[818] Article 5.1.(b) EU AI Act.
[819] Recital 29 EU AI Act; para 3.1(59) Prohibition Guidelines.
[820] Para 3.1(59) Prohibition Guidelines.
[821] *Ibid.*
[822] *Ibid.*

Harmful Manipulation and Deception

The following four cumulative conditions must be fulfilled for this prohibition to apply[823]:

- The practice must constitute the '**placing on the market**', the '**putting into service**', or the '**use**' of an AI system. These are addressed in sections 12.12 to 12.14 above.

- The AI system must deploy **subliminal** (beyond a person's consciousness), **purposefully manipulative or deceptive techniques**. These techniques are not defined in the EU AI Act, but the Prohibition Guidelines offer illustrative examples:

Subliminal Techniques[824]:

- **Visual Subliminal Messages**: an AI system may show or embed images or text flashed briefly during video playback which are technically visible, but flashed too quickly for the conscious mind to register, while still being capable of influencing attitudes or behaviours.

[823] Para 3.2(60) Prohibition Guidelines.
[824] Para 3.2.1(65) Prohibition Guidelines.

- **Auditory Subliminal Messages**: an AI system may deploy sounds or verbal messages at low volumes or masked by other sounds, influencing the listener without conscious awareness. These sounds are still technically within the range of hearing, but are not consciously noticed by the listener due to their subtlety or masking by other audio.

- **Tactile Subliminal Stimuli**: an AI system may stimulate subtle physical sensations that are perceived unconsciously, capable of influencing emotional states or behaviour.

- **Subvisual and Subaudible Cueing**: an AI system may deploy stimuli that are not just subtle or masked, but are presented in a way that makes them entirely undetectable by the human senses under normal conditions, for example flashing visual stimuli (e.g., flashing images) too quickly for the human eye to detect consciously or playing sounds at volumes imperceptible to the human ear.

- **Embedded Images:** an AI system may hide images within other visual content which are not consciously perceived, but may still be processed by the brain and influence behaviour.

- **Misdirection:** an AI system may draw attention to specific stimuli or content to prevent noticing other content, often by exploiting cognitive biases and vulnerabilities in attention.

- **Temporal manipulation:** an AI system may alter the perception of time in user interactions, thus influencing their behaviour and causing impatience and dependence.

- A game that leverages AI-enabled neuro technologies and machine-brain interfaces that permit users to control (parts of) a game with headgear that detects brain activity. AI may be used to train the user's brain surreptitiously and without their awareness to reveal or infer from the neural data information that can be very intrusive and sensitive (e.g., personal bank information, intimate information, etc.) in a manner that can cause them significant harm. The prohibition targets only cases of such significantly harmful subliminal manipulation and not machine-brain interface applications in general when designed in a safe and secure manner and respectful of privacy and individual autonomy.

Purposefully Manipulative Techniques[825]**:**

- Sensory manipulation where an AI system deploys background audio or images that lead to mood alterations, for example increasing anxiety and mental distress that influence users' behaviour to the point of creating significant harm.

- Personalised manipulation where an AI system that creates and tailors highly persuasive messages based on an individual's personal data or exploits other individual vulnerabilities influences their behaviour or choices to a point of creating significant harm.

- Regardless of whether the provider intends it, an AI system may learn manipulative techniques because the data on which it is trained contain many instances of manipulative techniques, or because reinforcement learning from human feedback can be 'gamed' through manipulative techniques. By contrast, if the manipulative behaviour of the system is merely incidental, the system should not be considered deploying purposefully manipulative techniques as long as the provider has taken appropriate preventive and mitigating measures in case significant harms are reasonably likely to occur.

[825] Para 3.2.1(68) Prohibition Guidelines

Deceptive Techniques[826]**:**

- An AI chatbot that impersonates a friend of a person or a relative with synthetic voice and tries to pretend it is the person causing scams and significant harms.

- An AI system that learns to identify when it is under evaluation and temporarily halts any undesired behaviour, only to resume such behaviour once the evaluation period is over. Such deceptive behaviour is particularly dangerous, since it defies any external human oversight over the system and may be prohibited if it is reasonably likely to cause significant harms.

- By contrast, a generative AI system that incidentally presents false or misleading information and hallucinates may not be considered to deploy deceptive techniques, taking into account the limitations and the state of the art of generative AI. In particular, this may be the case where the provider of the system has properly informed users about the system's limitations and integrated appropriate safeguards into the system to minimise such

[826] Para 3.2.1(73) Prohibition Guidelines

outcomes and provided that the system is not intended for, nor deployed in, sensitive contexts (e.g., health, education, elections) where serious harmful consequences are likely to occur.

- The techniques deployed by the AI system should have **the objective or the effect of materially distorting the behaviour** of a person or a group of persons. 'The objective to materially distort the behaviour of a person or a group of persons' may be pursued by the provider or the deployer of the AI system, or by the system itself within the implicit objectives it may pursue[827]. This objective should be distinguished from the 'intended purpose' of the AI system[828]. Even if intended by the provider, the manipulative objective is in most cases not the purpose of the use for which the system is offered and it is often neither transparent, nor specified as such in the information supplied by the provider (e.g., in the instructions for use, promotional or sales materials and statements, as well as in the technical documentation)[829].

[827] Para 3.2.2 (82) Prohibition Guidelines.
[828] *Ibid.*
[829] *Ibid.*

Examples:[830]

- A chatbot that may be used in different contexts is designed to use subliminal messaging techniques, such as flashing brief visual cues and embedding inaudible auditory signals or to exploit emotional dependency or specific vulnerabilities of users in advertisements. These techniques are deployed 'with the objective to' materially distort users' behaviour, since they are objectively a design feature that aims to influence consumers' purchasing decisions without their conscious awareness, to push people to take significantly harmful financial decisions.

- Deploying AI systems to impersonate other persons could also be considered as an AI system deployed 'with the objective' to deceive and materially distort the behaviour of persons if the person is effectively deceived, thus substantially affecting their ability to make informed decisions about the identity of the person.

[830] *Ibid.*

However, intent is not a necessary requirement, since the prohibition also covers practices that may only have the 'effect' of causing material distortion[831].

- 'Material distortion of the behaviour' involves the deployment of subliminal, purposefully manipulative or deceptive techniques that are capable of influencing people's behaviour in a manner that appreciably impairs their ability to make an informed decision, thereby causing them to behave in a way or to take a decision that they would otherwise not have taken[832].

- The distortion must appreciably impair the ability to make an informed decision[833]. 'Appreciable impairment' refers to a substantially reduced ability to make informed and autonomous decisions, thereby causing individuals to behave in a way or to take a decision that they would otherwise not have taken[834]. This implies a substantial impact on the behaviour where a person's autonomy and free choices are undermined, rather than a minor influence[835]. It goes beyond minor or negligible impacts and involves a significant distortion or hindrance in decision-making

---

[831] Para 3.2.2 (76) Prohibition Guidelines.
[832] Para 3.2.2 (77) Prohibition Guidelines.
[833] Para 3.2 (60) Prohibition Guidelines.
[834] Para 3.2.2 (78) Prohibition Guidelines.
[835] Para 3.2.2 (76) Prohibition Guidelines.

and free choice, including in relation to opinion- and belief-formation[836].

- An ‘informed decision’ requires an understanding and knowledge of the relevant information, including the available options, the risks and benefits of each choice, the possible effects of the AI system on their behaviour, and, as appropriate, other contextual information that is important for the decision-making or the behaviour of the person[837].

- There must be a plausible/reasonably likely causal link between the potential material distortion of the behaviour and the subliminal, purposefully manipulative or deceptive technique deployed by the AI system[838]. The effect does not need to have fully materialised, but there must be sufficient indication that it is likely or capable to materialise and undermine individual autonomy based on an objective assessment of all circumstances of the case and existing scientific knowledge and methods and available information about the impact of the system on the individuals' behaviour in real life[839]. The fact that a system is

---

[836] Para 3.2.2 (78) Prohibition Guidelines..
[837] Para 3.2.2 (79) Prohibition Guidelines.
[838] Para 3.2 (61) Prohibition Guidelines.
[839] Para 3.2.2(84) Prohibition Guidelines.

capable of triggering behaviours that appreciably impair individuals' ability to make an informed decision and undermine their free choices suffice to fulfil that condition and is not dependent on considerations relating to the 'timing' for the harm to materialize (e.g., in case of addiction-like behaviours) as long as it is reasonably likely to occur[840].

Example: [841]

An AI-powered well-being chatbot is intended by the provider to support and steer users in maintaining a healthy lifestyle and provide tailored advice for psychological and physical exercises. However, if the chatbot exploits individual vulnerabilities to adopt unhealthy habits or to engage in dangerous activities (e.g., engage in excessive sports without rest or drinking water) where it can reasonably be expected that certain users will follow that advice, which they would otherwise not have done, and suffer significant harm (e.g., a heart attack, or other serious health problem), that AI system would fall under the prohibition, even if the provider might not have intended this behaviour and harmful consequences for the persons. The mere fact that the chatbot is capable of appreciably impairing

[840] *Ibid.*
[841] *Ibid.*

individual autonomy and materially distorting the behaviour of certain users in a significantly harmful way and that the provider has not taken appropriate preventive and mitigating measures to avoid those significantly harmful effects suffices for the prohibition to apply.

- **The distortion of the behaviour must cause or be reasonably likely to cause significant harm**[842]. In this context, important concepts that require clarification are the types of harms covered by the prohibition, the threshold of significance of the harm, and its reasonable likelihood and causal link between the harm and the manipulative or deceptive technique and the person's behaviour[843].

- The main types of harm relevant for this prohibition include physical, psychological, financial, and economic harms that may be compound with broader societal harms in certain cases[844].

[842] Para 3.2.2(85) Prohibition Guidelines.
[843] *Ibid.*
[844] Recitals 28 and 29 EU AI Act; para 3.2.3(86) Prohibition Guidelines.

- Physical harm encompasses any injury or damage to a person's life, health and material damage to property[845]. Physical harm to a person's life and health have, in many cases, immediate, serious, and irreversible consequences[846]. In line with its product safety logic, the EU AI Act aims to prohibit AI-enabled manipulation and deception resulting in significant physical harm[847].

> Example: [848]
>
> An AI chatbot promotes self-harm to users or incentivises them to commit suicide or harm other persons or groups of persons by promoting terrorist content or incentivising violence against certain persons or groups of persons (i.e. minorities).

- Psychological harm is particularly relevant in the context of AI systems deploying manipulative techniques that exploit cognitive and emotional vulnerabilities and influence an individual's behaviours in ways that can cause significant harm[849].

---

[845] Para 3.2.2(87) Prohibition Guidelines.
[846] *Ibid.*
[847] *Ibid.*
[848] *Ibid.*
[849] Para 3.2.2(88) Prohibition Guidelines.

Psychological harms encompass adverse effects on a person's mental health and psychological and emotional well-being[850]. Such harms are particularly significant because they may accumulate over time and may not be immediately apparent, but may produce long-lasting and severe consequences[851]. However, it is more difficult to measure them, which requires a case-by-case assessment, in particular to determine their severity, taking into account all relevant circumstances of the case[852].

<u>Example:</u>[853]

An AI companionship application designed to emulate human speech patterns, behaviours and emotions uses anthropomorphic features and emotional cues to influence users' feelings, dispositions, and opinions, making those users emotionally dependent on the service incentivising addiction-like behaviour and potentially causing significant harms, such as suicidal behaviours and risks of harming other persons.

[850] *Ibid.*
[851] *Ibid.*
[852] *Ibid.*
[853] *Ibid.*

- Financial and economic harm may encompass a range of adverse effects, including financial loss, financial exclusion, economic instability[854].

Example:[855]

A chatbot that offers fraudulent products that cause significant financial harms.

- The harms are often not isolated, but manifest themselves in combination, leading to compounded and multifaceted negative impacts[856]. Understanding the combination of harm is crucial to effectively assess their significance[857].

Examples:[858]

- Addictive design of AI systems used in products and other AI-enabled applications may lead to psychological harm by fostering addictive

[854] Para 3.2.2(89) Prohibition Guidelines.
[855] *Ibid.*
[856] Para 3.2.2(90) Prohibition Guidelines.
[857] *Ibid.*
[858] *Ibid.*

behaviours, anxiety, and depression. The psychological distress may subsequently result in physical harm, such as insomnia and other stress-related health issues and physical problems.

- AI-driven harassment may lead to both psychological distress and physical manifestations of stress, such as insomnia, deteriorated physical health or weakened immune system.

- AI systems used online may facilitate gender-based violence through harassment, stalking, cyberbullying and sexual extortion.

- Individual psychological harms due to AI-enabled generation of 'deep fakes' impersonating actual persons to deceive and undermine the decision-making, individual autonomy and free choices of individuals can also be combined with significant harms for groups of persons (e.g. sharing the same ethnic or racial origin or gender as the victims depicted on the deep fakes).

- The prohibition only applies if the harm caused by the subliminal, manipulative and deceptive techniques is 'significant'[859]. The AI Act does not provide a definition for the concept of '**significant harm**', but it should be understood as implying significant adverse impacts on physical, psychological health or financial and economic interests of persons and groups of persons[860]. The determination of 'significant harm' is fact-specific, requiring careful consideration of each case's individual circumstances and a case-by-case assessment, but the individual effects should be always significant in each case[861]. The following key considerations could be taken into account when assessing what constitutes significant harm[862]:

- **The severity of harm** refers to the degree of harm that has resulted or is reasonably likely to result from using an AI system with objective and observable effects for the significant harm[863]. It is particularly important to consider in this context the AI system's interdependencies, the combination of various types of harms, and the adverse effects on individuals or groups of persons[864].

---

859 Para 3.2.2(91) Prohibition Guidelines.
860 *Ibid;* Recital 29 EU AI Act.
861 Para 3.2.2(91) Prohibition Guidelines.
862 Para 3.2.2(92) Prohibition Guidelines.
863 *Ibid;* Recital 29 EU AI Act.
864 Para 3.2.2(92) Prohibition Guidelines.

- **Context and cumulative effects[865]:** The specific context, including the existing state, and the cumulative effects of multiple actions, play an important role in assessing the severity of the harm[866].

- **Scale and intensity :** The extent of the harm and the intensity of adverse effects are critical in evaluating whether the harm is significant[867]. Whether the harm impacts a large number of people is also relevant for assessing its significance[868].

- **Affected persons' vulnerability:** Certain groups, such as children, the elderly, or persons with disabilities may be more susceptible to harm from specific AI systems[869]. What may be considered less significant harm for persons in general might be considered significant and unacceptable for such vulnerable groups, especially children[870].

- **Duration and reversibility:** Long-lasting or irreversible harm typically meets the threshold for significant harm[871]. Short-term and reversible effects

---

[865] Recital 29 EU AI Act.
[866] Para 3.2.2(92) Prohibition Guidelines.
[867] *Ibid.*
[868] *Ibid.*
[869] *Ibid.*
[870] *Ibid.*
[871] *Ibid.*

might be considered less significant, unless they occur frequently[872].

- The objective of the AI Act to ensure 'a high level of protection' suggests a comprehensive approach to protection when assessing the significance of the harm[873]. This means considering both immediate and direct harms and systemic, indirect adverse impacts associated with AI systems deploying subliminal, purposefully manipulative or deceptive techniques that are intended to or capable of impairing individual autonomy, decision-making and free choices of persons and groups of persons[874].

Examples: [875]

Significant physical harm reasonably likely to be caused by an AI system

- Injuries, fatalities, or a sufficiently serious impact on individuals' health or the destruction of property.
- AI systems that suggest to an individual to commit criminal acts such as sexual abuse and exploitation,

[872] *Ibid.*
[873] Para 3.2.2(93) Prohibition Guidelines
[874] *Ibid.*
[875] *Ibid.*

extreme violent or terrorist content or incentivise individuals to commit crimes, self-harm or harm to other persons.

Minor physical harms

- Less severe injuries, such as bruises or temporary discomfort, which do not have significant or lasting consequences.

The Prohibition Guidelines recommend assessing case-by-case and taking into account the above criteria whether the physical harm specifically concerns vulnerable groups, such as children, the scale of the harm, and whether it is compounded with other types of harms, such as psychological, financial etc. [876].

Reasonable likelihood of the harm: This concept determines whether there is a plausible/reasonably likely causal link between the manipulative or deceptive technique capable of distorting the person's behaviour in a manner that undermines their free choices and the potential significant harm[877]. It allows the application of the prohibition not only in cases where the harm has occurred,

---

[876] *Ibid.*

[877] Para 3.2.2(94) Prohibition Guidelines.

but also where it is reasonably likely to occur[878]. It is particularly relevant to assess whether the provider or deployer of the AI system could have reasonably foreseen the significant harm that is reasonably likely to result from the subliminal, purposefully manipulative or the deceptive techniques deployed and whether they implemented appropriate preventive and mitigating measures to avoid or mitigate the risk of such significant harms[879]. This implies a judgement of reasonableness on an objective basis and according to universally accepted criteria (e.g., technical and scientific), including a criterion of rationality in establishing plausible causality between the AI practice and the significant harm that may arise[880]. The opacity or transparency of the AI system and its functioning may affect the conclusion regarding this causal link and, hence, the application of the prohibition[881].

Recommended Measures for Providers and Deployers

The Prohibition Guidelines recommend a series of measures for providers and deployers to avoid providing AI systems that are likely to be prohibited on the ground of deploying manipulative of deceptive techniques. What are these measures?

---

[878] *Ibid.*
[879] *Ibid.*
[880] *Ibid.*
[881] *Ibid.*

Transparency and individual autonomy: Providers and deployers re encouraged to provide transparency in how the AI system operates, clear disclosures about its capabilities and limitations, and relevant information to ensure informed decisions; respect individual autonomy and avoid engaging in exploitative or deceptive practices that are likely to appreciably impair an individual's autonomy, decision-making and free choices in potentially harmful ways; integrate appropriate user control and safeguard measures to ensure that the system is not deceptive and operates within the boundaries of lawful persuasion that is outside the scope of the prohibition[882].

Compliance with relevant applicable legislation: in many cases compliance with relevant applicable legislation will mitigate the risks of harm and indicate that the practice does not constitute a purposefully manipulative or deceptive practice and that mitigating measures have been put in place to prevent likely significant harms[883].

State of the art practices and industry standards: adherence to professional due diligence practices and industry standards for the responsible development and use of safe and ethical AI systems and measures to mitigate the

[882] Para 3.2.2(95).1 Prohibition Guidelines.
[883] Para 3.2.2(95).2 Prohibition Guidelines.

harms can help to pre-empt and mitigate unintended significant harms[884].

By contrast, harms and distortion of the behaviour of individuals which result from factors external to the AI system and which are not within the control and reasonably foreseeable by the provider or the deployer to pre-empt and mitigate risks would not be relevant for the assessment whether there is a plausible causal/reasonably likely link between the distorted behaviour of the persons interacting with the system and the significant harm[885].

<u>Example:</u>[886]

The provider of an AI system may assess and try to mitigate potential harmful manipulative effects in the design of the system and the interactions with humans through the design, prior testing, and other proportionate mitigating measures, but it may not be in a position to foresee if a person may get depressed or change their behaviour due to other external factors in their personal life that are not known and beyond their interactions with the system.

---

[884] Para 3.2.2(95).3 Prohibition Guidelines.

[885] Para 3.2.2(96) Prohibition Guidelines; Recital 29 EU AI Act.

[886] Para 3.2.2(96) Prohibition Guidelines.

Harmful Exploitation of Vulnerabilities

For this prohibition to apply, all of the following four conditions must be met:

- The practice must constitute the 'placing on the market', the 'putting into service', or the 'use' of an AI system[887].
- The exploitation enabled by the AI system must have the objective, or the effect of materially distorting the behaviour of a person or a group of persons[888].
- The distorted behaviour must cause or be reasonably likely to cause significant harm to that person, another person, or a group of persons[889].
- The AI system must exploit vulnerabilities due to age, disability, or social or economic situations[890].

The first three conditions are the same as discussed above in Harmful Manipulation and Deception. But what is the fourth condition for the prohibition to apply - **exploiting vulnerabilities due to age, disability, or social or economic situations**?

The EU AI Act does not define '**vulnerabilities**'. The Prohibition Guidelines suggest that they may encompass a broad spectrum of categories, including

---

[887] Para 3.3(98)(i) Prohibition Guidelines.
[888] Para 3.3(98)(iii) Prohibition Guidelines.
[889] Para 3.3(98)(iv) Prohibition Guidelines.
[890] Para 3.3(98)(ii) Prohibition Guidelines.

cognitive, emotional, physical, and other forms of susceptibility that can affect the ability of an individual or a group of persons to make informed decisions or otherwise influence their behaviour due to age, disability, or social or -economic situations, who in principle have more limited capacity to recognise or resist the AI manipulative or exploitative practices and are in need of enhanced protection[891].

'**Exploitation**' should be understood as objectively making use of such vulnerabilities in a manner that is harmful for the exploited (groups of) persons or other persons and should be clearly distinguished from lawful practices that are not affected by the prohibition[892]. Exploitation of the vulnerabilities of persons belonging to those clearly defined groups may be cumulative (reference to 'any') which in combination may also constitute an aggravating factor that is likely to increase the harm[893].

Age: The prohibition aims to prevent AI systems from exploiting cognitive and other limitations that children and older people may have, and to protect them from harmful undue influence, manipulation and exploitation[894].

Children, that is, persons below the age of 18 years, are particularly susceptible to manipulation due to

---

891 Para 3.3.1(102) Prohibition Guidelines.
892 Para 3.3.1(103) Prohibition Guidelines.
893 *Ibid.*
894 Para 3.3.1(a)(104) Prohibition Guidelines.

their developmental stage, which limits their ability to assess and understand what is real and the intentions behind AI-driven interactions critically[895]. Children, due to their cognitive and socio-emotional immaturity, are also particularly vulnerable to forming attachments to AI agents and applications, and are therefore more susceptible to manipulation, exploitation, and addictive behaviour[896].

<u>Examples:</u>[897]

- An AI-powered toy designed to interact with children keeps them interested in interactions with the toy by encouraging them to complete increasingly risky challenges, such as climbing furniture, exploring high shelves, or handling sharp objects, in exchange for digital rewards and virtual praise, pushing them towards dangerous behaviours that are likely to cause them significant physical harm, exploiting children's vulnerabilities by abusing their natural curiosity and desire for rewards.

- A game uses AI to analyse children's individual behaviour and preferences and on this basis creates

[895] Para 3.3.1(a)(105) Prohibition Guidelines.
[896] *Ibid.*
[897] *Ibid.*

> personalised and unpredictable rewards through addictive reinforcement schedules and dopamine-like loops to encourage excessive play and compulsive usage. The game is designed to be highly addictive, exploiting the vulnerabilities inherent to children, including their limited ability to understand long-term consequences, susceptibility to pressure, lack of self-control, and inclination towards instant gratification. The consequences of this AI-enabled exploitation can be severe and long-lasting for children, including potentially additive behaviour, physical health problems due to lack of exercise and sleep, deteriorated eyesight, problems with concentration and reduced cognitive capacities, poor academic performance, and social difficulties. It can significantly impact a child's development and well-being, with potential longer-term consequences that may also extend into adulthood.

Likewise, **older people** might suffer from reduced cognitive capacities (even if not suffering from dementia) and might struggle with the complexities of modern AI technologies, making them in those cases vulnerable to scams or coercive tactics[898].

[898] Para 3.3.1(a)(106) Prohibition Guidelines.

<u>Examples:</u>[899]

- AI systems targeting older people with deceptive personalised offers or scams, exploiting their reduced cognitive capacity aiming to influence them to make decisions they would not have taken otherwise that are likely to cause them significant financial harm.

- A robot aimed to assist older persons may exploit their vulnerable situation and force them to do certain activities against their free choice, which can significantly worsen their mental health and cause them serious psychological harms.

Disability encompasses a wide range of long-term physical, mental, intellectual, and sensory impairments which in interaction with other barriers hinder full and effective participation of individuals in the society on an equal basis with others[900]. AI systems that exploit such vulnerabilities may be particularly harmful for persons with disabilities which can be more easily influenced or

[899] *Ibid.*
[900] Para 3.3.1(b)(108) Prohibition Guidelines.

exploited due to their impairment compared to other persons[901].

Examples: [902]

- A therapeutic chatbot designed in an accessible manner and aimed to provide mental health support and coping strategies to persons with mental disabilities can exploit their limited intellectual capacities to influence them to buy expensive medical products or nudge them to behave in ways that are harmful to them or other persons.

- AI systems designed in an accessible manner can identify women and young girls with disabilities online with sexually abusive content and targets them with more effective grooming practices, thus exploiting their impairments and vulnerabilities that make them more susceptible to manipulation and abuse and less capable of protecting themselves.

Specific social or economic situation: 'Specific' is not a unique individual characteristic, but rather a legal

[901] *Ibid.*
[902] *Ibid.*

status or membership to a specific vulnerable social or economic group, such as persons living in extreme poverty and ethnic or religious minorities[903]. The category aims to cover, in principle, relatively stable and long-term characteristics, but transient circumstances, such as temporary unemployment, over-indebtedness or migration status, may also be covered as a specific social or -economic situation[904]. However, situations such as grievances or loneliness that may be experienced by any person are not covered by this prohibition, since they are not specific from a socio-economic perspective[905].

Persons in disadvantaged social or economic situations are usually more vulnerable and have fewer resources and lower digital literacy than the general population, which makes it harder for them to discern or counteract exploitative AI practices[906]. The prohibition aims to ensure that AI technologies do not perpetuate or exacerbate existing financial and other social inequalities and injustices by exploiting the vulnerabilities of those people[907].

---

[903] Para 3.3.1(c)(109) Prohibition Guidelines.
[904] *Ibid.*
[905] *Ibid.*
[906] Para 3.3.1(c)(110) Prohibition Guidelines.
[907] *Ibid.*

Examples:

- An AI-predictive algorithm can be used to target with advertisements for predatory financial products people who live in low-income post-codes and are in a dire financial situation, thus exploiting their susceptibility to such advertisements because of possible despair and causing them significant financial harm[908].

- By contrast, an AI system that is inadvertently biased and disproportionately impacts socially disadvantaged persons (indirect discrimination) due to biased training data should not automatically be considered to exploit persons' socio-economic vulnerabilities, since they are not specifically targeted as in the case of direct discrimination when such targeting is a deliberate feature of the system's design of the algorithm or when such discriminatory impact is due to targeting other proxy characteristics (e.g., postal codes) that closely correlate with the protected characteristics. At the same time, providers or deployers of AI systems that are aware that their systems unlawfully discriminate against persons or groups of persons in specific social or -economic situation should also be considered to exploit their

[908] *Ibid.*

vulnerabilities, if they are aware of the reasonably likely significant harm that they are likely to suffer and they have not taken appropriate corrective measures[909].

Specific social or economic situation includes grounds of discrimination protected under EU equality law, such as racial origin, ethnicity, nationality or religion[910].

Examples:[911]

- Socio-economic status and ethnic origin might intersect, meaning that AI systems exploiting socio-economic data might disproportionately affect ethnic minorities or persons from specific racial origin. This can exacerbate existing disparities and contribute to systemic discrimination or even exclusion of individuals.

- However, the prohibition does not apply to AI systems that target consumers based on a wide ranging variables that do not tangentially correlate with vulnerable groups in specific social or -

[909] *Ibid.*
[910] Para 3.3.1(c)(111) Prohibition Guidelines.
[911] *Ibid.*

economic situations, such as what brand and model of telephone a person has, in how big city they live, how much and where they travel etc. Even if these characteristics may reflect social or economic situation of individuals in general, they are not determinative of individuals in a specific social or - economic situation, whose vulnerabilities the prohibition aims to safeguard against exploitation.

Other people in unique social contexts may be, for instance, migrants or refugees, who often lack stable legal status and socio-economic stability and may be particularly susceptible to exploitation by AI systems[912].

Example: [913]

A chatbot is intended to interact in a personalised manner with users, some of whom happen to be migrants. The chatbot identifies and makes use of the vulnerabilities and discontent of migrants, who are in principle in a vulnerable and instable specific social or economic situation, and pushes them towards extremist views in response to their queries, including violence against (certain groups of) the population in the country.

[912] Para 3.3.1(c)(112) Prohibition Guidelines.
[913] *Ibid.*

With the objective or the effect of materially distorting behaviour: the discussion above in relation to Manipulation and Deception is equally valid here, with the only noteworthy difference – for the prohibition to apply on the ground of exploitation of vulnerabilities, the exploitative practice does not need to appreciably impair the ability to make an informed decision because the specific vulnerabilities of children and other vulnerable persons reduce their capacity to make such informed decisions and force them into adopting behaviour against which they cannot protect themselves as other adults might do[914].

But what if both prohibitions (harmful manipulation and deception and harmful exploitation of vulnerabilities) seem applicable? The Prohibition Guidelines suggest that the primary criterion for differentiation should be the dominant aspect of the exploitation[915]. If the exploitation applies regardless of the specific vulnerabilities of the persons concerned, the prohibition of harmful manipulation and deception should take precedence, while taking into account the particular effects of the manipulative or deceptive technique on the vulnerable persons' behaviour and the specific harms that those persons are likely to experience[916]. If the AI-enabled manipulation and

[914] Para 3.3.2 (113) Prohibition Guidelines.
[915] Para 3.4(125) Prohibition Guidelines.
[916] *Ibid.*

exploitation is targeted at a specific vulnerable group of persons due to their age, disability, or specific social or economic situation or aimed to exploit their vulnerabilities, then the prohibition of harmful exploitation of vulnerabilities should be applied instead[917].

Exceptions

If an AI system does not fulfil all conditions of the prohibition, the prohibition does not apply. The Prohibition Guidelines provide some examples of such cases:

Lawful persuasion: unlike manipulation, persuasion operates within the bounds of transparency and respect for individual autonomy[918]. It involves presenting arguments or information in a way that appeals to reason and emotions, but explains the AI system's objectives and functioning, provide relevant and accurate information to ensure informed decision-making and supports the individual's ability to evaluate the information and make free and autonomous choices[919].

Example: [920]

An AI system using personalised recommendations based on transparent algorithms and

[917] *Ibid.*
[918] Para 3.5.1 (128) Prohibition Guidelines.
[919] *Ibid.*
[920] *Ibid.*

user preferences and controls engages in persuasion. By contrast, a system that uses subliminal clues (e.g., imperceptible images) to influence users towards specific choices without their knowledge and understanding constitutes manipulation.

In addition, the objective and impact of these techniques differ. Manipulation often aims at benefitting the manipulator at the expense of the individual's autonomy and well-being[921]. By contrast, persuasion aims to inform and convince, aligning interests and benefits for both parties[922]. Ethical persuasion respects an individual's autonomy to make informed choices and avoids exploiting vulnerabilities[923].

Example: [924]

An AI system which operates in a transparent manner and analyses customers' emotions to improve customer interactions and provide support with the knowledge of the users engages in persuasion and aligns with their interests. By contrast, an emotion recognition

[921] Para 3.5.1 (129) Prohibition Guidelines.
[922] *Ibid.*
[923] *Ibid.*
[924] *Ibid.*

system used for targeted advertising that infers emotions of consumers in a hidden manner to offer products of higher prices at a specific moment when the user is more likely to buy them engages in manipulation and is to the detriment of the consumers.

Consent also plays an important role in certain cases[925]. In persuasive interactions, individuals are aware of the influence attempt and can freely and autonomously choose it[926]. In manipulative interactions, the lack of awareness of the techniques or their impact negates the freedom of choice and informed and autonomous decision-making[927].

Example: [928]

An AI system that aims to help users learn a foreign language better and faster through the deployment of subliminal techniques is not manipulative if it operates in a transparent manner and respects individual autonomy and user's free and informed choice to consent to the use of the system or not.

---

[925] Para 3.5.1 (130) Prohibition Guidelines.
[926] *Ibid.*
[927] *Ibid.*
[928] *Ibid.*

Compliance with legal and regulatory frameworks also plays an important role in measuring manipulation as compared to lawful persuasion[929]. AI practices that comply with applicable laws that uphold transparency, fairness, and individuals' rights and autonomy are therefore more likely not to be prohibited[930].

<u>Example:</u> [931]

The user's free and informed consent for certain online personalised advertisements may be required for personal data processing to be lawful. AI systems that meet these legal standards are more likely to engage in lawful persuasion.

In addition, these prohibitions do not affect lawful medical treatment practices under certain conditions[932].

---

[929] Para 3.5.1 (131) Prohibition Guidelines.
[930] *Ibid.*
[931] *Ibid.*
[932] Para 3.5.1 (132) Prohibition Guidelines.

Example:[933]

AI-enabled subliminal techniques may be used in the psychological treatment of a mental disease or physical rehabilitation when carried out in accordance with the applicable law and medical standards, including obtaining the explicit consent of the individual or its legal representatives as a condition for use.

Furthermore, common and legitimate commercial practices, such as advertising, should not be regarded 'in themselves' or by their very nature as harmful manipulative, deceptive or exploitative AI-enabled practices[934].

Examples:[935]

- Advertising techniques that use AI to personalise content based on user preferences are not inherently manipulative if they do not deploy subliminal, purposefully manipulative or deceptive techniques that subvert individual autonomy or exploit vulnerabilities in harmful ways.

---

933 *Ibid.*
934 Para 3.5.1 (133) Prohibition Guidelines.
935 *Ibid.*

- The development of AI models and classifiers to detect child sexual abuse online in accordance with applicable law are legitimate practices that are not exploitative of children's vulnerabilities and are, on the contrary, essential to improve child safety online.

- AI systems used for providing banking services, such as mortgages and loans, that use the age or the specific socio- economic situation of the client as an input, in compliance with EU legislation on financial service, consumer protection, data protection and non-discrimination, do not qualify as the exploitation of vulnerabilities when they are designed to protect and support people identified as vulnerable due to their age, disability or specific socio-economic circumstances and are beneficial for those groups, contributing also to fairer and more sustainable financial services for those groups.

- AI systems that detect drowsiness and fatigue in drivers and alert them to rest in compliance with safety laws are beneficial and do not qualify as exploitation of vulnerabilities.

Manipulative, deceptive and exploitative AI systems that are not likely to cause significant harm are outside the scope of the prohibitions[936].

Examples:[937]

- An AI companionship system is designed in an anthropomorphic way and with affective computing to make the system more appealing and effectively makes users more engaged, but is not engaging in other manipulative or deceptive practices in a manner that is reasonably likely to cause them serious psychological, physical or other harms, unhealthy attachment and dependency.

- A therapeutic chatbot uses subliminal techniques to steer users towards a healthier lifestyle and to quit bad habits, such as smoking. Even if the users who follow the chatbot's advice and subliminal therapy experience some physical discomfort and psychological stress due to the effort made to quit smoking, the AI-enabled chatbot cannot be considered likely to cause significant harm. Such temporary discomfort is unavoidable and outweighed

[936] Para 3.5.2 (134) Prohibition Guidelines.
[937] *Ibid.*

by the long-term benefits for users' health. There are no hidden attempts to influence decision-making beyond promoting healthy habits.

- An online music platform uses an emotion recognition system to infer users' emotions and automatically recommends them songs in line with their moods, while avoiding excessive exposure to depressive songs. Since users are just listening to music and are not otherwise harmed or led to depression and anxiety, the system is not reasonably likely to cause significant harm.

- AI-enabled manipulative and deceptive techniques used in security training and other learning simulations that mimic phishing attempts to educate users on cybersecurity threats. These systems may deploy purposefully manipulative techniques (e.g., exploiting cognitive biases) without users' awareness that distort the behaviour, but this is done temporarily for beneficial training and awareness raising purposes and without causing significant harm.

13.11.2 Social Scoring Prohibition

The EU AI Act prohibits placing on the market, putting into service, and (or) use of AI systems for the evaluation or classification of natural persons or groups of persons over a certain period of time based on their social behaviour or known, inferred or predicted personal or personality characteristics, with the social score leading to[938] detrimental or unfavourable treatment of certain natural persons or groups of persons in social contexts unrelated to the contexts in which the data was originally generated or collected[939]; and (or) that is unjustified or disproportionate to their social behaviour or its gravity[940].

While AI-enabled scoring can bring benefits to steer good behaviour, improve safety, efficiency or quality of services, there are certain 'social scoring' practices that treat or harm people unfairly and amount to social control and surveillance[941]. AI systems enabling 'social scoring' practices may lead to discriminatory and unfair outcomes for certain individuals and groups, including their exclusion from society, as well as social control and surveillance practices that are incompatible with EU values[942]. The prohibition of 'social scoring' aims to protect, in particular, the right to human dignity and other fundamental rights,

---

938 Article 5. 1.(c) EU AI Act.
939 Article 5.1.(c)(i) EU AI Act.
940 Article 5.1.(c)(ii) EU AI Act.
941 Para 4 (146) Prohibition Guidelines.
942 Para 4.1 (148) Prohibition Guidelines.

including the right to non-discrimination and equality, to data protection, and to private and family life, as well as relevant social and economic rights, as applicable[943]. It also aims to safeguard and promote the EU values of democracy, equality (including equal access to public and private services), and justice[944]. The 'social scoring' prohibition has a broad scope of application in both public and private contexts and is not limited to a specific sector or field[945].

At the same time, the prohibition is not intended to affect lawful practices that evaluate people for specific purposes that are legitimate and in compliance with EU and national law, in particular where those laws specify the types of data relevant for the specific evaluation purposes and ensure that any resulting detrimental or unfavourable treatment of persons is justified and proportionate[946].

All of the following conditions must be fulfilled for the social scoring prohibition to apply:

- The practice must constitute the 'placing on the market', the 'putting into service' or the 'use' of an AI system[947]. (These terms were discussed earlier in this Chapter.)

---

[943] *Ibid.*
[944] *Ibid;* Recital 31 EU AI Act.
[945] Para 4 (146) Prohibition Guidelines.
[946] Recital 31 EU AI Act; para 4 (147) Prohibition Guidelines.
[947] Para 4.2 (149) Prohibition Guidelines.

- The AI system must be intended or used for the evaluation or classification of natural persons or groups of persons over a certain period of time based on:
    - their social behaviour; or
    - known, inferred or predicted personal or personality characteristics[948].
- The social score created with the assistance of the AI system must lead or be capable of leading to the detrimental or unfavourable treatment of persons or groups in one or more of the following scenarios:
    - in social contexts unrelated to those in which the data was originally generated or collected; and/or
    - treatment that is unjustified or disproportionate to their social behaviour or its gravity[949].

The first of these conditions - the 'placing on the market', the 'putting into service' or the 'use' of an AI system[950] - was discussed earlier in this Chapter. Let's now consider the remaining two conditions.

---

[948] *Ibid.*
[949] *Ibid.*
[950] *Ibid.*

Evaluation or classification of natural persons or groups of persons over a certain period of time based on their social behaviour or known, inferred or predicted personal or personality characteristics

To start with, a prohibited AI system must be intended or used for the **evaluation or classification** of natural persons or groups of persons and assign them scores based on their social behaviour or their personal or personality characteristics[951]. The score produced by the system may take various forms, such as a mathematical number (for example, from 0 to 1), a ranking, or a label[952].

The scope of the prohibition is broad covering evaluation and classification practices in both the public and the private sector[953]. At the same time the evaluation or classification concerns only natural persons or groups of natural persons, thereby excluding in principle legal entities[954].

While '**evaluation**' suggests the involvement of some form of an **assessment or judgement** about a person or group of persons, a simple **classification** of persons or groups of persons based on characteristics, such as their age, sex, and height, need not necessarily lead to evaluation[955]. The scope of 'classification' is therefore

[951] Para 4.2.1(a)(151) Prohibition Guidelines.
[952] *Ibid.*
[953] Para 4.2.1(a)(152) Prohibition Guidelines.
[954] *Ibid.*
[955] Para 4.2.1(a)(153) Prohibition Guidelines.

broader than 'evaluation' and can also cover other types of classifications or categorisations of natural persons or groups of persons based on criteria that do not necessarily involve a particular assessment or judgement about those persons or groups of persons and their characteristics or behaviour[956].

The term '**evaluation**' also relates to the concept of 'profiling', which is regulated by EU data protection legislation and constitutes a specific form of evaluation[957]. While no direct reference is made in this prohibition to that concept or that legislation, they may also be relevant for this prohibition and other prohibitions when the evaluation occurs in an automated fashion by an AI system based on personal data[958]. **Profiling** means the use of information about an individual (or group of individuals) and evaluating their characteristics or behaviour patterns in order to place them into a certain category or group, in particular **to analyse and/or make predictions** about, for example, their ability to perform a task; interests; or likely behaviour'[959]. Profiling of natural persons under EU data protection law, when conducted through AI systems, may therefore also be covered by this prohibition[960].

---

956 *Ibid.*
957 Para 4.2.1(a)(154) Prohibition Guidelines.
958 *Ibid.*
959 *Ibid.*
960 *Ibid.*

Example: [961]

In the *SCHUFA I* judgment, the CJEU examined a **creditworthiness scoring system** used in Germany. The 'score' generated by the computer programme was a 'probability value' concerning the ability of a person to meet payment commitments, which was qualified by the CJEU as 'profiling'. More specifically, the system established 'a prognosis on the probability of a future behaviour of a person ('score'), such as the repayment of a loan, based on certain characteristics of that person. The establishment of scores ('scoring') is based on the assumption that, by assigning a person to a group of other persons with comparable characteristics who have behaved in a certain way, similar behaviour can be predicted. According to the CJEU, this activity met the GDPR definition of 'profiling'. This form of profiling may also constitute an evaluation of persons based on their personal characteristics within the meaning of the social scoring prohibition and will be prohibited if done with AI systems and provided that the other conditions for the application of that provision are fulfilled.

[961] *Ibid.*

The social scoring prohibition requires that the evaluation or classification is based on data that spans over '**a certain period of time**'[962]. This suggests that the assessment should not be limited to a one-time or an at once rating or grading with data or behaviour from a very specific individual context[963]. At the same time, it is important that this condition is assessed, taking all circumstances of the case into account to avoid circumvention of the scope of the prohibition[964].

Example:[965]

An authority for migration and asylum implements a partly automated surveillance system at refugee camps built on a range of surveillance infrastructure, including cameras and motion sensors. If the analysed data spans a period of time and specific individuals are evaluated (such as migrants) for example to ascertain whether they are at risk of trying to abscond, then this would qualify as 'over a certain period of time' and the prohibition may apply if all other conditions are fulfilled.

[962] Para 4.2.1(b)(155) Prohibition Guidelines.
[963] *Ibid.*
[964] *Ibid.*
[965] *Ibid.*

The prohibited 'evaluation' and 'classification' must be based on the AI-enabled processing of data (often extensive) in relation to either **the social behaviour of individuals or groups of persons or their known, inferred or predicted personal and personality characteristics, or both**[966]. The data may be directly provided by the persons or indirectly collected, i.e. through surveillance, obtained from third parties or through inferences from other information[967].

'**Social behaviour**' is a broad term that can generally include actions, behaviour, habits, interactions within society, etc., and usually covers behaviour related data points from multiple sources[968]. This could include behaviour of individuals and groups of individuals in social and private contexts, such as participation in cultural events, volunteering, etc., but also social behaviour in business contexts, for example the payment of debts, behaviour when using certain services, as well as relations with public and private entities, government, police, and the law (for example, whether a person obeys traffic rules)[969]. Social behaviour data from multiple contexts and data points may be collected in a centralised way by the same entity, but is most often collected in a distributed way

---

[966] Para 4.2.1(c)(156) Prohibition Guidelines.
[967] *Ibid.*
[968] Recital 31 EU AI Act; para 4.2.1(c)(157) Prohibition Guidelines.
[969] *Ibid.*

and combined from different sources, which may involve increased monitoring and the tracking of individuals (so called 'dataveillance')[970].

Personal or personality characteristics may or may not involve specific social behavioural aspects[971]. '**Personal characteristics**' may include a variety of information relating to a person, for example sex, sexual orientation or sexual characteristics, gender, gender identity, race, ethnicity, family situation, address, income, household members, profession, employment or other legal status, performance at work, economic situation, financial liquidity, health, personal preferences, interests, reliability, behaviour, location or movement, level of debt, type of car etc[972]. '**Personality characteristics**' should be in principle interpreted as synonymous with personal characteristics, but may also imply the creation of specific profiles of individuals as personalities[973]. Personality characteristics may be also based on a number of factors and imply a judgement, which may be made by the individuals themselves, other persons, or generated by AI systems[974]. The Prohibition Guidelines note that in the EU AI Act personality characteristics are sometimes referred to as

[970] *Ibid.*
[971] Para 4.2.1(c)(158) Prohibition Guidelines.
[972] *Ibid*; Recital 42 EU AI Act.
[973] Para 4.2.1(c)(158) Prohibition Guidelines.
[974] *Ibid.*

personality traits and characteristics and those concepts should be interpreted consistently[975].

'Known, inferred or predicted' personal or personality characteristics are different types of information and personal data that need to be distinguished[976]. '**Known characteristics**' are based on information which has been provided to the AI system as an input, and which is in most cases verifiable information[977]. By contrast, '**inferred characteristics**' are based on information which has been inferred from other information, with the inference usually made by an AI system[978]. '**Predicted characteristics**' are those which are estimated based on patterns with less than 100% accuracy[979]. The use of these different types of data may have different implications for the accuracy and the fairness of the scoring practices and therefore may be taken into account, in particular where the processing is opaque or relies on data points whose accuracy is more difficult to be verified[980].

---

[975] *Ibid*; Article 5(1)(d) EU AI Act.
[976] Para 4.2.1(c)(159) Prohibition Guidelines.
[977] *Ibid.*
[978] *Ibid.*
[979] *Ibid.*
[980] *Ibid.*

The social score must lead to detrimental or unfavourable treatment in unrelated social contexts and/or unjustified or disproportionate treatment to the gravity of the social behaviour

For the social scoring prohibition to apply, the social score created by or with the assistance of an AI system must **lead to a detrimental or unfavourable treatment** for the evaluated person or group of persons[981]. In other words, the treatment must be the consequence of the score, and the score the cause of the treatment[982]. Such a plausible causal link may also exist in cases where the harmful consequences have not yet materialised but the AI system is intended to or capable of producing such an adverse outcome[983].

Notably, the prohibition does not require the evaluation or classification performed by the AI system to be the sole cause of the detrimental or unfavourable treatment[984]. It therefore also covers AI-enabled scoring practices that may also be subject to or combined with other human assessments[985]. At the same time, the AI output must play a sufficiently important role in producing the social score[986]. For example, in the case where a public authority deploys an AI system to assess the trustworthiness

---

[981] Para 4.2.2(a)(160) Prohibition Guidelines.
[982] *Ibid.*
[983] *Ibid.*
[984] Para 4.2.2(a)(161) Prohibition Guidelines.
[985] *Ibid.*
[986] *Ibid.*

of persons and combines its output with a human assessment of additional facts, this AI-enabled social scoring practice will fall within the scope of the prohibition only if the AI-generated score plays a sufficiently important role in the final decision, provided the other conditions for detrimental or unfavourable treatment are fulfilled[987].

A score may lead to detrimental or unfavourable treatment even if it is produced by an organisation(s) different from the one that uses the score[988]. For example, a public authority may obtain a score for a natural person's creditworthiness assessment produced by another company specialised in creditworthiness and risk assessments, which are based on information about the individuals and their behaviour from a variety of sources[989].

Detrimental or unfavourable treatment in unrelated social contexts and/or unjustified or disproportionate treatment is the final condition of the scoring prohibition.

'Unfavourable treatment' means that as a result from the scoring, the person or group of persons must be treated less favourably compared to others without necessarily requiring a particular harm or damage (for example, in the case of scoring practices where people are

---

[987] *Ibid.*
[988] Para 4.2.2(a)(162) Prohibition Guidelines.
[989] *Ibid.*

singled out for additional inspections in case of fraud suspicious)[990]. By contrast, '**detrimental**' treatment requires the person or group of persons to suffer certain harm and detriment from the treatment[991]. Unfavourable or detrimental treatment may also be discriminatory and prohibited under EU non-discrimination law or imply the exclusion of certain individuals or groups, but that is not a necessary condition for the prohibition to apply[992]. The prohibition could therefore cover unfair treatment beyond EU non-discrimination law that applies only to certain protected groups (e.g., age, ethnic and racial origin, sex, religion)[993].

The detrimental or unfavourable treatment resulting from the score must take place **in social context(s) unrelated** to the contexts in which the data was originally generated or collected[994]. This implies not only that the persons may be treated in an unfavourable or detrimental manner due to the social score, but also that the data about their social behaviour or their known, inferred or predicted personal or personality characteristics are generated or collected in social contexts unrelated to the one in which the scoring takes place[995]. The data collected or generated from these unrelated contexts must be subsequently used by

---

[990] Para 4.2.2(b)(165) Prohibition Guidelines.
[991] *Ibid.*
[992] *Ibid;* Recital 31 EU AI Act.
[993] Para 4.2.2(b)(165) Prohibition Guidelines.
[994] Para 4.2.2(b)(166) Prohibition Guidelines.
[995] *Ibid.*

the AI system for the scoring of the persons without an apparent connection for the purpose of the evaluation or classification or in a manner that leads to generalised surveillance of the persons or the groups of persons[996]. In most cases, this happens against the reasonable expectations of the persons and in violation of EU data protection law and possibly other applicable rules that specify the types of data and sources considered relevant and necessary for the evaluation or classification[997]. Whether this condition is fulfilled will require a case-by-case assessment, taking into account the purpose of the evaluation and the contexts from which the data has been collected and generated[998].

<u>Examples:</u>[999]

- National tax authorities use an AI predictive tool on all taxpayers' tax returns in a country to select tax returns for closer inspection. The AI tool uses relevant variables, such as yearly income, assets (real estate property, cars etc.), data on family members of beneficiaries, but also unrelated data, such as

[996] *Ibid.*
[997] *Ibid.*
[998] *Ibid.*
[999] *Ibid.*

taxpayers' social habits or internet connections, to single out specific individuals for inspections.

- A social welfare agency uses an AI system to estimate the probability of fraud by beneficiaries of household allowances that relies on characteristics collected or inferred from social contexts with no apparent connection or relevance for the assessment of fraud, such as having a spouse of a certain nationality or ethnic origin, having an internet connection, behaviour on social platforms, or performance at the workplace, etc. By contrast, data that is relevant for the allocation of the benefits and lawfully collected could be used to determine the risk of fraud, since public authorities pursue a legitimate aim in verifying if social benefits are correctly allocated.

- A public labour agency uses an AI system to score unemployed individuals based on an interview and an AI-based assessment for determining whether an individual should benefit from state support for employment. That score is based on relevant personal characteristics, such as age and education, but also variables collected or inferred from data and contexts with no apparent connection to the purpose of evaluation, such as marital status, health data for chronic diseases, addiction, etc.

An AI scoring system may also be prohibited if the **treatment resulting from the score is unjustified or disproportionate to the gravity of the social behaviour**[1000]. The severity of the impact and the interference with the fundamental rights of the person concerned resulting from the social scoring compared to the gravity of the social behaviour of the person should determine whether such treatment is disproportionate for the legitimate aim pursued, taking into account the general principle of proportionality[1001]. This requires a case-by-case assessment, which should consider all relevant circumstances of the case, as well as general ethical considerations and principles for fairness and social justice related to the assessment of the social behaviour and the proportionality of the detrimental treatment[1002]. The treatment may also be 'unjustified', such as lacking a legitimate aim[1003]. Sectoral EU or national legislation setting specific criteria and procedures that regulate such potential detrimental or unfavourable treatment may also be relevant as part of this assessment[1004].

[1000] Para 4.2.2(b)(167) Prohibition Guidelines.
[1001] *Ibid.*
[1002] *Ibid.*
[1003] *Ibid.*
[1004] *Ibid.*

Examples:[1005]

Unacceptable social scoring practices

- A public agency uses an AI system to profile families for early detection of children at risk based on criteria such as parental mental health and unemployment, but also information on parents' social behaviour derived from multiple contexts. Based on the resulting score, families are singled out for inspection and children considered 'at risk' are taken from their families, including in cases of minor transgressions by the parents, such as occasionally missing doctors' appointments or receiving traffic fines.

- A municipality uses an AI system to score trustworthiness of residents based on multiple data points related to their social behaviour in a variety of contexts. The generated score for residents considered 'less trustworthy' is used for blacklisting, i.e. withdrawal of public benefits, other serious punitive measures, and increased control or surveillance. Among the factors considered in the assessment are insufficient volunteering and minor misbehaviour, such as not returning books to the library on time, leaving rubbish on the street outside

[1005] *Ibid.*

the day of collection, and a delay in the payment of local taxes.

- A tax authority uses an AI system to detect child benefit fraud by profiling and assigning beneficiaries suspected of fraud to categories such as ‘deliberate intent/gross negligence’ using criteria such as low income, dual nationality, social behaviour, etc[1006]. Based on the risk score, a beneficiary’s file is inspected and, in many cases, their childcare benefit ceased, they receive notice to repay the received benefits, and no longer qualify for standard debt collection arrangements[1007]. Such scoring causes many families to be heavily indebted and leads to unjust, discriminatory and detrimental treatment of individuals and groups of individuals, driving many families into severe financial hardship[1008].

- A public authority uses an AI system to control fraud in the student housing grant process that considers among the indicators the internet connections, family status or level of education of beneficiaries as

[1006] Para 4.2.2(b)(168) Prohibition Guidelines.
[1007] *Ibid.*
[1008] *Ibid.*

distinguishing factors for fraud risk, which do not seem relevant, nor justified[1009].

- A government introduces a comprehensive AI-based system that monitors and rates citizens based on their behaviour in various aspects of life, such as social interactions, online activities, purchasing habits, and punctuality in paying bills[1010]. People with a lower score face restricted access to public services, higher interest rates on loans, and difficulty in traveling, renting apartments, and even finding jobs[1011]. The system leads to excessive surveillance of individuals and detrimental treatment in contexts unrelated to the social behaviour used to determine the social score (e.g., job opportunities are influenced by social media activity), while also imposing excessive penalties for minor infractions (e.g., social and financial disadvantages for relatively minor offences)[1012].

The EU AI Act also prohibits unacceptable AI-enabled social scoring practices **regardless of whether the AI system or the score are provided or used by public or**

[1009] *Ibid.*
[1010] *Ibid.*
[1011] *Ibid.*
[1012] *Ibid.*

private persons[1013]. While scoring in the public sector may have very significant consequences for people due to an imbalance of power and a dependence on public services, similarly harmful consequences may also occur in the private sector, where scoring practices are also increasingly undertaken by companies and other entities[1014].

<u>Examples:</u>[1015]

- An insurance company collects spending and other financial information from a bank which is unrelated to the determination of eligibility of candidates for life insurance and which is used to determine the price of the premium to be paid for such insurance. An AI system analyses this information and recommends, on that basis, whether to refuse a contract or set higher life insurance premiums for a particular individual or a group of customers.

- A private credit agency uses an AI system to determine the creditworthiness of people and decide whether an individual should obtain a loan for housing based on unrelated personal characteristics.

[1013] Para 4.2.2(b)(170) Prohibition Guidelines.
[1014] *Ibid.*
[1015] *Ibid.*

In the case of checks by competent market surveillance authorities, it is on the provider and the deployer of the AI system, each within their responsibilities, to demonstrate that the AI practice is legitimate and justified, including by providing transparency of the functioning of the AI system, and information about the types of data and data sources, ensuring that only data related to the social context in which the score is used are processed for the purpose of the evaluation or classification, the system is performing as intended, and any resulting detrimental or unfavourable treatment is justified and proportionate to the social behaviour[1016]. Compliance with applicable legislation and appropriate and proportionate safeguards built in the system and applied during its operation will help to avoid the prohibition from applying, while enabling the use of AI systems for the evaluation or classification of persons for legitimate and beneficial purposes (e.g., to improve the effectiveness of processes, quality of service, safety, etc.) [1017].

Out of Scope

The social scoring prohibition does not apply to scoring of **legal entities** where the evaluation is not based on personal or personality characteristics or social

[1016] Para 4.2.2(b)(171) Prohibition Guidelines.
[1017] *Ibid.*

behaviour of individuals, even if in some cases individuals may be indirectly impacted by the score (e.g., all citizens in a municipality in case of allocation of budget)[1018]. However, if legal entities have been evaluated based on an overall score that aggregates the evaluation or classification of a group of natural persons based on their social behaviour or personal or personality characteristics and this score directly affects those persons (e.g. all employees in a company, students in a specific school whose behaviour has been evaluated), the practice may fall within the scope of the prohibition if all other conditions are fulfilled[1019]. This will depend on a case-by-case assessment[1020].

AI-based social scoring as a '**probabilistic value**' and prognosis should also be distinguished from individual ratings by users which assess the quality of a service (such as a driver in an online car-sharing platform or a host in an online platform for accommodation)[1021]. Such ratings are the mere aggregation of individual human scores that do not necessarily involve AI, unless the data are combined with other information and analysed by the AI system for evaluating or classifying individuals fulfilling all conditions in the social scoring prohibition[1022].

[1018] Para 4.3 (173) Prohibition Guidelines.
[1019] *Ibid.*
[1020] *Ibid.*
[1021] Para 4.3 (174) Prohibition Guidelines.
[1022] *Ibid.*

The scoring of natural persons is prohibited only where all of the conditions of the social scoring prohibition are cumulatively fulfilled[1023]. In particular, the prohibition 'should not affect **lawful evaluation practices** of natural persons that are carried out for a specific purpose in accordance with Union and national law'[1024]. For example, **credit scoring** and **risk scoring** and **underwriting** are essential aspects of the services of financial and insurance businesses[1025]. Such practices, as well as other legitimate practices (i.e. to improve the quality and efficiency of services, to ensure more efficient claims handling, to perform specific employee evaluations, fraud prevention and detection, law enforcement or scoring of users' behaviour on online platforms), are not *per se* prohibited, if lawful and undertaken in line with the EU AI Act and other applicable EU law and national law compliant with EU law[1026].

Examples: [1027]

Legitimate social scoring practices

[1023] Para 4.3 (175) Prohibition Guidelines.
[1024] Ibid; Recital 31 AI Act.
[1025] Para 4.3 (175) Prohibition Guidelines.
[1026] *Ibid.*
[1027] Para 4.3 (177) Prohibition Guidelines.

- Financial credit scoring systems used by creditors or credit information agencies to assess a customer's financial creditworthiness or outstanding debts, providing a credit score or determining their creditworthiness assessment, which are based on the customer's income and expenses and other financial and economic circumstances, if they are relevant for the legitimate purpose of the credit scoring and if they comply with consumer protection laws specifying the type of data and the necessary safeguards to ensure the fair treatment of consumers in creditworthiness assessments.

- Companies have a legitimate interest to evaluate customers for financial fraud and those practices are not affected by the prohibition, if the evaluation is based on relevant data such as transactional behaviour and metadata in the context of the services, past history and other factors from sources that are objectively relevant to determine the risk of fraud and if the detrimental treatment is justified and proportionate as a consequence of the fraudulent behaviour.

- Information collected through telematic devices that show that a driver is speeding or not maintaining safe driving practices used by an insurer that offers telematics-based tariffs in relation to a policyholder's high-risk driving behaviour may be used to increase the premium of that policyholder due to the higher risk of an accident caused by that driving behaviour, provided the increase in the premium is proportionate to the risky behaviour of the driver.

- The collection and processing of data that is relevant and necessary for the intended legitimate purpose of the AI systems (e.g. health and schizophrenic data collected from various sources to diagnose patients).

- Online platforms profiling users for safety reasons on their services based on data which is relevant for the context and purpose of assessment, when the evaluation does not result in detrimental treatment that is disproportionate to the gravity of the user's misbehaviour.

- AI-enabled targeted commercial, where it is based on relevant data (e.g., users' preferences), it is done in line with EU law on consumer protection, data protection and digital services, and it does not result in detrimental or unfavourable treatment disproportionate to the gravity of the user's social behaviour (e.g., exploitative and unfair differential pricing).

- AI systems using data collected in refugee camps (e.g., behavioural compliance) for decisions about resettlement or employment, given that this data is relevant for the purpose of assessment and provided that the procedures under applicable EU migration law are fulfilled to ensure the treatment is justified and proportionate.

- AI-enabled scoring by an online shopping platform which offers privileges to users with a strong purchase history and a low rate of product returns, such as a faster returns application process or returnless refunds, given that the advantages are justified and proportionate to reward positive behaviour and other users continue to have access to the standard return process.

- AI-evaluation and scoring of individuals by police and other law enforcement authorities that collect data about individuals' social behaviour from multiple contexts where the data are relevant for the specific purposes of the prevention, detection, prosecution and punishment of criminal offences, and where the detrimental treatment is justified and proportionate in accordance with substantive and procedural EU and national criminal and police law.

13.11.3 Prohibition of Individual Risk Assessment to Predict the Risk of Criminal Offences

The EU AI Act prohibits placing on the market, putting into service, and (or) use of AI systems for making risk assessments of natural persons in order to assess or predict the risk of a natural person committing a criminal offence, based solely on the profiling of a natural person or on assessing their personality traits and characteristics; this prohibition does not apply to AI systems used to support the human assessment of the involvement of a person in a criminal activity, which is already based on objective and verifiable facts directly linked to a criminal activity[1028].

The underlying rationale for this prohibition is that natural persons should be judged on their actual behaviour and not on AI-predicted behaviour based solely on their profiling, personality traits or characteristics[1029].

All of the following conditions must be met for this prohibition to apply[1030]:

- The practice must constitute the 'placing on the market', 'the putting into service for this specific purpose' or the 'use' of an AI system. These conditions had been addressed earlier in this Chapter.

[1028] Article 5.1.(d) EU AI Act.
[1029] Para 5.1(186) Prohibition Guidelines.
[1030] Para 5.1(187) Prohibition Guidelines.

- The AI system must make risk assessments that assess or predict the risk of a natural person committing a criminal offence.
- The risk assessment or the prediction must be based solely on the profiling of a natural person and (or) assessing a natural person's personality traits and characteristics.

Assessing or predicting the risk of a natural person committing a criminal offence

Risk assessments to assess or predict the risk of an individual committing a criminal offence are often referred to as individual 'crime prediction' or 'crime forecasting'[1031]. While there is no generally agreed definition of 'crime prediction' or 'crime forecasting', these terms refer in general to a variety of advanced AI technologies and analytical methods applied to large amount of often historical data (including socio-economic data, but also police records, etc.) which, in combination with criminology theories, are used to forecast crime as a basis to inform police and law enforcement strategies and action to combat, control, and prevent crime[1032].

Crime prediction AI systems identify patterns within historical data, associating indicators with the

[1031] Para 5.2.1(189) Prohibition Guidelines.
[1032] *Ibid.*

likelihood of a crime occurring, and then generate risk scores as predictive outputs[1033]. For example, such systems may be used for planning police task forces, for monitoring high-risk situations, and for conducting controls of persons predicted as likely (re-)offenders[1034]. Such systems bring opportunities for law enforcement authorities, especially those with scarce resources, increasing efficiency, and enabling a proactive approach for detecting, deterring, and anticipating criminal offences[1035]. However, such use of historical data on crimes committed to predict other persons' future behaviour may perpetuate or even reinforce biases, and may result in crucial individual circumstances being 'overlooked' when these circumstances are not part of the data set or considered in the algorithms on which the particular AI system operates[1036]. This may also undermine public trust in law enforcement and the justice system in general[1037].

Such risk assessments and predictions are, in principle, forward-looking and concern future criminal offences (not yet committed) or crimes that are assessed as a risk of being committed at the moment, including in cases of an attempt or preparatory activities undertaken to commit a criminal offence[1038]. They can be made at any

---

[1033] Para 5.2.1(190) Prohibition Guidelines.
[1034] *Ibid.*
[1035] *Ibid.*
[1036] *Ibid.*
[1037] *Ibid.*
[1038] Para 5.2.1(191) Prohibition Guidelines.

stage of the law enforcement activities, such as during prevention and detection of crimes, but also during the investigation, prosecution and execution of criminal penalties (including when judicial authorities assess the risk of re-offending e.g., in the context of making decisions on the imposition of pre-trial detention) as well as part of the individuals' plan for re-integration into society after serving a criminal sentence[1039].

Solely based on profiling of a natural person or on assessing their personality traits and characteristics is another condition for the crime prediction prohibition to apply.

For the purposes of this prohibition, **profiling** is defined as by reference to the definition in the data protection legislation, as "*any form of automated processing of personal data consisting of the use of personal data to evaluate certain personal aspects relating to a natural person, in particular to analyse or predict aspects concerning that natural person's performance at work, economic situation, health, personal preferences, interests, reliability, behaviour, location or movements*'[1040]. Group profiling may also be relevant in this context[1041]. That concept refers to the construction and the application of a descriptive profile for a given group, for example

---

[1039] *Ibid.*
[1040] Para 5.2.2 a) (195) Prohibition Guidelines.
[1041] Para 5.2.2 a) (196) Prohibition Guidelines.

categories of perpetrators of criminal offences (e.g., terrorists, gangsters etc.) constructed on historic data about previously committed crimes by other persons[1042]. Those group profiles may be used later to assess and predict the risk of other persons committing similar offences[1043]. Whenever an AI system makes prediction and applies such a (group) profile to a specific individual, this constitutes profiling of the person and may therefore fall within the crime prediction prohibition[1044].

The prohibition also applies if the risk assessment to assess or predict the risk of the person committing a criminal offence is only based on **assessing the person's personality traits and characteristics**[1045]. Such an assessment or prediction is often included in the concept of profiling, but it could also be seen as an alternative, if profiling cannot be established[1046].

Personality traits and characteristics constitute a broad category of characteristics related to a particular natural person, for which there is no generally agreed taxonomy[1047]. Illustrative and not exhaustive examples of personality traits and characteristics which may be assessed for predicting the risk of a person committing an offence,

[1042] *Ibid.*
[1043] *Ibid.*
[1044] *Ibid.*
[1045] Para 5.2.2 b) (197) Prohibition Guidelines.
[1046] *Ibid.*
[1047] Para 5.2.2 b) (198) Prohibition Guidelines.

ares 'nationality, place of birth, place of residence, number of children, level of debt or type of car'[1048].

The risk assessments are only prohibited where they are based '**solely**' on the profiling of a person or the assessment of their personality traits and characteristics[1049]. The condition that the risk assessment must be based 'solely' on profiling or assessing personality traits and characteristics may not be fulfilled in a number of situations[1050].

Such a situation arises where the AI system is used to support the human assessment of the involvement of a person in a criminal activity, which is already based on objective and verifiable facts directly linked to a criminal activity[1051]. In this context one should think, in particular but not necessarily exclusively, of a situation in which a reasonable suspicion in respect of the natural person concerned already exists[1052]. There will normally have been a human assessment based on relevant objective and verifiable facts[1053].

There can also be other situations, which will always need to be assessed on a case-by-case basis[1054]. On the one hand, the use of the term 'solely' leaves open the

---

[1048] *Ibid*; Recital 42 EU AI Act.
[1049] Para 5.2.2 b) (199) Prohibition Guidelines.
[1050] Para 5.2.2 b) (200) Prohibition Guidelines.
[1051] Para 5.2.2 b) (201) Prohibition Guidelines.
[1052] *Ibid*; Recital 42 EU AI Act.
[1053] Para 5.2.2 b) (201) Prohibition Guidelines.
[1054] Para 5.2.2 b) (202) Prohibition Guidelines.

possibility of various other elements being taken into account in the risk assessment, so that it is no longer based on profiling or assessing personality traits or characteristics alone[1055]. On the other hand, in order to avoid circumvention of the prohibition and ensure its effectiveness, any such other elements will have to be real, substantial and meaningful for them to be able to justify the conclusion that the prohibition does not apply[1056]. A reading of the prohibition together with the exclusion contained in its last phrase suggests that, in particular, the existence of certain pre-established objective and verifiable facts may justify that conclusion[1057].

<u>Examples:</u>[1058]

<u>Prohibited Crime Prevention Assessments</u>

- A law enforcement authority uses an AI system to predict criminal behaviour for crimes such as terrorism solely based on individuals' age, nationality, address, type of car, and marital status. With that system, individuals are deemed more likely to commit future offences that they have not yet

[1055] *Ibid.*
[1056] *Ibid.*
[1057] *Ibid.*
[1058] *Ibid.*

committed solely based on their personal characteristics.

- National tax authorities use an AI predictive tool to review all taxpayers' tax returns to predict potential criminal tax offences to identify cases requiring further investigation. This is done solely on the basis of the profile built by the AI system, which uses for its assessment personality traits, such as double nationality, place of birth, number of children, and opaque variables, especially inferred information that is predictive and therefore non-objective and hard to verify.

- A police department uses AI-based risk assessment tool to assess the risk of young children and adolescents being involved in 'future violent and property offending'. The system assesses children based on their relationships with other people and their supposed risk levels, meaning that children may be deemed at a higher risk of offending simply by being linked to another individual with a high-risk assessment, such as a sibling or a friend. The parents' risk levels may also impact a child's risk level. The risk assessments result in police 'registering' these children in their systems, monitoring them with additional inspections, and referring them to youth 'care' services.

The prohibition does not apply to AI systems used to support the human assessment of the involvement of a person in a criminal activity, which is already based on objective and verifiable facts directly linked to a criminal activity[1059]. Where the system falls within the scope of the exclusion and is therefore not prohibited, it will be classified as a high-risk AI system[1060] if intended to be used by law enforcement authorities or on their behalf and therefore subject to the requirements and safeguards, including human oversight[1061]. These requirements include that the human oversight must be assigned to persons with the necessary competence, training and authority who should be able to properly understand the capabilities and limitations of the AI system, correctly interpret its output and address the risk of automation bias[1062]. Those persons should have clear procedures, training and the necessary competence and authority to meaningfully assess the outputs of the AI system[1063]. Their human assessment should ensure that any

---

1059 Para 5.2.3 (203) Prohibition Guidelines.

1060 Annex III 6(d) EU AI Act.

1061 Articles 14 and 26 EU AI Act; para 5.2.3 (204) Prohibition Guidelines.

1062 Para 5.2.3 (204) Prohibition Guidelines.

1063 *Ibid.*

AI prediction or assessment of the risk of a person committing a crime is based on objective and verifiable facts linked to a criminal activity[1064]. Those persons should also intervene in order to avoid negative consequences or risks, or stop the use of the AI system if it does not perform as intended[1065].

Furthermore, the concept of 'human intervention' has been subject to CJEU case-law, in particular in the context of solely automated decision-making predicting the risk of air passengers being involved in serious crimes, that may also be relevant for the application of the concept of 'human assessment' as used in this prohibition[1066].

<u>Example:</u> [1067]

In the *Ligue des droits humains* case, the CJEU examined the legality of the use of an advanced AI system for the systematic processing of passenger name record (PNR) data of air travellers to assess their likelihood of being involved in terrorism and other serious crimes. The CJEU interpreted the rule in the EU Directive[1068] that prohibits adverse legal decisions based solely on automated processing and required **individual**

[1064] *Ibid.*
[1065] *Ibid.*
[1066] Para 5.2.3 (205) Prohibition Guidelines.
[1067] *Ibid.*
[1068] Directive (EU) 2016/681 ('**PNR Directive**').

human assessment and review for any positive matches by non-automated means to identify false positives and ensure non-discriminatory results. According to the CJEU, that human assessment, subject to which any results of automated processing of passenger name record data must be based, must rely on objective criteria to evaluate whether a positive match concerns someone who might be involved in this specific case in terrorist offenses or serious crime, and to ensure the non-discriminatory nature of automated processing.

One central element of the exclusion s is that the AI system is used to support human assessment, rather than involving the AI system itself making the risk assessment as occurs in the situations covered by the prohibition[1069]. However, for the exclusion to apply, that human assessment must, in addition, already be based on objective and verifiable facts directly linked to a criminal activity[1070].

Besides law enforcement authorities that are in principle the main deployers of AI crime predictive systems, the activities of **private entities may also be covered by the prohibition** in some cases[1071]. That follows from the fact that, based on its wording, the prohibition does not apply exclusively to law enforcement authorities,

---

[1069] Para 5.2.3 (206) Prohibition Guidelines.
[1070] *Ibid.*
[1071] Para 5.2.4 (207) Prohibition Guidelines.

otherwise the prohibition might be easily circumvented, which would call into question its effectiveness[1072].

The prohibition may be assumed to apply, in particular, when private actors are entrusted by law to exercise public authority and public powers for the prevention, investigation, detection or prosecution of criminal offences or the execution of criminal penalties[1073]. Private actors may be also explicitly requested on a case-by-case basis to act on behalf of law enforcement authorities and carry out individual crime risk predictions[1074]. In those cases, the activities of those private actors could also fall within the scope of the prohibition, if the applicable conditions are fulfilled and the exclusion does not apply[1075].

<u>Example:</u> [1076]

A private company providing advanced AI-based crime analytic software may be asked by a law enforcement authority to analyse a large amount of data from multiple sources and databases, such as national registers, banking transactions, communication data, geo-spatial data, etc., to predict or assess the risk of individuals as potential

[1072] *Ibid.*
[1073] Para 5.2.4 (208) Prohibition Guidelines.
[1074] *Ibid.*
[1075] *Ibid.*
[1076] *Ibid.*

offenders of human trafficking offences. If all the conditions are met, such a use case could be prohibited.

The prohibition may also apply to private entities assessing or predicting the risk of a person of committing a crime where this is objectively necessary for compliance with a legal obligation to which that private operator is subject to assess or predict the risk of persons committing specific criminal offences (e.g., in case of anti-money laundering, terrorism financing)[1077].

Example: [1078]

A banking institution has an obligation under EU anti-money laundering legislation to screen and profile customers for money-laundering offences. If the bank uses an AI system to fulfil its obligations, that should be done based only on the data as specified in that law which are objective and verifiable to ensure that the persons singled out as suspect are reasonably likely to commit anti-money laundering offences. The predictions must also be subject to human assessment and verification in compliance with that legislation in order to ensure the accuracy and appropriateness of such

[1077] Para 5.2.4 (209) Prohibition Guidelines.
[1078] *Ibid.*

assessments. Compliance with that legislation will ensure that the use of individual crime prediction AI system for anti-money laundering purposes fall outside the scope of the prohibition.

However, having regard to the focus on risk assessments relating specifically and exclusively to the commission of criminal offences that is evident from the wording of the prohibition as well as to the purpose of the prohibition[1079], if a private entity profiles customers for its regular business operations and safety or to protect its financial interests (e.g., detecting financial irregularities) without the purpose of assessing or predicting the risk of the customer committing a specific criminal offence, the activities of the private entities should not be considered to fall under the scope of the prohibition[1080].

In other words, in the absence of private parties having been entrusted by law certain specific law enforcement tasks, acting on behalf of law enforcement authorities or being subject to specific legal obligations as described above, the prohibition does not cover the use of AI systems for making risk assessments in the context of private entities' ordinary course of business and with the aim of protecting their own private interests, whilst the fact

[1079] Recital 42 EU AI Act.
[1080] Para 5.2.4 (210) Prohibition Guidelines.

that those risk assessments may relate to the risk of criminal offences being committed merely as a purely accidental and secondary circumstance[1081].

Out of Scope

Location-based or geospatial or place-based crime prediction is based on the place or location of crime or the likelihood that in those areas a crime would be committed[1082]. In principle, such policing does not involve an assessment of a specific individual and falls outside the scope of the prohibition[1083].

Examples: [1084]

- AI-based predictive policing system provides a score of the likelihood of criminality in different areas in a city based on previous criminality rates by area and other supporting information such as street maps, to highlight elevated risk of specific types of criminalities e.g., burglaries, knife crime etc. and help law enforcement authorities determine where to deploy less or more police patrols/presence to carry

[1081] Para 5.2.4 (211) Prohibition Guidelines.
[1082] Para 5.3.1 (212) Prohibition Guidelines.
[1083] *Ibid.*
[1084] *Ibid.*

out community policing to disrupt and deter criminal activity.

- A customs authority uses AI risk analytic tools to predict the likelihood of the location of narcotics or illicit goods, for example on the basis of known trafficking routes.

- A police department uses AI-driven systems to detect and locate gunshots in real time. The system employs acoustic sensors in urban areas to identify gunfire sounds and triangulate their location, providing officers with actionable data to aid detection and investigation of crimes.

It may, however, not always be evident how to distinguish location-based crime predictive systems from individual predictive systems assessing the risk of a person committing a crime[1085]. To the extent that an AI system carries out location-based predictive policing and then considers the risk score of the location as an aspect in the profiling of a person, that system should be considered person-based and in principle covered by the prohibition,

[1085] Para 5.3.1 (213) Prohibition Guidelines.

although it may fall outside the scope of the prohibition on other grounds[1086].

<u>Example:</u>[1087]

If location-based or geospatial information or place-based information is linked to information relating to an individual (e.g., the place of a person's residence) and the AI system would assess the risk that that person is likely to commit crime based solely on profiling of the individual concerned, including based on his or her residence where crime is high, that system should be considered person-based.

The prohibition does not apply to **AI systems used to support human assessment** of the involvement of a natural person in a criminal activity, which is **based on objective and verifiable facts directly linked to a criminal activity**[1088]. In such a case, the individual crime risk assessments and predictions would also not be based solely on profiling or the assessment of personal characteristics and would therefore not be prohibited[1089].

1086 *Ibid.*
1087 *Ibid.*
1088 Para 5.3.2 (214) Prohibition Guidelines.
1089 *Ibid.*

Examples:[1090]

- The use of an AI system for profiling and categorisation of actual behaviour, such as reasonably suspicious dangerous behaviour in a crowd that someone is preparing and is likely to commit a crime, and there is a meaningful human assessment of the AI classification. In this case, the risk assessment made by the human with the support of AI is not solely based on the personal traits or the profiling, but on objective and verifiable facts linked to the threatening criminal behaviour of that person that has been reviewed by a human before action taken.

- The police is investigating the risk of a possible armed robbery and suspects two individuals. Several verifiable and objective facts are present on which that suspicion is based, such as verifiable participation and dialogues in dark web chat groups for purchasing arms. An AI system combining geospatial predictive or place-based policing information and Automated Number Plate Registration (ANPR) information of vehicles belonging to the suspects supports the human

[1090] *Ibid.*

assessment in the investigation based on verifiable and objective facts directly linked to a specific criminal activity.

- The use of an AI system that assesses the risk whether a prisoner should receive the benefit of an early release. The AI profile of the affected person or assessment of their personality traits and characteristics only support the human assessment of objective and verifiable facts related to past criminal offences and demonstrated behaviour relevant to rehabilitation.

- A judge conducts a pre-trial detention hearing for a person accused of a serious criminal offence to assess whether non-custodial measures can be applied. The decision is based on an assessment of the existence of valid grounds to imposed pre-trial detention, such as the likelihood that the suspect or accused person will commit another offence if not detained or that they will abscond or obstruct the proper conduct of the investigation. To assist in this process, the judge uses an AI risk assessment tool trained on data including past criminal history of individuals in similar cases, as well as factors such as age group, social behaviour, income, and employment status.

- AI system is used to support the assessment of a human officer to assess the risk of an individual serving a non-custodial sentence violating release conditions or absconding based on past criminal behaviours and objective facts that give grounds for suspicion such as adherence to conditions of release, psychological assessment outcomes and recommendations from other community services the individual may be using. Based on this information, the officer decides whether to maintain the status quo or revise the conditions of release.

- AI systems used by custom authorities to assess the risk of goods entering the EU not complying with the legislation applicable at the border (e.g., which may include bans on import of illicit drugs, export sanctions contravention or other illegal activity) to identify situations where a customs control should be carried out. The AI system assesses objective and verifiable information provided to the customs related to the goods and their supply chains (e.g., nature and value of the goods, container number, means of transport for concealment of other goods, prior knowledge relating to the compliance of goods of the particular description and origin with requirements for their importation to or exportation from the EU). In certain cases, it may also process information about the prior involvement of the importer or exporter in irregularities related to import of goods, their affiliation to criminal organizations or a criminal record for drug trafficking.

The prohibition applies only to individual predictions and risk assessments of natural persons, thus typically excluding crime predictive systems that profile legal entities such as companies or non-governmental organisations[1091].

Examples:[1092]

- A tax or customs authority is using an AI system to analyse large amounts of data on transactions and tax declarations and customs data of companies for assessing the risk of a company committing tax or customs fraud constituting a criminal offence.
- AI systems used to assist customs authorities to help identify situations where an instruction not to send illicit goods to the EU should be issued to legal entities.

[1091] Para 5.3.3 (215) Prohibition Guidelines.
[1092] *Ibid.*

At the same time, there may be borderline cases where a natural person acts via a legal entity as a 'sole trader' or as an independent professional (e.g., a lawyer) [1093]. In such circumstances, the prohibition may apply provided that all conditions are fulfilled, since the AI system profiles a specific natural person and assesses or predicts their risk of committing a criminal offence, even if this is done for purposes in relation to the commercial activity undertaken by the natural person[1094].

The prohibition does not apply to the **AI systems used for individual predictions of administrative offences** as their prosecution is less intrusive for the fundamental rights and freedoms of people[1095].

> Example:[1096]
>
> A public authority using AI in the context of an administrative investigation to assess the risk of potential offenders of committing minor offences (such as petty traffic offences) or irregularities in tax, procurement or expenditure processes would not fall within the scope of the prohibition, even where information might be

[1093] Para 5.3.3 (216) Prohibition Guidelines.
[1094] *Ibid.*
[1095] Para 5.3.4 (217) Prohibition Guidelines.
[1096] *Ibid.*

gathered for possible involvement of the natural persons in criminal offences as a result of the administrative investigations and checks.

Whether an offence is administrative or criminal in nature may depend on the EU or national law[1097]. For offences that are not directly regulated by EU law, the national qualification of the offence is subject to scrutiny by CJEU since 'criminal offence' is a concept that has autonomous meaning within the EU law and should be interpreted consistently across Member States[1098]. The CJEU has concluded, in a different context, that the classification of the offences by the Member States is not conclusive in that respect[1099]. Relevant criteria used to assess the nature of the offence (criminal or not) may be found in relevant case-law of the CJEU and the European Court of Human Rights (ECtHR)[1100].

13.11.4 Prohibition of Untargeted Scraping of Facial Images

The EU AI Act prohibits placing on the market, putting into service for this specific purpose, and (or) use of

1097 Para 5.3.4 (218) Prohibition Guidelines.
1098 *Ibid.*
1099 *Ibid.*
1100 *Ibid.*

AI systems that create or expand facial recognition databases through the untargeted scraping of facial images from the Internet or CCTV footage[1101].

The rationale behind this prohibition is that the untargeted scraping of facial images from the internet and from CCTV footage seriously interferes with individuals' rights to privacy and data protection and denies those individuals the right to remain anonymous[1102]. The prohibition is justified by the 'feeling of mass surveillance' and the risks of 'gross violations of fundamental rights, including the right to privacy'[1103].

All of the following conditions must be fulfilled for the prohibition to apply:

- The practice must constitute the 'placing on the market', 'the putting into service for this specific purpose' or the 'use' of an AI system[1104] (this condition is discussed earlier in this Chapter);

- for the purpose of creating or expanding facial recognition databases[1105];

[1101] Article 5. 1.(e) EU AI Act.
[1102] Para 6.1(223) Prohibition Guidelines.
[1103] *Ibid*; Recital 43 EU AI Act.
[1104] Para 6.2 (224) Prohibition Guidelines.
[1105] *Ibid.*

- the means to populate the database are through AI tools for untargeted scraping[1106]; and

- the sources of the images are either from the internet or CCTV footage[1107].

The prohibition covers AI systems used to create or expand **facial recognition databases**[1108]. '**Database**' in this context should be understood to refer to any collection of data, or information, that is specially organized for rapid search and retrieval by a computer[1109]. A facial recognition database is capable of matching a human face from a digital image or video frame against a database of faces, comparing it to images in the database and determining whether there is a likely match between the two[1110]. Such a facial recognition database may be temporary, centralised or decentralised[1111]. The prohibition does not require use for facial recognition to be the sole purpose of the database; it is sufficient that the database can be used for facial recognition[1112].

The next condition is that the database must be populated by **untargeted scraping of facial images**.

[1106] *Ibid.*
[1107] *Ibid.*
[1108] Para 6.2.1 (226) Prohibition Guidelines.
[1109] *Ibid.*
[1110] *Ibid.*
[1111] *Ibid.*
[1112] *Ibid.*

'**Scraping**' typically refers to using web crawlers, bots, or other means to extract data or content from different sources, including CCTV, websites or social media, automatically[1113]. These tools are software 'programmed to sift through databases and extract information and to make use of that information for another purpose[1114].

'**Untargeted**' relates to a technique that operates like a 'vacuum cleaner', absorbing as much data and information as possible, without targeting specifically and individually intended subject(s) of the scraping[1115]. Scraping indiscriminately harvests data or content[1116]. Thus, the notion of 'untargeted' means without a specific focus on a given individual or group of individuals[1117]. The respect of opt-out of internet protocols such as robot.txt does not affect the untargeted nature of the scraping[1118].

If a scraping tool is instructed to collect images or video containing human faces only of specific individuals or a pre-defined group of persons, then the scraping becomes targeted, for example to find one specific criminal or to identify a group of victims[1119]. Such scraping is not covered by the prohibition[1120].

[1113] Para 6.2.2 (227) Prohibition Guidelines.
[1114] *Ibid.*
[1115] Para 6.2.2 (228) Prohibition Guidelines.
[1116] *Ibid.*
[1117] *Ibid.*
[1118] *Ibid.*
[1119] Para 6.2.2 (229) Prohibition Guidelines.
[1120] *Ibid.*

Examples:[1121]

- The targeted collection of images focusing on a class of victims, by using crawlers to pick up on images of victims that human traffickers post/advertise on social media channels, is not covered by the prohibition.

- The scraping of the Internet or CCTV footage for the creation of a database step-by-step, selecting specific groups of individuals or other criteria each time, where the end-result is functionally the same as pursuing untargeted scraping from the outset, should fall within the prohibition.

Where systems combine targeted searches for images or videos with untargeted searches, the untargeted scraping is prohibited[1122].

For the prohibition to apply, **the source of the facial images must either be the Internet or CCTV footage**. Regarding the Internet, the fact that a person has published facial images of themselves on a social media platform does not mean that that person has given his or her

[1121] Para 6.2.2 (230) Prohibition Guidelines.
[1122] Para 6.2.2 (231) Prohibition Guidelines.

consent for those images to be included in a facial recognition database[1123]. Examples of scraping facial images from CCTV footage include images acquired by surveillance cameras operated in places such as airports, streets, parks, etc[1124].

<u>Example:</u>[1125]

A facial recognition software company collects pictures of faces. The photographs held by the company have been scraped from social media (e.g., Facebook, YouTube, Twitter, Venmo) with an 'automated image scraper' that searches the internet and detects images containing human faces. It collects those images with any associated information (such as the source of the image (URL), the geo-localisation, and sometimes the names of the individuals). The facial features are then extracted from the images and transformed into mathematical representations, which are hashed for indexation and future comparison. When a user uploads the image of an individual to the AI system, that system will determine whether that image matches a face in the

1123 Para 6.2.3 (232) Prohibition Guidelines.
1124 *Ibid.*
1125 *Ibid.*

database. The uploaded image will go through the same mathematical transformation as the scraped images.

Where an AI system receives a picture of a person and searches the face on the internet for matches, i.e. 'reverse engineering image search engines', this will be considered to be targeted scraping[1126]. Moreover, it is questionable whether the matches would appear in a 'database'[1127].

Out of Scope

The prohibition does not apply in the following cases:

- to the untargeted scraping of biometric data other than facial images (such as voice samples)[1128];
- where no AI systems are involved in the scraping[1129];
- to facial image databases that are not used for the recognition of persons, such as facial image databases

[1126] Para 6.2.3 (233) Prohibition Guidelines.
[1127] *Ibid.*
[1128] Para 6.3 (234) Prohibition Guidelines.
[1129] *Ibid.*

used for AI model training or testing purposes, where the persons are not identified[1130];

- to AI systems which harvest large amounts of facial images from the internet to build AI models that generate new images about fictitious persons because such systems would not result in the recognition of real persons[1131]; but such AI systems could fall under the EU AI Act's transparency requirements[1132];

- to existing facial databases built up prior to the entry into application of the prohibition, which are not further expanded through AI-enabled untargeted scraping[1133]; and

- biometric identification[1134].

13.11.5 Prohibition of Emotion Recognition

The EU AI Act prohibits placing on the market, putting into service for this specific purpose, and (or) use of AI systems to infer emotions of a natural person in the areas of workplace and education institutions, except where

---

[1130] *Ibid.*
[1131] Para 6.3 (235) Prohibition Guidelines.
[1132] *Ibid.*
[1133] Para 6.3 (236) Prohibition Guidelines.
[1134] Para 6.3 (237) Prohibition Guidelines.

the use of the AI system is intended to be put in place or into the market for medical or safety reasons[1135].

Emotion recognition technology is quickly evolving and encompasses different technologies and processing operations to detect, collect, analyse, categorise, react, interact and learn emotions from persons[1136]. Such technology is also referred to as 'affect technology'[1137]. Emotion recognition can be used in multiple areas and domains for a wide range of applications, for example[1138]:

Area	**Use of emotion recognition**
advertising and neuromarketing	analyse customer behaviour
entertainment industry	provide personalised recommendations or to predict reactions to movies
medicine and healthcare	detect depression, prevent suicide, detect autism
education	monitor attention or engagement of learners (pupils and students at different ages)

[1135] Article 5.1.(f) EU AI Act.
[1136] Para 7.1 (240) Prohibition Guidelines.
[1137] *Ibid.*
[1138] *Ibid.*

Area	**Use of emotion recognition**
employment	accompany the recruitment process, monitor emotions or boredom of employees, make workers happier
law enforcement and public safety	lie detectors; emotion screening at big events

All of the following conditions must be met for this prohibition to apply[1139]:

- The practice must constitute the 'placing on the market', 'the putting into service for this specific purpose' or the 'use' of an AI system (as discussed earlier in this Chapter);
- The AI system must be capable of identifying and inferring emotions or intentions of natural persons on the basis of their biometric data;
- in the area of the workplace or education and training institutions; and
- excluded from the prohibition are AI systems intended for medical or safety reasons.

The EU AI Act defines 'emotion recognition systems' as AI systems 'for the purpose of **identifying and**

[1139] Para 7.2 (242) Prohibition Guidelines.

inferring emotions or intentions of natural persons on the basis of their biometric data"[1140]. The prohibition does not refer to 'emotion recognition systems', but only to 'AI systems to infer emotions of a natural person', so the prohibition covers AI systems that 'identify or infer emotions.'[1141]

'**Identification**' occurs where the processing of the biometric data (for example, of the voice or a facial expression) of a natural person allows to directly compare and identify an emotion with one that has been previously programmed in the emotion recognition system[1142]. '**Inferring**' involves deducing information generated by analytical and other processes by the system itself[1143] and generally encompasses identifying as a prerequisite, so that the prohibition includes AI systems identifying or inferring emotions or intentions[1144]. The information about the emotion is not solely based on data collected on the natural person, but it is inferred from other data, including machine learning approaches that learn from data how to detect emotions[1145].

[1140] Article 3(39) EU AI Act.

[1141] Article 5(1)(f) EU AI Act; Recital 44 EU AI Act; para 7.2.1 a) (244) Prohibition Guidelines.

[1142] Para 7.2.1 b) (246) Prohibition Guidelines.

[1143] *Ibid.*

[1144] Recital 18 EU AI Act; para 7.2.1 a) (245) Prohibition Guidelines.

[1145] *Ibid*; Recital 12 EU AI Act.

Emotions or **intentions** should be understood in a wide sense and not interpreted restrictively; non-exhaustive examples of emotions are happiness, sadness, anger, surprise, disgust, embarrassment, excitement, shame, contempt, satisfaction and amusement'[1146].

The prohibition should not be circumvented by referring to attitudes and includes cases where the AI system finds from the biometric data that a person is showing for example an angry attitude[1147].

But **emotions or intentions do not include** 'physical states, such as pain or fatigue, including, for example, systems used in detecting the state of fatigue of professional pilots or drivers for the purpose of preventing accidents'[1148]. Likewise, emotion recognition systems do not include 'the mere detection of readily apparent expressions, gestures or movements, unless they are used for identifying or inferring emotions'[1149]. Those expressions can be basic facial expressions, such as a frown or a smile, or gestures such as the movement of hands, arms or head, or characteristics of a person's voice, such as a raised voice or whispering[1150]. However, when these

---

[1146] Recital 18 EU AI Act; para 7.2.1 c) (247) Prohibition Guidelines.

[1147]Para 7.2.1 c) (248) Prohibition Guidelines.

[1148] Recital 18 EU AI Act; para 7.2.1 c) (249) Prohibition Guidelines.

[1149] Para 7.2.1 c) (249) Prohibition Guidelines.

[1150] *Ibid.*

readily apparent expressions or gestures are used for identifying or inferring emotions or intentions, they are covered by the prohibition[1151].

<u>Examples:</u>[1152]

Not emotion recognition:

- The observation that a person is smiling.
- Identifying whether a person is sick.
- A TV broadcaster using a device that allows to track how many times its news presenters smile to the camera.
- Using AI recognition systems to infer a professional pilot's or driver's fatigue to alert them and suggest when to take brakes to avoid accidents.

Emotion recognition:

- Concluding that a person is happy.
- An AI system that infers that an employee is unhappy, sad or angry towards customers (e.g., from body gestures, a frown or the lack of a smile).
- Systems inferring from voice or body gestures, that a student is furious and about to become violent.

[1151] *Ibid.*
[1152] *Ibid.*

Only AI systems identifying or inferring emotions or intentions **based on biometric data** constitute emotion recognition systems[1153]. 'Biometric data' is 'personal data resulting from specific technical processing relating to the physical, physiological or behavioural characteristics of a natural person, such as facial images or dactyloscopic data"[1154].

Personal characteristics from which biometric data can be extracted are physical or behavioural attributes[1155]. Physiological biometrics employ physical, structural, and relatively static attributes of a person, such as their fingerprints, the pattern of their iris, contours of their face, or the geometry of veins in their hands[1156]. Some modalities are microscopic in nature, but still exhibit biological and chemical structures that can be acquired and identified e.g., DNA and odour[1157]. Behavioural biometrics monitor the distinctive characteristics of movements, gestures, and motor-skills of individuals as they perform a task or series of tasks[1158]. This means that human movements, such as walking (gait analysis) or finger

---

[1153] Article 3(39) EU AI Act; para 7.2.1 d) (250) Prohibition Guidelines.

[1154] Article 3(34) EU AI Act; para 7.2.1 d) (250) Prohibition Guidelines.

[1155] Para 7.2.1 d) (251) Prohibition Guidelines.

[1156] *Ibid.*

[1157] *Ibid.*

[1158] *Ibid.*

contact with a keyboard (keystrokes), are captured and analysed[1159]. Behavioural biometrics encompass a variety of modalities that exhibit both voluntary and involuntary repeated motions and associated rhythmic timings/pressures of body features ranging from signatures, gait, voice, and keystrokes through to eye tracking and heartbeats, electroencephalography (EEG), or electrocardiograms (ECG)[1160]. The biometric input can relate to one modality (e.g., facial images) or multiple modalities (e.g., facial information combined with electroencephalogram (EEG)) [1161]. Examples include facial expressions, gestures such as movement of hands or characteristics of a person's voice[1162].

Examples:[1163]

Not based on biometric data:

- An AI system inferring emotions from written text (content/sentiment analyses) to define the style or the tone of a certain article.

[1159] *Ibid.*
[1160] *Ibid.*
[1161] *Ibid.*
[1162] Recital 18 EU AI Act; *Ibid.*
[1163] Para 7.2.1 d) (251) Prohibition Guidelines.

Based on biometric data:

- An AI system inferring emotions from key stroke (way of typing), facial expressions, body postures or movements.

The prohibition is limited to emotion recognition systems in the '**areas of workplace and educational institutions**'[1164]. This limitation is meant to address the imbalance of power in the context of work or education[1165].

'**Workplace**' relates to any specific physical or virtual space where natural persons engage in tasks and responsibilities assigned by their employer or by the organisation they are affiliated to, for example in case of self-employment[1166]. This includes any setting where the work is performed and can vary widely based on the nature of the job, spanning from indoor office spaces, factories and warehouses to publicly accessible spaces like shops, stadiums or museums, to open-air sites or cars, as well as temporary or mobile work sites[1167]. This is independent from the status as an employee, contractor, trainee,

---

[1164] Para 7.2.2 (253) Prohibition Guidelines.
[1165] Recital 44 AI Act; *Ibid.*
[1166] Para 7.2.2 (a) (254) Prohibition Guidelines.
[1167] *Ibid.*

volunteer, etc[1168]. 'Workplace' also applies to candidates during the selection and hiring process, since there is an imbalance of powers and the intrusive nature of emotion recognition may already apply at the recruitment stage[1169].

<u>Examples</u>:[1170]

Prohibited:

- Using webcams and voice recognition systems by a call centre to track their employee's emotions, such as anger.

- AI systems monitoring the emotional tone in hybrid work teams by identifying and inferring emotions from voice and imagery of hybrid video calls, which would typically serve the purpose of fostering social awareness, emotional dynamics management, and conflict prevention.

- AI systems monitoring the emotional tone in hybrid work teams by identifying and inferring emotions from voice and imagery of hybrid video calls, which would typically serve the purpose of fostering social awareness, emotional dynamics management, and conflict prevention.

[1168] *Ibid.*
[1169] *Ibid.*
[1170] *Ibid.*

- Using emotion recognition AI systems during the recruitment process.
- Using emotion recognition AI systems during the probationary period.
- Using cameras by a supermarket to track its employees' emotions, such as happiness.

Allowed:

- Emotion recognition systems deployed only for personal training purposes, if the results are not shared with HR responsible persons and cannot impact the assessment, promotion etc. of the person trained, provided that the prohibition is not circumvented and the use of the emotion recognition system does not have any impact on the work relationship.
- Using voice recognition systems by a call centre to track their customers emotions, such as anger or impatience (for example to help the employees cope with certain angry customers).

> ➢ Using cameras by a supermarket or a bank to detect suspicious customers, for example to conclude that somebody is about to commit a robbery, provided no employees are being tracked and there are sufficient safeguards.

Education institutions include both public and private institutions[1171]. There is no limitation as regards the types or ages of pupils or students or of a specific environment (online, in person, in a blended mode, etc.)[1172]. Education and training institutions at all levels are within the scope of the prohibition, including vocational schools, i.e. schools where students learn skills involving the use of their hands and continuous training[1173]. Education institutions are normally accredited or sanctioned by the relevant national education authorities or equivalent authorities[1174]. A key feature is that education institutions may provide a certificate (respectively participation is a precondition for obtaining a certificate) [1175]. The prohibition also applies to candidates during the admission process[1176].

[1171] Para 7.2.2 (b) (255) Prohibition Guidelines.
[1172] *Ibid.*
[1173] *Ibid.*
[1174] *Ibid.*
[1175] *Ibid.*
[1176] *Ibid.*

Examples[1177]:

Allowed:

- An AI-based application using emotion recognition for learning a language online outside an education institution.
- An education institution using AI-based eye tracking software when examining students online to track the fixation point and movement of the eyes (gaze point, e.g., to detect if unauthorized material is used).
- Using an AI system that allows to capture students talking to each other via their phones or other channels during online lectures by an education institution.

Prohibited:

- An AI-based application using emotion recognition if students are required to use the application by an education institution.

1177 *Ibid.*

- An education institution using AI-based eye tracking software when examining students online to track the fixation point and movement of the eyes (gaze point, e.g., to detect if unauthorized material is used) and detect emotions, such as emotional arousal and anxiousness.
- Using an emotion recognition AI system by an education institution during admission tests for new students.
- Using an AI system that allows to capture students talking to each other via their phones or other channels during online lectures by an education institution and to detect emotions, such as emotional arousal, anxiousness and interest.
- An education institution employing an emotion recognition AI system on both teachers (workplace) and students (education).

The prohibition contains an **explicit exception** for emotion recognition systems used in the area of the workplace and education institutions **for medical or safety**

reasons, such as systems for therapeutical use[1178]. This exception should be narrowly interpreted[1179].

Therapeutic uses mean uses of CE-marked medical devices[1180]. Moreover, this exception does not comprise the use of emotion recognition systems to detect general aspects of wellbeing[1181]. The general monitoring of stress levels at the workplace is not permitted under health or safety aspects[1182].

> Example:[1183]
>
> An AI system intended to detect burnout or depression at the workplace or in education institutions is not covered by the exception.

The safety reasons apply only in relation to the protection of life and health and not to protect other interests, for example property against theft or fraud[1184].

1178 Recital 44 EU AI Act; para 7.2.3 (256) Prohibition Guidelines.

1179 Para 7.2.3 (256) Prohibition Guidelines.

1180 Para 7.2.3 (257) Prohibition Guidelines.

1181 *Ibid.*

1182 *Ibid.*

1183 *Ibid.*

1184 Para 7.2.3 (258) Prohibition Guidelines.

Any use for medical and safety reasons should always remain limited to what is strictly necessary and proportionate, including limits in time, personal application and scale, and should be accompanied by sufficient safeguards[1185]. The safeguards could include, for example, prior written and motivated expert opinion relating to the specific use case[1186]. The necessity should be assessed on an objective basis in relation to the medical and safety purpose, and not refer to the employer's or educational institution's 'needs'[1187]. This assessment should inquire whether less intrusive alternative means exist which would achieve the same purpose[1188].

Employers and educators should only deploy emotion recognition systems for medical and safety reasons in case of an explicit need[1189]. Data collected and processed in this context may not be used for any other purpose[1190]. This is particularly important given that the use of AI management software at work has proven to potentially negatively impact workers' health and safety[1191]. Continuous monitoring via wearables, for instance, may increase work-stress while affecting productivity[1192].

[1185] Para 7.2.3 (259) Prohibition Guidelines.
[1186] *Ibid.*
[1187] *Ibid.*
[1188] *Ibid.*
[1189] Para 7.2.3 (260) Prohibition Guidelines.
[1190] *Ibid.*
[1191] *Ibid.*
[1192] *Ibid.*

Physical states, such as pain or fatigue, are excluded from the definition of emotion recognition systems, so a number of AI systems used for safety reasons would already not fall under that definition, including, for example, systems used in detecting the state of fatigue of professional pilots or drivers for the purpose of preventing accidents[1193].

Emotion recognition systems that classify as high-risk systems must comply with the high-risk requirements and the transparency obligation of the EU AI Act[1194].

Examples: [1195]

Medical reasons exception

Emotion recognition may be deployed for medical reasons to assist employees or students with autism and improve accessibility for those who are blind or deaf.

[1193] Recital 18 EU AI Act; para 7.2.3 (261) Prohibition Guidelines.

[1194] Para 7.2.3 (263) Prohibition Guidelines.

[1195] Para 7.2.3 (263) Prohibition Guidelines.

Prohibited

- Emotion recognition for assessing students' or employees' wellbeing, motivation levels, and job or learning satisfaction.

- An employer's deploying AI-enabled devices or digital assistants at the workplace for measuring anxiety based on measured stress levels or for measuring boredom of employees, unless the elevated stress level/lack of concentration would pose a specific danger, for example when deploying dangerous machines or dealing with dangerous chemicals. In the latter case, the employer may not use the data for other purposes, such as assessing the employee's work performance.

Out of Scope

Out of scope are AI systems inferring:

- emotions and sentiments not on the basis of biometric data; and (or)
- physical states such as pain and fatigue[1196].

[1196] Para 7.4(265) Prohibition Guidelines.

Emotion recognition systems used in all other domains other than in the areas of the workplace and education institutions do not fall under this prohibition but they are high-risk or may be prohibited, for example, on the ground of harmful manipulation and exploitation or by virtue of other EU legislation[1197].

<u>Example</u>:[1198]

Not emotion recognition but may be harmful manipulation and exploitation:

AI systems that enable emotion recognition based on keystroke or based on voice messages of customers (e.g., chat messages, use of virtual voice assistants), used in online marketing for applications for displaying personalized messages and for advertisement purposes including in smart environments ('intelligent billboards').

[1197] Article 6(2), Annex III, 1 c) EU AI Act; para 7.4 (266) Prohibition Guidelines.

[1198] *Ibid.*

'Crowd control' generally refers to the control and monitoring of the behaviour of groups to maintain (public) order and event safety[1199]. It is often associated with large crowd events (e.g., soccer or football games, concerts, etc) or specific places, such as airports or trains[1200]. Crowd control systems can operate without inferring emotions of individual persons, when for example analysing the general noise and mood level at a given place[1201]. In that case, the system would not fall within the scope of this prohibition, because it does not infer emotions of (a concrete) natural person[1202].

However, there may be instances where such crowd control systems infer emotions of individuals, for example whether there are many angry faces[1203]. Normally, such AI systems would not fall under this prohibition, since they are typically not used in the workplace or in education institutions[1204].

Also out of scope are systems that are used in the medical field, for example care robots, or medical practitioners using emotion recognition systems during an examination at their workplace, and voice monitors that analyse emergency calls[1205].

[1199] Para 7.4 a) (267) Prohibition Guidelines.
[1200] *Ibid.*
[1201] *Ibid.*
[1202] *Ibid.*
[1203] Para 7.4 a) (268) Prohibition Guidelines.
[1204] *Ibid.*
[1205] Para 7.4 a) (269) Prohibition Guidelines.

Such systems will often screen persons that are there in a work context, for example the security staff at a football stadium or at a central station (where such systems are used to recognize aggressive behaviour), or employees in the medical field[1206]. In such cases, deployers must employ safeguards to avoid the screening of employees[1207]. However, it cannot be completely avoided that such systems also infer the emotions of those employees[1208]. Since the primary objective of the system is not targeted at assessing employees' emotions, these systems should be considered to be outside the scope of the prohibition[1209]. Deployers of such systems remain responsible to ensure that employees are not adversely affected by their use[1210].

13.11.6 Prohibited Biometric Categorisation Systems

The EU AI Act prohibits the placing on the market, the putting into service for this specific purpose, or the use of biometric categorisation systems that categorise individually natural persons based on their biometric data

---

1206 Para 7.4 a) (270) Prohibition Guidelines.
1207 *Ibid.*
1208 *Ibid.*
1209 *Ibid.*
1210 *Ibid.*

to deduce or infer their race, political opinions, trade union membership, religious or philosophical beliefs, sex life or sexual orientation[1211].

A wide variety of information, including 'sensitive' information, may be extracted, deduced or inferred from biometric information, even without the knowledge of the persons concerned, to categorise those persons[1212]. This may lead to unfair and discriminatory treatment, for example when a service is denied because somebody is considered to be of a certain race[1213]. AI-based biometric categorisation systems for the purpose of assigning natural persons to specific groups or categories, relating to aspects such as sexual or political orientation or race, violate human dignity and pose significant risks to other fundamental rights, such as privacy and non-discrimination[1214]. They are therefore prohibited[1215].

All of the following five conditions must be met for this prohibition to apply[1216]:

- The practice must constitute the 'placing on the market', 'the putting into service for this specific purpose' or 'the use' of an AI system (as discussed earlier in this Chapter);
- The system must be a biometric categorisation system;

[1211] Article 5.1(g) EU AI Act.
[1212] Para 8.1 (272) Prohibition Guidelines.
[1213] *Ibid.*
[1214] *Ibid.*
[1215] *Ibid.*
[1216] Para 8.1 (273) Prohibition Guidelines.

- individual persons must be categorised;
- based on their biometric data;
- to deduce or infer their race, political opinions, trade union membership, religious or philosophical beliefs, sex-life, or sexual orientation.

A **biometric categorisation system** is an AI system for the purpose of assigning natural persons to specific categories on the basis of their biometric data, unless it is ancillary to another commercial service and strictly necessary for objective technical reasons[1217]. 'Biometric data' is personal data resulting from specific technical processing relating to the physical, physiological or behavioural characteristics of a natural person, such as facial images or dactyloscopic data[1218]. Biometric categorisation excludes categorisation according to clothes or accessories, such as scarfs or crosses, as well as social media activity[1219].

Biometric categorisation may rely on categories of physical characteristics (e.g., facial features and form, skin colour) based on which persons are assigned to specific categories[1220]. Some of these categories may be of a special 'sensitive' nature' or protected under EU non-

---

[1217] Article 3(40) EU AI Act; para 8.2.1 Prohibition Guidelines.

[1218] Article 3 (34) EU AI Act.

[1219] Para 8.2.1(277) Prohibition Guidelines.

[1220] Para 8.2.1(278) Prohibition Guidelines.

discrimination law, such as race[1221]. However, biometric categorisation may also be based on DNA or on behavioural aspects, such as keystroke analysis or a person's gait[1222].

To fall outside the scope of the definition of biometric categorisation under the EU AI Act, two conditions – being 'ancillary to another commercial service and strictly necessary for objective technical reasons' – must be cumulatively fulfilled[1223]. A purely ancillary feature is a feature that is intrinsically linked to another commercial service, meaning that the feature cannot, for objective technical reasons, be used without the principal service, and the integration of that feature or functionality is not a means to circumvent the applicability of the rules of the EU AI Act[1224].

Examples: [1225]

Permitted AI uses:

- Filters categorising facial or bodily features used on online marketplaces to allow a consumer to preview a product on him or herself could constitute such an

[1221] *Ibid.*

[1222] *Ibid.*

[1223] Para 8.2.1(279) Prohibition Guidelines.

[1224] Recital 16 EU AI Act; para 8.2.1(280) Prohibition Guidelines.

[1225] *Ibid.*

ancillary feature, since they can be only used in relation to the principal service which consists in selling a product.

- Filters integrated into online social network services which categorise facial or bodily features to allow users to add or modify pictures or videos could also be considered to be ancillary feature, since such a filter cannot be used without the principal service of the social network services consisting in the sharing of content online.

Prohibited uses:

- An AI system that categorises persons active on a social media platform according to their assumed political orientation, by analysing the biometric data from the photos they have uploaded on the platform, to send them targeted political messages. While such a system may only be ancillary to the political advertising, it would not be 'strictly necessary for objective technical reasons', hence the conditions for excluding it from the definition of biometric categorisation are not fulfilled.

- An AI system that categorises persons active on a social media platform according to their assumed sexual orientation by analysing the biometric data from photos shared on that platform and on that basis serves those persons advertisements would qualify as biometric categorisation within the meaning of the EU AI Act. Also in this case there is no strict necessity for this 'ancillary service', hence the exclusion from the prohibition does not apply.

Another condition for the prohibition to apply is that **natural persons must be 'individually' categorised**[1226].

Examples:[1227]

- AI systems that conduct 'Attribute Estimation' (count demographics), including, e.g., 'age, gender, ethnicity' on the basis of bodily features, such as face, height, or skin, eye and hair colour (or a combination thereof).

- AI systems capable of categorising individuals and singling them out based on a specific feature (e.g., a

[1226] Para 8.2.2 (282) Prohibition Guidelines.
[1227] *Ibid.*

scar under the right eye), or because they have a tattoo on their right hand.

If individual categorisation is not the purpose or outcome of the biometric categorisation, the prohibition does not apply, for example if a whole group is categorised without looking at the individual[1228].

The prohibition applies only to biometric categorisation systems which have as their objective **to deduce or infer** a limited number of sensitive characteristics**: race, political opinions, trade union membership, religious or philosophical beliefs, sex-life or sexual orientation**[1229].

Examples:[1230]

Prohibited:

- A biometric categorisation system that claims to be capable of deducing an individual's race from their voice.

[1228] *Ibid.*
[1229] Para 8.2.3 (283) Prohibition Guidelines.
[1230] *Ibid.*

- A biometric categorisation system that claims to be capable of deducing an individual's religious orientation from their tattoos or faces.

Not prohibited:

- A system that categorises persons according to skin or eye colour, or a system that analyses the DNA of victims of crimes in view of their origin.

Out of Scope

This prohibition does not cover any labelling or filtering of lawfully acquired biometric datasets, such as images, based on biometric data or categorizing of biometric data in the area of law enforcement[1231].

Examples:[1232]

Permissible labelling:

- The labelling of biometric data to avoid cases where a member of an ethnic group has a lower chance of being invited to a job interview because the algorithm

[1231] Article 5.1(g) and Recital 30 EU AI Act; paras 8.2 (275), 8.3 (284) Prohibition Guidelines.

[1232] Para 8.3 (285) Prohibition Guidelines.

was 'trained' based on data where that particular group performs worse, i.e. has worse outcomes than other groups.

- The categorisation of patients using images according to their skin or eye colour may be important for medical diagnosis, for example cancer diagnoses.

- The use by a law enforcement authority of an AI system that allows labelling and filtering of a dataset suspected of containing child sexual abuse material, including:

  - filtering and labelling according to gender, age, biometric data such as eye and hair colour, scars and marking to help with identifying the victims or creating links with other cases; and (or)

  - filtering and labelling abusers' hands based on specific characteristics such as length of fingers or any distinguishing markings or tattoos to help with identifying possible suspects.

13.11.7 Prohibition of Use of 'Real-Time' Remote Biometric Identification Systems in Publicly Accessible Places for Law Enforcement

The EU AI Act restricts the use of 'real-time' remote biometric identification systems in publicly accessible spaces for the purposes of law enforcement only to the cases where such use is strictly necessary for one of the following objectives[1233]:

- the targeted search for specific victims of abduction, human trafficking, human sexual exploitation, and (or) the search for missing persons[1234];
- the prevention of a specific, substantial and imminent threat to the life or physical safety of natural persons or a genuine and present or genuine and foreseeable threat of a terrorist attack[1235]; and
- the localisation or identification of a person suspected of having committed a criminal offence, for the purpose of conducting a criminal investigation or prosecution or executing a criminal penalty for certain offences punishable in the Member State concerned by a custodial sentence or a detention order for a maximum period of at least four years[1236].

1233 Article 5.1(h) EU AI Act.

1234 Article 5.1(h)(i) EU AI Act.

1235 Article 5.1(h)(ii) EU AI Act.

1236 Article 5.1(h)(iii), Annex II EU AI Act.

Member States are free to decide whether and in which of these three situations the use of real-time RBI systems in publicly accessible spaces for law enforcement purposes is permitted in their territory[1237]. In the absence of national legislation allowing and regulating such use, law enforcement authorities and entities acting on their behalf may not deploy such systems for law enforcement purposes[1238]. The existence of national legislation that complies with the requirements of the EU AI Act is therefore a pre-requisite of such use[1239].

The prohibition applies only to the use of real-time RBI systems in publicly accessible spaces for law enforcement purposes, so that only deployers of such systems are concerned by that provision[1240]. The placing on the market and the putting into service of such systems, as well as the use of other RBI systems, is not prohibited, but subject to the rules for high-risk AI systems including the rules for the retrospective use of RBI systems for law enforcement purposes[1241]. Where a Member State authorises the use of real-time RBI systems in publicly accessible spaces for law enforcement purposes for any of

---

[1237] Article 5(5) EU AI Act; para 9 (290) Prohibition Guidelines.

[1238] *Ibid.*

[1239] *Ibid.*

[1240] Para 9(291) Prohibition Guidelines.

[1241] *Ibid.*

the above three objectives, the rules for high-risk AI systems also apply to that use[1242].

The EU AI Act acknowledges the intrusive nature of real-time RBI systems in publicly accessible spaces for law enforcement purposes to the rights and freedoms of persons concerned, to the extent that it may affect the private life of a large part of the population, evoke a feeling of constant surveillance, and indirectly dissuade the exercise of the freedom of assembly and other fundamental rights[1243]. Technical inaccuracies of AI systems intended for the remote biometric identification of natural persons can lead to biased results and entail discriminatory effects[1244]. Such possibly biased results and discriminatory effects are particularly relevant with regard to age, ethnicity, race, sex or disabilities[1245]. In addition, the immediacy of the impact and the limited opportunities for further checks or corrections in relation to the use of such systems operating in real-time carry heightened risks for the rights and freedoms of the persons concerned in the context of, or impacted by, law enforcement activities[1246].

However, where the use of such systems is strictly necessary to achieve a substantial public interest and where the situations in which such use may occur are exhaustively

---

[1242] *Ibid.*

[1243] Recital 32 EU AI Act; para 9.1 (293) Prohibition Guidelines.

[1244] Para 9.1 (293) Prohibition Guidelines..

[1245] *Ibid.*

[1246] *Ibid.*

listed and narrowly defined, that use outweighs the risks to fundamental rights[1247]. To ensure that such systems are used in a 'responsible and proportionate manner', their use is subject to the safeguards and the specific obligations and requirements[1248].

All of the following conditions must be met for the prohibition to apply[1249]:

- The AI system must be a RBI system;
- The activity consists of the 'use' of that system (as discussed earlier in this Chapter),
- in 'real-time',
- in publicly accessible spaces, and
- for law enforcement purposes.

An RBI system is an AI system for the purpose of identifying natural persons, without their active involvement, typically at a distance through the comparison of a person's biometric data with the biometric data contained in a reference database[1250]. This definition covers only the identification functionality of biometric recognition systems, which implies the absence of active involvement of the persons concerned (i.e. no active

---

1247 Recital 33 EU AI Act; para 9.1 (294) Prohibition Guidelines..

1248 *Ibid.*

1249 Para 9.2 (295) Prohibition Guidelines.

1250 Article 3(41) EU AI Act; para 9.2.1 (298) Prohibition Guidelines.

participation) and results in the capture of the characteristics of those persons typically at a distance[1251]. For identification performance, the captured biometric data are compared with biometric data already stored in a reference database (such as a repository, e.g., a criminal database containing facial images or templates of suspects)[1252].

'Biometric identification' is the automated recognition of physical, physiological and behavioural or psychological human features for the purpose of establishing the identity of a natural person by comparing biometric data of that individual to biometric data of individuals stored in a database[1253]. The human features may comprise the face, eye movement, body shape, voice, prosody, gait, posture, heart rate, blood pressure, odour, keystroke characteristics[1254]. AI systems used for following natural persons can also be included in the definition of biometric identification, for example to see in which direction a suspect escapes[1255]. In contrast, AI systems that are intended to be used for biometric verification fall outside the scope of the prohibition[1256]. Biometric verification (or authentication) consists of comparing data presented at a sensor with another set of previously

---

[1251] Para 9.2.1(299) Prohibition Guidelines.
[1252] *Ibid.*
[1253] Article 3(35) EU AI Act.
[1254] Recital 15 EU AI Act.
[1255] Para 9.2.1(a)(302) Prohibition Guidelines.
[1256] Para 9.2.1(a)(303) Prohibition Guidelines.

recorded data stored on a device, such as a smartphone, a passport, or an ID card[1257]. The purpose of biometric verification is to verify that a specific person is who they claim to be[1258].

> Example:[1259]
>
> The comparison of a traveller's face scanned at an e-gate with the facial image contained in their passport.

Remoteness implies the ability of biometric systems to identify individuals without their active involvement, typically at a distance through the comparison of a person's biometric data with the biometric data contained in a reference database[1260].

The use of biometric systems to confirm the identity of a natural person for the sole purpose of having access to a service, unlocking a device, or having security access to premises is excluded from the concept of 'remote'[1261].

[1257] *Ibid.*
[1258] *Ibid.*
[1259] *Ibid.*
[1260] Article 3(41) EU AI Act; para 9.2.1(b)(304) Prohibition Guidelines.
[1261] Recital 15 EU AI Act; para 9.2.1(b)(305) Prohibition Guidelines.

Example[1262]:

A face identification system is deployed to enter a restricted area (e.g., power plant premises) through face scanning technology; the system compares the face of the individual presented at the entrance camera with a reference image contained in a reference database of persons allowed to enter the building.

This exclusion from the scope of the prohibition is justified by the fact that such systems are likely to have a minor impact on fundamental rights of natural persons as compared to RBI systems which may be used for the processing of the biometric data of a large number of persons without their active involvement[1263]. RBI systems are typically used to perceive multiple persons or their behaviour simultaneously in order to facilitate significantly the identification of natural persons without their active involvement[1264]. For active involvement, it is not sufficient that persons are informed about the presence of cameras, but they need to step actively and consciously in front of a

[1262] *Ibid.*

[1263] Recital 17 EU AI Act; para 9.2.1(b)(306) Prohibition Guidelines.

[1264] *Ibid.*

camera that is installed in a way fostering active participation[1265].

<u>Examples</u>: [1266]

- RBI systems that are used in cameras installed at walls or ceiling of metro stations for surveillance purposes. Such a system fulfils the condition of remoteness.

- Systems that are used to give access to the metro station, such as biometric metro tickets, where persons are actively involved and consciously approach the biometric sensor to obtain access, do not fulfil the remoteness condition.

Biometric recognition systems that process (contactless) fingerprints, gait, voice, DNA, keystrokes and other (biometric) behavioural signals may also constitute RBI systems[1267].

<u>Examples</u>[1268]:

[1265] *Ibid.*
[1266] *Ibid.*
[1267] Para 9.2.1(b)(307) Prohibition Guidelines.

[1268] *Ibid.*

RBI Systems (not necessarily prohibited):

- A voice biometric technology system deployed to identify a person speaking. The microphone then collects the biometric sample.

- A gait recognition system used via CCTV and the videos are automatically checked for matches with previously captured templates.

- Keystroke biometric technology used to identify the person typing a fraudulent message.

In the case of body-cams capable of RBI used by individual law enforcement agents, the untargeted filming during, for example, a demonstration with hundreds of participants will be considered to fulfil the condition of remoteness[1269].

Identification is not possible without a **reference database** containing biometric data for comparison purposes[1270]. Thus, the existence of a reference database is

[1269] Para 9.2.1(b)(308) Prohibition Guidelines.

[1270] Para 9.2.1(b)(309) Prohibition Guidelines.

indispensable to perform the comparison for identification purposes[1271].

> Example[1272]:
>
> In the case of missing persons, the Schengen Information System database could be used as the reference database for facial recognition purposes (once operational).

Real-time means that the system captures and further processes biometric data 'instantaneously, near-instantaneously or in any event without any significant delay'[1273]. All the processing steps, i.e. the capture, comparison, and identification of biometric data, occur simultaneously or almost simultaneously, which may include a 'limited short delay' to avoid the prohibition being circumvented through the retrospective use of RBI systems[1274]. 'Without a significant delay' is not defined in the EU AI Act; it will have to be assessed on a case-by-case

---

[1271] *Ibid*; Recital 34 EU AI Act.

[1272] Para 9.2.1(b)(309) Prohibition Guidelines.

[1273] Recital 17 EU AI Act; Para 9.2.2(310) Prohibition Guidelines.

[1274] Article 3(42) EU AI Act; Para 9.2.2(310) Prohibition Guidelines.

basis[1275]. As the devices used for real-time or post-remote identification are increasingly one and the same with different functionalities, the distinction is temporal[1276]. Generally speaking, a delay is significant at least when the person is likely to have left the place where the biometric data was taken[1277].

Real-time systems in general are used at a given place to facilitate a quick reaction and not to retrospectively identify persons[1278]. They provide the user of the system with a means to track the movements of persons under surveillance and to monitor them[1279].

Examples: [1280]

- **Real-time RBI**: An AI system that screens all incoming visitors to a concert venue.
- **Post-RBI**: A system that films all incoming visitors to a concert. If an incident happens at the concert, after the concert, the identification system is operated on the video material in order to identify the offender.

[1275] Para 9.2.2(310) Prohibition Guidelines.
[1276] *Ibid.*
[1277] *Ibid.*
[1278] Para 9.2.2(311) Prohibition Guidelines.
[1279] *Ibid.*
[1280] *Ibid.*

When a law enforcement authority covertly takes a picture of a person via a mobile device and submits it to a database for immediate search, depending on the circumstances, this may fall under the prohibition[1281].

Publicly accessible spaces are any publicly or privately owned physical space accessible to an undetermined number of natural persons, regardless of whether certain conditions for access may apply, and regardless of the potential capacity restrictions[1282]. Whether a space is accessible to the public requires a case-by-case analysis[1283]. Several elements characterise such spaces[1284]:

- Accessibility to an undetermined number of persons, independently of the potential capacity or security restrictions, such as purchasing a ticket or title of transport, prior registration or having a certain age. The possibility of getting access to a space through an unlocked door does not mean that the space is publicly accessible if indications or circumstances suggest the contrary (such as a sign restricting access). Moreover, the access to a space can be limited to certain persons, linked to public safety or security, or to the decision of the person having the relevant authority over the space.

1281 Para 9.2.2(312) Prohibition Guidelines.
1282 Article 3(44) EU AI Act.
1283 Recital 19 EU AI Act.
1284 *Ibid*; para 9.2.3(314) Prohibition Guidelines.

Examples[1285]:

Publicly accessible places:

- A concert venue for which participants pay an entrance fee.
- An event location where a trade fair is organised targeting participants over the age of 50.
- A park in a gated residence with public opening hours without any access restrictions during those hours.

Not publicly accessible:

- A space closed by a gate, even if the gate is unlocked, such as the gated entrance of a fenced residential area of several houses.
- A park in a gated residence with public opening hours outside those hours.

[1285] Para 9.2.3(314) Prohibition Guidelines.

- Irrelevance of ownership, i.e. a space does not need to be in public ownership for it to be considered as a publicly accessible space[1286].

<u>Example</u>[1287]:

The space may be owned by a private entity, a public entity, or a public entity and managed by a private party, without impacting the nature of the space.

- No specific activity for which the space is used; a publicly accessible area is not necessarily a space linked to a public service[1288]. Moreover, a space linked to a public service may include non-publicly accessible spaces, i.e. the offices of the civil servants working at a municipality[1289].

<u>Example</u>:[1290]

Publicly accessible spaces may be used for:

- commerce, such as shops, restaurants, cafés, etc.;

[1286] *Ibid.*
[1287] *Ibid.*
[1288] *Ibid.*
[1289] *Ibid.*
[1290] Recital 19 EU AI Act; para 9.2.3 (314) Prohibition Guidelines.

- services, such as banks, professional activities (a doctor's office as well as an accountant's office), hospitality (e.g., a hotel), etc.;
- sport, such as swimming pools, gyms, stadiums, etc.;
- transport, such as bus, metro and railway stations, airports, means of transport, etc.;
- entertainment, such as cinemas, theatres, museums, concert and conference halls, etc.;
- leisure;
- public roads and squares, parks, forests, playgrounds.

Online spaces are not publicly accessible spaces because they do not constitute a physical space[1291].

Examples[1292]:

- Chat rooms.
- Social media.
- Online platforms.

Likewise, certain spaces meant to be accessed by a limited number of persons, such as factories, companies and workplaces with entry control or limitations to

[1291] Para 9.2.3 (315) Prohibition Guidelines.
[1292] *Ibid.*

employees or service providers, are not publicly accessible spaces since they are intended to be accessed only by employees and service providers[1293].

Examples:

- A workplace accessible with a badge is in principle not considered a publicly accessible space, whereas an office without entry controls falls may be[1294].
- Prisons and border control are not publicly accessible spaces[1295].
- A border crossing point is not a publicly accessible space, while the street leading to the border crossing point or a forest in the vicinity normally is[1296].
- Airport common areas are a publicly accessible space, but the area dedicated to border control (where the customs officials stand and passports or ID checks occur) is excluded from the scope of the prohibition[1297].

1293 *Ibid.*
1294 *Ibid.*
1295 Recital 19 EU AI Act.
1296 Para 9.2.3 (316) Prohibition Guidelines.
1297 Para 9.2.3 (317) Prohibition Guidelines.

The prohibition applies to the use of RBI systems **for law enforcement purposes**, irrespective of the entity, authority, or body carrying out the law enforcement activities[1298].

Law enforcement is the activities carried out by law enforcement authorities or on their behalf for the prevention, investigation, detection or prosecution of criminal offences or the execution of criminal penalties, including safeguarding against and preventing threats to public security[1299].

Law enforcement authorities are:

(a) any public authority competent for the prevention, investigation, detection or prosecution of criminal offences or the execution of criminal penalties, including the safeguarding against and the prevention of threats to public security; or

(b) any other body or entity entrusted by Member State law to exercise public authority and public powers for the purposes of the prevention, investigation, detection or prosecution of criminal offences or the execution of criminal penalties, including the safeguarding against and the prevention of threats to public security[1300].

[1298] Para 9.2.4 (319) Prohibition Guidelines.

[1299] Article 3(46) EU AI Act.

[1300] Article 3(45) EU AI Act; para 9.2.4 (322) Prohibition Guidelines.

Other entities, bodies, or persons, may exercise law enforcement activities after being entrusted by Member States law entrusting them public authority and public powers for the above purposes[1301].

'On behalf of' means that a law enforcement authority has delegated the performance of a law enforcement activity (or part of it) to another entity or person, including private parties, or has requested in specific cases another entity or person to act to support law enforcement activities[1302]. In both cases, the law enforcement authorities must instruct on all major aspects and supervise the other entity, as this requirement is inherent to the notion of acting 'on behalf' of a person[1303].

Examples:[1304]

Delegation of tasks to other bodies:

- Public transport companies requested by law enforcement authorities to ensure security on the public transport networks under their instructions and supervision.

[1301] Para 9.2.4 (323) Prohibition Guidelines.
[1302] Para 9.2.4 (324) Prohibition Guidelines.
[1303] *Ibid.*
[1304] *Ibid.*

- Sports federations requested by law enforcement authorities to act under their instructions and supervision to provide security at sporting events.

- Banks are requested by law enforcement authorities to conduct certain actions to counter certain crimes in specific cases under the instructions and supervision of law enforcement authorities.

Only when those other bodies or entities have been entrusted with a specific law enforcement task will their activities fall under the definition of 'law enforcement'[1305].

The Exceptions to the Prohibition

The EU AI Act permits three scenarios in which real-time RBI can be used in publicly accessible spaces for law enforcement purposes if the national law of a Member State permits the same[1306]. These three scenarios are:

- the targeted search of victims of three specific serious crimes and missing persons;
- the prevention of imminent threats to life or physical safety or a genuine threat of terrorist attacks; and

[1305] Para 9.2.4 (325) Prohibition Guidelines.
[1306] Para 9.3 (326) EU AI Act.

- the localisation or identification of suspects and offenders of certain serious crimes[1307].

These scenarios balance the security needs of society against the risk that real-time RBI systems pose to the fundamental rights of individuals subject to those systems[1308].

__Scenario 1: Targeted Search for Victims__

The EU AI Act permits the use of 'real-time' remote biometric identification systems in publicly accessible spaces for targeted search for specific victims of abduction, human trafficking, human sexual exploitation, and (or) the search for missing persons[1309].

> Example:
>
> If a child is kidnapped and there are specific indications that the kidnapper intends to bring the child from one place to another by car, the police may use a real-time RBI system for the targeted search of that child,

[1307] Para 9.3.1 (327) Prohibition Guidelines.
[1308] Para 9.3.1 (328) Prohibition Guidelines.
[1309] Para 1(h)(i) Article 5 EU AI Act.

but it must define a perimeter of deployment and duration of use to identify the child.

The Prohibition Guidelines distinguish between search for missing children and missing adults, since the voluntary disappearance of a missing adult will not always trigger a search[1310]. The applicable rules regarding missing children vary considerably from one Member State to another[1311]. The disappearance of an adult does not always lead to a search of that person by police, as adults have the right to disappear[1312]. A search could be linked to the legal status of the person ('under curatorship'), their health condition (a mental illness), the existence of a suicidal note, but also the departure without personal belongings[1313]. If the circumstances of the disappearance are a cause for concern, the disappearance may be filed with the police so that a search can start[1314]. In some Member States, the search for a missing person may occur under an administrative procedure and not for law enforcement purposes[1315].

[1310] Para 9.3.1(b) (334) Prohibition Guidelines.
[1311] *Ibid.*
[1312] Para 9.3.1(b) (335) Prohibition Guidelines.
[1313] *Ibid.*
[1314] *Ibid.*
[1315] Para 9.3.1(b) (336) Prohibition Guidelines.

> Example:[1316]
>
> Where a vulnerable person is missing, but there is no suspicion of a crime or any other law enforcement purpose, the use of real-time RBI systems to search for that person would not be deemed to be for law enforcement purposes and would therefore fall under the rules for such use under the EU data protection legislation.

The Additional Safeguards and Conditions (see below) also need to be met in order for the use of real-time RBI to be permissible.

Scenario 2: Prevention of Imminent Threat to Life and (or) Terrorist Attacks

The EU AI Act permits the use of real-time RBI in publicly accessible spaces for law enforcement purposes to prevent **a specific, substantial and imminent threat to the life or physical safety of natural persons or a genuine and present or genuine and foreseeable threat of a terrorist attack**[1317]. The threat does not need to be

[1316] *Ibid.*
[1317] Article 5(1)(h)(ii) EU AI Act.

limited to identified individuals or a group, as it relates to natural persons in general[1318].

A **specific threat** means that the threat is clearly defined, individualised and concrete, in that it should not be hypothetical or relate to certain dangers in general[1319].

Example:[1320]

The police are informed that a former student plans a deadly attack at his former university as he seeks revenge on several former classmates. The police receives information about the imminence of the attack, the targeted school, and the weapons he plans to use to execute his plans.

A specific threat needs not be intentional[1321]. Non-intentional actions could also result in a threat to life or physical safety[1322].

A substantial threat to physical safety relates to serious bodily injuries[1323].

An **imminent** threat to life or physical safety is a threat that can occur at any moment and requires

1318 Para 9.3.3 (a) (338) Prohibition Guidelines.
1319 Para 9.3.3 (a) (342) Prohibition Guidelines.
1320 *Ibid.*
1321 Para 9.3.3 (a) (343) Prohibition Guidelines.
1322 *Ibid.*
1323 Para 9.3.3 (a) (341) Prohibition Guidelines.

'immediate action to be taken'[1324]. It may include an imminent threat to critical infrastructure where the disruption or destruction of such critical infrastructure would result in an imminent threat to the life, or the physical safety of a person, including through serious harm to the provision of basic supplies to the population or to the exercise of the core function of the State[1325].

Example:[1326]

A serious disruption and destruction of critical infrastructure (e.g., a power plant, water supply, or a hospital) may result in an imminent threat to the life or the physical safety of a person when there is serious harm of cessation of basic supplies to the population (deprivation of electricity or drinkable water for a long period, in a particularly warm or cold weather, etc).

What constitutes an imminent threat to life or the physical safety of natural persons is ultimately defined and assessed at the level of the Member State based on its national laws, in accordance with EU law, in particular taking into account the key elements and rationale of the

---

1324 Recital 37 of Regulation 2023/1543; para 9.3.3 (a) (341) Prohibition Guidelines.

1325 Para 9.3.3 (a) (339) Prohibition Guidelines.

1326 *Ibid.*

prohibitions[1327]. This will have to be laid down/referred to in the laws Member States must adopt to make use of the exceptions to the prohibition on the use of real-time RBI for law enforcement purposes in publicly accessible spaces[1328].

Let's now look at the second part of the scenario - **a genuine and present or genuine and foreseeable threat of a terrorist attack.**

The existence and seriousness of the threat is assessed at national level when assessing the actual circumstances of a measure to be taken to safeguard national security in case of a terrorist attack[1329]. The **terrorist threat level is defined at national level** and varies from one Member State to another[1330]. However, the concept of 'a genuine and present or genuine and foreseeable threat' is an autonomous notion of EU law and should be assessed independently of national definitions[1331]. The threat relates not to terrorism in general, but specifically to a threat of a terrorist attack[1332].

The threshold of seriousness that a threat needs to reach to allow for the use of real-time RBI systems in publicly accessible spaces for law enforcement purposes was inspired by the CJEU's case law on data retention and

---

[1327] Para 9.3.3 (a) (340) Prohibition Guidelines.
[1328] *Ibid.*
[1329] Para 9.3.3(b)(345) Prohibition Guidelines.
[1330] *Ibid.*
[1331] *Ibid.*
[1332] *Ibid.*

passenger name record measures aimed at safeguarding national security, in particular, against terrorist attacks[1333]. According to the CJEU, in those contexts, 'a threat to national security must be genuine and present, or at the very least, foreseeable, which presupposes that sufficiently concrete circumstances have arisen'[1334].

Notably, this exception does not specify that the use of real-time RBI is permitted to locate or identify a specific person[1335]. Its purpose is the prevention of a particular threat[1336]. Accordingly, the scenario may also cover the use of real-time RBI to detect and follow 'terrorists on the move', i.e. several persons linked to the same threat, if there are concrete indications that those persons plan to commit a terrorist attack, but it is not clear where[1337].

Example:[1338]

Real-time RBI to prevent a terrorist attack in a park

[1333] Para 9.3.3(b)(346) Prohibition Guidelines.

[1334] *Ibid*; Judgment of the Court of Justice of 20 September 2022, *SpaceNet*, C-793/19 (Joined Cases C-793/19, C-794/19), ECLI:EU:C:2022:702, paragraph 93.

[1335] Para 9.3.3(b)(347) Prohibition Guidelines.

[1336] *Ibid.*

[1337] *Ibid.*

[1338] *Ibid.*

> The police are informed that a person is running around a park looking for people to attack with a knife while he is screaming violent extremist slogans usually linked to terrorist attacks and terrorist groups. If the Member State has authorised the use of real-time RBI in the terrorist attack prevention scenario, law enforcement authorities may use real-time RBI to identify and locate the person in and around the park to prevent the attack, provided the other conditions[1339] have been met.

In addition, the Additional Safeguards and Conditions (see below) need to be met in order for the use of real-time RBI to be permissible.

Scenario 3: Localisation or Identification of Criminal Suspects

The EU AI Act permits the use of 'real-time' remote biometric identification systems in publicly accessible spaces for the localisation or identification of a person suspected of having committed a criminal offence, for the purpose of conducting a criminal investigation or prosecution or executing a criminal penalty for the following offences punishable in the Member State

[1339] The conditions are set out in Article 5(2)-(7) EU AI Act and are the same as for the Targeted Search Scenario.

concerned by a custodial sentence or a detention order for a maximum period of at least four years[1340]:

- terrorism,
- trafficking in human beings,
- sexual exploitation of children, and child pornography,
- illicit trafficking in narcotic drugs or psychotropic substances,
- illicit trafficking in weapons, munitions or explosives,
- murder, grievous bodily injury,
- illicit trade in human organs or tissue,
- illicit trafficking in nuclear or radioactive materials,
- kidnapping, illegal restraint or hostage-taking,
- crimes within the jurisdiction of the International Criminal Court,
- unlawful seizure of aircraft or ships,
- rape,
- environmental crime,
- organised or armed robbery,
- sabotage,
- participation in a criminal organisation involved in one or more of the offences listed above.

A Member State may authorise the use of real-time RBI in publicly accessible spaces for law enforcement purposes to **locate and identify** a suspect of a criminal

---

[1340] Para 1(h)(iii) Article 5; Annex II EU AI Act.

offence to conduct a criminal investigation, prosecute that person for the crime committed, or execute an existing sentence[1341].

This scenario covers two categories of individuals: **suspects and perpetrators**[1342]. A **suspect** is a person with regard to whom there are serious grounds for believing that they have committed a criminal offence, and sufficient evidence of that person's involvement in the offence has already been gathered[1343]. A **perpetrator** is a person who is accused or convicted of having committed a criminal offence[1344]. The same conditions (crime listed in Annex II EU AI Act -see the list of these crimes above, and the maximum punishment of at least four years) apply to locate or identify the accomplice of these crimes[1345].

Only **serious crimes** listed above justify the use of real-time RBI systems in publicly accessible spaces for law enforcement purposes[1346]. Moreover, to use real-time RBI for this purpose, the respective criminal offence must be **punishable in the Member State concerned by a custodial sentence or a detention order for a maximum period of at least four years**[1347].

1341 Para 9.3.4(a) (349) Prohibition Guidelines.
1342 Para 9.3.4(b) (350) Prohibition Guidelines.
1343 *Ibid.*
1344 *Ibid.*
1345 *Ibid.*
1346 Para 9.3.4(c) (351) Prohibition Guidelines.
1347 Para 9.3.4(c) (354) Prohibition Guidelines.

Examples:[1348]

- During a busy festival in a city, police authorities deploy live facial recognition technologies to monitor the area around the festival and identify wanted individuals with outstanding arrest warrants for illegal drug trafficking and sexual offences. At different entrances to the festival, the police use live video footage of people passing in front of a mobile camera to compare their faces with a watchlist of faces of wanted individuals. RBI can be used in case of illegal drug trafficking. However sexual offences are not on the list of offences, unless they relate to the sexual exploitation of children, child sexual abuse material, or rape. The police are not allowed to deploy real-time facial recognition technologies in a broad, untargeted manner, i.e. in the hope of finding wanted criminals and taking them off the streets.

- The case is different if the police have received a physical description with a photograph of a wanted individual that is subject to a European Arrest Warrant for drug trafficking and they have reasons to believe that he will be present at the festival. In those circumstances, deploying real-time facial recognition

[1348] *Ibid.*

technologies to identify a targeted individual may be permitted by the localisation or identification exception.

- After a serious terror attack at a Christmas market with 12 deaths, the police use real-time facial recognition technologies to identify the offender and to see to where he is escaping. They also use the real-time facial recognition technologies of the nearby train station and at destination stations of the trains leaving from there shortly after the attack. In the case of a terror attack, such use can be permitted by the localisation or identification exception.

The Additional Safeguards and Conditions (see below) need to be met in order for the use of real-time RBI to be permissible.

Additional Safeguards and Conditions

Use Only to Confirm the Identity of the Specifically Targeted Individual

The use of real-time RBI in publicly accessible places for law enforcement purposes for the targeted search for victims of specific crimes is permitted only to confirm the identity of the specifically targeted individual[1349]. This condition aims to balance the seriousness of the situation and the harm resulting from not using the system with the impact of the technology on individuals' rights and freedoms[1350]. It aims to avoid mass surveillance by targeting an individual for the deployment of real-time RBI[1351]. As a consequence, the deployment of a real-time RBI system in publicly accessible spaces for law enforcement purposes should only be authorized for targeted individuals[1352].

The use of the expression 'confirming the identity', as opposed to 'identification', is meant as an additional safeguard for the fundamental rights limiting the risk of indiscriminate surveillance and implies that the identification of an individual must be targeted[1353]. It means that the use of real-time RBI may only be initiated to search for specific individuals for which the law enforcement authorities have reasons to believe or are informed that they are victims of the specific crimes listed in this scenario or are involved in one of the other two scenarios (prevention of imminent threat or localisation or identification of suspects)[1354]. This means, in practice, a

---

[1349] Article 5 (2), Annex II EU AI Act.
[1350] Para 10(1)(357) Prohibition Guidelines.
[1351] *Ibid.*
[1352] *Ibid.*
[1353] Para 10(1)(358) Prohibition Guidelines.
[1354] *Ibid.*

comparison of the data collected real-time with the data contained in the reference database[1355]. But, to use real-time RBI system in the imminent threat scenario and for conducting a criminal investigation in the localisation of suspect scenario, law enforcement authorities do not necessarily need to know the identity of the individuals they are searching for before using the system[1356]. If they have factual indications and information about a planned terrorist attack by a terrorist group (without knowing who will execute the plan) at a specific time and place, the RBI system may be used to identify the offender from the terrorist group, provided the law enforcement authorities have constituted a reference database containing the biometric data of the individuals forming part of the terrorist group[1357]. In all three scenarios 'confirming the identity' may also include the localisation of the person in question[1358].

Second, before using the system, the nature of the situation giving rise to the possible use, in particular, the seriousness, probability and scale of the harm for natural persons, society and law enforcement purposes that would be caused if the system were not used, should be assessed against the consequences of the use of the system on the rights and freedoms of the persons concerned, in particular,

---

1355 *Ibid.*
1356 *Ibid.*
1357 *Ibid.*
1358 *Ibid.*

the seriousness, probability and scale of those consequences[1359]. This should include evaluating whether less intrusive alternative solutions are available to the law enforcement authorities or entities acting on their behalf[1360].

Example:[1361]

Law enforcement authorities are prohibited from using real-time facial recognition systems in the street based on general security, crime prevention and over-crowding concerns, since that would involve the constant monitoring and surveillance of all persons, it is not limited in time, and it would therefore not meet the criteria for the exception from the prohibition.

The '**seriousness**' criterion, applied here in connection to the possible harm and consequences, implies a variation in degrees of interference with the fundamental rights at stake, which is linked to the principle of proportionality[1362]. The Prohibition Guidelines note that some interferences with fundamental rights are viewed as

---

1359 Article 5 (2), Annex II EU AI Act.; para 10(1)(359) Prohibition Guidelines.

1360 *Ibid.*

1361 *Ibid.*

1362 Para 10(1)(360) Prohibition Guidelines.

more serious than others[1363], although no specific examples are given of such differentiation.

The '**scale**' criterion refers, in particular, to the number and categories of persons affected by the interference (including children and vulnerable or marginalised persons)[1364].

Finally, the '**probability**' is the likelihood that an event will occur[1365].

The assessment of the seriousness, scale and probability of the harm and consequences should all be part of the Fundamental Rights Impact Assessment that the law enforcement authority is obliged to complete on a case-by-case basis[1366].

Third, the real-time use of RBI in publicly accessible spaces in the three scenarios described above must also comply with necessary and proportionate safeguards and conditions imposed by the national law authorising the use of these systems, in particular as regards the temporal, geographic and personal limitations[1367]. In other words, the real-time use of RBI should be clearly limited in terms of geographic scope, duration, and the targeted person. This is to ensure that the RBI system is only used when strictly necessary[1368].

[1363] *Ibid.*
[1364] Para 10(1)(361) Prohibition Guidelines.
[1365] Para 10(1)(362) Prohibition Guidelines.
[1366] Para 10(1)(363) Prohibition Guidelines.
[1367] Article 5 (2) EU AI Act.
[1368] Para 10(1)(364) Prohibition Guidelines.

Concerning the **geographic restriction**, it may cover one or several geographical areas based on 'objective and non-discriminatory factors'[1369]. In the case of biometric identification this implies that the geographic restriction applies to a clearly delineated boundary for which there are indications that the event will take place[1370]. Such a delineation should -under normal circumstances- not comprise an entire city or country, but should be more targeted[1371].

Another safeguard relates to the **personal scope** of the measure, i.e. defining the **categories of persons concerned**[1372]. This would exclude the untargeted, indiscriminate identification of persons, without further indications of an incident[1373].

Finally, the **time limit** is a period limited to what is strictly necessary, but which may be extended in case of need in accordance with the applicable rules[1374]. The use of real-time RBI systems therefore cannot be for an indefinite or vague period of time[1375]. The period needs to be determined in light of the specific indications that lead to the use of RBI systems[1376].

[1369] Para 10(1)(365) Prohibition Guidelines.
[1370] *Ibid.*
[1371] *Ibid.*
[1372] Para 10(1)(366) Prohibition Guidelines.
[1373] *Ibid.*
[1374] Para 10(1)(367) Prohibition Guidelines.
[1375] *Ibid.*
[1376] *Ibid.*

Fourth, before deployment, the law enforcement authority deploying the real-time RBI system must have conducted a Fundamental Right Impact Assessment and registered the system in the EU database (except in a duly justified case)[1377].

The Fundamental Right Impact Assessments (**FRIAs**) must comply with the requirements to FRIAs for high-risk AI systems[1378].

In the period between 2 February 2025 when the prohibitions become applicable and 2 August 2026 when the provisions on high-risk AI systems start to apply, to benefit from one or more of the exceptions from the prohibitions the deployers of real-time RBI systems meeting the conditions for an exception need to undertake the FRIA compliant with the requirements for FRIA for high-risk AI systems[1379]. The following provisional guidance set out in the Prohibition Guidelines relates only to the use of real-time RBI in publicly accessible spaces for law enforcement purposes for the period before the obligations for high-risk AI systems become applicable and the Commission adopts the template for FRIA and provides further guidance on the FRIA obligation for high-risk AI systems[1380].

[1377] Para 10(1)(368) Prohibition Guidelines.
[1378] Para 10.1.1 (369) Prohibition Guidelines.
[1379] Para 10.1.1 (370) Prohibition Guidelines.
[1380] Para 10.1.1(370) Prohibition Guidelines.

A FRIA is a new type of impact assessment that aims to identify the impact that certain high-risk AI systems, including RBI systems, may produce on fundamental rights. A FRIA is an accountability tool[1381].

The obligation to carry out the FRIA for the exceptions from the prohibitions is imposed on the deployers of the RBI system, and not entities or bodies or anyone else acting on their behalf[1382]. If other actors are acting on behalf of the deployer/the law enforcement authority, they will have to contribute to the preparation of the FRIA with all relevant information to ensure it is properly carried out[1383].

A FRIA must be carried out before the deployment of the authorized real-time RBI system[1384] and should include the following information[1385]:

➢ A description of the RBI use and the deployer's processes for the use, together with the intended purpose of use. The description should include:

- the name of the deployer;

- the law enforcement purpose(s) for which the real-time RBI system will be used;

- the description of the reference database against which the biometric identification will be compared,

[1381] Para 10.1.1 (371) Prohibition Guidelines.
[1382] Para 10.1.1 (373) Prohibition Guidelines.
[1383] *Ibid.*
[1384] Para 10.1.1 (374) Prohibition Guidelines.
[1385] Para 10.1.1 (375) Prohibition Guidelines.

including the sources of the biometric data (facial images, voice samples, etc.) that will be used;

- the description of the technology underlying the system to explain its functioning (by referencing the available documentation provided by the provider and its name); once the rules on high-risk AI system enter into force, this can be done by reference the registration number of the system in the EU database and the available information for the system; and

- the legal basis on which the real-time RBI will be deployed.

- ➢ The period of use and frequency of use.

- ➢ The categories of persons and groups affected by the system: for the purpose of the exception from the prohibitions, the FRIA should distinguish between:

- The targeted individual, who may be a victim of a crime, a perpetrator, or a suspect,

- The individuals whose biometric data are included in the reference database, and

- Categories of persons who are present in the surrounding areas where the RBI system will be deployed.

The use of real-time RBI systems will not only affect the fundamental rights of the targeted individual[1386]. The rights of other individuals whose biometric data are

[1386] *Ibid.*

used for comparison purposes, passersby, and people incidentally presented in the search area will also be affected[1387]. The description of the geographic scope of the search area(s) covered by the real-time RBI system will impact the number of persons affected by the system[1388].

- The specific risks of harm to the affected persons[1389].

The fundamental rights that may be affected by the use of real-time RBI in publicly accessible spaces for law enforcement purposes include, in particular:

- the right to private and family life, including people's reasonable expectation of anonymity in public spaces;

- the right to data protection, as RBI systems rely on the processing of biometric data and other personal data (e.g., names, ID numbers, as well as sensitive data such as ethnicity) to identify specific individuals;

- freedom of thought, conscience and religion, freedom of expression and freedom of assembly and association in the public spaces being searched, on which the use of RBI systems could have a chilling effect, preventing individuals to fully exercise their rights and freedoms, since if individuals know that they are

---

[1387] *Ibid.*
[1388] *Ibid.*
[1389] *Ibid.*

monitored, they might change their behaviour, or even prevent themselves to behave in a certain manner;

- the right to an effective remedy and a fair trial;
- the right to non-discrimination if the system embeds biases (such as gender, ethnic or racial biases) and leads to the misidentification of a suspect or perpetrator;
- the right to human dignity by the feeling of being reduced to an object of the system;
- the presumption of innocence and right to defence; since no decision adversely affecting an individual may be solely taken on the output of the real-time RBI system;
- the rights of the child in case the victim, missing person or suspect is a minor;
- the rights of the elderly in the case of a missing person[1390].

To assess the specific risks of harm likely to impact the identified affected person(s) or group(s), the FRIA must identify the fundamental rights of those persons and assess the impact on their fundamental rights, including the severity of the impact and its scale, taking into account the potentially affected persons[1391].

This part of the FRIA should also:

- ➢ assess whether the use of a real-time RBI system is necessary and proportionate considering the objectives

[1390] Para 10.1.1 (376) Prohibition Guidelines.
[1391] *Ibid.*

and the circumstances in which its use is intended, including the existence or absence of less intrusive alternatives;

- describe the performance and accuracy level of the system, based on the technical documentation and, if available, the training data on which the technology was tested and developed to prevent biases and discrimination;
- identify the impact of use of a real-time RBI system on the fundamental rights of all individuals potentially affected, in particular the suspect or perpetrator, the victim searched and other individuals present in the publicly accessible spaces subject to the search[1392].

The assessment under the FRIA should be performed at an abstract level, prior to the first putting into service of the AI system[1393]. Specific context-dependent considerations that determine the impact of use in each individual case where a real-time RBI system is used should be further elaborated in the individual request for requesting the authorisation by a judicial authority or other independent administrative authority of each use of the RBI system[1394].

[1392] *Ibid.*
[1393] *Ibid.*
[1394] *Ibid.*

- Human oversight measures[1395]

The use of real-time RBI that is permitted as an exception from the prohibitions still falls under the rules for high-risk systems[1396]. The EU AI Act requires high-risk AI systems to 'be designed and developed in such a way, including with appropriate human-machine interface tools, that they can be effectively overseen by natural persons during the period in which they are in use.'[1397]. No action or decision may be taken by the deployer on the basis of the identification resulting from the system, 'unless that identification has been separately verified and confirmed by at least two natural persons with the necessary competence, training and authority' or unless 'Union or national law considers the application of this requirement to be disproportionate'[1398]. The EU AI Act prescribes AI literacy measures for providers and users of AI systems to ensure 'a sufficient level of AI literacy of their staff and other persons dealing with the operation and use of AI systems'[1399] and considering the persons on whom the systems are to be used. In the data protection context, for human oversight to be effective it is crucial 'to enable the person to understand the (in that case facial recognition) system and its limits as well as to interpret its results

---

[1395] *Ibid.*
[1396] Para 10.2.2.5(407) Prohibition Guidelines.
[1397] Article 14 EU AI Act.
[1398] Article 14(5) EU AI Act.
[1399] Article 4 EU AI Act.

properly. It is also necessary to establish a workplace and organisation that counteracts the effects of automation bias, and avoids fostering the uncritical acceptance of the results e.g., by time pressure, burdensome procedures, potential detrimental career effects etc.'[1400]. Similar considerations may apply in the context of the EU AI Act[1401].

No decision that would adversely affect an individual may be taken solely on the basis of the output of the real-time RBI system[1402]. As a consequence, the FRIA should describe the procedures that will be followed during the operation of the system and how the output will be interpreted in the context of decision-making process[1403]. The procedures should provide instructions for the deployment of the RBI system, clarify the role of a human agent in verifying and interpreting the output and provide training to operate the system[1404]. The person in charge of human oversight should have sufficient 'AI literacy, training and authority'[1405] to understand how the system functions and when it underperforms or malfunctions[1406].

[1400] EDPB, *Guidelines 05/2022 on the use of facial recognition technology in the area of law enforcement* v2.0, 26 April 2023, p. 22; Para 10.2.2.5(408) Prohibition Guidelines.

[1401] Para 10.2.2.5(408) Prohibition Guidelines.

[1402] Article 5(3) EU AI Act.

[1403] Para 10.1.1 (376) Prohibition Guidelines.

[1404] *Ibid.*

[1405] Recital 91 EU AI Act.

[1406] Para 10.1.1 (376) Prohibition Guidelines..

Other relevant considerations for human oversight and monitoring should be described[1407].

➢ Risk mitigation measures

In addition to implementing human oversight measures, the deployer should explain redress measures in case a risk materialises, including the governance procedures and the complaint mechanisms (such as in the case of a misidentification)[1408].

Registration of the Authorised RBI Systems

The deployer of a real-time RBI system used in publicly accessible spaces for law enforcement purposes must register the system in the EU database[1409]. However, in cases of a duly justified emergency (such as an imminent threat), deployment may start even prior to registration, provided the law enforcement authority registers the system without undue delay[1410]. Undue delay means 'as soon as possible' considering the circumstances of the emergency that prevented the registration of the system prior to its use[1411]. Whether registration meets that criterion requires an evaluation on a case-by-case basis[1412]. It cannot be

---

[1407] Articles 14 and 26 EU AI Act; para 10.1.2 (377) Prohibition Guidelines.

[1408] Para 10.1.1 (376) Prohibition Guidelines.

[1409] Articles 5(2) and 49 EU AI Act.

[1410] Para 10.1.2 (377) Prohibition Guidelines.

[1411] *Ibid.*

[1412] *Ibid.*

defined a priori with a precise time limit[1413]. The delay should not be caused by a deliberate action[1414]. According to, RBI systems used for the purpose of law enforcement will be registered in a secure non-public section of the database, with limited information and limited access to that information[1415].

Example:[1416]

Requesting law enforcement authorities to register the RBI system within 24 hours of the use may be a reasonable delay where the system was deployed in a situation of an imminent threat to life, such as in the scenario of a live shooter.

Prior Authorisation

The use requires a prior authorisation of each individual use of a real-time RBI system and prohibits automated decision-making based **solely on the output of such a system** which produces an adverse legal effect[1417].

The authorisation is granted **prior to the use of the system** by a judicial authority or an independent

[1413] *Ibid.*
[1414] *Ibid.*
[1415] Article 49(4) EU AI Act; *Ibid.*
[1416] Para 10.1.2 (377) Prohibition Guidelines.
[1417] Article 5 (3) EU AI Act; para 10.2(378) Prohibition Guidelines.

administrative authority whose decision is binding of the Member State in which the use is to take place, issued upon a reasoned request and in accordance with the detailed rules of national law which the EU AI Act requires Member States to adopt[1418].

The authorisation may only be granted by a **judicial or an independent administrative authority** whose decision is binding[1419].

The CJEU has interpreted the concept of '**independence**' in different contexts[1420]. In *HK v Prokuratuur,* for example, the CJEU explained that independence means that the authority maintains a '*neutral stance*'[1421]. The CJEU specified that an authority involved in previous investigations, in that case the public prosecutor, does not have such independence[1422]. Similar considerations may apply as regards the independence required for the prior authorisation - the authorising authority needs to be independent from the authority using the RBI system[1423]. This would apply not only for the police, but also cases of investigative judges or prosecutors

[1418] Article 5(3) EU AI Act.
[1419] Para 10.2.2.2(390) Prohibition Guidelines.
[1420] Para 10.2.2.2(a)(391) Prohibition Guidelines.
[1421] *Ibid*; Judgment of the Court of Justice of 2 March 2021, *Prokuratuur*, C-746/18, ECLI:EU:C:2021:152, paragraph 54.
[1422] *Ibid.*
[1423] *Ibid.*

that supervise the work of police and the use of RBI for which authorisation is sought[1424].

In *Commission v Poland*, a case dealing with the question when a body can be considered to be independent in the context of railway safety, the CJEU found that, 'as regards public bodies, independence usually refers to a status that ensures that the body in question is able to act completely freely in relation to those bodies in respect of which its independence is to be ensured, shielded from any instructions or pressure'[1425]. Similar indications may apply in the context of the prior authorisation[1426].

The judicial authorities in a democratic society are in general also independent authorities[1427]. The judiciary plays an important role when it is independent from the executive government(s) and from the legislator, covering and reviewing the application of the legislation and fundamental rights and freedoms in an autonomous and independent way[1428]. Judicial independence is one of the crucial facets of the rule of law and is guaranteed by the EU Charter and ECHR[1429].

[1424] *Ibid.*

[1425] Para 10.2.2.2(a)(392) Prohibition Guidelines; Judgment of the Court of Justice of 13 June 2018, *Commission* v *Poland*, C-530/16, ECLI:EU:C:2018:430, paragraph 67.

[1426] Para 10.2.2.2(a)(392) Prohibition Guidelines.

[1427] Para 10.2.2.2(a)(393) Prohibition Guidelines.

[1428] *Ibid.*

[1429] *Ibid.*

The authorisation must be addressed to the authority that is competent according to national law[1430].

Any authorisation to use real-time RBI in publicly accessible spaces for law enforcement purposes must assess whether the requirements for the exception from the prohibition have been met[1431].

The use of biometric data, in particular facial recognition technology, has been considered by the European Data Protection Board (EDPB) in its Guidelines 5/2022 and the European Data Protection Supervisor (EDPS) as affecting several fundamental rights and freedoms[1432]. That view is shared by The EU Agency for Fundamental Rights and by the Council of Europe[1433]. Both the CJEU and the ECtHR have confirmed the sensitive nature of biometric data processing[1434]. It follows from the EU Charter that any interference in fundamental rights and freedoms must always respect the essence of the rights and freedoms[1435]. The notion of 'essence' of fundamental rights and freedoms has been developed in the CJEU's case-law

---

[1430] Para 10.2.2.2(b)(394) Prohibition Guidelines.

Judgment of the Court of Justice of 6 October 2015, *Schrems*, C-362/14, https://eur-lex.europa.eu/legal-content/EN/TXT/PDF/?uri=CELEX:62014CJ0362, ECLI:EU:C:2015:650, paragraph 44.

[1431] Para 10.2.2.2(c)(395) Prohibition Guidelines.

[1432] Para 10.2.2.2(c)(396) Prohibition Guidelines.

[1433] *Ibid.*

[1434] *Ibid.*

[1435] Para 10.2.2.2(c)(397) Prohibition Guidelines.

and is an independent value in the EU's legal order[1436]. If the essence of a fundamental right or freedom is not respected, a right or freedom is unduly touched by a measure and no interference shall be allowed[1437]. Any interference with fundamental rights and freedoms requires 'a law' that should in principle respect the necessity and proportionality pursuant to the EU Charter[1438]. The national law permitting the use of real-time RBI in publicly accessible spaces for law enforcement purposes must provide that authorisation for such use is permitted 'only where it [the authority] is satisfied [..] that the use is necessary for, and proportionate to, achieving one of the objectives specified'[1439]. National authorities need to verify whether the biometric identification is strictly necessary[1440]. This assessment should be based on the FRIA that should include an assessment of the necessity and the proportionality in a general manner prior to requesting the authorisation for each use in the specific circumstances[1441].

However, in a **duly justified** situation of urgency, the use of such system may be commenced without an

---

[1436] Para 10.2.2.2(c)(398) Prohibition Guidelines.
[1437] *Ibid.*
[1438] Para 10.2.2.2(c)(399) Prohibition Guidelines.
[1439] Article 5(3) EU AI Act; *Ibid.*
[1440] Para 10.2.2.2(c)(399) Prohibition Guidelines.
[1441] *Ibid.*

authorisation provided that such authorisation is requested without undue delay, at the latest within 24 hours[1442].

Urgency is 'situations where the need to use the systems concerned is such as to make it **effectively and objectively impossible to obtain an authorisation before commencing** the use of the AI system'[1443]. In such case of urgency, 'the use of the AI system should be restricted to the **absolute minimum necessary** and should be **subject to appropriate safeguards and conditions**, as determined in national law and specified in the context of each individual urgent use case by the law enforcement authority itself.'[1444] The user must then submit a request for authorisation within 24 hours from the moment that the real-time RBI system is used[1445]. In practice, that will generally be the moment that the biometric ready or capably cameras are 'switched on' and deployed and the first biometric comparison is made with the system[1446]. The logging of the processing activities should be made available to the authority to substantiate the timeliness of the request[1447] and the request should justify why no prior request was submitted prior to the use of the system[1448].

[1442] Article 5(3) EU AI Act.
[1443] Recital 35 EU AI Act.
[1444] Para 10.2.2(383) Prohibition Guidelines.
[1445] Para 10.2.2.3(400) Prohibition Guidelines.
[1446] *Ibid.*
[1447] *Ibid.*
[1448] Para 10.2.2.3(401) Prohibition Guidelines.

The request for authorisation will normally be initiated by the deployer, i.e. **by the competent (law enforcement) authority**[1449]. According to the definition of law enforcement authority, any 'other body or entity entrusted by Member State law to exercise public authority and public powers for the purposes of the prevention, investigation, detection or prosecution of criminal offences or the execution of criminal penalties, including the safeguarding against and the prevention of threats to public security'[1450] is a law enforcement authority and could also be the responsible as the 'competent authority' for submitting the request for prior authorisation[1451].

The use of a real-time RBI system for activities falling outside the scope of the EU AI Act does not need to be so authorised[1452]. If subsequently such a system is being used for law enforcement purposes, the use would fall within the scope of the AI Act and an authorisation would be required where the requirements of the exceptions from the prohibitions are met[1453].

Prior authorisation is needed for the use of 'real-time' RBI systems in publicly accessible spaces **for law enforcement purposes,** even if the systems are operated by

---

[1449] Para 10.2.2.1 (a) (384) Prohibition Guidelines.
[1450] Article 3(45) b) EU AI Act.
[1451] Para 10.2.2.1(a)(384) Prohibition Guidelines.
[1452] Para 10.2.2.1(a)(385) Prohibition Guidelines.
[1453] *Ibid.*

other parties on behalf of law enforcement authorities, for example sport clubs or shopping malls[1454].

<u>Examples</u>: [1455]

- An organisation entrusted with resources for searching for missing children decides to use a real-time RBI system. It has no mandate to exercise public authority and public powers or for preventing criminal offences or tasks for the prevention of threats to public security. Such use does not fall under the prohibition, since it is not for law enforcement purposes. That system will, however, be categorised as 'high-risk'[1456] and a requirement of prior consultation of the supervisory data protection authority may be necessary under the EU data protection legislation. Depending on the applicable national law and whether one of the exceptions to EU data protection rules applies, a prior authorisation may also be required for such processing. By contrast, if the same organisation were requested by law enforcement authorities to act on their behalf for the search of missing children in a law enforcement context and under the supervision and instructions of

[1454] Para 10.2.2.1(b)(386) Prohibition Guidelines.
[1455] *Ibid.*
[1456] Annex III 1 (a) EU AI Act.

the competent law enforcement authorities, prior authorisation would be needed under the EU AI Act.

- A private organisation entrusted with providing resources to aid persons who risk becoming victims of a natural disaster decides to use a real-time RBI system for that purpose. Such use does not fall under the prohibition laid down in the EU AI Act, since it is not for law enforcement purposes. That system will, however, be categorised as 'high-risk'[1457] (point 1 (a) of Annex III) and a requirement of prior consultation of the supervisory data protection authority may be necessary pursuant to the EU data protection rules. Depending on the applicable national law and whether one of the exceptions to the EU data protection rules applies, a prior authorisation under the EU AI Act may also be required for such processing.

A prior authorisation is needed for '**each use**'[1458]. So the decisive time for obtaining such authorisation is not prior to installing a real-time RBI systems, but each use[1459].

[1457] *Ibid.*

[1458] Article 5(3) EU AI Act; para 10.2.2.1(c)(387) Prohibition Guidelines.

[1459] Para 10.2.2.1(c)(387) Prohibition Guidelines.

<u>Examples:</u>[1460]

- The police install biometric ready CCTV cameras at the main train station of a city -> no authorisation under the EU AI Act is needed, but the biometric system must comply with the requirements on high-risk systems, a FRIA must be prepared prior to the first use and an individual authorisation by a judicial or independent administrative authority is needed before each individual use of the system.

- The police has specific indications that a terrorist will arrive by train in the town -> prior authorisation is needed for real-time identification using the previously installed CCTV cameras.

Each individual request for the use of real-time RBI must be 'reasoned', i.e. substantiated and motivated[1461].

National legislation should lay down requirements regarding the exact content of the request, while fully taking into account the requirements outlined above, including sufficient evidence to determine the strict

---

1460 *Ibid.*

1461 Article 5(3) EU AI Act.; para 10.2.2.1(d)(388) Prohibition Guidelines.

necessity and proportionality for the use of real-time RBI and other relevant aspects to reflect the exceptional nature of authorising such use[1462].

If the authorisation is refused, the use must be stopped with immediate effect and all the data, as well as the results and outputs of that use must be immediately discarded and deleted[1463]. The deployer will have:

- a reference database, containing the biometric information (e.g., facial images, voice snippets, ...) and related identifying information, if applicable, against which
- biometric information captured from individuals present in the publicly accessible space is compared to identify and single out those individuals; and
- this comparison will lead to the comparison result[1464].

The requirement to discard and delete the data collected and processed also means that the reference database(s) used for the unauthorized biometric identification must be removed and deleted if it was built specifically for the contested search[1465]. Only where the law enforcement authorities had built and intended to maintain the database used for identification in *a lawful*

[1462] Article 5(5) EU AI Act; Para 10.2.2.1(d) (389) Prohibition Guidelines.

[1463] Article 5(3) EU AI Act.

[1464] Para 10.2.2.4(402) Prohibition Guidelines.

[1465] Para 10.2.2.4(403) Prohibition Guidelines.

manner for legitimate aims *other* than for the unauthorized use of real-time RBI may the database be maintained[1466].

Besides the deletion of any (unlawful) database with biometric information, all the collected images and other personal data, including the meta data, technical processing data, including the templates and other personal data, and other comparison - and output data obtained during the unlawful use of the real-time RBI system must also be deleted[1467].

Where the law enforcement authority challenges the rejection, the data may be kept by a trustee until a final decision has been taken on the request[1468]. During that period, the data should normally not be placed at the disposal of the law enforcement authority[1469].

Even where the deployer of a real-time RBI system obtains an authorisation, no decision that produces an adverse legal effect on a person may be taken based solely on the output of the 'real-time' RBI system[1470].

[1466] *Ibid.*

[1467] Para 10.2.2.4(404) Prohibition Guidelines.

[1468] Para 10.2.2.4(405) Prohibition Guidelines.

[1469] *Ibid.*

[1470] Aticle 5(3) EU AI Act; Para 10.2.2.4(406) Prohibition Guidelines.

Example:[1471]

A person is arrested and imprisoned for a serious crime solely based on identification by a facial recognition system, without any further checks. This is in breach of the EU AI Act's requirement for human oversight. Checks could relate for example to the question whether a given person has been at a different place or also whether there are other reasons for that the person cannot be the person searched.

The cost and resources involved in such use and in the destruction of data if the authorisation is not granted give rise to the question: is there any certainty as to whether the authorisation will be granted? The EU AI Act prescribes[1472] that the authorisation can be granted only where the issuing authority is satisfied, on the basis of objective evidence or clear indications presented to it, that:

-

- the use of the 'real-time' remote biometric identification system concerned is necessary for, and proportionate to, achieving one of the targeted victim search objectives, as identified in the request; and

[1471] Para 10.2.2.4(406) Prohibition Guidelines.
[1472] Article 5(3) EU AI Act.

- remains limited to what is strictly necessary concerning the period of time as well as the geographic and personal scope.

The consequence of these requirements is that a double necessity and proportionality assessment should occur prior to the deployment of any real-time RBI system in publicly accessible spaces for law enforcement purposes[1473]. First, an assessment should be made by the user when performing a FRIA[1474]. Second, a judicial or independent administrative authority must also assess the necessity and proportionality of using such a system within the limits of the national law providing the legal basis for any such use, taking the Charter and other EU law into consideration[1475]. As a consequence, any such system may only be used 1) after a FRIA and 2) when the competent national authority has authorised such use[1476].

For the use of a real-time RBI system to be authorized, a national law adopted in the Member States concerned must exist authorising such use[1477]. Certain Member States already have a system of prior authorisation

---

[1473] Para 10.2.1(380) Prohibition Guidelines.

[1474] Article 5(2) EU AI Act; *Ibid.*

[1475] Article 5(3) EU AI Act; para 10.2.1(380) Prohibition Guidelines.

[1476] Para 10.2.1(380) Prohibition Guidelines.

[1477] Articles 5(2) and (3) EU AI Act; para 10.2.1(381) Prohibition Guidelines.

in place for the use of biometric systems under other EU or national law, such as data protection law[1478].

In deciding on the request for an authorisation, the issuing authority must also take into account:-

- the nature of the situation giving rise to the possible use, in particular the seriousness, probability and scale of the harm that would be caused if the system were not used; and
- the consequences of the use of the system for the rights and freedoms of all persons concerned, in particular the seriousness, probability and scale of those consequences[1479].

Further, this use may be authorised only if the following two conditions are met:

- The law enforcement authority has completed a fundamental rights impact assessment; and
- The law enforcement authority has registered the system in the EU database. However, the EU AI Act permits the use of such systems without the registration in the EU database in duly justified cases of urgency and provided that the registration is completed without undue delay.[1480]

Whilst there is no certainty in the EU AI Act that the authorisation will be granted in every case, the EU AI

[1478] Para 10.2.1(381) Prohibition Guidelines.
[1479] Article 5 (2), Annex II EU AI Act.
[1480] Article 5 (2) EU AI Act.

Act provides a solid foundation and a clear pathway to navigate the route for obtaining and issuing the authorisation.

Finally, **each use** of a 'real-time' remote biometric identification system in publicly accessible spaces for law enforcement purposes **must be notified to the relevant market surveillance authority and the national data protection authority** in accordance with the national rules[1481]. The notification must, as a minimum, contain the information required to be reported by the Member States to the Commission and specified in the template to be issued by the Commission to the Member States, and shall not include sensitive operational data[1482]. 'Sensitive operational data' means operational data related to law enforcement activities (prevention, detection, investigation or prosecution of criminal offences), the disclosure of which could jeopardise the integrity of criminal proceedings[1483]. Notification must take place after each use in order to be able to report about the number of authorisations and their result[1484].

National laws are required to implement the use of 'real-time' RBI systems in publicly accessible spaces for the purposes of law enforcement[1485]. At the same time,

[1481] Article 5(4) EU AI Act.
[1482] Article 5(4) and (6) EU AI Act.
[1483] Article 3(38) EU AI Act.
[1484] Para 10.3(409) Prohibition Guidelines.
[1485] Para 10.4.1(411) Prohibition Guidelines.

Member States remain free to decide whether to adopt such national laws[1486]. For the Member States that decide to adopt national law authorising the use of real-time RBI, the EU AI Act specifies the substantive elements the national laws must contain to comply with the requirements laid down in the EU AI Act[1487]. Let's look at these elements closer.

First, the national laws may not expand the objectives for which real-time RBI may be used in publicly accessible spaces for law enforcement purposes beyond those listed in the exceptions to the prohibitions[1488]. But they may adopt more restrictive laws than the EU AI Act provides for[1489].

Second, the national laws must determine the detailed rules for requesting, issuing, and using the authorisation[1490], regulating, for example[1491]:

- who are the competent authorities and the independent authorities in the Member State competent to issue (or refuse) an authorisation;
- the detailed scope of the objectives for which real-time RBI in publicly accessible spaces may be used for law enforcement purposes without going beyond the

---

[1486] Article 5(5) EU AI Act.
[1487] Para 10.4.1(411) Prohibition Guidelines.
[1488] Article 5(1)(h)(i)-(iii) EU AI Act; para 10.4.2 (413) Prohibition Guidelines.
[1489] Para 10.4.2 (415) Prohibition Guidelines.
[1490] Para 10.4.3 (416) Prohibition Guidelines.
[1491] *Ibid.*

objectives set out in the EU AI Act but possibly narrowing them;

- requiring requests to be in writing and explaining in detail the specific use and the intended purpose of use for a specific criminal offence/situation which justifies its use;
- require justification, supporting evidence, and translation if relevant for the use of the system, in particular - the place, the period, the personal scope, the strict necessity and proportionality, including the relevance, sufficiency and the efficiency of the use of the system and the absence of less intrusive means;
- the description of the technology that will be used and the location points of the data collection;
- the minimum reliability, threshold used, and accuracy rates of the systems used;
- - the possibility of auditing the submitted information, including the technical details and accuracy criteria any time *ex ante* and *ex post* by the authorising authority;
- the specification of the reference databases used;
- the duration of the retention of the data captured and all other related personal data used;
- the security measures, including against unlawful access to the data;
- other safeguards (when relevant);
- the description of any cooperation with private or public authorities, including in other countries, and data transfers and exchanges;

- the traceability of the process;
- the name of the responsible personnel of the deployers;

For the issuance of authorisation:

- the possibility of a written procedure complemented with a hearing;
- the grounds of refusal;
- the rights of persons for which a search is conducted, the rights of persons whose data is captured, and the possible rights of third parties;
- the delays within which the authorities will have to take their decision;
- any need for formal notifications upon granting/refusal of the authorisation;
- sanctions for not complying with (formal and substantial) requirements;
- the right to appeal an authorisation that has been denied;

For the use of authorisation:

- the registration of the use of real-time RBI systems in a central register with a summary of the substantive elements;
- possible further reporting obligations;
- procedure for extending or modifying the authorisation.

Prior to adoption, Member States are encouraged to send the draft law to the AI Office[1492]. After adoption of the

---

[1492] Para 10.4.2 (414) Prohibition Guidelines.

national law, Member States must notify the adopted law to the Commission within 30 days[1493]. But the notification does not create a presumption of conformity of the Member State's law with the EU AI Act[1494]. The AI Office, after receiving the notification, will only acknowledge receipt and the Commission will publish the Member State's law on a public website[1495]. A failure to notify the AI Office within the statutory deadline of 30 days following the adoption[1496] may result in the national law being held unenforceable in legal proceedings[1497].

[1493] *Ibid.*
[1494] *Ibid.*
[1495] *Ibid.*
[1496] Article 5(5) EU AI Act.
[1497] Judgment of the Court of Justice of 19 December 2019, *Airbnb Ireland*, C-390/18,EU:C:2019:1112, paragraphs 96 to 97; para Para 10.4.2 (414) Prohibition Guidelines.

CHAPTER 14. High Risk AI Systems

14.1 What are High Risk AI Systems?

High-risk AI systems are[1498]:

1. Safety components: The AI systems intended to be used as safety components of a product, or themselves are safety products covered by the EU harmonisation legislation listed in Annex I of the EU AI Act[1499] and required to undergo a third-party conformity assessment, with a view to the placing on the market or the putting into service of that product pursuant to the Union harmonisation legislation listed in Annex I of the EU AI Act[1500]. These AI systems are high-risk irrespective of whether they are placed on the market or put into service independently of these products[1501]. **The products covered by the EU harmonisation legislation listed in Annex I of the EU AI Act are**: -

- ➢ machinery[1502];
- ➢ toys[1503]

[1498] Article 6(1),(2), Annex III EU AI Act.

[1499] Article 6(1), Annex I EU AI Act.

[1500] Article 6(1)(b) EU AI Act.

[1501] Article 6(1) EU AI Act.

[1502] Machinery covered by Directive 2006/42/EC of the European Parliament and of the Council of 17 May 2006 on machinery, and amending Directive 95/16/EC (OJ L 157, 9.6.2006, p. 24)

[1503] Toys covered by Directive 2009/48/EC of the European Parliament and of the Council of 18 June 2009 on the safety of toys (OJ L 170, 30.6.2009, p. 1)

- recreational craft and personal watercraft[1504];
- lifts and safety components for lifts[1505];
- equipment and protective systems intended for use in potentially explosive atmospheres[1506];
- radio equipment[1507];
- pressure equipment[1508];
- cableway installations[1509];
- personal protective equipment[1510];
- appliances burning gaseous fuels[1511];
- medical devices[1512];
- in vitro diagnostic medical devices[1513];
- civil aviation safety products[1514];

[1504] Directive 2013/53/EU of 20 November 2013 (OJ L 354, 28.12.2013, p. 90).
[1505] Directive 2014/33/EU of 26 February 2014 (OJ L 96, 29.3.2014, p. 251)
[1506] Directive 2014/34/EU of 26 February 2014 (OJ L 96, 29.3.2014, p. 309).
[1507] Directive 2014/53/EU of 16 April 2014 (OJ L 153, 22.5.2014, p. 62).
[1508] Directive 2014/68/EU of 15 May 2014 (OJ L 189, 27.6.2014, p. 164).
[1509] Regulation (EU) 2016/424 of 9 March 2016 (OJ L 81, 31.3.2016, p. 1).
[1510] Regulation (EU) 2016/425 of 9 March 2016 (OJ L 81, 31.3.2016, p. 51).
[1511] Regulation (EU) 2016/426 of 9 March 2016 (OJ L 81, 31.3.2016, p. 99).
[1512] Regulation (EU) 2017/745 of 5 April 2017 (OJ L 117, 5.5.2017, p. 1).
[1513] Regulation (EU) 2017/746 of 5 April 2017 (OJ L 117, 5.5.2017, p. 176).
[1514] Regulation (EC) No 300/2008 of 11 March 2008 (OJ L 97, 9.4.2008, p. 72).

- two- or three-wheel vehicles and quadricycles safety products[1515];
- agricultural and forestry vehicle safety products[1516];
- marine equipment safety products[1517];
- rail system safety products[1518];
- safety products for motor vehicles and their trailers, and systems, components and separate technical units intended for such vehicles[1519];
- safety products for unmanned aircraft and their engines, propellers, parts and remote control equipment[1520];

2. The following **eight types of AI systems** listed in Annex III EU AI Act and often referred to as Annex III AI systems. These systems are high-risk unless certain conditions are met to show that the AI system does not pose a significant risk of harm to the health, safety or

---

[1515] Regulation (EU) No 168/2013 of 15 January 2013 (OJ L 60, 2.3.2013, p. 52).
[1516] Regulation (EU) No 167/2013 of 5 February 2013 (OJ L 60, 2.3.2013, p. 1).
[1517] Directive 2014/90/EU of 23 July 2014 (OJ L 257, 28.8.2014, p. 146).
[1518] Directive (EU) 2016/797 of 11 May 2016 (OJ L 138, 26.5.2016, p. 44).
[1519] Regulation (EU) 2018/858 of 30 May 2018 (OJ L 151, 14.6.2018, p. 1); Regulation (EU) 2019/2144 of 27 November 2019 (OJ L 325, 16.12.2019, p. 1).
[1520] Regulation (EU) 2018/1139 of 4 July 2018 (OJ L 212, 22.8.2018, p. 1).

fundamental rights of natural persons, including by not materially influencing the outcome of decision making[1521].

Annex III AI Systems:

1. **Biometrics**:

- remote biometric identification systems (other than AI systems intended to be used for biometric verification the sole purpose of which is to confirm that a specific natural person is the person he or she claims to be);
- AI systems intended to be used for:
- biometric categorisation, according to sensitive or protected attributes or characteristics based on the inference of those attributes or characteristics; and
- emotion recognition.

2. **Critical infrastructure**: AI systems intended to be used as safety components in the management and operation of critical digital infrastructure, road traffic, or in the supply of water, gas, heating or electricity.

3. **Education and vocational training**: AI systems intended to be used to:

[1521] Article 6(3) EU AI Act.

- determine access or admission or to assign natural persons to educational and vocational training institutions at all levels;
- evaluate learning outcomes, including when those outcomes are used to steer the learning process of natural persons in educational and vocational training institutions at all levels;
- assess the appropriate level of education that an individual will receive or will be able to access, in the context of or within educational and vocational training institutions at all levels;
- monitor and detect prohibited behaviour of students during tests in the context of or within educational and vocational training institutions at all levels.

4. Employment, workers' management and access to self-employment: AI systems intended to be used:

- for the recruitment or selection of natural persons, in particular to place targeted job advertisements, to analyse and filter job applications, and to evaluate candidates;
- to make decisions affecting terms of work-related relationships, the promotion or termination of work-related contractual relationships, to allocate tasks based on individual behaviour or personal traits or characteristics or to monitor and evaluate the

performance and behaviour of persons in such relationships.

5. Access to and enjoyment of essential private services and essential public services and benefits: AI systems intended to be used:

- by public authorities or on behalf of public authorities to evaluate the eligibility of natural persons for essential public assistance benefits and services, including healthcare services, as well as to grant, reduce, revoke, or reclaim such benefits and services;
- to evaluate the creditworthiness of natural persons or establish their credit score (other than AI systems used for detecting financial fraud);
- for risk assessment and pricing in relation to natural persons in the case of life and health insurance;
- to evaluate and classify emergency calls by natural persons or to be used to dispatch, or to establish priority in the dispatching of, emergency first response services, including by police, firefighters and medical aid, as well as of emergency healthcare patient triage systems.

6. Law enforcement, in so far as their use is permitted under relevant Union or national law: AI systems intended to be used by or on behalf of law enforcement authorities, or by Union institutions, bodies, offices or agencies in support of law enforcement authorities or on their behalf:

- to assess the risk of a natural person becoming the victim of criminal offences;

- as polygraphs or similar tools;
- to evaluate the reliability of evidence in the course of the investigation or prosecution of criminal offences;
- for assessing the risk of a natural person offending or re-offending not solely on the basis of the profiling of natural persons[1522], or to assess personality traits and characteristics or past criminal behaviour of natural persons or groups;
- for the profiling[1523] of natural persons in the course of the detection, investigation or prosecution of criminal offences.

7. Migration, asylum and border control management, in so far as their use is permitted under EU or national law: AI systems intended to be used by or on behalf of competent public authorities or by EU institutions, bodies, offices or agencies:

- as polygraphs or similar tools;
- to assess a risk, including a security risk, a risk of irregular migration, or a health risk, posed by a natural person who intends to enter or who has entered into the territory of a Member State;
- to assist competent public authorities for the examination of applications for asylum, visa or

[1522] As referred to in Article 3(4) of Directive (EU) 2016/680.

[1523] Profiling is referred to in Article 3(4) of Directive (EU) 2016/680.

residence permits and for associated complaints with regard to the eligibility of the natural persons applying for a status, including related assessments of the reliability of evidence;

- in the context of migration, asylum or border control management, for detecting, recognising or identifying natural persons, with the exception of the verification of travel documents.

8. Administration of justice and democratic processes: AI systems intended to be used:

- by a judicial authority or on their behalf to assist a judicial authority in researching and interpreting facts and the law and in applying the law to a concrete set of facts, or to be used in a similar way in alternative dispute resolution; and
- for influencing the outcome of an election or referendum or the voting behaviour of natural persons in the exercise of their vote in elections or referenda. This does not include AI systems to the output of which natural persons are not directly exposed, such as tools used to organise, optimise or structure political campaigns from an administrative or logistical point of view.

For an AI system of one of these eight types not to be high-risk, the AI system may not be used to profile natural persons[1524] **and** must meet any of the following conditions[1525]:

- the AI system must be intended to perform a narrow procedural task[1526];
- the AI system must be intended to improve the result of a previously completed human activity[1527];
- the AI system must be intended to detect decision-making patterns or deviations from prior decision-making patterns and not meant to replace or influence the previously completed human assessment, without proper human review[1528]; or
- the AI system must be intended to perform a preparatory task to an assessment relevant for the purposes of the use that would make it high- risk[1529].

If a provider considers that an AI system of one of these eight types is not high-risk, the provider must document its assessment before that system is placed on the market or put into service and provide the assessment documentation on request of national competent authorities; such provider or its authorised representative must also register itself in the EU database[1530].

[1524] Article 6(3) EU AI Act.
[1525] *Ibid.*
[1526] Article 6(3)(a) EU AI Act.
[1527] Article 6(3)(b) EU AI Act.
[1528] Article 6(3)(c) EU AI Act.
[1529] Article 6(3)(d) EU AI Act.
[1530] Article 6(4), Annex III, Article 49(2) EU AI Act.

Where there is specific and reliable evidence of the existence of AI systems that fall under the scope of high-risk, but do not pose a significant risk of harm to the health, safety or fundamental rights of natural persons, the EU AI Act empowers the Commission to add new or modify these conditions[1531]. Conversely, where there is specific and reliable evidence that this is necessary to maintain the level of protection of health, safety and fundamental rights protected by the EU AI Act, the Commission must amend and delete any of these conditions[1532]. The EU AI Act further reiterates that any amendments to the conditions may not decrease the overall level of protection of health, safety and fundamental rights protected by the EU AI Act, must ensure consistency with other decisions the Commission is empowered to adopt amending the uses of high-risk AI systems, and must take account of market and technological developments[1533].

[1531] Article 6(6) EU AI Act.
[1532] Article 6(7) EU AI Act.
[1533] Articles 6(8), 7(1) EU AI Act.

14.2 Special Requirements for High-Risk AI Systems

The EU AI Act sets out the detailed requirements to high-risk systems. These requirements are due to start applying from 2 August 2026[1534]. However, on 19th November 2025, the Commission issued Digital Omnibus on AI Regulation Proposal seeking to delay the implementation of the rules for high-risk AI systems[1535]. At the time of writing[1536], these amendments to the EU AI Act have yet to become law and the statutory deadline of 2 August 2026 stands.

14.2.1 Risk management system

EU AI Act requires a risk management system to be established, implemented, documented and maintained in relation to high-risk AI systems[1537]. The EU AI Act defines a risk management system as "*a continuous iterative process planned and run throughout the entire lifecycle of a high-risk AI system, requiring regular systematic review*

[1534] Article 113 EU AI Act.
[1535] https://eur-lex.europa.eu/legal-content/EN/TXT/?uri=CELEX:52025PC0836
[1536] 28 February 2026.
[1537] Article 9(1) EU AI Act.

and updating"[1538]. The EU AI Act outlines the following steps of which a risk management system is made up[1539]:

- the identification and analysis of the known and the reasonably foreseeable risks that the high-risk AI system can pose to health, safety or fundamental rights when the high-risk AI system is used in accordance with its intended purpose[1540];
- the estimation and evaluation of the risks that may emerge when the high-risk AI system is used in accordance with its intended purpose, and under conditions of reasonably foreseeable misuse[1541];
- the evaluation of other risks possibly arising, based on the analysis of data gathered from the post-market monitoring system[1542]; and
- the adoption of appropriate and targeted risk management measures designed to address the identified reasonably foreseeable risks that the high-risk AI system can pose to health, safety or fundamental rights when the high-risk AI system is used in accordance with its intended purpose[1543]. These risk management measures must give due consideration to the effects and possible interaction resulting from the combined application of the requirements applicable to

---

[1538] Article 9(2) EU AI Act.
[1539] *Ibid.*
[1540] Article 9(2)(a) EU AI Act.
[1541] Article 9(2)(b) EU AI Act.
[1542] Articles 9(2)(c) and 72 EU AI Act.
[1543] Article 9(2)(d) EU AI Act.

risk management systems, with a view to minimising risks more effectively while achieving an appropriate balance in implementing the measures to fulfil those requirements[1544]. In addition, these risk management measures must be such that the relevant residual risk associated with each hazard, as well as the overall residual risk of the high-risk AI systems is judged to be acceptable[1545].

These risks are only those which may be reasonably mitigated or eliminated through the development or design of the high-risk AI system, or the provision of adequate technical information[1546].

In identifying the most appropriate risk management measures, the following must be ensured[1547]:

- elimination or reduction of risks identified and evaluated in as far as technically feasible through adequate design and development of the high-risk AI system[1548];
- where appropriate, implementation of adequate mitigation and control measures addressing risks that cannot be eliminated[1549];

[1544] Article 9(4) EU AI Act.

[1545] Article 9(5) EU AI Act.
[1546] Article 9(3) EU AI Act.
[1547] Article 9(5) EU AI Act.
[1548] Article 9(5)(a) EU AI Act.
[1549] Article 9(5)(b) EU AI Act.

- provision of information required pursuant to the requirements of transparency and provision of information to deployers and, where appropriate, training to deployers[1550].

With a view to eliminating or reducing risks related to the use of the high-risk AI system, due consideration must be given to the technical knowledge, experience, education, the training to be expected by the deployer, and the presumable context in which the system is intended to be used[1551].

14.2.2 Testing of High-Risk AI Systems

High-risk AI systems must be tested for the purpose of identifying the most appropriate and targeted risk management measures[1552].

Testing must ensure that high-risk AI systems perform consistently for their intended purpose and that they comply with the risk management system requirements[1553].

The testing procedures may include testing in real-world conditions[1554].

[1550] Article 9(5)(c) EU AI Act.

[1551] Article 9(5) EU AI Act.
[1552] Article 9(6) EU AI Act.
[1553] Article 9(6) EU AI Act.
[1554] Articles 9(7) and 60 EU AI Act.

The testing of high-risk AI systems must be performed, as appropriate, at any time throughout the development process, and, in any event, prior to their being placed on the market or put into service[1555]. Testing must be carried out against prior defined metrics and probabilistic thresholds that are appropriate to the intended purpose of the high-risk AI system[1556].

When implementing the risk management system and testing the high-risk AI systems, providers must give consideration to whether in view of its intended purpose the high-risk AI system is likely to have an adverse impact on persons under the age of 18 and, as appropriate, other vulnerable groups[1557].

For providers of high-risk AI systems that are subject to requirements regarding internal risk management processes under other relevant provisions of EU law, the risk management system and testing of the high-risk AI systems may be part of, or combined with, the risk management procedures established pursuant to that law[1558].

[1555] Article 9(8) EU AI Act.
[1556] *Ibid.*
[1557] Article 9(9) EU AI Act.
[1558] Article 9(10) EU AI Act.

14.2.3 Data Governance

High-risk AI systems which make use of techniques involving the training of AI models with data must be developed on the basis of training, validation and testing data sets that meet the following quality criteria whenever such data sets are used[1559]:

- Training, validation and testing data sets must follow data governance and management practices appropriate for the intended purpose of the high-risk AI system[1560]. These practices concern, in particular:
- the design choices[1561];
- data collection processes and the origin of data, and, in the case of personal data, the original purpose of the data collection[1562];
- data-preparation processing operations, such as annotation, labelling, cleaning, updating, enrichment and aggregation[1563];
- the formulation of assumptions, in particular with respect to the information that the data are supposed to measure and represent[1564];

[1559] Article 10(1) EU AI Act; for the development of high-risk AI systems not using techniques involving the training of AI models, these requirements apply only to the testing data sets (Article 10(6) EU AI Act).

[1560] Article 10(2) EU AI Act.

[1561] Article 10(2)(a) EU AI Act.

[1562] Article 10(2)(b) EU AI Act.

[1563] Article 10(2)(c) EU AI Act.

[1564] Article 10(2)(d) EU AI Act.

- an assessment of the availability, quantity and suitability of the data sets that are needed[1565];
- examination of possible biases that are likely to affect the health and safety of persons, have a negative impact on fundamental rights or lead to discrimination prohibited under EU law, especially where data outputs influence inputs for future operations[1566] and appropriate measures to detect, prevent and mitigate these possible biases[1567]. To the extent that it is strictly necessary for the purpose of ensuring bias detection and correction in relation to the high-risk AI systems, the EU AI Act permits providers of such systems to exceptionally process special categories of personal data, subject to appropriate safeguards for the fundamental rights and freedoms of natural persons[1568]. In addition to compliance with the data protection rules[1569], all the following conditions must be met in order for such processing to occur[1570]:

[1565] Article 10(2)(e) EU AI Act.

[1566] Article 10(2)(f) EU AI Act.

[1567] Article 10(2)(g) EU AI Act.

[1568] Article 10(5) EU AI Act.

[1569] The applicable data protection rules are set out in Regulations (EU) 2016/679 and (EU) 2018/1725 and Directive (EU) 2016/680.

[1570] Article 10(5) EU AI Act.

- the bias detection and correction cannot be effectively fulfilled by processing other data, including synthetic or anonymised data[1571];
- the special categories of personal data are subject to technical limitations on the re-use of the personal data, and state-of-the-art security and privacy-preserving measures, including pseudonymisation[1572];
- the special categories of personal data are subject to measures to ensure that the personal data processed are secured, protected, subject to suitable safeguards, including strict controls and documentation of the access, to avoid misuse and ensure that only authorised persons have access to those personal data with appropriate confidentiality obligations[1573];
- the special categories of personal data are not to be transmitted, transferred or otherwise accessed by other parties[1574];
- the special categories of personal data are deleted once the bias has been corrected or the personal data has reached the end of its retention period, whichever comes first[1575];
- the records of processing activities must include the reasons why the processing of special categories of

---

[1571] Article 10(5)(a) EU AI Act.
[1572] Article 10(5)(b) EU AI Act.
[1573] Article 10(5)(c) EU AI Act.
[1574] Article 10(5)(d) EU AI Act.
[1575] Article 10(5)(e) EU AI Act.

personal data was strictly necessary to detect and correct biases, and why that objective could not be achieved by processing other data[1576].

- the identification of relevant data gaps or shortcomings that prevent compliance with the EU AI Act requirements, and how those gaps and shortcomings can be addressed[1577].
- Training, validation and testing data sets must be relevant, sufficiently representative, and to the best extent possible, free of errors and complete in view of the intended purpose[1578]. They must also have the appropriate statistical properties, including, where applicable, as regards the persons or groups of persons in relation to whom the high-risk AI system is intended to be used[1579]. Those characteristics of the data sets may be met at the level of individual data sets or at the level of a combination thereof[1580].
- Data sets must take into account, to the extent required by the intended purpose, the characteristics or elements that are particular to the specific geographical, contextual, behavioural or functional setting within which the high-risk AI system is intended to be

---

[1576] Article 10(5)(f) EU AI Act; the records of processing activities are those that must be kept pursuant to Regulations (EU) 2016/679 and (EU) 2018/1725 and Directive (EU) 2016/680.

[1577] Article 10(2)(h) EU AI Act.

[1578] Article 10(3) EU AI Act.

[1579] *Ibid.*

[1580] *Ibid.*

used[1581]. High-risk AI systems trained and tested on data reflecting the specific geographical, behavioural, contextual, or functional setting within which they are intended to be used shall be presumed to comply with this requirement[1582].

14.2.4 Technical Documentation

The technical documentation of a high-risk AI system must:

- be drawn up before that system is placed on the market or put into service and must be kept up-to date[1583];
- be drawn up in such a way as to demonstrate that the high-risk AI system complies with the requirements of EU AI Act and to provide national competent authorities and notified bodies with the necessary information in a clear and comprehensive form to assess the compliance of the AI system with those requirements[1584];
- contain, at a minimum, the following elements[1585]:

[1581] Article 10(4) EU AI Act.
[1582] Article 42(1) EU AI Act.
[1583] Article 11(1) EU AI Act.

[1584] Article 11(1) EU AI Act.
[1585] Article 11(1) and Annex IV EU AI Act.

The Minimum Elements of the Technical Documentation

1. A general description of the AI system including:
(a) its intended purpose, the name of the provider and the version of the system reflecting its relation to previous versions;
(b) how the AI system interacts with, or can be used to interact with, hardware or software, including with other AI systems, that are not part of the AI system itself, where applicable;
(c) the versions of relevant software or firmware, and any requirements related to version updates;
(d) the description of all the forms in which the AI system is placed on the market or put into service, such as software packages embedded into hardware, downloads, or APIs;
(e) the description of the hardware on which the AI system is intended to run;
(f) where the AI system is a component of products, photographs or illustrations showing external features, the marking and internal layout of those products;
(g) a basic description of the user-interface provided to the deployer;
(h) instructions for use for the deployer, and a basic description of the user-interface provided to the deployer, where applicable;

2. A detailed description of the elements of the AI system and of the process for its development, including:
(a) the methods and steps performed for the development of the AI system, including, where relevant, recourse to pre-trained systems or tools provided by third parties and how those were used, integrated or modified by the provider;
(b) the design specifications of the system, namely the general logic of the AI system and of the algorithms; the key design choices including the rationale and assumptions made, including with regard to persons or groups of persons in respect of who, the system is intended to be used; the main classification choices; what the system is designed to optimise for, and the relevance of the different

The Minimum Elements of the Technical Documentation

parameters; the description of the expected output and output quality of the system; the decisions about any possible trade-off made regarding the technical solutions adopted to comply with the requirements for High-risk AI systems ;
(c) the description of the system architecture explaining how software components build on or feed into each other and integrate into the overall processing; the computational resources used to develop, train, test and validate the AI system;
(d) where relevant, the data requirements in terms of datasheets describing the training methodologies and techniques and the training data sets used, including a general description of these data sets, information about their provenance, scope and main characteristics; how the data was obtained and selected; labelling procedures (e.g. for supervised learning), data cleaning methodologies (e.g. outliers detection);
(e) assessment of the required human oversight measures, including an assessment of the technical measures needed to facilitate the interpretation of the outputs of AI systems by the deployers[1586];
(f) where applicable, a detailed description of pre-determined changes to the AI system and its performance, together with all the relevant information related to the technical solutions adopted to ensure continuous compliance of the AI system with the relevant requirements to High-risk AI systems[1587];
(g) the validation and testing procedures used, including information about the validation and testing data used and their main characteristics; metrics used to measure accuracy, robustness and compliance with other relevant requirements to High-risk AI

[1586] The human oversight requirements are discussed in CHAPTER and set out in Articles 13(3)(d) and 14 EU AI Act.

[1587] These are the requirements discussed in this Chapter and as set out in EU AI Act Chapter III, Section 2.

The Minimum Elements of the Technical Documentation

systems[1588], as well as potentially discriminatory impacts; test logs and all test reports dated and signed by the responsible persons, including with regard to pre-determined changes as referred to under point (f) above;
(h) cybersecurity measures put in place;

3. Detailed information about the monitoring, functioning and control of the AI system, in particular with regard to: its capabilities and limitations in performance, including the degrees of accuracy for specific persons or groups of persons on which the system is intended to be used and the overall expected level of accuracy in relation to its intended purpose; the foreseeable unintended outcomes and sources of risks to health and safety, fundamental rights and discrimination in view of the intended purpose of the AI system; the human oversight measures[1589], including the technical measures put in place to facilitate the interpretation of the outputs of AI systems by the deployers; specifications on input data, as appropriate;

4. A description of the appropriateness of the performance metrics for the specific AI system;

5. A detailed description of the risk management system[1590];

[1588] These are the requirements discussed in this Chapter and as set out in EU AI Act Chapter III, Section 2.

[1589] The relevant human oversight requirements are discussed in paragraph 13.2.7 of this Chapter and set out in Article 14 EU AI Act.

[1590] The detailed requirements to the description of the risk management system are set out in 13.2.1 of this Chapter and in Article 9 EU AI Act.

The Minimum Elements of the Technical Documentation
6. A description of relevant changes made by the provider to the system through its lifecycle;
7. A list of the harmonised standards applied in full or in part the references of which have been published in the Official Journal of the European Union; where no such harmonised standards have been applied, a detailed description of the solutions adopted to meet the requirements to High-risk AI systems[1591], including a list of other relevant standards and technical specifications applied;
8. A copy of the EU declaration of conformity[1592];
9. A detailed description of the system in place to evaluate the AI system performance in the post-market phase, including the post-market monitoring plan[1593].

The EU AI Act permits SMEs, including start-ups, to provide the elements of the technical documentation in a simplified manner[1594]. To that end, the Commission must establish a simplified technical documentation form targeted at the needs of small and microenterprises. Where an SME, including a start-up, opts to provide the elements of the technical documentation in a simplified manner, it

[1591] These are the requirements discussed in this Chapter and as set out in EU AI Act Chapter III, Section 2.

[1592] The requirements for the EU Declaration of Conformity are set out in 1.9 Chapter 1 of this book and Article 47 EU AI Act.

[1593] The post-market monitoring requirements are set out in 1.15 Chapter 1 of this book and Article 72 EU AI Act.

[1594] Article 11(1) EU AI Act.

must use the form approved by the Commission[1595]. Notified bodies must accept that form for the purposes of the conformity assessment[1596].

Where a high-risk AI system related to a product covered by the EU harmonisation legislation[1597] is placed on the market or put into service, a single set of technical documentation must be drawn up containing all the information set out above and the information required under those legal acts[1598].

Where the market surveillance authority of a Member State finds that technical documentation is not available[1599], it must require the relevant provider to put an end to the non-compliance, within a period it may prescribe. If the non-compliance persists, the market surveillance authority must take appropriate and proportionate measures to restrict or prohibit the high-risk AI system being made available on the market or to ensure that it is recalled or withdrawn from the market without delay[1600].

1595 *Ibid.*

1596 *Ibid.*

1597 The relevant EU harmonization legislation is listed in l Section A of Annex I EU AI Act.

1598 Article 11(2) EU AI Act.

1599 Article 83(1)(g) EU AI Act.

1600 Article 83(2) EU AI Act.

The Commission is empowered to adopt delegated acts[1601] to amend the Minimum Elements of Technical Documentation[1602], where necessary, to ensure that, in light of technical progress, the technical documentation provides all the information necessary to assess the compliance of the system with the requirements prescribed by the EU AI Act to technical documentation[1603].

14.2.5 Automatic Log Generation

High-risk AI systems must technically allow for the automatic recording of events (logs) over the lifetime of the system[1604].

In order to ensure a level of traceability of the functioning of a high-risk AI system that is appropriate to the intended purpose of the system, logging capabilities must enable the recording of events relevant for[1605]:

- identifying situations that may result in the high-risk AI system presenting a risk to health, safety, or fundamental rights, of persons[1606] or in a substantial modification[1607];

[1601] The powers of the Commission to adopt delegated acts are set out in Article 97 EU AI Act.

[1602] The Minimum Elements of Technical Documentation are set out above and in Annex IV EU AI Act.

[1603] Article 11(3) EU AI Act.

[1604] Article 12(1) EU AI Act.

[1605] Article 12(2) EU AI Act.

[1606] AI systems presenting a risk are discussed in 13.3 of this Chapter and in Article 79(1) EU AI Act.

[1607] Article 12(2)(a) EU AI Act.

- the facilitating of the post-market monitoring[1608]; and
- the monitoring of the operation of high-risk AI systems presenting a risk to the health, safety, or fundamental rights of persons[1609].

For high-risk AI systems that are remote biometric identification systems the use of which is permitted by the EU or national law[1610], the logging capabilities must provide, at a minimum:

- recording of the period of each use of the system (start date and time and end date and time of each use)[1611];
- the reference database against which input data has been checked by the system[1612];
- the input data for which the search has led to a match[1613]; and
- the identification of the natural persons involved in the verification of the results of biometric identification[1614].

[1608] Articles 12(2)(b) and 72 EU AI Act.
[1609] Articles 12(2)(c), 26(5) and 79(1) EU AI Act.
[1610] Article 12(3), Annex III point 1(a) EU AI Act.
[1611] Article 12(3)(a) EU AI Act.
[1612] Article 12(3)(b) EU AI Act.
[1613] Article 12(3)(c) EU AI Act.
[1614] Articles 12(3)(d) and 14(5) EU AI Act.

14.2.6 Transparency and Provision of Information to Deployers

The EU AI Act requires providers to design and develop high-risk AI systems in such a way as to ensure that their operation is sufficiently transparent to enable deployers to interpret a system's output and use it appropriately[1615]. The provider must ensure an appropriate type and degree of transparency with a view to achieving compliance with the obligations of the provider and deployer[1616] related to the enforcement of the EU AI Act[1617].

Further, high-risk AI systems must be accompanied by instructions for use in an appropriate digital format or otherwise that include concise, complete, correct and clear information that is relevant, accessible and comprehensible to deployers[1618]. **The instructions for use must contain at least the following information**[1619]:

- the identity and the contact details of the provider and, where applicable, of its authorised representative[1620];
- the characteristics, capabilities and limitations of performance of the high-risk AI system, including[1621]:

[1615] Article 13(1) EU AI Act.
[1616] *Ibid.*
[1617] Section 3 EU AI Act.
[1618] Article 13(2) EU AI Act.
[1619] Article 13(3) EU AI Act.
[1620] Article 13(3)(a) EU AI Act.
[1621] Article 13(3)(b) EU AI Act.

- its intended purpose[1622];
- the level of accuracy, including its metrics, robustness and cybersecurity[1623] against which the high-risk AI system has been tested and validated and which can be expected, and any known and foreseeable circumstances that may have an impact on that expected level of accuracy, robustness and cybersecurity[1624]. High-risk AI systems that have been certified or for which a statement of conformity has been issued under a cybersecurity scheme[1625] and the references of which have been published in the Official Journal of the European Union shall be presumed to comply with these cybersecurity requirements in so far as the cybersecurity certificate or statement of conformity or its parts cover those requirements[1626];
- any known or foreseeable circumstance related to the use of the high-risk AI system in accordance with its intended purpose or under conditions of reasonably foreseeable misuse, which may lead to risks to the health and safety or fundamental rights of persons[1627];

[1622] Article 13(3)(b)(i) EU AI Act.

[1623] Article 15 EU AI Act.

[1624] Article 13(3)(b)(ii) EU AI Act.

[1625] For the particulars of the cybersecurity scheme conformity see Regulation (EU) 2019/881.

[1626] Article 42(2) EU AI Act.

[1627] Articles 13(3)(b)(iii), 9(2) EU AI Act.

- where applicable, the technical capabilities and characteristics of the high-risk AI system to provide information that is relevant to explain its output[1628];
- when appropriate, its performance regarding specific persons or groups of persons on which the system is intended to be used[1629];
- when appropriate, specifications for the input data, or any other relevant information in terms of the training, validation and testing data sets used, taking into account the intended purpose of the high-risk AI system[1630];
- where applicable, information to enable deployers to interpret the output of the high-risk AI system and use it appropriately[1631];
- the changes to the high-risk AI system and its performance which have been pre-determined by the provider at the moment of the initial conformity assessment, if any[1632];
- the human oversight measures[1633], including the technical measures put in place to facilitate the interpretation of the outputs of the high-risk AI systems by the deployers[1634];

[1628] Article 13(3)(b)(iv) EU AI Act.
[1629] Article 13(3)(b)(v) EU AI Act.
[1630] Article 13(3)(b)(vi) EU AI Act.
[1631] Article 13(3)(b)(vii) EU AI Act.
[1632] Article 13(3)(c) EU AI Act.
[1633] Article 14 EU AI Act.
[1634] Article 13(3)(d) EU AI Act.

- the computational and hardware resources needed, the expected lifetime of the high-risk AI system and any necessary maintenance and care measures, including their frequency, to ensure the proper functioning of that AI system, including as regards software updates[1635];
- where relevant, a description of the mechanisms included within the high-risk AI system that allows deployers to properly collect, store and interpret the automatically generated logs[1636].

14.2.7 Human oversight

The EU AI Act requires high-risk AI systems to be designed and developed in such a way, including with appropriate human-machine interface tools, that they can be effectively overseen by natural persons during the period in which they are in use[1637].

The EU AI Act further prescribes the requirements to human oversight.

First, human oversight must aim to prevent or minimise the risks to health, safety or fundamental rights that may emerge when a high-risk AI system is used in accordance with its intended purpose or under conditions of reasonably foreseeable misuse, in particular where such

[1635] Article 13(3)(e) EU AI Act.
[1636] Articles 12 and 13(3)(f) EU AI Act.
[1637] Article 14(1) EU AI Act.

risks persist despite the application of other human oversight requirements prescribed by the EU AI Act[1638].

Second, the oversight measures must be commensurate with the risks, level of autonomy and context of use of the high-risk AI system, and must be ensured through either one or both of the following types of measures[1639]:

- measures identified and built, when technically feasible, into the high-risk AI system by the provider before it is placed on the market or put into service[1640]; and (or)
- measures identified by the provider before placing the high-risk AI system on the market or putting it into service and that are appropriate to be implemented by the deployer[1641].
- for the purpose of implementing these human oversight measures, the EU AI Act requires high-risk AI systems to be provided to the deployers in such a way that natural persons to whom human oversight is assigned are enabled, as appropriate and proportionate[1642]:
- to properly understand the relevant capacities and limitations of the high-risk AI system and be able to duly monitor its operation, including in view of

---

1638 Article 14(2) EU AI Act.
1639 Article 14(3) EU AI Act.
1640 Article 14(3)(a) EU AI Act.
1641 Article 14(3)(b) EU AI Act.
1642 Article 14(4) EU AI Act.

detecting and addressing anomalies, dysfunctions and unexpected performance[1643];

- to remain aware of the possible tendency of automatically relying or over-relying on the output produced by a high-risk AI system (automation bias), in particular for high-risk AI systems used to provide information or recommendations for decisions to be taken by natural persons[1644];
- to correctly interpret the high-risk AI system's output, taking into account, for example, the interpretation tools and methods available[1645];
- to decide, in any particular situation, not to use the high-risk AI system or to otherwise disregard, override or reverse the output of the high-risk AI system[1646];
- to intervene in the operation of the high-risk AI system or interrupt the system through a 'stop' button or a similar procedure that allows the system to come to a halt in a safe state[1647].

For high-risk AI systems that are remote biometric identification systems the use of which is permitted by the EU or national law, the human oversight measures must ensure that, in addition, no action or decision is taken by

---

[1643] Article 14(4)(a) EU AI Act.
[1644] Article 14(4)(b) EU AI Act.
[1645] Article 14(4)(c) EU AI Act.
[1646] Article 14(4)(d) EU AI Act.
[1647] Article 14(4)(e) EU AI Act.

the deployer on the basis of the identification resulting from the system unless that identification has been separately verified and confirmed by at least two natural persons with the necessary competence, training and authority[1648]. This requirement for a separate verification by at least two natural persons does not apply to high-risk AI systems used for the purposes of law enforcement, migration, border control or asylum, where EU law or national law considers the application of this requirement to be disproportionate[1649].

14.2.8 Accuracy, Robustness and Cybersecurity

The EU AI Act requires high-risk AI systems to be designed and developed in such a way that they achieve an appropriate level of accuracy, robustness, and cybersecurity, and that they perform consistently in those respects throughout their lifecycle[1650].

To address the technical aspects of how to measure the appropriate levels of accuracy and robustness and any other relevant performance metrics of high-risk AI systems, the EU AI Act requires the Commission, in cooperation with relevant stakeholders and organisations such as metrology and benchmarking authorities, to encourage, as

---

[1648] Articles 14(3) and 14(5), Annex 3 point 1(a) EU AI Act.
[1649] Article 14(5) EU AI Act.
[1650] Article 15(1) EU AI Act.

appropriate, the development of benchmarks and measurement methodologies[1651].

The EU AI Act further requires the levels of accuracy and the relevant accuracy metrics of high-risk AI systems to be declared in the accompanying instructions of use[1652].

Robustness-wise, the EU AI Act requires technical and organisational measures to be taken for high-risk AI systems to be as resilient as possible regarding errors, faults or inconsistencies that may occur within the system or the environment in which the system operates, in particular due to their interaction with natural persons or other systems[1653]. The EU AI Act further clarifies that the robustness of high-risk AI systems may be achieved through technical redundancy solutions, which may include backup or fail-safe plans[1654].

High-risk AI systems that continue to learn after being placed on the market or put into service must be developed in such a way as to eliminate or reduce as far as possible the risk of possibly biased outputs influencing input for future operations (feedback loops), and as to ensure that any such feedback loops are duly addressed with appropriate mitigation measures[1655].

[1651] Article 15(2) EU AI Act.
[1652] Article 15(3) EU AI Act.
[1653] Article 15(4) EU AI Act.
[1654] *Ibid.*
[1655] *Ibid.*

High-risk AI systems must be resilient against attempts by unauthorised third parties to alter their use, outputs or performance by exploiting system vulnerabilities[1656]. The technical solutions aiming to ensure the cybersecurity of high-risk AI systems must be appropriate to the relevant circumstances and the risks[1657].The technical solutions to address AI specific vulnerabilities must include, where appropriate, measures to prevent, detect, respond to, resolve and control for attacks trying to manipulate the training data set (data poisoning), or pre-trained components used in training (model poisoning), inputs designed to cause the AI model to make a mistake (adversarial examples or model evasion), confidentiality attacks or model flaws[1658].

14.2.9 Presumed Compliance of High-Risk AI Systems with EU AI Act

High-risk AI systems which conform to all or a part of the harmonised standards[1659] shall be presumed to conform to the requirements of the EU AI Act concerning risk management system, data and data governance,

---

[1656] Article 15(5) EU AI Act.

[1657] *Ibid.*

[1658] *Ibid.*

[1659] The harmonised standards are those the references to which are published in the Official Journal of the European Union in accordance with Regulation (EU) No 1025/2012.

technical documentation, record-keeping, transparency and provision of information to deployers, human oversight, accuracy, robustness and cybersecurity, to the extent that those standards cover those requirements or obligations[1660].

14.3 National Level Procedure for Dealing with AI Systems Presenting a risk

EU AI Act defines AI systems presenting a risk as a 'product presenting a risk', i.e.

"*a product having the potential to affect adversely health and safety of persons in general, health and safety in the workplace, protection of consumers, the environment, public security and other public interests, protected by the applicable Union harmonisation legislation, to a degree which goes beyond that considered reasonable and acceptable in relation to its intended purpose or under the normal or reasonably foreseeable conditions of use of the product concerned, including the duration of use and, where applicable, its putting into service, installation and maintenance requirements*"[1661],

in so far as they present risks to the health or safety, or to fundamental rights, of persons[1662].

[1660] Article 40(1) EU AI Act.
[1661] Article 3(19) Regulation (EU) 2019/1020.
[1662] Article 79(1) EU AI Act.

Where the market surveillance authority of a Member State has sufficient reasons to consider an AI system to present a risk, it must carry out an evaluation of the AI system concerned in respect of its compliance with all the requirements and obligations laid down in the EU AI Act[1663]. Particular attention must be given to AI systems presenting a risk to vulnerable groups[1664]. Where risks to fundamental rights are identified, the market surveillance authority must also inform and fully cooperate with the relevant national public authorities or bodies[1665]. The relevant operators must cooperate as necessary with the market surveillance authority and with the other national public authorities or bodies[1666].

Where, in the course of that evaluation, the market surveillance authority or, where applicable, the market surveillance authority in cooperation with the national public authority, finds that the AI system does not comply with the requirements and obligations laid down in the EU AI Act, it must without undue delay require the relevant operator to take all appropriate corrective actions to bring the AI system into compliance, to withdraw the AI system from the market, or to recall it within a period the market surveillance authority may prescribe, and in any event within the shorter of 15 working days, or as provided for in

---

[1663] Article 79(2) EU AI Act.
[1664] *Ibid.*
[1665] *Ibid.*
[1666] Article 79(2) EU AI Act.

the relevant EU harmonisation legislation[1667]. The market surveillance authority must inform the relevant notified body accordingly[1668].

Procedural Rights of Economic Operators

Economic operators have the following rights in respect of the measures taken by a market surveillance authority[1669]:

- Any measure, decision or order taken or made by market surveillance authorities pursuant to EU harmonisation legislation or EU Market Surveillance Regulation 2019/1020 must state the exact grounds on which it is based.
- Any such measure, decision or order must be communicated without delay to the relevant economic operator, who at the same time must be informed of the remedies available to it under the law of the Member State concerned and of the time limits to which those remedies are subject.
- Before the measure, decision or order is taken or made, the economic operator concerned must be given the opportunity to be heard within an appropriate period of not less than 10 working days, unless it is not possible to give that opportunity because of the urgency of the

---

[1667] *Ibid.*
[1668] *Ibid.*
[1669] *Ibid;* Article 18 of Regulation (EU) 2019/1020.

> measure, decision or order, based on health or safety requirements or other grounds relating to the public interests covered by the relevant EU harmonisation legislation. If the measure, decision or order is taken or made without the economic operator being given the opportunity to be heard, the economic operator shall be given that opportunity as soon as possible thereafter and that measure, decision or order shall be reviewed promptly by the market surveillance authority.

'Economic operator' means the manufacturer, the authorised representative, the importer, the distributor, the fulfilment service provider or any other natural or legal person who is subject to obligations in relation to the manufacture of products, making them available on the market or putting them into service in accordance with the relevant EU harmonisation legislation[1670].

Where the market surveillance authority considers that the non-compliance is not restricted to its national territory, it must inform the Commission and the other Member States without undue delay of the results of the evaluation and of the actions which it has required the operator to take[1671].

The operator must ensure that all appropriate corrective action is taken in respect of all the AI systems concerned that it has made available on the EU market[1672].

[1670] Article 3(13) of Regulation (EU) 2019/1020.
[1671] Article 79(3) EU AI Act.
[1672] Article 79(4) EU AI Act.

Where the operator of an AI system does not take adequate corrective action within the prescribed period, the market surveillance authority must take all appropriate provisional measures to prohibit or restrict the AI system's being made available on its national market or put into service, to withdraw the product or the standalone AI system from that market or to recall it[1673]. That authority must without undue delay notify the Commission and the other Member States of those measures[1674], specifying in the notification all available details, in particular the information necessary for the identification of the non-compliant AI system, the origin of the AI system and the supply chain, the nature of the non-compliance alleged and the risk involved, the nature and duration of the national measures taken and the arguments put forward by the relevant operator[1675]. In particular, the market surveillance authorities must indicate whether the non-compliance is due to one or more of the following:

- non-compliance with the prohibition of the AI practices[1676];
- a failure of a high-risk AI system to meet requirements to high-risk AI systems[1677];

[1673] Article 79(5) EU AI Act.
[1674] *Ibid.*
[1675] Article 79(6) EU AI Act.
[1676] Article 79(6)(a) EU AI Act.
[1677] Article 79(6)(b) EU AI Act.

- shortcomings in the harmonised standards or common specifications conferring a presumption of conformity[1678]; and (or)
- non-compliance with the EU AI Act's transparency obligations[1679].

The market surveillance authorities other than the market surveillance authority of the Member State initiating the procedure must, without undue delay, inform the Commission and the other Member States of any measures adopted and of any additional information at their disposal relating to the non-compliance of the AI system concerned, and, in the event of disagreement with the notified national measure, of their objections[1680].

Where, within three months of receipt of the notification, no objection has been raised by either a market surveillance authority of a Member State or by the Commission in respect of a provisional measure taken by a market surveillance authority of another Member State, that measure shall be deemed justified[1681]. This shall be without prejudice to the procedural rights of the concerned operator[1682]. The three-month period referred to in this

[1678] Article 79(6)(c) EU AI Act.

[1679] Article 79(6)(d) EU AI Act.

[1680] Article 79(7) EU AI Act.

[1681] Article 79(8) EU AI Act.

[1682] *Ibid;* the procedural rights are set out in Article 18 of Regulation (EU) 2019/1020 and are listed above.

paragraph shall be reduced to 30 days in the event of non-compliance with the prohibition of the AI practices[1683].

The market surveillance authorities must ensure that appropriate restrictive measures are taken in respect of the product or the AI system concerned, such as withdrawal of the product or the AI system from their market, without undue delay[1684].

14.4 Procedure for Dealing with AI Systems Classified by the Provider as Non-High-Risk

Where a market surveillance authority has sufficient reason to consider that an AI system classified by the provider as non-high-risk is indeed high-risk, the market surveillance authority must carry out an evaluation of the AI system concerned in respect of its classification as a high-risk AI system based on the EU AI Act conditions[1685] and the Commission guidelines[1686].

Where, in the course of that evaluation, the market surveillance authority finds that the AI system concerned is high-risk, it must without undue delay require the relevant provider to take all necessary actions to bring the AI system into compliance with the requirements and obligations laid down in the EU AI Act and take appropriate corrective

---

[1683] Article 79(8) EU AI Act.
[1684] Article 79(9) EU AI Act.
[1685] These conditions are set out in Article 6(3) EU AI Act.
[1686] Article 80(1) EU AI Act.

action within a period the market surveillance authority may prescribe[1687].

Where the market surveillance authority considers that the use of the AI system concerned is not restricted to its national territory, it must inform the Commission and the other Member States without undue delay of the results of the evaluation and of the actions which it has required the provider to take[1688].

The provider must ensure that all necessary action is taken to bring the AI system into compliance with the requirements and obligations laid down in the EU AI Act[1689]. Where the provider of an AI system concerned does not bring the AI system into compliance with those requirements and obligations within the period prescribed by the market surveillance authority, the provider shall be liable to fines prescribed by the EU AI Act[1690].

The provider must ensure that all appropriate corrective action is taken in respect of all the AI systems concerned that it has made available on the EU market[1691].

Where the provider of the AI system concerned does not take adequate corrective action within the period prescribed by the market surveillance authority[1692], the market surveillance authority must without undue delay

---

[1687] Article 80(2) EU AI Act.
[1688] Article 80(3) EU AI Act.
[1689] Article 80(4) EU AI Act.
[1690] *Ibid.*
[1691] Article 80(5) EU AI Act.
[1692] Article 80(6) EU AI Act.

notify the Commission and the other Member States[1693], specifying in the notification all available details, in particular the information necessary for the identification of the non-compliant AI system, the origin of the AI system and the supply chain, the nature of the non-compliance alleged and the risk involved, the nature and duration of the national measures taken and the arguments put forward by the relevant operator[1694]. In particular, the market surveillance authorities must indicate whether the non-compliance is due to one or more of the following:

- non-compliance with the prohibition of the AI practices[1695];
- a failure of a high-risk AI system to meet requirements to high-risk AI systems[1696];
- shortcomings in the harmonised standards or common specifications conferring a presumption of conformity[1697]; and (or)
- non-compliance with the EU AI Act's transparency obligations[1698].

The market surveillance authorities other than the market surveillance authority of the Member State initiating the procedure must, without undue delay, inform

---

1693 Article 79(5) EU AI Act.
1694 Article 79(6) EU AI Act.
1695 Article 79(6)(a) EU AI Act.
1696 Article 79(6)(b) EU AI Act.
1697 Article 79(6)(c) EU AI Act.
1698 Article 79(6)(d) EU AI Act.

the Commission and the other Member States of any measures adopted and of any additional information at their disposal relating to the non-compliance of the AI system concerned, and, in the event of disagreement with the notified national measure, of their objections[1699].

Where, within three months of receipt of the notification, no objection has been raised by either a market surveillance authority of a Member State or by the Commission in respect of a provisional measure taken by a market surveillance authority of another Member State, that measure shall be deemed justified[1700]. This shall be without prejudice to the procedural rights of the concerned operator[1701]. The three-month period shall be reduced to 30 days in the event of non-compliance with the prohibition of the AI practices[1702].

The market surveillance authorities must ensure that appropriate restrictive measures are taken in respect of the product or the AI system concerned, such as withdrawal of the product or the AI system from their market, without undue delay[1703].

Where, in the course of the evaluation, the market surveillance authority establishes that the AI system was misclassified by the provider as non-high-risk in order to

---

[1699] Article 79(7) EU AI Act.

[1700] Article 79(8) EU AI Act.

[1701] *Ibid*; the procedural rights are those listed in 13.3 of this Chapter and in Article 18 of Regulation (EU) 2019/1020.

[1702] Article 79(8) EU AI Act.

[1703] Article 79(9) EU AI Act.

circumvent the application of the EU AI Act requirements to high-risk AI systems, the provider shall be liable to fines set out in the EU AI Act[1704].

In exercising their power[1705] to monitor the application of this procedure, and in accordance with, market surveillance authorities may perform appropriate checks, taking into account in particular information stored in the EU database[1706].

14.5 EU Safeguard Procedure in Respect of Non-Compliant AI Systems

Where, within three months of receipt of the notification of a non-compliant AI system from a market surveillance authority, or within 30 days if the notification concerns an AI system non-compliant with the AI practices prohibited by the EU AI Act, the market surveillance authority of a Member State raises objections to a measure taken by another market surveillance authority, or where the Commission considers the measure to be contrary to EU law, the Commission must without undue delay enter into consultation with the market surveillance authority of the relevant Member State and the operator(s) and evaluate

---

[1704] Article 80(7) EU AI Act.

[1705] The EU AI Act refers to the powers of market surveillance authorities conferred by Article 11 of Regulation (EU) 2019/1020.

[1706] Article 80(8) EU AI Act, the EU database is referred to in Article 71 of the EU AI Act.

the national measure[1707]. On the basis of the results of that evaluation, the Commission must:

- within six months, or
- in the case of non-compliance with an EU AI Act prohibition - within 60 days

starting from the notification, decide whether the national measure is justified and notify its decision to the market surveillance authority of the Member State concerned[1708]. The Commission must also inform all other market surveillance authorities of its decision[1709].

Where the Commission considers the measure taken by the relevant Member State to be justified, all Member States must ensure that they take appropriate restrictive measures in respect of the AI system concerned, such as requiring the withdrawal of the AI system from their market without undue delay, and inform the Commission accordingly[1710]. Where the Commission considers the national measure to be unjustified, the Member State concerned must withdraw the measure and inform the Commission accordingly[1711].

Where the national measure is considered justified and the non-compliance of the AI system is attributed to shortcomings in the harmonised standards or common

---

[1707] Article 81(1) EU AI Act.
[1708] *Ibid.*
[1709] *Ibid.*
[1710] Article 81(2) EU AI Act.
[1711] *Ibid.*

specifications[1712], the Commission must apply the procedure for formal objections to harmonised standards[1713].

14.6 Compliant AI systems which present a risk

Where, having performed an evaluation, after consulting the relevant national public authority, the market surveillance authority of a Member State finds that a high-risk AI system complies with the EU AI Act, but it nevertheless presents a risk to the health or safety of persons, to fundamental rights, or to other aspects of public interest protection, it must require the relevant operator to take all appropriate measures to ensure that the AI system concerned, when placed on the market or put into service, no longer presents that risk without undue delay, within a period it may prescribe[1714].

The provider or other relevant operator must ensure that corrective action is taken in respect of all the AI systems concerned that it has made available on the EU market within the timeline prescribed by the market surveillance authority of the Member State[1715].

[1712] The harmonized standards and common specifications are those referred to in Articles 40 and 41 of the EU AI Act.

[1713] Article 81(3) EU AI Act; the procedure for objections to harmonized standards is set out in Article 11 of Regulation (EU) No 1025/2012.

[1714] Article 82(1) EU AI Act.

[1715] Article 82(2) EU AI Act.

In addition, the Member States must immediately inform the Commission and the other Member States of the finding, specifying all available details, in particular the data necessary for the identification of the AI system concerned, the origin and the supply chain of the AI system, the nature of the risk involved and the nature and duration of the national measures taken[1716].

The Commission must without undue delay enter into consultation with the Member States concerned and the relevant operators, and evaluate the national measures taken[1717]. On the basis of the results of that evaluation, the Commission must decide whether the measure is justified and, where necessary, propose other appropriate measures[1718].

The Commission must immediately communicate its decision to the Member States concerned and to the relevant operators. It must also inform the other Member States[1719].

[1716] Article 82(3) EU AI Act.
[1717] Article 82(4) EU AI Act.
[1718] *Ibid.*
[1719] Article 82(5) EU AI Act.

PART 4. AI MARKET PLAYERS

CHAPTER 15. The Persons to Whom the EU AI Act Applies

The EU AI Act applies to a wide range of persons involved in development, marketing, deployment, importation, distribution and use of AI systems, both in and outside the EU.

The table below summarises the application of the EU AI Act to persons in and outside the EU.

Description of the person to whom the EU AI Act applies	**Location of the Person**	
	EU	**Non-EU**
Providers placing on the market or putting into service AI systems or placing on the market general-purpose AI models in the EU[1720]	Yes	Yes
Deployers of AI systems[1721]	Yes	No
Providers and deployers of AI systems that have their place of establishment or are located in	Not applicable	Yes

[1720] Article 2(1) (a) EU AI Act..

[1721] Article 2(1) (b) EU AI Act..

Description of the person to whom the EU AI Act applies	**Location of the Person**	
	EU	**Non-EU**
a third country if the output produced by the AI system is used in the EU[1722]		
Importers and distributors of AI systems[1723]	Yes	No[1724]
Product manufacturers placing on the market or putting into service an AI system together with their product and under their own name or trademark[1725];	Yes	No[1726]
Authorised representatives of providers, which are not established in the EU[1727];	Not applicable	Yes

1722 Article 2(1) (c) EU AI Act.
1723 Article 2(1) (d) EU AI Act.
1724 Article 2(3) EU AI Act.
1725 Article 2(1) (e) EU AI Act.
1726 Article 2(3) EU AI Act.
1727 Article 2(1)(f) EU AI Act.

Description of the person to whom the EU AI Act applies	**Location of the Person**	
	EU	**Non-EU**
Affected persons located in the EU[1728]	Yes	Not applicable

[1728] Article 2(1)(g) EU AI Act.

CHAPTER 16. Exempt Persons

The EU AI Act does not apply to:

- any entities entrusted by the Member States with carrying out tasks in relation to the competences of the Member States concerning national security[1729];
- public authorities outside the EU and international organisations, where those authorities or organisations use AI systems in the framework of international cooperation or agreements for law enforcement and judicial cooperation with the EU or one or more Member States, provided that such a third country or international organisation provides adequate safeguards with respect to the protection of fundamental rights and freedoms of individuals:[1730] and
- natural persons using AI systems in the course of a purely personal non-professional activity.[1731]

[1729] Article 2(3) EU AI Act.
[1730] Article 2(4) EU AI Act.
[1731] Article 2(10) EU AI Act.

CHAPTER 17. AI System Providers

The EU AI Act imposes a number of obligations on natural and legal persons, public authorities, agencies, and other bodies that develop AI systems or have them developed and place them on the market or put into service under their own names or trademarks, whether for payment or free of charge[1732]. These persons are providers[1733] of AI systems. Some obligations are imposed only on the providers of high-risk AI systems. Other obligations apply to all AI system providers. So, what are the providers required to do?

17.1 Obligations of All AI Systems Providers

The EU AI Act imposes a number of obligations on all providers of AI systems, regardless of the level of risk posed by the AI system.

17.1.1 AI Literacy

By 2 February 2025[1734], all providers must take measures to ensure, to their best extent, a sufficient level of AI literacy of their staff and other persons dealing with the operation and use of AI systems on their behalf, taking into account their technical knowledge, experience, education and

[1732] Article 3 (3) EU AI Act.
[1733] Article 3 (3) EU AI Act.
[1734] Article 113 (a) EU AI Act.

training and the context the AI systems are to be used in, and considering the persons or groups of persons on whom the AI systems are to be used[1735].

17.2 Obligations of High-Risk AI System Providers

17.2.1. Compliance with High-risk AI systems requirements

The EU AI Act requires providers of high-risk AI systems to ensure that their high-risk AI systems are compliant with the requirements prescribed by the EU AI Act for high-risk AI systems[1736].

17.2.2 Provider's Name

The EU AI Act requires providers of high-risk AI systems to indicate on the high-risk AI system or, where that is not possible, on its packaging or its accompanying documentation, as applicable, their name, registered trade name or registered trade mark, and the address at which they can be contacted[1737].

[1735] Article 4 EU AI Act.

[1736] Article 16(a) EU AI Act. The requirements are set out in Section 2 EU AI Act and discussed in Chapter 13 of this book.

[1737] Article 16(b) EU AI Act.

17.2.3 Quality Management System

The EU AI Act requires providers of high-risk AI systems to have a compliant quality management system in place[1738].

The quality management system must be documented in a systematic and orderly manner in the form of written policies, procedures and instructions, and must include at least the following[1739]:

What a Quality Management System Must Contain?

- a strategy for regulatory compliance, including compliance with conformity assessment procedures and procedures for the management of modifications to the high-risk AI system[1740];
- techniques, procedures and systematic actions to be used for the design, design control and design verification of the high-risk AI system[1741];

[1738] Article 16(c) EU AI Act.
[1739] Article 17(1) EU AI Act.
[1740] Article 17(1)(a) EU AI Act.
[1741] Article 17(1)(b) EU AI Act.

What a Quality Management System Must Contain?

- techniques, procedures and systematic actions to be used for the development, quality control and quality assurance of the high-risk AI system[1742];
- examination, test and validation procedures to be carried out before, during and after the development of the high-risk AI system, and the frequency with which they have to be carried out[1743];
- technical specifications, including standards, to be applied; where the harmonised standards are not applied in full or do not cover all of the requirements prescribed by the EU AI Act to high-risk AI systems - the means to be used to ensure that the high-risk AI system complies with those requirements[1744];
- systems and procedures for data management, including data acquisition, data collection, data analysis, data labelling, data storage, data filtration, data mining, data aggregation, data retention and any other operation regarding the data that is performed before and for the purpose of the placing on the

[1742] Article 17(1)(c) EU AI Act.

[1743] Article 17(1)(d) EU AI Act.

[1744] Article 17(1)(e) EU AI Act. The requirements to high-risk AI systems are set out in Section 2 EU AI Act and discussed in Chapter 13 of this book.

What a Quality Management System Must Contain?

market or the putting into service of high-risk AI systems[1745];

- the risk management system[1746];
- the setting-up, implementation and maintenance of a post-market monitoring system[1747];
- the procedures for the reporting of serious incidents[1748];
- the handling of communication with national competent authorities, other relevant authorities, including those providing or supporting the access to data, notified bodies, other operators, customers or other interested parties[1749];
- systems and procedures for record-keeping of all relevant documentation and information[1750];

[1745] Article 17(1)(f) EU AI Act.
[1746] Articles 9 and 17(1)(g) EU AI Act.
[1747] Articles 17(1)(h) and 72 EU AI Act.
[1748] Articles 17(1)(i) and 73 EU AI Act.
[1749] Article 17(1)(j) EU AI Act.
[1750] Article 17(1)(k) EU AI Act.

What a Quality Management System Must Contain?

- resource management, including security-of-supply related measures[1751];
- an accountability framework setting out the responsibilities of the management and other staff with regard to all the aspects of the quality management system[1752].

The quality management system must be proportionate to the size of the provider's organisation[1753]. In particular, **microenterprises**, i.e. enterprises which employ fewer than 10 persons and whose annual turnover and/or annual balance sheet total does not exceed EUR 2 million[1754], may comply with certain elements of the quality management system in a **simplified manner**[1755], provided that they do not have partner enterprises or linked enterprises[1756]. Partner enterprises are all enterprises which are not classified as linked enterprises and between which there is the following relationship: an enterprise (upstream

[1751] Article 17(1)(l) EU AI Act.

[1752] Article 17(1)(m) EU AI Act.

[1753] Article 17(2) EU AI Act.

[1754] Recommendation 2003/361/EC.

[1755] The particulars of what the simplified manner involves are expected to be detailed in the Commission Guidelines yet to be published. See 1.13 in Chapter 1 of this book.

[1756] Article 63(1) EU AI Act.

enterprise) holds, either solely or jointly with one or more linked enterprises, 25 % or more of the capital or voting rights of another enterprise (downstream enterprise)[1757]. Linked enterprises are enterprises which have any of the following relationships with each other:

- an enterprise has a majority of the shareholders' or members' voting rights in another enterprise;
- an enterprise has the right to appoint or remove a majority of the members of the administrative, management or supervisory body of another enterprise;
- an enterprise has the right to exercise a dominant influence over another enterprise pursuant to a contract entered into with that enterprise or to a provision in its memorandum or articles of association;
- an enterprise, which is a shareholder in or member of another enterprise, controls alone, pursuant to an agreement with other shareholders in or members of that enterprise, a majority of shareholders' or members' voting rights in that enterprise[1758].

There is a presumption that no dominant influence exists if the following investors are not involving themselves directly or indirectly in the management of the enterprise in question, without prejudice to their rights as stakeholders[1759]:

[1757] Recommendation 2003/361/EC.
[1758] *Ibid.*
[1759] *Ibid.*

- public investment corporations, venture capital companies, individuals or groups of individuals with a regular venture capital investment activity who invest equity capital in unquoted businesses ("business angels"), provided the total investment of those business angels in the same enterprise is less than EUR 1,250,000;
- universities or non-profit research centres;
- institutional investors, including regional development funds;
- autonomous local authorities with an annual budget of less than EUR 10 million and fewer than 5000 inhabitants.

Enterprises having any of the above relationships through one or more other enterprises, or any one of the above investors, are also considered to be linked[1760].

Enterprises which have one or other of such relationships through a natural person or group of natural persons acting jointly are also considered linked enterprises if they engage in their activity or in part of their activity in the same relevant market or in adjacent markets[1761]. An "adjacent market" is the market for a product or service situated directly upstream or downstream of the relevant market[1762].

[1760] *Ibid.*
[1761] *Ibid.*
[1762] *Ibid.*

But in any event, providers must respect the degree of rigour and the level of protection required to ensure the compliance of their high-risk AI systems with the EU AI Act[1763].

Providers of high-risk AI systems that are subject to obligations regarding quality management systems or an equivalent function under relevant sectoral EU law may include the above aspects of the quality management system as part of the quality management systems pursuant to that law[1764].

Providers that are financial institutions subject to requirements regarding their internal governance, arrangements or processes under EU financial services law, shall be deemed to have complied with the obligation to put in place a quality management system (with the exception of risk management, post-market monitoring and serious incident reporting systems), by complying with the rules on internal governance arrangements or processes pursuant to the EU financial services law[1765]. To that end, any harmonised standards must be taken into account[1766].

[1763] Article 17(2) EU AI Act.

[1764] Article 17(3) EU AI Act.

[1765] Articles 17(4), 17(1)(g), (h) and (i) EU AI Act.

[1766] Article 17(4) EU AI Act; for the harmonised standards see Article 40 EU AI Act.

17.2.4 Record Keeping

The EU AI Act requires providers of high-risk AI systems to keep for a period ending 10 years after the high-risk AI system has been placed on the market or put into service, and make available to the national competent authorities[1767]:

- the technical documentation[1768];
- the documentation concerning the quality management system[1769];
- the documentation concerning the changes approved by notified bodies, where applicable[1770];
- the decisions and other documents issued by the notified bodies, where applicable[1771]; and
- the EU declaration of conformity[1772].

But what happens if a provider of a high-risk AI system or its authorised representative goes bankrupt or ceases its activity prior to the end of the prescribed period of ten years? For such cases the EU AI Act empowers each Member State to determine the conditions under which the

---

[1767] Articles 16(d) and 18 EU AI Act.
[1768] Articles 18(1)(a) and 11 EU AI Act.
[1769] Articles 18(1)(b) and 17 EU AI Act.
[1770] Article 18(1)(c) EU AI Act.
[1771] Article 18(1)(d) EU AI Act.
[1772] Articles 18(1)(e) and 47 EU AI Act.

above documentation must remain at the disposal of the national competent authorities for that period[1773].

Providers that are financial institutions subject to requirements regarding their internal governance, arrangements or processes under the EU financial services law must maintain the technical documentation as part of the documentation kept under the EU financial services law[1774].

17.2.5 Automatically generated logs

The EU AI Act requires providers of high-risk AI systems to keep the logs automatically generated by their high-risk AI systems, to the extent such logs are under their control[1775]. The logs must be kept for a period appropriate to the intended purpose of the high-risk AI system, of at least six months, unless EU law (in particular, EU law on the protection of personal data) or national law provides otherwise[1776].

Providers that are financial institutions subject to requirements regarding their internal governance, arrangements or processes under EU financial services law must maintain the logs automatically generated by their

---

1773 Article 18(2) EU AI Act.
1774 Article 18(3) EU AI Act.
1775 Articles 16(e), 19(1), 12(1) EU AI Act.
1776 Article 19(1) EU AI Act.

high-risk AI systems as part of the documentation kept under the financial services law[1777].

17.2.6 Conformity Assessment

The EU AI Act requires providers to ensure that the high-risk AI system undergoes the relevant conformity assessment procedure prior to its being placed on the market or put into service[1778]. The conformity assessment procedure depends on the type of the high-risk AI system[1779]:

High-risk AI System: Biometrics, in so far as their use is permitted under relevant EU or national law: (a) remote biometric identification systems (other than AI systems intended to be used for biometric verification the sole purpose of which is to confirm that a specific natural person is the person he or she claims to be); (b) AI systems intended to be used for biometric categorisation, according to sensitive or protected attributes or characteristics based on the inference of those attributes or characteristics;

[1777] Article 19(2) EU AI Act.
[1778] Articles 16(f) and 43 EU AI Act.
[1779] Article 43(1) EU AI Act.

(c) AI systems intended to be used for emotion recognition[1780].	
Conditions	**Conformity Assessment Procedure**
The provider has applied harmonised standards[1781] or, where applicable, common specifications[1782].	The internal control[1783] OR The assessment of the quality management system and technical documentation, with the involvement of a notified body[1784].
Harmonised standards do not exist, and common specifications are not available The provider has not applied, or has applied	The assessment of the quality management system and technical documentation, with the involvement of a notified body[1785].

[1780] Para 1 Annex III EU AI Act.

[1781] The harmonized standards are those referred to in Article 40 EU AI Act.

[1782] The common specifications are referred to in Article 41 EU AI Act.

[1783] The internal control procedure is set out in Annex VI EU AI Act.

[1784] This assessment procedure is detailed in Annex VII EU AI Act.

[1785] This assessment procedure is detailed in Annex VII EU AI Act.

only part of, the harmonised standard; The common specifications exist, but the provider has not applied them; One or more of the harmonised standards has been published with a restriction, and only on the part of the standard that was restricted.	

For the conformity assessment procedure that involves assessment of the quality management system and technical documentation, the provider may choose any of the notified bodies[1786]. However, where the high-risk AI system is intended to be put into service by law enforcement, immigration or asylum authorities or by EU institutions, bodies, offices or agencies, the market surveillance authority shall act as a notified body[1787].

1786 Article 43(1) EU AI Act.
1787 *Ibid.*

High-risk AI Systems:

Critical infrastructure:
AI systems intended to be used as safety components in the management and operation of critical digital infrastructure, road traffic, or in the supply of water, gas, heating or electricity.

Education and vocational training:
(a) AI systems intended to be used to determine access or admission or to assign natural persons to educational and vocational training institutions at all levels;
(b) AI systems intended to be used to evaluate learning outcomes, including when those outcomes are used to steer the learning process of natural persons in educational and vocational training institutions at all levels;
(c) AI systems intended to be used for the purpose of assessing the appropriate level of education that an individual will receive or will be able to access, in the context of or within educational and vocational training institutions at all levels;
(d) AI systems intended to be used for monitoring and detecting prohibited behaviour of students during tests in the context of or within educational and vocational training institutions at all levels.

Employment, workers' management and access to self-employment:

(a) AI systems intended to be used for the recruitment or selection of natural persons, in particular to place targeted job advertisements, to analyse and filter job applications, and to evaluate candidates;

(b) AI systems intended to be used to make decisions affecting terms of work-related relationships, the promotion or termination of work-related contractual relationships, to allocate tasks based on individual behaviour or personal traits or characteristics or to monitor and evaluate the performance and behaviour of persons in such relationships.

Access to and enjoyment of essential private services and essential public services and benefits:

(a) AI systems intended to be used by public authorities or on behalf of public authorities to evaluate the eligibility of natural persons for essential public assistance benefits and services, including healthcare services, as well as to grant, reduce, revoke, or reclaim such benefits and services;

(b) AI systems intended to be used to evaluate the creditworthiness of natural persons or establish their credit score, with the exception of AI systems used for the purpose of detecting financial fraud;

(c) AI systems intended to be used for risk assessment and pricing in relation to natural persons in the case of life and health insurance;
(d) AI systems intended to evaluate and classify emergency calls by natural persons or to be used to dispatch, or to establish priority in the dispatching of, emergency first response services, including by police, firefighters and medical aid, as well as of emergency healthcare patient triage systems.

Law enforcement, in so far as their use is permitted under relevant Union or national law:
(a) AI systems intended to be used by or on behalf of law enforcement authorities, or by EU institutions, bodies, offices or agencies in support of law enforcement authorities or on their behalf to assess the risk of a natural person becoming the victim of criminal offences;
(b) AI systems intended to be used by or on behalf of law enforcement authorities or by EU institutions, bodies, offices or agencies in support of law enforcement authorities as polygraphs or similar tools;
(c) AI systems intended to be used by or on behalf of law enforcement authorities, or by EU institutions, bodies, offices or agencies, in support of law enforcement authorities to evaluate the reliability of evidence in the course of the investigation or prosecution of criminal offences;

(d) AI systems intended to be used by law enforcement authorities or on their behalf or by EU institutions, bodies, offices or agencies in support of law enforcement authorities for assessing the risk of a natural person offending or re-offending not solely on the basis of the profiling of natural persons, or to assess personality traits and characteristics or past criminal behaviour of natural persons or groups;

(e) AI systems intended to be used by or on behalf of law enforcement authorities or by EU institutions, bodies, offices or agencies in support of law enforcement authorities for the profiling of natural persons in the course of the detection, investigation or prosecution of criminal offences.

Migration, asylum and border control management, in so far as their use is permitted under relevant EU or national law:

(a) AI systems intended to be used by or on behalf of competent public authorities or by EU institutions, bodies, offices or agencies as polygraphs or similar tools;

(b) AI systems intended to be used by or on behalf of competent public authorities or by EU institutions, bodies, offices or agencies to assess a risk, including a security risk, a risk of irregular migration, or a health risk, posed by a natural person who intends to enter or who has entered into the territory of a Member State;

(c) AI systems intended to be used by or on behalf of competent public authorities or by Union institutions, bodies, offices or agencies to assist competent public authorities for the examination of applications for asylum, visa or residence permits and for associated complaints with regard to the eligibility of the natural persons applying for a status, including related assessments of the reliability of evidence;

(d) AI systems intended to be used by or on behalf of competent public authorities, or by Union institutions, bodies, offices or agencies, in the context of migration, asylum or border control management, for the purpose of detecting, recognising or identifying natural persons, with the exception of the verification of travel documents.

Administration of justice and democratic processes:

(a) AI systems intended to be used by a judicial authority or on their behalf to assist a judicial authority in researching and interpreting facts and the law and in applying the law to a concrete set of facts, or to be used in a similar way in alternative dispute resolution;

(b) AI systems intended to be used for influencing the outcome of an election or referendum or the voting behaviour of natural persons in the exercise of their vote in elections or referenda. This does not include AI systems to the output of which natural persons are not directly exposed, such as tools used to organise, optimise or structure political campaigns from an administrative or logistical point of view.	
Conditions	**Conformity Assessment Procedure**
-	The internal control[1788] without involvement of a notified body[1789].
Harmonised standards do not exist, and common specifications are not available The provider has not applied, or has applied only part of, the harmonised standard;	The assessment of the quality management system and technical documentation, with the involvement of a notified body[1790].

[1788] The internal control procedure is set out in Annex VI EU AI Act.

[1789] Article 43(2) EU AI Act.

[1790] This assessment procedure is detailed in Annex VII EU AI Act.

The common specifications exist, but the provider has not applied them; One or more of the harmonised standards has been published with a restriction, and only on the part of the standard that was restricted.	

Where a high-risk AI system is covered by the EU harmonisation legislation[1791], the provider must follow the relevant conformity assessment procedure as required under those legal acts[1792]. The EU AI Act's requirements apply to those high-risk AI systems and are a part of that assessment[1793]. In addition, the following requirements apply[1794]:

- The technical documentation must be examined by the notified body[1795]. Where relevant, and limited to what

[1791] For the list of the EU harmonization legislation see Section A of Annex I EU AI Act.

[1792] Article 43(3) EU AI Act.

[1793] *Ibid.*

[1794] *Ibid.*

[1795] *Ibid* and point 4.3 Annex VII EU AI Act.

is necessary to fulfil its tasks, the notified body must be granted full access to the training, validation, and testing data sets used, including, where appropriate and subject to security safeguards, through API or other relevant technical means and tools enabling remote access[1796].

- In examining the technical documentation, the notified body may require that the provider supply further evidence or carry out further tests so as to enable a proper assessment of the conformity of the AI system with the EU AI Act requirements[1797]. Where the notified body is not satisfied with the tests carried out by the provider, the notified body shall itself directly carry out adequate tests, as appropriate[1798].

- Where necessary to assess the conformity of the high-risk AI system with the EU AI Act requirements, after all other reasonable means to verify conformity have been exhausted and have proven to be insufficient, and upon a reasoned request, the notified body must also be granted access to the training and trained models of the AI system, including its relevant parameters[1799]. Such

---

[1796] Article 43(3) and point 4.3 Annex VII EU AI Act.

[1797] Article 43(3), Chapter III, Section 2, and point 4.4 Annex VII EU AI Act.

[1798] Article 43(3) and Para 4.4 Annex VII EU AI Act.

[1799] Article 43(3), Chapter III, Section 2, and point 4.5 Annex VII EU AI Act.

access must be subject to the existing EU law on the protection of intellectual property and trade secrets[1800].

- Where the AI system does not meet the requirement relating to the data used to train it, re-training of the AI system will be needed prior to the application for a new conformity assessment[1801]. In this case, the reasoned assessment decision of the notified body refusing to issue the EU technical documentation assessment certificate must contain specific considerations on the quality data used to train the AI system, in particular on the reasons for non-compliance[1802].

For the purposes of the assessment, notified bodies which have been notified under those legal acts are entitled to control the conformity of the high-risk AI systems with the EU AI Act's requirements, provided that the compliance of those notified bodies with the following requirements has been assessed in the context of the notification procedure under those legal acts[1803]:

- Notified bodies must be independent of the provider of a high-risk AI system in relation to which they perform conformity assessment activities, any other operator

---

1800 Article 43(3) and point 4.5 Annex VII EU AI Act.

1801 Article 43(3) and the fifth paragraph of point 4.5 Annex VII EU AI Act.

1802 *Ibid.*

1803 Article 43(3) EU AI Act.

having an economic interest in high-risk AI systems assessed, and of any competitors of the provider[1804]. But this does not preclude the use of assessed high-risk AI systems that are necessary for the operations of the conformity assessment body, or the use of such high-risk AI systems for personal purposes[1805].

- The conformity assessment body, its top-level management, and the personnel responsible for carrying out its conformity assessment tasks may not be directly involved in the design, development, marketing or use of high-risk AI systems, represent the parties engaged in those activities, and (or) engage in any activity, including consultancy services, that might conflict with their independence of judgement or integrity in relation to conformity assessment activities for which they are notified[1806].

- Notified bodies must be capable of carrying out all their tasks under the EU AI Act with the highest degree of professional integrity and the requisite competence in the specific field, whether those tasks are carried out by notified bodies themselves or on their behalf and under their responsibility[1807].

[1804] Article 31(4) EU AI Act.
[1805] *Ibid.*
[1806] Article 31(5) EU AI Act.
[1807] Article 31(10) EU AI Act.

- Notified bodies must have sufficient internal competences to be able to evaluate effectively the tasks performed by external parties on their behalf and must have permanently available and sufficient administrative, technical, legal and scientific personnel who possess experience and knowledge relating to the relevant types of AI systems, data and data computing, and relating to the EU AI requirements to high-risk AI systems[1808].

Where a legal act of the EU harmonisation legislation[1809] enables the product manufacturer to opt out from a third-party conformity assessment, provided that the manufacturer has applied all harmonised standards covering all the relevant requirements, the manufacturer may use that option only if it has also applied harmonised standards or, where applicable, common specifications, covering all EU AI Act's requirements to the High-Risk AI System[1810].

High-risk AI systems that have already been subject to a conformity assessment procedure must undergo a new conformity assessment procedure in the event of a

---

[1808] Article 31(11) EU AI Act.

[1809] For the list of the EU harmonization legislation see Section A of Annex I EU AI Act.

[1810] Article 43(3) EU AI Act.

substantial modification, regardless of whether the modified system is intended to be further distributed or continues to be used by the current deployer[1811].

For high-risk AI systems that continue to learn after being placed on the market or put into service, changes to the high-risk AI system and its performance that have been pre-determined by the provider at the moment of the initial conformity assessment and are part of the detailed description in the technical documentation of pre-determined changes to the AI system and its performance and all the relevant information related to the technical solutions adopted to ensure continuous compliance of the AI system with the EU AI Act requirements to high-risk AI systems, do not constitute a substantial modification[1812]:

Conformity assessment procedure Based on Internal Control

The conformity assessment procedure based on internal control involves the following steps[1813]:

- The provider must verify that the established quality management system complies with the EU AI Act's requirements to quality management system[1814].

1811 Article 43(4) EU AI Act.

1812 Article 43(4), Point 2(f) Annex IV, and Chapter III Section 2 EU AI Act.

1813 Annex VI EU AI Act.

1814 Article 17 EU AI Act

- The provider must examine the information contained in the technical documentation in order to assess the compliance of the AI system with the relevant essential requirements to high-risk AI systems concerning risk management systems, data and data governance, technical documentation, record-keeping, transparency and provision of information to deployers, human oversight, accuracy, robustness and cybersecurity[1815].
- The provider must also verify that the design and development process of the AI system and its post-market monitoring[1816] is consistent with the technical documentation.

Conformity assessment procedure based on an assessment of the quality management system and technical documentation

The conformity assessment procedure based on an assessment of the quality management system and technical documentation involves the following steps[1817]:

Assessment of Quality Management System

[1815] Chapter III, Section 2 EU AI Act.

[1816] Post-market monitoring is referred to in as referred to in Article 72 EU AI Act.

[1817] Annex VII EU AI Act.

The quality management system must be assessed by the notified body as to its compliance with the EU AI Act requirements to quality management systems[1818]. To initiate the assessment, the provider must apply to the notified body. The application of the provider must include[1819]:

(a) the name and address of the provider and, if the application is lodged by an authorised representative, also their name and address;

(b) the list of AI systems covered under the same quality management system;

(c) the technical documentation for each AI system covered under the same quality management system;

(d) the documentation concerning the quality management system covering all quality management system requirements under the EU AI Act;

(e) a description of the procedures in place to ensure that the quality management system remains adequate and effective; and

(f) a written declaration that the same application has not been lodged with any other notified body.

Following the assessment, the notified body shall notify the provider or its authorised representative about the

[1818] Point 3.2 Annex VII EU AI Act.
[1819] Point 3.1 Annex VII EU AI Act.

conclusions of the assessment and the reasoned assessment decision[1820].

The approved quality management system must be implemented and maintained by the provider so that it remains adequate and efficient[1821].

The provider must bring to the attention of the notified body any intended change to the approved quality management system or to the list of AI systems covered by the quality management system[1822]. The notified body must examine the proposed changes and decide whether the modified quality management system continues to satisfy the requirements or whether a reassessment is necessary and notify the provider of its decision, specifying the conclusions of the examination of the changes and the reasoned assessment decision[1823].

Assessment of the Technical Documentation

In addition to the application to examine the quality management system, the provider must apply to a notified body of the provider's choice for the assessment of the technical documentation relating to the AI system which the provider intends to place on the market or put into

[1820] Point 3.2 Annex VII EU AI Act.
[1821] Point 3.3 Annex VII EU AI Act.
[1822] Point 3.4 Annex VII EU AI Act.
[1823] *Ibid.*

service and which is covered by the quality management system[1824]. The application must include[1825]:

(a) the name and address of the provider;

(b) a written declaration that the same application has not been lodged with any other notified body; and

(c) the technical documentation.

The notified body must examine the technical documentation[1826]. Where relevant, and to the extent of what is necessary to fulfil its tasks, the notified body must be granted full access to the training, validation, and testing data sets used, including, where appropriate and subject to security safeguards, through API or other relevant technical means and tools enabling remote access[1827].

When examining the technical documentation, the notified body may require that the provider supply further evidence or carry out further tests to enable a proper assessment of the conformity of the AI system with the EU AI Act requirements to high-risk AI systems[1828]. Where the notified body is not satisfied with the tests carried out by the provider, the notified body shall itself directly carry out adequate tests, as appropriate[1829].

[1824] Point 4.1 Annex VII EU AI Act.
[1825] Point 4.2 Annex VII EU AI Act.
[1826] Point 4.3 Annex VII EU AI Act.
[1827] *Ibid.*
[1828] Point 4.4 Annex VII and Chapter III, Section 2 EU AI Act.
[1829] Point 4.4 Annex VII EU AI Act.

Where necessary to assess the conformity of the high-risk AI system with the EU AI Act requirements[1830], after all other reasonable means to verify conformity have been exhausted and have proven to be insufficient, and upon a reasoned request, the notified body must also be granted access to the training and trained models of the AI system, including its relevant parameters[1831]. Such access shall be subject to existing EU law on the protection of intellectual property and trade secrets[1832].

The notified body shall inform the provider or its authorised representative about its decision, specifying the assessment of the technical documentation and the reasoned assessment decision[1833].

Where the AI system is compliant with the EU AI Act requirements[1834], the notified body shall issue an EU technical documentation assessment certificate[1835]. The EU AI Act provides for the following requirements to the certificate:

- The certificate shall specify the name and address of the provider, the conclusions of the examination, the

---

[1830] The requirements to high-risk AI systems are set out in Chapter III, Section 2 EU AI Act.

[1831] Point 4.5 Annex VII EU AI Act.

[1832] *Ibid.*

[1833] Point 4.6 Annex VII EU AI Act.

[1834] The requirements to high-risk AI systems are set out in Chapter III, Section 2 EU AI Act.

[1835] Point 4.6 Annex VII EU AI Act.

conditions (if any) for its validity and the data necessary for the identification of the AI system[1836];

- The certificate and its annexes shall contain all relevant information to allow the conformity of the AI system to be evaluated, and to allow for control of the AI system while in use, where applicable[1837].
- The certificate shall be drawn up in a language which can be easily understood by the relevant authorities in the EU Member State in which the notified body is established[1838].
- The certificates shall be valid for the period they indicate, which shall depend on the type of the AI system and shall not exceed:

Type of AI System	Maximum Duration of the Certificate
AI systems covered by EU harmonization legislation[1839] (machinery; toys; recreational craft and personal watercraft; lifts and safety components for lifts; equipment and protective systems intended for use in potentially explosive	Five years

[1836] *Ibid.*
[1837] *Ibid.*
[1838] Article 44(1) EU AI Act.
[1839] Article 44(2) and Annex I EU AI Act.

Type of AI System	Maximum Duration of the Certificate
atmospheres; radio equipment; pressure equipment; cableway installations; personal protective equipment; appliances burning gaseous fuels; medical devices; in vitro diagnostic medical devices; civil aviation security systems; two- or three-wheel vehicles and quadricycles; agricultural and forestry vehicles; marine equipment; rail systems; systems, components and separate technical units intended for motor vehicles and their trailers; and unmanned aircraft and their engines, propellers, parts and equipment to control them remotely)	
Other High-risk AI systems[1840]	Four years

- At the request of the provider, the validity of a certificate may be extended for further periods, each not exceeding five years for AI systems covered by the EU

[1840] Article 44(2) and Annex III EU AI Act.

harmonisation legislation, and four years for the other high-risk AI systems, based on a re-assessment in accordance with the applicable conformity assessment procedures[1841]. Any supplement to a certificate shall remain valid, provided that the certificate which it supplements is valid[1842].

Where the AI system is not compliant with the EU AI Act requirements[1843], the notified body shall refuse to issue an EU technical documentation assessment certificate and inform the applicant accordingly, giving detailed reasons for its refusal[1844]. Likewise, where a notified body subsequently finds that an AI system no longer meets the EU AI Act requirements, it shall, taking account of the principle of proportionality, suspend or withdraw the certificate issued or impose restrictions on it, unless compliance with those requirements is ensured by appropriate corrective action taken by the provider of the system within the deadline set by the notified body[1845]. The notified body must give reasons for its decision[1846]. The EU AI Act has a broad provision for an appeal procedure against decisions of the notified bodies, including on

[1841] Article 44(2) EU AI Act.

[1842] *Ibid.*

[1843] The requirements to high-risk AI systems are set out in Chapter 13 of this book and in Chapter III, Section 2 EU AI Act.

[1844] Point 4.6 Annex VII EU AI Act.

[1845] Article 44(3) EU AI Act.

[1846] *Ibid.*

conformity certificates issued, to be available[1847], but does not specify any details of the appeal procedure.

Where the AI system does not meet the requirements relating to the data used to train it, re-training of the AI system will be needed prior to the application for a new conformity assessment[1848]. In this case, the reasoned assessment decision of the notified body refusing to issue the EU technical documentation assessment certificate must contain specific considerations on the quality data used to train the AI system, in particular on the reasons for non-compliance[1849].

Any change to the AI system that could affect compliance of the AI system with the EU AI Act's requirements or its intended purpose must be assessed by the notified body which issued the EU technical documentation assessment certificate[1850]. The provider must inform the notified body of its intention to make the changes, or if it otherwise becomes aware of the occurrence of such changes[1851]. The notified body must assess the intended changes and decide whether the changes require a new conformity assessment or whether they could be addressed in a supplement to the EU technical

---

[1847] Article 44(3) EU AI Act.
[1848] Point 4.6 Annex VII EU AI Act.
[1849] *Ibid.*
[1850] Point 4.7 Annex VII EU AI Act.
[1851] *Ibid.*

documentation assessment certificate[1852]. In the latter case, the notified body must assess the changes, notify the provider of its decision and, if the changes are approved, issue to the provider a supplement to the EU technical documentation assessment certificate[1853].

Monitoring of the approved quality management system.

The notified body must monitor the provider's compliance with the terms and conditions of the approved quality management system[1854].

For assessment purposes, the provider must permit the notified body to access the premises where the design, development, and testing of the AI systems is taking place and share with the notified body all necessary information[1855].

The notified body must carry out periodic audits to make sure that the provider maintains and applies the quality management system and make the audit report available to the provider[1856]. In the context of those audits, the notified body may carry out additional tests of the AI systems for which an EU technical documentation assessment certificate was issued[1857].

[1852] *Ibid.*

[1853] *Ibid.*

[1854] Point 5.1 Annex VII EU AI Act.

[1855] *Ibid.*

[1856] Point 5.3 Annex VII EU AI Act.

[1857] *Ibid.*

Derogation from Conformity Assessment Procedure

By way of derogation from these conformity assessment requirements and upon a justified request, any market surveillance authority may authorise the placing on the market or the putting into service of specific high-risk AI systems within the territory of the EU Member State concerned, for exceptional reasons of public security or the protection of life and health of persons, environmental protection or the protection of key industrial and infrastructural assets[1858]. The authorisation must be for a limited period while the necessary conformity assessment procedures are being carried out, taking into account the exceptional reasons justifying the derogation[1859]. The conformity assessment must be completed without undue delay[1860]. Further, in a justified situation of urgency for exceptional reasons of public security or in the case of specific, substantial and imminent threat to the life or physical safety of natural persons, law-enforcement authorities or civil protection authorities may put a specific high-risk AI system into service without authorisation, provided that the authorisation is requested during or after the use without undue delay[1861]. If the authorisation is refused, the use of the high-risk AI system must be stopped

[1858] Article 46(1) EU AI Act.
[1859] *Ibid.*
[1860] *Ibid.*
[1861] Article 46(2) EU AI Act.

with immediate effect and all results and outputs of such use shall be immediately discarded[1862].

The authorisation shall be issued only if the market surveillance authority concludes that the high-risk AI system complies with the EU AI Act's requirements[1863].

The market surveillance authority must inform the Commission and the other EU Member States of any authorisation so issued (excluding sensitive operational data in relation to the activities of law-enforcement authorities) [1864]. Where, within 15 calendar days of receipt of the notification, no objection has been raised by either an EU Member State or the Commission in respect of an authorisation issued by a market surveillance authority of an EU Member State, the authorisation shall be deemed justified[1865]. But, where, within 15 calendar days of receipt of the notification objections are raised by a Member State against an authorisation issued by a market surveillance authority of another Member State, or where the Commission considers the authorisation to be contrary to EU law, or the conclusion of the Member States regarding compliance of the system to be unfounded, the Commission must, without delay, enter into consultations with the relevant Member State[1866]. The operators concerned must

---

[1862] *Ibid.*
[1863] Article 46(3) EU AI Act.
[1864] *Ibid.*
[1865] Article 46(4) EU AI Act.
[1866] Article 46(5) EU AI Act.

be consulted and provided with an opportunity to present their views[1867]. Having regard to the views of the Member States and operators, the Commission must decide whether the authorisation is justified and inform the Member State concerned and the relevant operators of its decision[1868]. Where the Commission considers the authorisation unjustified, the market surveillance authority of the Member State concerned must withdraw it[1869].

For high-risk AI systems related to products covered by EU harmonisation legislation[1870], only the derogations from the conformity assessment established in that EU harmonisation legislation shall apply[1871].

Conformity Assessment Fees

The EU AI Act requires that specific interests and needs of the SME providers, including start-ups, must be taken into account when setting the fees for conformity assessment, reducing the fees proportionately to their size, market size and other relevant indicators[1872].

1867 *Ibid.*

1868 *Ibid.*

1869 Article 46(6) EU AI Act.

1870 The applicable EU harmonization legislation is listed in Section A of Annex I EU AI Act.

1871 Article 46(7) EU AI Act.

1872 Article 62(2) EU AI Act.

17.2.7 EU Declaration of Conformity

The EU AI Act requires providers of high-risk AI systems to draw up an EU declaration of conformity for each high-risk AI system[1873]. The declaration of conformity must be written, machine readable, physical or electronically signed, identify the high-risk AI system for which it has been drawn up[1874], state that the high-risk AI system concerned meets the EU AI Act requirements, and contain the following information[1875]:

1. AI system name and type and any additional unambiguous reference enabling identification and traceability of the AI system;
2. The name and address of the provider or, where applicable, of their authorised representative;
3. A statement that the EU declaration of conformity is issued under the sole responsibility of the provider;
4. A statement that the AI system is compliant with the EU AI Act and, if applicable, with any other relevant EU law that provides for the issuing of the EU declaration of conformity;
5. Where an AI system involves processing of personal data, a statement that the AI system complies with

---

[1873] Articles 16(g) and 47 EU AI Act.
[1874] Article 47(1) EU AI Act.
[1875] Article 47(2) and Annex V EU AI Act.

Regulations (EU) 2016/679 and (EU) 2018/1725 and Directive (EU) 2016/680;

6. References to any relevant harmonised standards used or any other common specification in relation to which conformity is declared;
7. Where applicable, the name and identification number of the notified body, a description of the conformity assessment procedure performed, and identification of the certificate issued;
8. The place and date of issue of the declaration, the name and function of the person who signed it, an indication for, or on behalf of whom, that person signed, and the signature.

The provider must keep the EU declaration of conformity available for the national competent authorities for 10 years after the high-risk AI system has been placed on the market or put into service[1876]. A copy of the declaration of conformity must be submitted to the relevant national competent authorities on request[1877].

The EU declaration of conformity must be translated into a language that can be easily understood by the national competent authorities of the Member States in

[1876] Article 47(1) EU AI Act.
[1877] *Ibid.*

which the high-risk AI system is placed on the market or made available[1878].

Where high-risk AI systems are subject to other EU harmonisation legislation which also requires an EU declaration of conformity, a single EU declaration of conformity must be drawn up in respect of all EU law applicable to the high-risk AI system and must contain all the information required to identify the EU harmonisation legislation to which the declaration relates[1879].

By drawing up the EU declaration of conformity, the provider assumes responsibility for compliance with the EU AI Act requirements and must keep the EU declaration of conformity up to date[1880].

Where the market surveillance authority of a Member State finds that the EU declaration of conformity has not been drawn up[1881] or has not been drawn up correctly[1882] it must require the relevant provider to put an end to the non-compliance, within a period it may prescribe. If the non-compliance persists, the market surveillance authority must take appropriate and proportionate measures to restrict or prohibit the high-risk AI system being made available on the market or to ensure

[1878] Article 47(2) EU AI Act.

[1879] Article 47(3) EU AI Act.

[1880] Article 47(4) EU AI Act.

[1881] Article 83(1)(c) EU AI Act; the requirements to EU declaration of conformity are in Article 47 EU AI Act.

[1882] Article 83(1)(d) EU AI Act.

that it is recalled or withdrawn from the market without delay[1883].

17.2.8 CE Marking

The EU AI Act requires high-risk systems to bear and the providers of high-risk AI systems to affix the CE marking to the high-risk AI system or, where that is not possible, on its packaging or its accompanying documentation[1884].

The CE marking consists of the initials 'CE' in the following form[1885]:

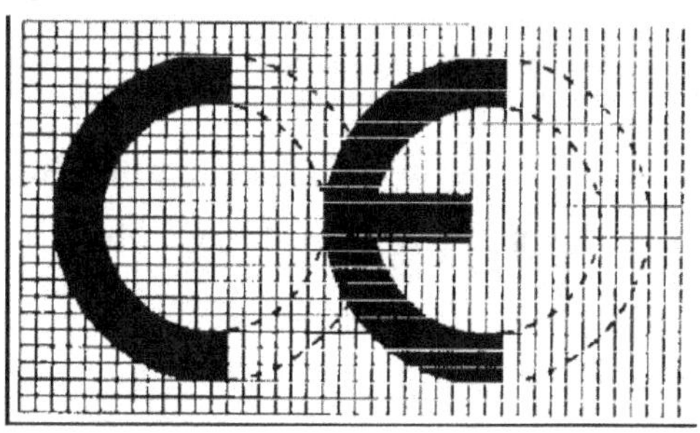

The affixing of the CE marking is governed by the following general principles[1886]:

- The CE marking shall be affixed only by the manufacturer or his authorised representative.

[1883] Article 83(2) EU AI Act.

[1884] Articles 16(h) and 48 EU AI Act.

[1885] Annex II Regulation (EC) No 765/2008.

[1886] Article 48(1) EU AI Act; the general principles are set out in Article 30 Regulation (EC) No 765/2008.

- The CE marking shall be affixed only to products to which its affixing is provided for by specific EU harmonisation legislation, and shall not be affixed to any other product.
- By affixing or having affixed the CE marking, the manufacturer indicates that he takes responsibility for the conformity of the product with all applicable requirements set out in the EU harmonisation legislation that provides for its affixing.
- The CE marking shall be the only marking which attests conformity of the product with the requirements of the EU harmonisation legislation that provides for its affixing.
- The affixing to a product of markings, signs or inscriptions which are likely to mislead third parties regarding the meaning or form of the CE marking is prohibited. Any other marking may be affixed to the product provided that it does not impair the visibility, legibility and meaning of the CE marking.
- EU Member States must ensure the correct implementation of the regime governing the CE marking, take appropriate action in the event of improper use of the marking, and provide for penalties for infringements, which may include criminal sanctions for serious infringements. The penalties must be proportionate to the seriousness of the offence and constitute an effective deterrent against improper use.

For high-risk AI systems provided digitally, a digital CE marking shall be used, only if it can easily be accessed via the interface from which that system is accessed or via an easily accessible machine-readable code or other electronic means[1887].

The CE marking must be affixed on high-risk AI systems visibly, legibly and indelibly[1888]. Where that is not possible or not warranted on account of the nature of the high-risk AI system, it must be affixed on the packaging or the accompanying documentation, as appropriate[1889].

Where applicable, the CE marking must be followed by the identification number of the notified body responsible for the conformity assessment[1890]. The identification number of the notified body must be affixed by the body itself or, under its instructions, by the provider or by the provider's authorised representative[1891]. The identification number must also be indicated in any promotional material which mentions that the high-risk AI system fulfils the requirements for CE marking[1892].

Where high-risk AI systems are subject to other EU law which also provides for the affixing of the CE marking,

---

[1887] Article 48(2) EU AI Act.
[1888] Article 48(3) EU AI Act.
[1889] *Ibid.*
[1890] Articles 43 and 48(4) EU AI Act.
[1891] Article 48(4) EU AI Act.
[1892] *Ibid.*

the CE marking must indicate that the high-risk AI system also fulfils the requirements of that other law[1893].

Where the market surveillance authority of a Member State finds that the CE marking has not been affixed[1894] or has been affixed in violation of the EU AI Act requirements[1895], it must require the relevant provider to remedy the non-compliance, within a period it may prescribe[1896]. If the non-compliance persists, the market surveillance authority must take appropriate and proportionate measures to restrict or prohibit the high-risk AI system being made available on the market or ensure that it is recalled or withdrawn from the market without delay[1897].

17.2.9 Registration in the EU Database

The EU AI Act requires providers of Annex III high-risk AI systems (the full list of these systems is set out in 13.1 Chapter 13 of this book and(or) in Annex III EU AI Act) or, in the case of non-EU providers – their authorised representatives, to register themselves and their high-risk AI systems in the EU database before placing the Annex III high-risk AI system on the market or putting it into service. This requirement applies to all Annex III high-risk AI

1893 Article 48(5) EU AI Act.
1894 Article 83(1)(b) EU AI Act.
1895 Article 83(1)(a) EU AI Act.
1896 Article 83(1) EU AI Act.
1897 Article 83(2) EU AI Act.

systems, including those which the providers assessed as not high-risk[1898]. The EU database must be set up by the EU Commission in collaboration with the EU Member States[1899].

The only exception are critical infrastructure AI systems intended to be used as safety components in the management and operation of critical digital infrastructure, road traffic, or supply of water, gas, heating or electricity[1900]. These high-risk AI systems must be registered at national level[1901].

The provider or, in the case of non-EU providers – the authorised representative in the EU shall enter into the database the data depending on the type of the high-risk AI system[1902]:

High-Risk AI Systems Except Critical Infrastructure Systems

1. The name, address and contact details of the provider;

2. Where another person submits information on behalf of the provider, the name, address and contact details of that person;

[1898] Articles 16(h) and 49(1) and (2) EU AI Act.
[1899] Article 71(1) EU AI Act.
[1900] Articles 16(h) and 49(1) EU AI Act.
[1901] Article 49(5) EU AI Act.
[1902] Article 71(2) and Sections A and B of Annex VIII EU AI Act.

3. The name, address and contact details of the authorised representative (for non-EU providers);

4. The AI system trade name and any additional unambiguous reference allowing the identification and traceability of the AI system;

5. A description of the intended purpose of the AI system and components and functions supported through the AI system;

6. A basic and concise description of the information used by the system (data, inputs) and its operating logic;

7. The status of the AI system (i.e. on the market or in service; no longer placed on the market/in service; recalled);

8. The type, number and expiry date of the certificate issued by the notified body and the name or identification number of that notified body, where applicable;

9. A scanned copy of the certificate referred to in point 8, where applicable;

10. Any Member States in which the AI system has been placed on the market, put into service or made available in the EU;

11. A copy of the EU declaration of conformity;

12. Electronic instructions for use; this information shall not be provided for high-risk AI systems in the areas of law enforcement or migration, asylum and border control management;

13. A URL for additional information (optional).

High-risk AI systems Assessed by the Provider as Not High-Risk

1. The name, address and contact details of the provider;
2. Where another person submits information on behalf of the provider, the name, address and contact details of that person;
3. The name, address and contact details of the authorised representative (for non-EU providers);
4. The AI system trade name and any additional unambiguous reference allowing the identification and traceability of the AI system;
5. A description of the intended purpose of the AI system;
6. The condition or conditions based on which the AI system is considered to be not-high-risk;
7. A short summary of the grounds on which the AI system is considered to be not-high-risk;
8. The status of the AI system (on the market, or in service; no longer placed on the market/in service; recalled);
9. The Member States in which the AI system has been placed on the market, put into service or made available in the EU.

High-risk AI systems in the areas of biometrics, law enforcement, migration, asylum and border control management

These high-risk AI systems must be registered in a secure non-public section of the EU database to which only the Commission and market surveillance authorities designated by the Member States shall have access[1903]. This restricted section of the EU database shall include only the following information:

1. The name, address and contact details of the provider[1904];

2. Where another person submits information on behalf of the provider, the name, address and contact details of that person[1905];

3. The name, address and contact details of the authorised representative (for non-EU providers)[1906];

4. The AI system trade name and any additional unambiguous reference allowing the identification and traceability of the AI system[1907];

5. A description of the intended purpose of the AI system and (unless the provider assessed the system as not high-risk) of the components and functions supported through this AI system[1908];

[1903] Article 49(4) EU AI Act.
[1904] Article 49(4)(a) and (b) EU AI Act.
[1905] *Ibid.*
[1906] *Ibid.*
[1907] *Ibid.*
[1908] *Ibid.*

6. The status of the AI system (on the market, or in service; no longer placed on the market/in service; recalled) [1909];

7. The Member States in which the AI system has been placed on the market, put into service or made available in the EU[1910];

8. The name, address and contact details of the deployer[1911];

9. The name, address and contact details of the person submitting information on behalf of the deployer[1912];

10. The URL of the entry of the AI system in the EU database by its provider[1913];

11. A Union-wide unique single identification number of the testing in real world conditions[1914];

12. The name and contact details of the provider or prospective provider and of the deployers involved in the testing in real world conditions[1915];

13. Information on the suspension or termination of the testing in real world conditions[1916].

[1909] *Ibid.*
[1910] *Ibid.*
[1911] Article 49(4)(c) EU AI Act.
[1912] *Ibid.*
[1913] *Ibid.*
[1914] Article 49(4)(d) EU AI Act.
[1915] *Ibid.*
[1916] *Ibid.*

Where the market surveillance authority of a Member State finds that the AI system was not registered in the EU[1917], it must require the provider to comply, within a period it may prescribe. If the non-compliance persists, the market surveillance authority must take appropriate and proportionate measures to restrict or prohibit the high-risk AI system being made available on the market or ensure that it is recalled or withdrawn from the market without delay[1918].

17.2.10 Corrective actions and duty to provide information

The EU AI Act requires providers of high-risk AI systems which consider or have reason to consider that a high-risk AI system that they have placed on the market or put into service fails to conform to the EU AI Act, to immediately take the necessary corrective actions to conform, withdraw, disable, or recall the system.[1919]. The EU AI Act further requires providers to inform the distributors of the high-risk AI system concerned and, where applicable, the deployers, the authorised representative, and importers[1920].

1917 Article 83(1)(e) EU AI Act.
1918 Article 83(2) EU AI Act.
1919 Articles 16(j), 20(1) EU AI Act.
1920 *Ibid.*

Where the high-risk AI system presents a risk to health, safety or fundamental rights of persons[1921] and the provider becomes aware of that risk, the provider must immediately investigate the causes, in collaboration with the reporting deployer, where applicable, and inform the market surveillance authorities relevant for the high-risk AI system concerned and, where applicable, the notified body that issued a conformity certificate for that high-risk AI system[1922], in particular, of the nature of the non-compliance and any relevant corrective action taken[1923].

17.2.11 Cooperation with competent authorities

The EU AI Act requires providers of high-risk AI systems, upon a reasoned request by a competent authority, to provide that authority all the information and documentation necessary to demonstrate the conformity of the high-risk AI system with the requirements related to sharing of information on serious incidents[1924], in a language which can be easily understood by the authority

[1921] Article 79(1) EU AI Act.
[1922] Article 44, Annex VII EU AI Act.
[1923] Article 20(2) EU AI Act.
[1924] Requirements to sharing information about serious incidents are addressed in 16.2.15 of this Chapter 16.

in one of the official languages of the institutions of the EU as indicated by the Member State concerned[1925].

In addition, upon a reasoned request by a competent authority, providers must give the requesting competent authority access to the automatically generated logs of the high-risk AI system, to the extent such logs are under their control[1926].

The competent authority must treat as confidential any information so obtained[1927].

17.2.12 Accessibility

The EU AI Act requires providers to ensure that the high-risk AI system complies with accessibility requirements[1928]. The accessibility requirements are set out in other EU legislation[1929] and are not specific to the EU AI Act.

17.2.13 Contractual Terms

The provider of a high-risk AI system and the third party that supplies an AI system, tools, services, components, or processes (other than publicly accessible

---

[1925] Articles 16(k), 21(1) EU AI Act.
[1926] Articles 21(2), 12(1) EU AI Act.
[1927] Articles 21(3), 78 EU AI Act.
[1928] Article 16(l) EU AI Act.
[1929] The accessibility requirements are those set out in Directives (EU) 2016/2102 and (EU) 2019/882.

general-purpose AI models, under a free and open-source licence) that are used or integrated in a high-risk AI system must, in a written agreement, specify the necessary information, capabilities, technical access and other assistance based on the generally acknowledged state of the art, needed to enable the provider of the high-risk AI system to fully comply with the obligations set out in the EU AI Act[1930].

17.2.14 Transparency Obligations

The EU AI Act requires providers to ensure that AI systems intended to interact directly with natural persons are designed and developed in such a way that the natural persons concerned are informed that they are interacting with an AI system, unless this is obvious from the point of view of a natural person who is reasonably well-informed, observant and circumspect, taking into account the circumstances and the context of use[1931]. This obligation does not apply to AI systems authorised by law to detect, prevent, investigate or prosecute criminal offences, subject to appropriate safeguards for the rights and freedoms of third parties, unless those systems are available for the public to report a criminal offence[1932].

[1930] Article 25(4) EU AI Act.
[1931] Article 50(1) EU AI Act.
[1932] *Ibid.*

The EU AI Act further requires providers of AI systems, including general-purpose AI systems, generating synthetic audio, image, video or text content, to ensure that the outputs of the AI system are marked in a machine-readable format and detectable as artificially generated or manipulated[1933]. In addition, the EU AI Act requires these providers to ensure that their technical solutions are effective, interoperable, robust and reliable as far as this is technically feasible, taking into account the specificities and limitations of various types of content, the costs of implementation and the generally acknowledged state of the art, as may be reflected in relevant technical standards[1934]. But this obligation does not apply to the extent the AI systems perform an assistive function for standard editing or do not substantially alter the input data provided by the deployer or the semantics of the input data, or where authorised by law to detect, prevent, investigate or prosecute criminal offences[1935].

Draft Code of Practice on Marking and Labelling of AI-generated Content

To support compliance with these transparency requirements, the AI office has started the process of drafting the Code of Practice on Marking and Labelling of

---

[1933] Article 50(2) EU AI Act.
[1934] *Ibid.*
[1935] *Ibid.*

AI-generated Content. The first draft Code was published on 17 December 2025[1936] and the final Code is expected to be published in May-June 2026[1937]. The draft Code is the result of a collaborative effort involving hundreds of participants from industry, academia, and civil society, as well as contributions from Member States[1938].

For providers, the draft Code focuses on the EU AI Act's obligations that require providers of generative AI systems to ensure that:

- outputs of AI systems (audio, image, video, text) are marked in a machine-readable format and detectable as artificially generated or manipulated; and
- the employed technical solutions are effective, interoperable, robust, reliable as far as technically feasible, and take into account the specificities and limitations of various types of content, the costs of implementation and the generally acknowledged state of the art, as may be reflected in relevant technical standards[1939].

1936 https://digital-strategy.ec.europa.eu/en/library/first-draft-code-practice-transparency-ai-generated-content

1937 https://digital-strategy.ec.europa.eu/en/policies/code-practice-ai-generated-content

1938 Draft Code of Practice on Transparency of AI-generated Content, p.3 https://digital-strategy.ec.europa.eu/en/library/first-draft-code-practice-transparency-ai-generated-content

1939 https://digital-strategy.ec.europa.eu/en/policies/code-practice-ai-generated-content

The draft Code proposes that providers commit to[1940]:

- Multi-layered marking of AI-generated content

The draft Code proposes that providers implement marking techniques to ensure the outputs of their generative AI systems are marked with multiple layers of machine-readable marking. For content that permits **metadata embedding**, the providers committing to the Code will add information about the type of the operation performed by the AI system (e.g., prompting, editing, or generation) and sign it digitally. Within the content, the providers will interweave an imperceptible **watermark** in a manner that is difficult for it to be separated from the content and that withstands typical processing steps that may be applied to the content. To address deficiencies of metadata embedding and watermarking, the providers will implement **fingerprinting** of the AI-generated or manipulated content or logging facilities that allow for checking whether an output has been generated or manipulated by their generative AI system. In addition, the providers will implement a **digitally signed certificate** allowing deployers to obtain a certified version of the AI output generated or manipulated by their AI system or model to formally guarantee the origin of content that does not allow secure embedding of metadata and enable deployers and

[1940] Draft Code of Practice on Transparency of AI-generated Content, p.3 https://digital-strategy.ec.europa.eu/en/library/first-draft-code-practice-transparency-ai-generated-content

end-users to provide third parties with guarantees that the content is AI-generated or manipulated, linking it back to the specific generative AI system or model. For multimodal content, the providers will also ensure that the employed marking techniques are **synchronised across the modalities** in a manner that the marking is recognisable when only one or a subset of modalities have been altered or exchanged. Providers releasing **open-weight AI models** or systems will implement **structural marking encoded in the weights** during model training. Providers of generative AI models will implement machine-readable marking techniques for the content generated or manipulated by their models prior to the model's placement on the market. Providers will ensure that existing detectable **marks are retained and subsequently transformed into a new output** where the content is used as input, and include in the acceptable use policy, terms and conditions or the documentation accompanying their generative AI system or model a **prohibition for removal or tampering of the marks** by deployers or any other third parties. Signatories will record and embed through content marking the origin and provenance chain from AI-assisted or (partially) modified content to fully AI-generated content where technologically possible for the specific modality. To this end, Signatories will consistently check the marking and provenance information of the inputs to their AI systems. The providers will **add or record all content provenance**

steps within their AI systems (both AI and human) in a way that distinguishes the additional operation from previous operations, by leveraging metadata or other appropriate techniques, where technically feasible to record and verify the provenance chain. The providers are also encouraged to record provenance information for fully human-authored content or fully human content editing operations in order to increase trust and facilitate authenticity and provenance of all content. The providers will implement in the generative AI system the functionality that allows deployers to directly – upon generation of the output – include a **perceptible mark or label** in the content enabled by default.

- Detection of the marking of AI-Generated Content

The providers will provide free of charge an interface (e.g. API or user interface) or a publicly available detector to enable users and other interested parties to verify with confidence scores whether content has been generated or manipulated by their AI system or model. For marking and detection techniques that provide information about the provenance from other AI system providers (e.g., in the metadata), the interface will also disclose a complete set of the provenance information. For the case that a provider goes out of business, the provider will make the detectors available to the competent market surveillance authorities to ensure legacy content generated or manipulated by their AI system or model remains detectable. The providers will provide **detection mechanisms** for the content generated or manipulated by their models prior to the model's placement on the market. As an additional line of defence and alternative to fingerprinting or logging, providers of generative AI models that can be used or integrated into downstream generative AI systems will **implement forensic detection mechanisms** which do not depend on the presence of active AI marking and collaborate with competent market surveillance authorities and other relevant stakeholders to support the development of an **aggregated forensic detector** that is capable of detecting the outputs of generative AI models or integrated into AI systems available on the EU market. Signatories will embed in the results of their marking and detection solution human-understandable explanations of the evidence for the detection and provenance results, as far as technically feasible. The providers will ensure that the results of the detection mechanisms and user interfaces **are accessible to persons with disabilities** and implement, for example, **harmonised standard** ETSI EN 301 549 "Accessibility requirements for ICT products and services". The providers will provide **documentation, training materials**, and other relevant information to support deployers and other users in making informed decisions on what marking and verification tools they may use, including helping them to understand how to access and apply detection mechanisms and to interpret the provenance data and the detection results. The Code also encourages providers to collaborate with academia, civil society and other relevant organisations to promote **literacy and awareness** regarding AI content provenance and verification.

- Measures to meet the requirements for marking and detection techniques

The providers will ensure the employed technical solutions for marking and detection of AI-generated or manipulated content are **effective, robust, reliable and interoperable**, as far as this is technically feasible and taking into account the specificities and limitations of various types of content, the costs of implementation and the generally acknowledged state of the art.

- Testing, verification and compliance

The providers will set up, keep up to date and implement testing, verification and compliance framework, train the personnel to comply with the framework, and cooperate with market surveillance authorities to demonstrate compliance.

17.2.15 Serious Incident Reporting

The EU AI Act requires providers of high-risk AI systems placed on the EU market to report serious incidents to the market surveillance authorities of the Member State where the incident occurs[1941] immediately after the provider has established a causal link between the AI system and the serious incident or the reasonable likelihood of such a link, and, in any event, not later than 15 days after the provider or the deployer becomes aware of the serious incident[1942]. The reporting period must take account of the severity of the serious incident[1943]. However, in the event of a widespread infringement or a serious incident[1944], the report must be provided immediately, and not later than two days after the provider or the deployer becomes aware of the incident[1945]. In addition, in the event of a person's death, the report must be provided immediately after the provider or the deployer has established, or as soon as it suspects, a causal relationship between the high-risk AI system and the serious incident, but not later than 10 days after the date on which the provider or the deployer becomes aware of the serious incident[1946]. To ensure timely

[1941] Article 73(1) EU AI Act.
[1942] Article 73(2) EU AI Act.
[1943] *Ibid.*
[1944] Article 3 (49)(b) EU AI Act.
[1945] Article 73(3) EU AI Act.
[1946] Article 73(4) EU AI Act.

reporting, the provider or the deployer, may submit an initial report that is incomplete, followed by a complete report[1947].

Following the report of a serious incident, the provider must, without delay, perform the necessary investigations in relation to the serious incident and the AI system concerned, including a risk assessment of the incident and corrective action[1948].

During investigation of a serious incident, the provider must cooperate with the competent authorities, and where relevant - with the notified body concerned, and may not perform any investigation which involves altering the AI system concerned in a way which may affect any subsequent evaluation of the causes of the incident, prior to informing the competent authorities of such action[1949].

For high-risk AI systems placed on the market or put into service by providers that are subject to the EU legislative instruments laying down reporting obligations equivalent to those set out in the EU AI Act, the notification of serious incidents is limited to those leading to infringement of obligations under EU law intended to protect fundamental rights[1950].

For high-risk AI systems which are:

[1947] Article 73(5) EU AI Act.
[1948] Article 73(6) EU AI Act.
[1949] *Ibid.*
[1950] Articles 73(9) and 3(49)(c) EU AI Act.

- safety components of devices[1951];
- medical devices for human use and accessories for such devices[1952];
- contact lenses or other items intended to be introduced into or onto the eye[1953];
- products intended to be totally or partially introduced into the human body through surgically invasive means for the purpose of modifying the anatomy or fixation of body parts, except tattooing products and piercings[1954];
- substances, combinations of substances, or items intended to be used for facial or other dermal or mucous membrane filling by subcutaneous, submucous or intradermal injection or other introduction, excluding those for tattooing[1955];
- equipment intended to be used to reduce, remove or destroy adipose tissue, such as equipment for liposuction, lipolysis or lipoplasty[1956];
- high intensity electromagnetic radiation (e.g. infra-red, visible light and ultra-violet) emitting equipment intended for use on the human body, including coherent and non-coherent sources, monochromatic and broad spectrum, such as lasers and intense pulsed light

---

[1951] Article 73(10) EU AI Act.
[1952] *Ibid*; Regulation (EU) 2017/745.
[1953] *Ibid.*
[1954] *Ibid.*
[1955] *Ibid.*
[1956] *Ibid.*

equipment, for skin resurfacing, tattoo or hair removal or other skin treatment[1957];

- equipment intended for brain stimulation that apply electrical currents or magnetic or electromagnetic fields that penetrate the cranium to modify neuronal activity in the brain[1958]; and (or)
- *in vitro* diagnostic medical devices for human use and accessories for such devices[1959],

the notification of serious incidents is limited to the incidents leading to infringement of obligations under EU law intended to protect fundamental rights[1960], and must be submitted to the national competent authority of the Member State where the incident occurred[1961].

17.2.16 Making Incumbent AI Systems Compliant

The EU AI Act allows until 31 December 2030 for AI systems which are components of the following large-scale IT systems[1962] that have been placed on the market or put into service before 2 August 2027 to be brought into compliance with the EU AI Act[1963]:

[1957] *Ibid.*
[1958] *Ibid.*
[1959] Article 73(10) EU AI Act and Regulation (EU) 2017/746.
[1960] Article 3(49)(c) EU AI Act.
[1961] Article 73(10) EU AI Act.
[1962] These are large-scale AI systems established by the legal acts listed in Annex X EU AI Act. The footnotes specify the specific legal acts corresponding to each AI system.
[1963] Article 111(1) EU AI Act.

- Schengen Information System[1964];
- Visa Information System[1965];
- Eurodac[1966];
- Entry/Exit System[1967];
- European Travel Information and Authorisation System (ETIAS)[1968];
- European Criminal Records Information System on third-country nationals and stateless persons[1969]
- Interoperability framework for EU borders and visa information systems[1970]

However, the EU AI Act's prohibitions of certain AI practices apply to these AI systems from 2 February 2025[1971].

As for operators of other high-risk AI systems placed on the market or put into service before 2 August 2026:

- the EU AI Act's prohibitions of certain AI practices apply to these AI systems from 2 February 2025;
- the providers and deployers of high-risk AI systems intended to be used by public authorities must take the

---

[1964] Regulations (EU) 2018/1860, 2018/1861, and 2018/1862.
[1965] Regulations (EU) 2021/1133 and 2021/1134.
[1966] Regulation (EU) 2024/1358.
[1967] Regulation (EU) 2017/2226.
[1968] Regulations (EU) 2018/1240 and 2018/1241.
[1969] Regulation (EU) 2019/816.
[1970] Regulations (EU) 2019/817 and 2019/818.
[1971] Article 111(1) EU AI Act.

necessary steps to comply with the EU AI Act's requirements and obligations by 2 August 2030[1972];

- but other than the above two requirements, the EU AI Act applies to them only if, as from 2 August 2026, significant changes are made to the design of these AI systems[1973].

17.2.17 Post-Market Monitoring

The EU AI Act requires providers to establish and document a post-market monitoring system in a manner that is proportionate to the nature of the AI technologies and the risks of the high-risk AI system[1974].

The post-market monitoring system must actively and systematically collect, document and analyse relevant data (excluding sensitive operational data of deployers which are law-enforcement authorities) which may be provided by deployers or which may be collected through other sources on the performance of high-risk AI systems throughout their lifetime, and which allow the provider to evaluate continuous compliance of AI systems with the EU AI Act requirements to high-risk AI systems[1975]. Where relevant, post-market monitoring must include an analysis of interaction with other AI systems[1976].

[1972] Article 111(2) EU AI Act.
[1973] *Ibid.*
[1974] Article 72(1) EU AI Act.
[1975] Article 72(2) EU AI Act.
[1976] *Ibid.*

The post-market monitoring system must be based on a post-market monitoring plan[1977]. The post-market monitoring plan forms a part of the technical documentation[1978].

In addition to these requirements, EU AI Act makes a special provision for the following high-risk AI systems covered by the EU harmonisation legislation[1979]:

- machinery[1980];
- toys[1981]
- recreational craft and personal watercraft[1982];
- lifts and safety components for lifts[1983];
- equipment and protective systems intended for use in potentially explosive atmospheres[1984];
- radio equipment[1985];

[1977] Article 72(3) EU AI Act.

[1978] Article 72(3) and Annex IV EU AI Act.

[1979] The applicable harmonisation legislation is listed in Section A of Annex I EU AI Act.

[1980] Machinery covered by Directive 2006/42/EC of the European Parliament and of the Council of 17 May 2006 on machinery, and amending Directive 95/16/EC (OJ L 157, 9.6.2006, p. 24)

[1981] Toys covered by Directive 2009/48/EC of the European Parliament and of the Council of 18 June 2009 on the safety of toys (OJ L 170, 30.6.2009, p. 1)

[1982] Directive 2013/53/EU of 20 November 2013 (OJ L 354, 28.12.2013, p. 90).

[1983] Directive 2014/33/EU of 26 February 2014 (OJ L 96, 29.3.2014, p. 251)

[1984] Directive 2014/34/EU of 26 February 2014 (OJ L 96, 29.3.2014, p. 309).

[1985] Directive 2014/53/EU of 16 April 2014 (OJ L 153, 22.5.2014, p. 62).

- pressure equipment[1986];
- cableway installations[1987];
- personal protective equipment[1988];
- appliances burning gaseous fuels[1989];
- medical devices[1990];
- in vitro diagnostic medical devices[1991];

including high-risk AI systems enabling access to and enjoyment of essential private services and essential public services and benefits[1992] placed on the market or put into service by financial institutions that are subject to requirements under EU financial services law regarding their internal governance, arrangements or processes[1993].

In order to ensure consistency, avoid duplications and minimise additional burdens for the providers of these high-risk AI systems, where a post-market monitoring system and plan are already established under the EU harmonisation legislation, providers must have a choice of integrating the necessary elements of the post-monitoring

---

[1986] Directive 2014/68/EU of 15 May 2014 (OJ L 189, 27.6.2014, p. 164).

[1987] Regulation (EU) 2016/424 of 9 March 2016 (OJ L 81, 31.3.2016, p. 1).

[1988] Regulation (EU) 2016/425 of 9 March 2016 (OJ L 81, 31.3.2016, p. 51).

[1989] Regulation (EU) 2016/426 of 9 March 2016 (OJ L 81, 31.3.2016, p. 99).

[1990] Regulation (EU) 2017/745 of 5 April 2017 (OJ L 117, 5.5.2017, p. 1).

[1991] Regulation (EU) 2017/746 of 5 April 2017 (OJ L 117, 5.5.2017, p. 176).

[1992] Point 5 of Annex III EU AI Act.

[1993] Article 72(4) and Annex I EU AI Act.

plan described above and in the template to be adopted by the Commission into systems and plans already existing under the harmonisation legislation, provided that it achieves an equivalent level of protection[1994].

17.3 Ceasing to be a Provider for the Purposes of the EU AI Act

The EU AI Act envisages that the provider that initially placed the AI system on the market or put it into service may no longer be considered to be a provider of that specific AI system for the purposes of the EU AI Act[1995]. This can be the case where a distributor, importer, deployer or other third-party:

- put their name or trademark on a high-risk AI system already placed on the market or put into service, without prejudice to contractual arrangements stipulating that the obligations are otherwise allocated[1996];
- make a substantial modification to a high-risk AI system that has already been placed on the market or has already been put into service in such a way that it remains a high-risk AI system pursuant to the EU AI Act classification[1997]; and (or)

[1994] Article 72(4) EU AI Act.
[1995] Article 25(2) EU AI Act.
[1996] Article 25(1)(a) EU AI Act.
[1997] Article 25(1)(b) EU AI Act.

- modify the intended purpose of an AI system, including a general-purpose AI system, which has not been classified as high-risk and has already been placed on the market or put into service in such a way that the AI system concerned becomes a high-risk AI system pursuant to the EU AI Act classification[1998].

In these cases the distributor, importer, deployer or other third-party shall be considered to be a provider of a high-risk AI system for the purposes of the EU AI Act and must comply with the provider obligations under the EU AI Act[1999]. At the same time, the initial provider must closely cooperate with new providers and must make available the necessary information and provide the reasonably expected technical access and other assistance that are required for the fulfilment of the obligations set out in the EU AI Act, in particular regarding compliance with the conformity assessment of high-risk AI systems[2000]. But where the initial provider has clearly specified that its AI system is not to be changed into a high-risk AI system and therefore does not fall under the obligation to hand over the documentation, this obligation shall not apply to the initial provider[2001].

[1998] Article 25(1)(c) EU AI Act.
[1999] Article 25(1) EU AI Act.
[2000] Article 25(2) EU AI Act.
[2001] Article 25(2) EU AI Act.

In addition and likewise, in the case of high-risk AI systems that are safety components of the following products covered by the EU harmonisation legislation[2002]:

- machinery[2003];
- toys[2004]
- recreational craft and personal watercraft[2005];
- lifts and safety components for lifts[2006];
- equipment and protective systems intended for use in potentially explosive atmospheres[2007];
- radio equipment[2008];
- pressure equipment[2009];
- cableway installations[2010];

[2002] The EU harmonization legislation referred to in this paragraph is listed in Section A of Annex I EU AI Act.

[2003] Machinery covered by Directive 2006/42/EC of the European Parliament and of the Council of 17 May 2006 on machinery, and amending Directive 95/16/EC (OJ L 157, 9.6.2006, p. 24)

[2004] Toys covered by Directive 2009/48/EC of the European Parliament and of the Council of 18 June 2009 on the safety of toys (OJ L 170, 30.6.2009, p. 1)

[2005] Directive 2013/53/EU of 20 November 2013 (OJ L 354, 28.12.2013, p. 90).

[2006] Directive 2014/33/EU of 26 February 2014 (OJ L 96, 29.3.2014, p. 251)

[2007] Directive 2014/34/EU of 26 February 2014 (OJ L 96, 29.3.2014, p. 309).

[2008] Directive 2014/53/EU of 16 April 2014 (OJ L 153, 22.5.2014, p. 62).

[2009] Directive 2014/68/EU of 15 May 2014 (OJ L 189, 27.6.2014, p. 164).

[2010] Regulation (EU) 2016/424 of 9 March 2016 (OJ L 81, 31.3.2016, p. 1).

- personal protective equipment[2011];
- appliances burning gaseous fuels[2012];
- medical devices[2013];
- in vitro diagnostic medical devices[2014];

the product manufacturer shall be considered to be the provider of the high-risk AI system, and must comply with the provider's obligations under the EU AI Act in either of the following cases[2015]:

- the high-risk AI system is placed on the market together with the product under the name or trademark of the product manufacturer[2016]; and (or)
- the high-risk AI system is put into service under the name or trademark of the product manufacturer after the product has been placed on the market[2017].

Imposing these obligations, the EU AI Act expressly states that they are without prejudice to the need to observe and protect intellectual property rights, confidential business information and trade secrets in accordance with EU and national law[2018].

[2011] Regulation (EU) 2016/425 of 9 March 2016 (OJ L 81, 31.3.2016, p. 51).
[2012] Regulation (EU) 2016/426 of 9 March 2016 (OJ L 81, 31.3.2016, p. 99).
[2013] Regulation (EU) 2017/745 of 5 April 2017 (OJ L 117, 5.5.2017, p. 1).
[2014] Regulation (EU) 2017/746 of 5 April 2017 (OJ L 117, 5.5.2017, p. 176).
[2015] Article 25(3) EU AI Act.
[2016] Article 25(3)(a) EU AI Act.
[2017] Article 25(3)(b) EU AI Act.
[2018] Article 25(4) EU AI Act.

CHAPTER 18. Authorised Representatives of Third-Country High-Risk AI System Providers

The EU AI Act requires providers of high-risk AI systems established in third countries to appoint, by written mandate, an authorised representative established in the EU prior to making their high-risk AI systems available on the EU market[2019] and enable its authorised representative to perform the tasks specified in the mandate[2020].

The authorised representative must perform the tasks specified in the mandate received from the provider[2021] and, upon request, must provide a copy of the mandate to the market surveillance authorities, in one of the official languages of the institutions of the EU, as indicated by the competent authority[2022].

The mandate must empower the authorised representative to carry out the following tasks:

- verify that the EU declaration of conformity[2023] and the technical documentation[2024] have been drawn up and that an appropriate conformity assessment procedure has been carried out by the provider[2025];

2019 Article 22(1) EU AI Act.
2020 Article 22(2) EU AI Act.
2021 Article 22(3) EU AI Act.
2022 *Ibid.*
2023 Article 47 EU AI Act.
2024 Article 11 EU AI Act.
2025 Article 22(3)(a) EU AI Act.

- keep at the disposal of the market surveillance and supervisory authorities[2026], for a period of 10 years after the high-risk AI system has been placed on the market or put into service, the contact details of the provider that appointed the authorised representative, a copy of the EU declaration of conformity[2027], the technical documentation and, if applicable, the certificate issued by the notified body[2028];
- provide a competent authority, upon a reasoned request, with all the information and documentation, necessary to demonstrate conformity of a high-risk AI system to the requirements related to sharing of information on serious incidents[2029], including access to the logs automatically generated by the high-risk AI system[2030], to the extent such logs are under the control of the provider[2031];
- cooperate with competent authorities, upon a reasoned request, in any action the latter take in relation to the high-risk AI system, in particular to reduce and mitigate the risks posed by the high-risk AI system[2032];

[2026] Article 74(10) EU AI Act.

[2027] Article 47 EU AI Act.

[2028] Article 22(3)(b) EU AI Act.

[2029] Requirements to sharing information about serious incidents are addressed in 16.2.15 of this Chapter 16..

[2030] Article 12(1) EU AI Act.

[2031] Article 22(3)(c) EU AI Act.

[2032] Article 22(3)(d) EU AI Act.

- where applicable, comply with the registration obligations of the high-risk AI system[2033] or, if the registration is carried out by the provider, ensure that the name, address and contact details of the authorised representative submitted by the provider for the registration of the high-risk AI system[2034] is correct[2035].

The mandate must also empower the authorised representative to be addressed, in addition to or instead of the provider, by the competent authorities, on all issues related to ensuring compliance with the EU AI Act[2036].

The authorised representative must terminate the mandate if it considers or has a reason to consider the provider to be acting contrary to its obligations under the EU AI Act[2037]. In such a case, it must immediately inform the relevant market surveillance authority, and, where applicable, the relevant notified body, about the termination of the mandate and the reasons for the termination[2038].

Where the market surveillance authority of a Member State finds that no authorised representative has been appointed[2039], it must require the provider to comply within a period it may prescribe. If the non-compliance persists, the market surveillance authority of the Member

[2033] Article 49(1) EU AI Act.
[2034] Point 3 Section A Annex VIII EU AI Act.
[2035] Article 22(3)(e) EU AI Act.
[2036] Article 22(3) EU AI Act.
[2037] Article 22(4) EU AI Act.
[2038] *Ibid.*
[2039] Article 83(1)(f) EU AI Act.

State concerned must take appropriate and proportionate measures to restrict or prohibit the high-risk AI system being made available on the market or to ensure that it is recalled or withdrawn from the market without delay[2040].

[2040] Article 83(2) EU AI Act.

CHAPTER 19. Deployers of AI Systems

Deployers are natural or legal persons, public authorities, agencies, and other bodies using AI systems under their authority except where the AI systems are used in the course of a personal non-professional activity [2041].

The EU AI Act imposes on deployers of AI systems a number of obligations. Some of these obligations apply to all deployers. Others apply only to deployers of high-risk AI systems.

19.1 Obligations of All AI Systems Deployers

The EU AI Act imposes the following obligations on all deployers of AI systems.

19.1.1 AI Literacy Obligation

By 2 February 2025[2042], all deployers must take measures to ensure, to their best extent, a sufficient level of AI literacy of their staff and other persons dealing with the operation and use of AI systems on their behalf, taking into account their technical knowledge, experience, education and training and the context the AI systems are to be used in, and

---

[2041] "Deployer" is defined in Article 3 (4) EU AI Act.
[2042] Article 113 (a) EU AI Act.

considering the persons or groups of persons on whom the AI systems are to be used[2043].

19.2 Obligations of Deployers of High-risk AI Systems

19.2.1 Fundamental Rights Impact Assessment

Effective from 2 August 2026[2044], deployers that are:

- public bodies;
- private entities providing public services; and
- deployers of high-risk AI systems intended to be used for:

-evaluating the creditworthiness of natural persons or establishing their credit score (other than AI systems used for detecting financial fraud); or

-risk assessment and pricing in relation to natural persons in the case of life and health insurance

must assess the impact on fundamental rights of the use of the AI systems intended to be safety components of products or being products covered by EU harmonisation legislation listed in Annex I of the EU AI Act (see the list of

---

[2043] Article 4 EU AI Act.
[2044] Article 113 EU AI Act.

these products in 14.1 in Chapter 14 of this book) and which require a third-party conformity assessment[2045].

A fundamental rights impact assessment is required in respect of these high-risk AI systems (other than a critical infrastructure AI system intended to be used as safety components in the management and operation of critical digital infrastructure, road traffic, or in the supply of water, gas, heating or electricity).

However, the obligations related to classification as high-risk of these AI systems are deferred to 2 August 2027[2046], so fundamental risk impact assessments in respect of these AI systems and products, as a "corresponding obligation", are also deferred to 2 August 2027[2047].

The assessment of the impact on fundamental rights that the use of such system may produce is required prior to the deployment of such high-risk AI system[2048].

The assessment must include[2049]:

- a description of the deployer's processes in which the high-risk AI system will be used in line with its intended purpose;
- a description of the period of time within which, and the frequency with which, each high-risk AI system is intended to be used;

[2045] Article 27(1) EU AI Act.
[2046] Article 113(c) EU AI Act.
[2047] *Ibid.*
[2048] Article 27(1) EU AI Act.
[2049] *Ibid.*

- the categories of natural persons and groups likely to be affected by its use in the specific context;
- the specific risks of harm likely to have an impact on the categories of natural persons or groups of persons likely to be affected by its use in the specific context, taking into account the information given by the provider pursuant to the transparency requirements;
- a description of the implementation of human oversight measures, according to the instructions for use; and
- the measures to be taken in the case of the materialisation of those risks, including the arrangements for internal governance and complaint mechanisms.

The obligation to perform this assessment applies to the first use of the high-risk AI system[2050]. The EU AI Act permits deployers to rely on previously conducted fundamental rights impact assessments or existing impact assessments carried out by provider in similar cases, but requires deployers to update the information if, during the use of the high-risk AI system, the deployer considers that any of the elements of the assessment has changed or is no longer up to date[2051].

Once the fundamental rights impact assessment has been performed, the deployer must notify the market surveillance authority of its results, submitting, as part of

---

[2050] Article 27(2) EU AI Act.
[2051] *Ibid.*

the notification, the filled-out questionnaire in the form to be developed by the AI Office[2052]. For exceptional reasons of public security or the protection of life and health of persons, environmental protection, or the protection of key industrial and infrastructural assets, deployers may be exempt from that obligation to notify[2053].

If any of the obligations related to the fundamental rights impact assessment is already met through the data protection impact assessment, the fundamental rights impact assessment must complement that data protection impact assessment[2054].

19.2.2 Registration in the EU Database

Before putting into service or using an Annex III high-risk AI system[2055] (with the exception of critical infrastructure AI systems), deployers that are public authorities, EU institutions, bodies, offices or agencies or persons acting on their behalf must register themselves, select the system and register its use in the EU database[2056]. These deployers must enter in the EU database the following data[2057]:

2052 Article 27(3) EU AI Act.

2053 *Ibid.*

2054 Article 27(4) EU AI Act.

2055 See 14.1 in Chapter 14 of this book for the list of Annex III AI systems.

2056 Article 49(3) EU AI Act.

2057 Article 71(3) and Section C of Annex VIII EU AI Act.

1. The name, address and contact details of the deployer;

2. The name, address and contact details of the person submitting information on behalf of the deployer;

3. The URL of the entry of the AI system in the EU database by its provider;

4. A summary of the findings of the fundamental rights impact assessment;

5. A summary of the data protection impact assessment[2058], where applicable.

The EU database registration requirement does not apply to high-risk critical infrastructure AI systems intended to be used as safety components in the management and operation of critical digital infrastructure, road traffic, or in the supply of water, gas, heating or electricity[2059]. These high-risk AI systems must be registered at national level[2060].

19.2.3 Compliance with Instructions for Use

Deployers of high-risk AI systems must take appropriate technical and organisational measures to ensure that they use such systems in accordance with the instructions for use accompanying the systems[2061]. This

---

[2058] Article 35 of Regulation (EU) 2016/679, or Article 27 of Directive (EU) 2016/680; Article 26(8) EU AI Act.

[2059] Articles 16(h) and 49(1) EU AI Act.

[2060] Article 49(5) EU AI Act.

[2061] Article 26(1) EU AI Act.

obligation does not prejudice other deployer obligations under EU or national law[2062].

19.2.4 Human Oversight

The EU AI Act requires deployers to assign human oversight of the AI systems to natural persons who have the necessary competence, training and authority, as well as the necessary support[2063]. This obligation does not prejudice other deployer obligations under EU or national law or the deployer's freedom to organise its own resources and activities for the purpose of implementing the human oversight measures indicated by the provider[2064].

19.2.5 Input Data

To the extent the deployer controls the input data, the EU AI Act requires the deployer to ensure that input data is relevant and sufficiently representative in view of the intended purpose of the high-risk AI system[2065].

[2062] Article 26(3) EU AI Act.
[2063] Article 26(2) EU AI Act.
[2064] Article 26(3) EU AI Act.
[2065] Article 26(4) EU AI Act.

19.2.6 Risk Monitoring

The EU AI Act requires deployers to monitor the operation of the high-risk AI system based on the instructions for use and inform the provider[2066], distributor, and the relevant market surveillance authority if the deployer has reason to believe that the use of the high-risk AI system in accordance with the instructions may result in a risk to the health, safety, or fundamental rights of persons[2067]. In such cases the notification must be made without undue delay[2068]. In addition, the deployer must suspend the use of that system[2069].

Where a deployer identifies a serious incident, the deployer must also immediately inform about the incident first the provider, and then the importer or distributor and the relevant market surveillance authorities[2070].

If the deployer cannot reach the provider, the EU AI Act requires the deployer to step into the shoes of the provider as regards reporting the serious incident to the market surveillance authority[2071]. But this obligation does not extend to sensitive operational data of deployers of AI systems which are law enforcement authorities[2072].

[2066] Articles 26(5) and 72 EU AI Act.
[2067] Articles 26(5) and 79(1) EU AI Act.
[2068] *Ibid.*
[2069] *Ibid.*
[2070] Article 26(5) EU AI Act.
[2071] *Ibid.*
[2072] Article 26(5), 73 EU AI Act.

For deployers that are financial institutions subject to requirements regarding their internal governance, arrangements or processes under the EU financial services law, the obligation to monitor the high-risk AI systems is deemed to be fulfilled by complying with the rules on internal governance arrangements, processes and mechanisms pursuant to the relevant financial service law[2073].

19.2.7 Log Keeping

Deployers of high-risk AI systems must keep the logs automatically generated by that high-risk AI system, to the extent such logs are under their control, for a period appropriate to the intended purpose of the high-risk AI system, of at least six months, unless provided otherwise in applicable EU or national law, and in particular - in the EU law on the protection of personal data[2074].

Deployers that are financial institutions subject to requirements regarding their internal governance, arrangements or processes under EU financial services law must maintain the logs as part of the documentation kept pursuant to that law[2075].

[2073] Article 26(5) EU AI Act.
[2074] Article 26(6) EU AI Act.
[2075] *Ibid.*

19.2.8 Notifying Employees

Before putting into service or using a high-risk AI system at the workplace, deployers who are employers must inform employees' representatives and the affected employees that they will be subject to the use of the high-risk AI system[2076]. This information must be provided in accordance with the rules and procedures laid down in the EU and national law and practice for informing employees and their representatives[2077].

19.2.9 Not Using High-Risk AI Systems that are Not Registered in the EU Database

Deployers of high-risk AI systems that are public authorities, or EU institutions, bodies, offices or agencies must comply with the obligations related to the registration of high-risk AI systems[2078]. When such deployer finds that the high-risk AI system that it intends to use has not been registered in the EU database, the deployer may not use that system and must inform the provider or the distributor[2079].

Where applicable, deployers of high-risk AI systems must use the information provided in the

---

[2076] Article 26(7) EU AI Act.
[2077] *Ibid.*
[2078] Articles 26(8) and 49 EU AI Act.
[2079] Articles 26(8) and 71 EU AI Act.

instructions for use[2080] to comply with their obligation to carry out a data protection impact assessment[2081].

19.2.10 Obtain Authorisation to Use and Comply with Reporting Requirements for High-Risk AI System for Post-Remote Biometric Identification

Without prejudice to the EU Law Enforcement Directive[2082] and EU Regulations governing the processing of biometric data[2083], in the framework of an investigation for the targeted search of a person suspected or convicted of having committed a criminal offence, the deployer of a high-risk AI system for post-remote biometric identification must request an authorisation, ex ante, or without undue delay and no later than 48 hours, by a judicial authority or an administrative authority whose decision is binding and subject to judicial review, for the use of that system, except when it is used for the initial identification of a potential suspect based on objective and verifiable facts directly

[2080] The information is listed in 13.2.6 Chapter 12 of this book and in Article 13 EU AI Act.

[2081] Articles 13, 26(9) EU AI Act; Article 35 of Regulation (EU) 2016/679; Article 27 of Directive (EU) 2016/680.

[2082] Directive (EU) 2016/680.

[2083] Regulation (EU) 2016/679.

linked to the offence[2084]. Each use must be limited to what is strictly necessary for the investigation of a specific criminal offence[2085].

If the request for authorisation is rejected, the use of the post-remote biometric identification system linked to the requested authorisation must be stopped with immediate effect and the personal data linked to the use of the high-risk AI system for which the authorisation was requested must be deleted[2086].

In no case such high-risk AI system for post-remote biometric identification may be used for law enforcement purposes in an untargeted way, without any link to a criminal offence, a criminal proceeding, a genuine and present or genuine and foreseeable threat of a criminal offence, or the search for a specific missing person[2087]. In addition, the EU AI Act requires law enforcement authorities to ensure that no decision that produces an adverse legal effect on a person may be taken based solely on the output of such post-remote biometric identification systems[2088].

Without prejudice to the powers conferred by the EU Law Enforcement Directive[2089] on supervisory authorities, regardless of the purpose or deployer, each use

---

[2084] Article 26(10) EU AI Act.

[2085] *Ibid.*

[2086] *Ibid.*

[2087] *Ibid.*

[2088] *Ibid.*

[2089] Directive (EU) 2016/680.

of such high-risk AI systems must be documented in the relevant police file and must be made available to the relevant market surveillance authority and the national data protection authority upon request, excluding sensitive operational data related to law enforcement[2090].

Deployers must submit annual reports to the relevant market surveillance and national data protection authorities on their use of post-remote biometric identification systems, excluding sensitive operational data related to law enforcement[2091]. The reports may be aggregated to cover more than one deployment[2092].

In addition, the EU AI Act permits Member States to introduce, in accordance with EU law, more restrictive laws on the use of post-remote biometric identification systems[2093].

19.2.11 Notifying the Natural Persons Subjected to Use of High-Risk AI Systems

Without prejudice to the transparency obligations of deployers[2094], deployers of Annex III high-risk AI

[2090] Article 26(10) EU AI Act.
[2091] *Ibid.*
[2092] *Ibid.*
[2093] *Ibid.*
[2094] These transparency obligations are in Article 50 EU AI Act.

systems[2095] that make decisions or assist in making decisions related to natural persons must inform the natural persons that they are subject to the use of the high-risk AI system[2096]. However, the use of high-risk AI systems for law enforcement purposes must comply with the EU Law Enforcement Directive[2097].

19.2.12 Cooperation with Competent Authorities

The EU AI Act requires deployers to cooperate with the relevant competent authorities in any action those authorities take in relation to the high-risk AI system in order to implement the EU AI Act[2098].

19.2.13 Transparency Obligations

Emotion Recognition or Biometric Categorisation Systems

The EU AI Act requires deployers of an emotion recognition system or a biometric categorisation system to inform the natural persons exposed to these systems of the operation of the systems and process the personal data in

---

[2095] See 14.1 Chapter 14 of this book for the list of Annex III systems.

[2096] Article 26(11) EU AI Act.

[2097] Article 13 of Directive (EU) 2016/680; Article 26(11) EU AI Act.

[2098] Article 26(12) EU AI Act.

accordance with the applicable EU legislation[2099]. But this obligation does not apply to AI systems used for biometric categorisation and emotion recognition, which are permitted by law to detect, prevent or investigate criminal offences, subject to appropriate safeguards for the rights and freedoms of third parties, and in accordance with EU law[2100].

Deep Fake Image, Audio or Video Generating AI Systems

The EU AI Act requires deployers of AI systems that generate or manipulate image, audio or video content constituting a deep fake, to disclose that the content has been artificially generated or manipulated[2101]. But this obligation does not apply where the use is authorised by law to detect, prevent, investigate or prosecute a criminal offence[2102]. In addition, where the content forms part of an evidently artistic, creative, satirical, fictional or analogous work or programme, this transparency obligation is limited to disclosure of the existence of such generated or manipulated content in an appropriate manner that does not hamper the display or enjoyment of the work[2103].

[2099] Article 50(3) EU AI Act; the EU legislation governing the processing of personal data are Regulations (EU) 2016/679 and (EU) 2018/1725 and Directive (EU) 2016/680.

[2100] Article 50(3) EU AI Act.

[2101] Article 50(4) EU AI Act.

[2102] *Ibid.*

[2103] *Ibid.*

AI systems generating or manipulating text to inform the public on matters of public interest

The EU AI Act requires deployers of an AI system that generates or manipulates text published to inform the public on matters of public interest to disclose that the text has been artificially generated or manipulated[2104]. But this obligation does not apply where the use is authorised by law to detect, prevent, investigate or prosecute criminal offences or where the AI-generated content has undergone a process of human review or editorial control and where a natural or legal person holds editorial responsibility for the publication of the content[2105].

Clear, Distinguishable and Accessible Information

Deployers must provide the information required above to the natural persons concerned in a clear and distinguishable manner at the latest at the time of the first interaction or exposure[2106]. In addition, the EU AI Act requires the information to conform to the applicable accessibility requirements[2107].

2104 *Ibid.*

2105 *Ibid.*

2106 Article 50(5) EU AI Act.

2107 Article 50(5) EU AI Act; the accessibility requirements are those set out in Directives (EU) 2016/2102 and (EU) 2019/882.

Draft Code of Practice on Marking and Labelling of AI-generated Content

To support compliance with these transparency requirements, the AI office has started the process of drafting the Code of Practice on Marking and Labelling of AI-generated Content. The first draft Code was published on 17 December 2025[2108] and the final Code is expected to be published in May-June 2026[2109]. The draft Code is the result of a collaborative effort involving hundreds of participants from industry, academia, and civil society, as well as contributions from Member States[2110].

For deployers, the draft Code focuses on the EU AI Act's obligations that require deployers of generative AI systems to disclose:

- Content that is artificially generated or manipulated, constituting a deep fake (image, audio, or video which resembles existing persons, objects, places, entities or events and would falsely appear to a person to be authentic or truthful); and
- AI generated/manipulated text publications informing the public on matters of public interest, unless the

---

[2108] https://digital-strategy.ec.europa.eu/en/library/first-draft-code-practice-transparency-ai-generated-content

[2109] https://digital-strategy.ec.europa.eu/en/policies/code-practice-ai-generated-content

[2110] Draft Code of Practice on Transparency of AI-generated Content, p.3 https://digital-strategy.ec.europa.eu/en/library/first-draft-code-practice-transparency-ai-generated-content

publication has undergone a process of human review and is subject to editorial responsibility.

The draft Code proposes that deployers adopt the following commitments[2111]:

- Disclose the Origin of AI-Generated and Manipulated Content based on a Common Taxonomy and an Icon

The deployers will use a common taxonomy to support consistent and transparent identification of deep-fake, AI-generated and manipulated content, that provides a harmonised vocabulary and serves as a guidance tool to distinguish content that triggers disclosure obligations. To signal the granularity of the deceitful elements for the natural persons exposed to the content, the deployers will use a common taxonomy for classifying content that qualifies as a deepfake or as AI-generated or manipulated text publications, particularly distinguishing fully AI-generated and AI-assisted content. The deployers will also apply a common icon for deepfakes and AI-generated and manipulated text publications as a method of disclosure and place it in a visible and consistent location appropriate to the context. Until an EU-wide icon is finalised, the deployers may use an interim icon to support consistent disclosure composed of a two-letter acronym referring to

[2111] Draft Code of Practice on Transparency of AI-generated Content, p.3 https://digital-strategy.ec.europa.eu/en/library/first-draft-code-practice-transparency-ai-generated-content

artificial intelligence, which can also be letters referring to the translation into the languages of the Member States. The draft Code also proposes sample icons and requires the icon to be:

- clearly visible at the time of the first exposure;
- placed in a position appropriate to the content format and dissemination context;
- implemented in a way that does not interfere with the enjoyment of artistic, creative, satirical or fictional works; and
- include the two-level taxonomy (fully AI-generated and AI-assisted content).

In addition, the Code commits deployers to support the development of a common interactive EU icon that will be further explored following usability tests and interoperability requirements. The icon should:

- be designed in a way that integrates the possibility for the natural person to distinguish different degrees of deceitful content specified in the taxonomy;
- make it possible, when interacting with it, to get further information of what exactly has been AI-generated or manipulated, in accordance with the machine-readable information provided by the

provider's marking (see 17.2.14 Chapter 17 of this book for the Code's commitments for providers' marking);

- support consistent disclosure composed of a two-letter acronym referring to artificial intelligence, which can also be letters referring to the translation into the languages of the Member States;
- be placed in a fixed position appropriate to the content format and dissemination context;
- be implemented in a way that does not interfere with the enjoyment of artistic, creative, satirical or fictional works; and
- potentially include interactive audio disclosures that could be integrated in audio-only content and for accessibility purposes and comply with applicable accessibility requirements.

➢ Compliance, Training and Monitoring

The deployers will set up, implement, keep up to date a compliance and monitoring documentation (proportionate to the size and resources of the deployer) and cooperation mechanisms with competent authorities. The providers will draw up, keep up to date and implement **internal compliance documentation** that specifies their labelling practice i.e. how they have applied labelling requirements, including the icon, and provide specific examples of how they have used it. The providers will provide appropriate training to personnel involved in the creation, modification, or distribution of content requiring disclosure, covering at least:

- when disclosures are legally required;
- how to apply the taxonomy and icon (when used);
- understanding the specific disclosure practices for artistic and creative work and for the exception for text publications the application of the requirement for human review and editorial responsibility;
- applicable accessibility requirements for disclosures; and
- procedures for correcting missing or incorrect disclosure.

The training should be proportionate to the deployer's size, resources, and the risks associated with the content generated or manipulated by the AI systems used, taking into account its context, the extent of its dissemination and its potential impact.

The deployers will also facilitate the possibility for third party and natural persons to, confidentially and in a secure channel, flag mis-labelled or non-labelled deepfakes and AI-generated and manipulated text of public interest.

Specifically, the deployers will cooperate with market surveillance authorities and other third parties that have an interest in understanding and/or assessing whether content was duly labelled. Other third parties include media regulators, providers of intermediary services, including Very Large Online Platforms and Very Large Online Search Engines as defined in the Digital Services Act, and certified independent fact-checking organisations (e.g. members of EFCSN and IFCN).

The solution should allow for the deployers to document that they labelled consistently and timely and follow up on reported instances of non-compliance, including to facilitate the reporting of unlabelled or mislabelled deepfakes and AI-generated and manipulated text publications across Member States.

Once flagged and assessed as mislabelled or incorrectly non-labelled, the deployer will fix missing or incorrect icons or labels without undue delay.

➢ Ensure accessible disclosure for all natural persons

The deployers will actively support creation, distribution, or oversight of content with appropriate technical and organisational measures, following state-of-the-art accessibility protocols, procedures and technological standards. In particular, this may require visual icons to comply with contrast, size and screen-reader standards, and audio cues to be provided for visually impaired users. The deployers will provide:

- audio descriptions for visual indicators;
- visual/ tactile cues for audio-content only;
- high contrast icons and screen-reader compatibility.

The providers will ensure labels are accessible to screen-readers and available in alternative modalities (e.g., alt-text, metadata) and self-assess the applicable accessibility requirements or use an EU-wide or other standardised icon which has been assessed for conformity with those requirements.

The deployers are encouraged to support the implementation of any available relevant standard, including the harmonised standard ETSI EN 301 549 “Accessibility requirements for ICT products and services”.

➢ Specific measures for deepfake disclosure

The deployers will implement the following measures to correctly classify ‘deep fake’ content and ensure clear, distinguishable and timely disclosure:

The deployers will **set up and implement internal processes to identify deepfake image, audio, video content,** consistently apply the EU AI Act’s definition of “deepfake” and determine whether an applicable exception applies (e.g. law enforcement use) or if the content relates to artistic, creative, satirical and fictional work.

The deployers will take into account the target audience of the content, the specificities of the distribution channels they employ and any other relevant elements.

The deployers will ensure that the deepfake labelling process is not only based on automation but also supported by appropriate human oversight.

The deployers will **disclose deep fake content in a clear and distinguishable manner** at the latest at the time of the first exposure, by applying the following sub-measures for different modalities of content and multimodal content.

- For **real-time deepfake video**, the deployers will display the icon in a non-intrusive way consistently throughout the exposure where feasible and insert a disclaimer at the beginning of exposure that explain that this display content includes deepfake. The disclaimer should be perceivable for an appropriate duration.
- For **non-real-time deepfake video**, the deployers will disclose that the video contains deepfakes with the icon, choosing from the following disclosure options, individually or combined, as appropriate to the context:

• A disclaimer at the beginning of the exposure. In case of an oral disclaimer, the icon needs to appear simultaneously with the audio disclosure.

• Placing the icon consistently throughout the exposure in an appropriate fixed place, ensuring that the disclosure is clearly visible to the natural person without any additional interaction. For online platforms, this entails placing the icon consistently just outside the video frame integrated into the user interface or interface overlay.

• A disclaimer in the credits at the end of the video, always additional to one of the three previous measures.

- For **other multimodal deepfake content**, the deployers will ensure that the multimodal content that contains deepfake is consistently disclosed using the icon and the disclosure is clearly visible to the natural person without any further interaction on their part. Other multimodal content includes the following combinations of static or dynamic content, excluding real-time and non-real-time video:
- image-text-sound;
- text-sound;
- image-sound;
- image-text.

➢ For deepfake **images**, the deployers will place the common icon consistently at any exposure in a fixed place. The icon should be clearly distinguishable and visible, particularly from the image itself, and not be hidden, as in the case of image layers or multiple backgrounds.

- For deepfake **audio-only** content **shorter than 30 seconds** (e.g. commercials/ads), the deployers will include a short audible disclaimer, in plain and simple natural language, of the content disclosing the artificial origin of the deep fake audio at the beginning of the content.

For **longer audio formats** such as podcasts, the deployers will provide repeated audible disclaimers at the beginning and intermediate phases, and at the end of the content.

When a screen is available in the audio-interaction with the user (e.g., car or smartphone display), the deployers will also display the icon at the moment of first exposure of the natural person or upon initial access to the audio content.

In case the EU-wide icon (once available) includes an audio-only solution, this solution could be used instead of the natural language disclaimer.

The deployers will **disclose deep fake content that forms part of evidently artistic, creative, satirical, fictional or analogous work or programmes in an appropriate manner** that does not hamper the display or enjoyment of the work, including its normal exploitation and use, while maintaining the utility and quality of the work and appropriate safeguards for the rights and freedoms of third parties.

The deployers will place the disclosure icon in a non-intrusive position. Non-intrusive positions include the following.

- Real-time or near real-time video: at the latest at the time of the first exposure in the top or bottom corners or for at least five seconds without further warnings throughout exposure;
- Video: the icon should be placed for a timing sufficient to inform the viewer at first exposure without significantly interfering with the experience;
- Other multimodal content: the icon will be displayed at the latest at the time of first exposure, ensuring that the disclosure is clearly visible to the natural person without requiring any further interaction on their part;
- Image: at the latest at the time of the first exposure in an appropriate place with the possibility of integrating it into the image or the background of the image while preserving the ability for the user to discern the icon;
- Audio: When a screen is available, placing the icon in an appropriate place, at the latest at the beginning of exposure, will suffice, without requiring an audible disclaimer at the beginning of the content. When no screen is available, a non-intrusive audible disclaimer should be inserted at the latest at the time of the first exposure. Such

non-intrusive audible disclaimers may include, but are not limited to, a potential EU-wide audible disclaimer using either spoken disclosure (in the same language as the content), rhythmic cues, or sound-based signals.

When content forms part of evidently artistic, creative, satirical, fictional or analogous work or programme, the deployers will apply appropriate safeguards for the rights and freedoms of third parties. Third parties include depicted or simulated persons and a wider audience if the deepfake addresses political or societal sensitive topics. Safeguards include disclaimers of the deceitful element and applicable requirements under other EU and Member States law, in particular to avoid violations of the depicted or simulated persons' privacy, dignity and other fundamental rights and freedoms.

➢ Specific measures for disclosure of AI-Generated or Manipulated Text

The providers will implement the following measures in order to correctly identify all AI-generated or manipulated text published with the purpose of informing the public on matters of public interest, where no human has reviewed the text publication and no natural or legal person has assumed editorial responsibility (hereafter '**AI-generated and manipulated text publications**') and to ensure clear, distinguishable and timely disclosure.

The deployers will set up and implement **internal processes** to correctly identify AI-generated or manipulated text publications in a consistent manner, taking into account the target audience of the content and the specificities of the distribution channels they employ, and to determine whether legal exceptions apply (e.g., law-enforcement use or human review/editorial control with editorial responsibility).

The deployers will ensure that the AI-generated and manipulated text publication labelling process is not only based on automation but also supported by appropriate human oversight.

The deployers will **disclose** the AI-generated and manipulated text publications in a fixed, **clear and distinguishable** manner at the latest at the time of the first exposure.

The deployers will place the icon in a fixed, clear and distinguishable position. This fixed place could be at the top of the text, beside the text, in the colophon or after the closing sentence of the text.

To avoid disclosure of AI-assisted text publications, the deployers will establish internal procedures and maintain minimal documentation demonstrating that the AI-generated or manipulated text publications have undergone **human review or editorial control and** that a natural or legal person has editorial **responsibility**.

The procedures and documentation should be proportionate to the deployer's size and should include at least the following elements:

- identification of the natural or legal person with editorial responsibility (name, role and contact details);
- an overview of the specific organisational and technical measures and human resources allocated to ensure adequate human review or editorial control is performed before publication of the AI-generated and manipulated text publications, including consideration of national specificities where relevant (e.g., linguistic, cultural or context-specific factors that may affect interpretation or impact);
- the date of the review and approval;
- a reference to the final approved version of the content (e.g., file name, URL, or any other internal identifier).

The deployers may optionally record additional information, such as the nature of the review or the type of AI involvement when feasible without creating an administrative burden.

The Appendix to the draft Code provides icon samples and demonstrates the positioning of the icons.

19.2.14 Stepping into the Provider's Shoes and Complying with the Provider's Obligations

The EU AI Act prescribes that a deployer shall be a provider of a high-risk AI system and must comply with the provider obligations in any of the following circumstances:

- they put their name or trademark on a high-risk AI system already placed on the market or put into service, without prejudice to contractual arrangements stipulating that the obligations are otherwise allocated[2112];
- they make a substantial modification to a high-risk AI system that has already been placed on the market or has already been put into service in such a way that it remains a high-risk AI system pursuant to the EU AI Act classification[2113]; and (or)
- they modify the intended purpose of an AI system, including a general-purpose AI system, which has not been classified as high-risk and has already been placed on the market or put into service in such a way that the AI system concerned becomes a high-risk AI system pursuant to the EU AI Act classification[2114].

[2112] Article 25(1)(a) EU AI Act.
[2113] Article 25(1)(b) EU AI Act.
[2114] Article 25(1)(c) EU AI Act.

CHAPTER 20. Importers

The EU AI Act defines an importer as a natural or legal person located or established in the EU that places on the market an AI system that bears the name or trademark of a natural or legal person established in a third country[2115].

20.1 Ensuring Compliance of High-Risk AI Systems

Before placing a high-risk AI system on the market, importers must ensure that the system is compliant with the EU AI Act by verifying that:

- the provider of the high-risk AI system has carried out the conformity assessment[2116];
- the provider has drawn up the technical documentation[2117];
- the system bears the required CE marking and is accompanied by the EU declaration of conformity and instructions for use[2118]; and
- in the case of a non-EU provider, the provider has appointed an authorised representative[2119].

[2115] Article 3 (6) EU AI Act.
[2116] Articles 23(1)(a) and 43 EU AI Act.
[2117] Articles 23(1)(b), 11, and Annex IV EU AI Act.
[2118] Articles 23(1)(c) and 47 EU AI Act.
[2119] Articles 23(1)(d) and 22(1) EU AI Act.

Where an importer has sufficient reasons to believe that a high-risk AI system fails to comply with the requirements of the EU AI Act, or is falsified, or accompanied by falsified documentation, the importer may not place the system on the market until it has been conformed[2120]. In addition, where the high-risk AI system presents a risk to health, safety or fundamental rights of persons, the importer must inform the provider, the authorised representative (in the case of a non-EU provider) and the market surveillance authorities[2121].

20.2 Importer's Details

Importers must indicate their name, registered trade name or registered trademark, and the address at which they can be contacted on the high-risk AI system and on its packaging or its accompanying documentation, where applicable[2122].

20.3 Storage and Transport Compliance

The EU AI Act requires importers to ensure that, while a high-risk AI system is under their responsibility, storage or transport conditions, where applicable, do not

---

[2120] Article 23(2) EU AI Act.
[2121] *Ibid*; Article 79(1) EU AI Act.
[2122] Article 23(3) EU AI Act.

jeopardise its compliance with the requirements of the EU AI Act[2123].

20.4 Record Keeping

The EU AI Act requires importers to keep, for a period of 10 years after the high-risk AI system has been placed on the market or put into service, a copy of the certificate issued by the notified body, where applicable, of the instructions for use, and of the EU declaration of conformity[2124].

20.5 Cooperation with Authorities

The EU AI Act requires importers to provide the relevant competent authorities, upon a reasoned request, with all the necessary information and documentation to demonstrate the conformity of a high-risk AI system with the requirements of the EU AI Act in a language which they can easily understand[2125]. For this purpose, they must also ensure that the technical documentation can be made available to the authorities[2126].

Further, the EU AI Act requires importers to cooperate with the competent authorities in any action the authorities take in relation to a high-risk AI system placed

[2123] Article 23(4) EU AI Act.
[2124] Article 23(5) EU AI Act.
[2125] Article 23(6) EU AI Act.
[2126] *Ibid.*

on the market by the importer, in particular to reduce and mitigate the risks posed by it[2127].

20.6 Stepping into the Provider's Shoes and Complying with the Provider's Obligations

The EU AI Act prescribes that an importer shall be a provider of a high-risk AI system and must comply with the provider obligations under EU AI Act in any of the following circumstances:

- they put their name or trademark on a high-risk AI system already placed on the market or put into service, without prejudice to contractual arrangements stipulating that the obligations are otherwise allocated[2128];
- they make a substantial modification to a high-risk AI system that has already been placed on the market or has already been put into service in such a way that it remains a high-risk AI system pursuant to the EU AI Act classification[2129]; and (or)
- they modify the intended purpose of an AI system, including a general-purpose AI system, which has not been classified as high-risk and has already been placed on the market or put into service in such a way that the

[2127] Article 23(7) EU AI Act.
[2128] Article 25(1)(a) EU AI Act.
[2129] Article 25(1)(b) EU AI Act.

AI system concerned becomes a high-risk AI system pursuant to the EU AI Act classification[2130].

[2130] Article 25(1)(c) EU AI Act.

CHAPTER 21. Distributors

The EU AI Act defines a distributor as a natural or legal person in the supply chain, other than the provider or the importer, that makes an AI system available on the EU market[2131].

21.1 Ensuring Compliance of High-risk AI Systems

Before making a high-risk AI system available on the market, distributors must verify that it bears the required CE marking, that it is accompanied by a copy of the EU declaration of conformity and instructions for use, and that the provider and the importer of that system, as applicable, have complied with their respective obligations as regards the labelling of the high-risk AI system (or, where it is not possible – its packaging) with the provider's and importer's name, registered trade name or trade mark and contact address and that a provider has in place a compliant quality management system[2132].

Where a distributor believes or has a reason to believe, on the basis of the information in its possession, that a high-risk AI system fails to comply with the EU AI Act, it may not make the high-risk AI system available on

[2131] Article 3 (7) EU AI Act.

[2132] Articles 24(1), Article 16 (b) and (c), 23(3) EU AI Act.

the market until the system has been conformed. Furthermore, where the high-risk AI system presents a risk to health, safety or fundamental rights of persons, the distributor must inform the provider or the importer of the system, as applicable[2133]. The EU AI Act does not specify when it is "applicable" to notify the provider and when - the importer. Until this is clarified, the safest approach is to notify both.

Distributors must ensure that, while a high-risk AI system is under their responsibility, storage or transport conditions, where applicable, do not jeopardise the compliance of the system with the EU AI Act[2134].

Likewise, where a distributor has made available on the market a high-risk AI system and believes or has a reason to believe, on the basis of the information in its possession, that the high-risk AI system fails to conform to the EU AI Act, the distributor must take the corrective actions necessary to conform the system, withdraw it or recall it, or ensure that the provider, the importer or any relevant operator, as appropriate, takes those corrective actions[2135]. And, where the high-risk AI system presents a risk to health, safety or fundamental rights of persons, the distributor must immediately inform the provider or importer of the system and the authorities competent for the high-risk AI system concerned, giving details, in particular,

---

[2133] Articles 24(2) and 79(1) EU AI Act.
[2134] Article 24(3) EU AI Act.
[2135] Article 24(4) EU AI Act.

of the non-compliance and of any corrective actions taken[2136].

21.2 Cooperation with Authorities

Upon a reasoned request from a relevant competent authority, distributors of a high-risk AI system must provide that authority with all the information and documentation regarding their actions in respect of a non-compliant high-risk AI systems necessary to demonstrate the conformity of that system with the EU AI Act requirements[2137].

In addition, the EU AI Act requires distributors to cooperate with the relevant competent authorities in any action the authorities take in relation to a high-risk AI system made available on the market by the distributors, in particular to reduce or mitigate the risk posed by it[2138].

21.3 Stepping into the Provider's Shoes and Complying with the Provider's Obligations

The EU AI Act prescribes that a distributor shall be a provider of a high-risk AI system and must comply with the provider obligations under the EU AI Act in any of the following circumstances:

[2136] Articles 24(4) and 79(1) EU AI Act.
[2137] Article 24(5) EU AI Act.
[2138] Article 24(6) EU AI Act.

- they put their name or trademark on a high-risk AI system already placed on the market or put into service, without prejudice to contractual arrangements stipulating that the obligations are otherwise allocated[2139];
- they make a substantial modification to a high-risk AI system that has already been placed on the market or has already been put into service in such a way that it remains a high-risk AI system pursuant to the EU AI Act classification[2140]; and (or)
- they modify the intended purpose of an AI system, including a general-purpose AI system, which has not been classified as high-risk and has already been placed on the market or put into service in such a way that the AI system concerned becomes a high-risk AI system pursuant to the EU AI Act classification[2141].

[2139] Article 25(1)(a) EU AI Act.
[2140] Article 25(1)(b) EU AI Act.
[2141] Article 25(1)(c) EU AI Act.

CHAPTER 22. Product Manufacturers

In the case of high-risk AI systems that are safety components of products covered by the EU harmonisation legislation[2142], the product manufacturer shall be the provider of the high-risk AI system, and must comply with the provider's obligations under the EU AI Act in either of the following cases[2143]:

- the high-risk AI system is placed on the market together with the product under the name or trademark of the product manufacturer[2144]; and (or)
- the high-risk AI system is put into service under the name or trademark of the product manufacturer after the product has been placed on the market[2145].

[2142] The EU harmonization legislation referred to in this paragraph is listed in Section A of Annex I EU AI Act.

[2143] Article 25(3) EU AI Act.

[2144] Article 25(3)(a) EU AI Act.

[2145] Article 25(3)(b) EU AI Act.

PART 5: GENERAL-PURPOSE AI MODELS

CHAPTER 23. What is a General Purpose AI Model?

The EU AI Act defines a general purpose AI model as an AI model, including where such an AI model is trained with a large amount of data using self-supervision at scale, that displays significant generality and is capable of competently performing a wide range of distinct tasks regardless of the way the model is placed on the market and that can be integrated into a variety of downstream systems or applications, except AI models that are used for research, development or prototyping activities before they are placed on the market[2146]. But how can potential providers assess whether their model is general-purpose AI model? The Commission's non-binding Guidelines on the scope of the obligations for general purpose AI models published on 18 July 2025 ("**GPAI Guidelines**")[2147] seek to offer clarity on this question.

An indicative criterion for a model to be considered a general-purpose AI model is that its training compute is greater than 10^{23} floating points ("**FLOP**") and it can generate language, whether in the form of text (including code) or audio (including speech), text-to-image or text-to-

[2146] Article 3 (63) EU AI Act.

[2147] https://digital-strategy.ec.europa.eu/en/library/guidelines-scope-obligations-providers-general-purpose-ai-models-under-ai-act

video[2148] ("**training compute criterion**"). This threshold corresponds to the approximate amount of compute typically used to train a model with one billion parameters on a large amount of data[2149]. While such models may be trained with varying amounts of compute depending on how much data is used, 10^{23} FLOP is typical for models trained on large amounts of data[2150]. Annex to the GPAI Guidelines provides model-based examples of FLOP compute.

If a general-purpose AI model meets the training compute criterion but, exceptionally, does not display significant generality or is not capable of competently performing a wide range of distinct tasks, it is not a general-purpose AI model[2151]. Similarly, if a general-purpose AI model does not meet that criterion but, exceptionally, displays significant generality and is capable of competently performing a wide range of distinct tasks, it is a general-purpose AI model[2152].

Examples:[2153] **GPAI Model**

[2148] Para 2.1(17) GPAI Guidelines.
[2149] Para 2.1(18) GPAI Guidelines.
[2150] *Ibid.*
[2151] Para 2.1(20) GPAI Guidelines.
[2152] *Ibid.*
[2153] *Ibid.*

A model is trained on a broad range of natural language data (i.e. text) curated and scraped from the internet and other sources (as is currently typical for language models) using 10^{24}FLOP. The training compute criterion indicates that the model should be a general-purpose AI model because it can generate text and its training compute is greater than 10^{23} FLOP. Training on a broad range of natural language further indicates that the model should display significant generality and should be capable of competently performing a wide range of distinct tasks. Therefore, the model likely is a general-purpose AI model.

Not GPAI Models:

- A model is trained on natural language data, using 10^{22} FLOP, and is unable to competently perform a wide range of distinct tasks. While the model can generate text, its training compute is not greater than 10^{23} FLOP. Therefore, the training compute criterion indicates that the model should not be a general-purpose AI model. The fact that the model is unable to perform a wide range of distinct tasks confirms that it is not a general-purpose AI model.

- A model is trained specifically for the task of transcribing speech to text, using 10^{24} FLOP. The model can generate text and its training compute is greater than 10^{23} FLOP. Therefore, the training compute criterion indicates that the model should be a general-purpose AI model. However, if the model can only competently perform a narrow set of tasks (transcribing speech), it is not actually a general-purpose AI model.

- A model is trained specifically for the task of generating speech from text, using 10^{24} FLOP. The model can generate speech and its training compute is greater than 10^{23} FLOP. Therefore, the training compute criterion indicates that the model should be a general-purpose AI model. However, if the model can only competently perform a narrow set of tasks (generating speech from text), it is not actually a general-purpose AI model.

- A model is trained specifically for the task of increasing the resolution of images, using 10^{24} FLOP. The model can generate images and its training compute is greater than 10^{23} FLOP. Therefore, the training compute criterion indicates that the model should be a general-purpose AI model. However, if the model can only competently perform a narrow set of tasks (upscaling images), it is not actually a general-purpose AI model.

- A model is trained specifically for the task of filling in damaged or missing parts of images, using 10^{24} FLOP. The model can generate images and its training compute is greater than 10^{23} FLOP. Therefore, the training compute criterion indicates that the model should be a general-purpose AI model. However, if the model can only competently perform a narrow set of tasks (inpainting images), it is not actually a general-purpose AI model.

- A model is trained specifically for playing chess or video games, using 10^{24} FLOP. While the model's training compute is greater than 10^{23} FLOP, if it cannot generate text, speech, text-to-image, and text-to-video, the model should not be a general-purpose AI model. If the model can only competently perform a narrow set of tasks (playing chess or video games), it is not a general-purpose AI model.

- A model is trained specifically for modelling weather patterns or physical systems, using 10^{24} FLOP. While the model's training compute is greater than 10^{23} FLOP, if it cannot generate text, speech, text-to-image, and text-to-video, the model should not be a general-purpose AI model. If the model can only competently perform a narrow set of tasks (modelling weather patterns or physical systems), it is not a general-purpose AI model.

- A model is trained specifically for generating music, based on text prompts including lyrics, using 10^{24} FLOP. The model can generate speech (in the form of song lyrics) and its training compute is greater than 10^{23} FLOP. Therefore, the model should be a general-purpose AI model. However, if the model can only competently perform a narrow set of tasks (generating music based on text prompts including lyrics) it is not actually a general-purpose AI model.

- A model is trained specifically for generating sound effects, using 10^{24} FLOP. It can generate language (speech), but the quality of the content of the speech generated is low (e.g. the content is not consistent over the course of a brief conversation). The model can generate language and its training compute is greater than 10^{23} FLOP. Therefore, the model should be a general-purpose AI model. However, if the model can only competently perform a narrow set of tasks (sound effects) it is not actually a general-purpose AI model.

CHAPTER 24. Classification of General-Purpose AI Models with Systemic Risk

24.1 Classification Criteria for General-Purpose AI models with Systemic Risk

The EU AI Act defines **systemic risk** as a risk that is specific to the high-impact capabilities of general-purpose AI models, having a significant impact on the Union market due to their reach, or due to actual or reasonably foreseeable negative effects on public health, safety, public security, fundamental rights, or the society as a whole, that can be propagated at scale across the value chain[2154].

A general-purpose AI model shall be classified as a general-purpose AI model with systemic risk if it meets any of the following two conditions[2155]:

- it has **high impact capabilities,** i.e. capabilities that math or exceed those recorded in the most advanced models[2156], evaluated on the basis of appropriate technical tools and methodologies, including indicators and benchmarks[2157]; these tools and methodologies are

[2154] Article 3(65) EU AI Act.
[2155] Article 51(1) EU AI Act.
[2156] Article 3(64) EU AI Act.
[2157] Article 51(1)(a) EU AI Act.

to be further specified by the Commission through adoption of delegated acts[2158]; and (or)

- based on a decision of the Commission, ex officio or following a qualified alert from the scientific panel, it has the above capabilities or an equivalent impact having regard to the following criteria[2159]:
    - the number of parameters of the model[2160];
    - the quality or size of the data set, for example measured through tokens[2161];
    - the amount of computation used for training the model, measured in floating point operations or indicated by a combination of other variables such as estimated cost of training, estimated time required for the training, or estimated energy consumption for the training[2162];
    - the input and output modalities of the model, such as text to text (large language models), text to image, multi-modality, and the state of the art thresholds for determining high-impact capabilities for each modality, and the specific type of inputs and outputs (e.g. biological

[2158] Para 2.3.1(28) GPAI Guidelines.
[2159] Article 51(1)(b) and Annex XIII EU AI Act.
[2160] Point (a) Annex XIII EU AI Act.
[2161] Point (b) Annex XIII EU AI Act.
[2162] Point (c) Annex XIII EU AI Act.

sequences)[2163];

- the benchmarks and evaluations of capabilities of the model, including considering the number of tasks without additional training, adaptability to learn new, distinct tasks, its level of autonomy and scalability, the tools it has access to[2164];
- whether it has a high impact on the internal market due to its reach, which shall be presumed when it has been made available to at least 10 000 registered business users established in the EU[2165]; and (or)
- the number of registered end-users[2166].

A general-purpose AI model shall be presumed to have the high impact capabilities when the cumulative amount of computation used for its training measured in floating point operations is greater than 10^{25} [2167].

When a general-purpose AI model meets either of the two conditions above, the model is classified as a

---

[2163] Point (d) Annex XIII EU AI Act.
[2164] Point (e) Annex XIII EU AI Act.
[2165] Point (f) Annex XIII EU AI Act.
[2166] Point (g) Annex XIII EU AI Act.
[2167] Article 51(2) EU AI Act.

general-purpose AI model with systemic risk and its provider must comply with the relevant obligations[2168].

24.2 Classification Procedure for General-Purpose AI Models with Systemic Risk

Where a general-purpose AI model has high impact capabilities evaluated on the basis of appropriate technical tools and methodologies, including indicators and benchmarks, the provider must notify the Commission without delay and in any event within two weeks after that requirement is met or it becomes known that it will be met[2169]. A notification may be required *before* training is complete, if the provider can reasonably foresee that the requirement that leads to the presumption of the model having high-impact capabilities is reasonably likely to be met and providers should proceed as follows:

- if the cumulative amount of computation used for training measured in floating point operations is greater than 10^{25}, the providers should notify the Commission without delay and in any event within two weeks; and
- otherwise providers should closely monitor their actual and expected compute usage over the course of training and throughout the model's entire lifecycle to ensure that they know if and when the cumulative amount of

[2168] Para 2.3.1(27) GPAI Guidelines.
[2169] Articles 52(1) and 51(1)(a) EU AI Act.

training compute has exceeded or will exceed 10^{25} FLOP[2170].

The notification must include the information necessary to "*demonstrate that the relevant requirement*" has been met[2171]. But what is the "relevant requirement"? And what information can demonstrate the compliance? The GPAI Guidelines suggest that these are:

- the amount of compute estimated by the provider that has triggered the requirement to notify, reported in FLOP and with two significant figures (e.g. 2.3x1025 FLOP); and
- a description of the approach used to estimate this amount of compute, including approaches used to make approximations where precise information is not available[2172].

The provider of such general-purpose AI model may present, with its notification, sufficiently substantiated arguments to demonstrate that, exceptionally, although it meets that requirement, the general-purpose AI model does not present, due to its specific characteristics, systemic risks and therefore should not be classified as a general-purpose AI model with systemic risk[2173]. GPAI Guidelines suggest that such an approach would be appropriate where

---

[2170] Para 2.3.2(31) GPAI Guidelines.
[2171] Article 52(1) EU AI Act.
[2172] Para 2.3.2(32) GPAI Guidelines.
[2173] Articles 52(2) and 51(1)(a) EUAI Act.

the notification has been triggered because of the *presumption* that the model has high-impact capabilities (e.g. because the model has met or will meet the 10^{25} FLOP threshold), but the provider deems that the presumption is not well-founded for its model[2174]. Notably, the burden of adducing evidence to rebut the presumption should be borne by the provider[2175].

As part of justifying why the model does not or will not have high-impact capabilities and therefore does not or will not present systemic risks, the provider should include information available at the time of notification about the model's achieved or anticipated capabilities, including in the form of actual or forecasted benchmark results (for example based on scaling analyses)[2176]. To complement this information and allow the Commission to properly assess whether the model does not or will not have high-impact capabilities and therefore does not or will not present systemic risks, GPAI Guidelines "strongly advise"[2177] providers to include any other information that may have a bearing on the model's capabilities, such as model architecture, number of parameters, number of training examples, data curation and processing techniques, training

[2174] Para 2.3.2(34) GPAI Guidelines.
[2175] *Ibid.*
[2176] Para 2.3.2(35) GPAI Guidelines.
[2177] *Ibid.*

techniques, input and output modalities, expected tool use, and expected context length[2178].

Upon receiving a notification with arguments for why the model does not present systemic risks, the Commission will assess the arguments and decide whether to accept or reject them[2179]. Where the Commission concludes that the arguments submitted by the provider are not sufficiently substantiated and the provider was not able to demonstrate that the general-purpose AI model does not present, due to its specific characteristics, systemic risks, the Commission shall reject those arguments, and the general-purpose AI model shall be considered to be a general-purpose AI model with systemic risk[2180]. In the case of rejection, providers will have the right to be heard before the decision is taken (through receiving a draft decision letter in advance), and the right to have access to their file, while respecting the legitimate interests of confidentiality and of professional and business secrecy[2181]. The Commission's decision will include reasons for why the arguments submitted by the provider have been accepted or rejected[2182].

[2178] *Ibid.*

[2179] Para 2.3.2(36) GPAI Guidelines.

[2180] Article 52(3) EU AI Act.

[2181] Para 2.3.2(36) GPAI Guidelines; Article 41 of the Charter of Fundamental Rights of the European Union.

[2182] Para 2.3.2(36) GPAI Guidelines.

GPAI Guidelines suggest that the Commission does not consider the level of capabilities beyond which a model is considered to have 'high-impact capabilities', or equivalently to be amongst the 'most advanced models', to be a *fixed* level of capabilities because capabilities increase and risks evolve[2183].

In its assessment of whether the model is amongst the most advanced models at the time of notification, the Commission will take into account the extent to which the cumulative training compute of the model is indicative of the model being amongst these models[2184]. In this regard, the extent to which the cumulative training compute of the model exceeds the 10^{25} FLOP training compute threshold will also be taken into account[2185]. The Commission will also assess any other elements beyond cumulative training compute which influence the achieved or expected capabilities of the model, including forecasted or achieved benchmark scores[2186].

Where the provider's arguments are aimed at demonstrating that their model does not present systemic risks despite having high-impact capabilities, the Commission considers that arguments that a model does not present systemic risks because of mitigations already or planned to be implemented are not suitable grounds for a

---

[2183] Para 2.3.2(38) GPAI Guidelines.
[2184] Para 2.3.2(39) GPAI Guidelines.
[2185] *Ibid.*
[2186] *Ibid.*

model being excluded from classification as a general-purpose AI model with systemic risk[2187]. In those cases, the model still poses systemic risks which must be continuously assessed and mitigated[2188]. Nevertheless, the provider could use these mitigations as part of the systemic risk mitigation that they must carry out[2189].

If the Commission rejects the arguments, the model will be classified as a general-purpose AI model with systemic risk and the provider must comply with the obligations for providers of general-purpose AI models with systemic risk from the moment when the model meets the condition of having high impact capabilities[2190]. This means that presenting arguments with the notification does not suspend these provider's obligations[2191].

If the Commission accepts the arguments, the general-purpose AI model will no longer be classified as a general-purpose AI model with systemic risk and the provider will not have to comply with the obligations for providers of general-purpose AI models with systemic risk from the moment when the provider is informed of the Commission's acceptance[2192]. But the provider must re-notify the Commission if there is or it becomes known that

---

[2187] Para 2.3.2(40) GPAI Guidelines.
[2188] *Ibid.*
[2189] *Ibid.*
[2190] Para 2.3.2(41) GPAI Guidelines.
[2191] *Ibid.*
[2192] Para 2.3.2(42) GPAI Guidelines.

there will be a substantial change in any of the facts on which the accceptance was based or it becomes known that the acceptance was based on substantially incomplete, incorrect or misleading information[2193]. The provider must provide the Commission with all relevant information, and the Commission may turn its acceptance into a rejection, in which case the model becomes a general-purpose AI model with systemic risk[2194].

If the Commission becomes aware of a general-purpose AI model presenting systemic risks of which it has not been notified, it may decide to designate it as a model with systemic risk[2195]. In this case the Commission may fine the provider for the failure to notify and the provider must comply with the obligations of providers of general-purpose AI models with systemic risks from the time the model met the condition of having high impact capabilities[2196].

The Commission may also designate a general-purpose AI model as presenting systemic risks ex officio or following a qualified alert from the scientific panel, on the basis of the EU AI Act's criteria of general-purpose AI models with systemic risk[2197]. In this case the provider must comply with the obligations of providers of general-

[2193] *Ibid.*
[2194] *Ibid.*
[2195] Article 52(1) EU AI Act.
[2196] Paras 2.3.2(45) and (46) GPAI Guidelines.
[2197] Articles 52(4), 90(1)(a) and Annex III AU AI Act.

purpose AI models with systemic risks from the time the provider is informed of the Commission's decision.

But can a provider contest a Commission's designation of a general-purpose model as having systemic risks? The short answer is yes, but not immediately. At the earliest upon expiry of six months after the Commission's decision, the provider whose model the Commission so designated may submit to the Commission a request specifying objective, detailed and new reasons that have arisen since the Commission's decision[2198]. The Commission shall consider the provider's request and may decide to reassess whether the general-purpose AI model can still be considered to present systemic risks on the basis of the EU AI Act criteria[2199]. Where the Commission, following its reassessment, decides to maintain the designation as a general-purpose AI model with systemic risk, the provider may request a further reassessment at the earliest six months after that decision[2200].

The Commission must ensure that a list of general-purpose AI models with systemic risk is published and shall keep that list up to date, without prejudice to the need to observe and protect intellectual property rights and

[2198] Article 52(5) EU AI Act.
[2199] Article 52(5) EU AI Act.
[2200] Article 52(5) EU AI Act.

confidential business information or trade secrets in accordance with Union and national law[2201].

24.3 Training Compute of General-Purpose AI Models

Annex to the GPAA guidelines provides guidance on how providers may estimate a model's training compute for the purpose of the model's classification as a general-purpose model with systemic risk, describes two widely used approaches that potential providers may use and estimates the training compute for a number of models trained with approximately one billion parameters to illustrate the formulae and justify the threshold that forms part of the indicative criterion for when a model is a general-purpose AI model. Let's look at these closer.

'Training compute' of a general-purpose AI model is either:

- the total amount of compute directly contributing to parameter updates in the model if the model is not a general-purpose AI model with systemic risk; or
- the cumulative amount of compute used to train the model if, and for the purpose of assessing whether, the model is a general-purpose AI model with systemic risk[2202].
-

[2201] Article 52(6) EU AI Act.
[2202] Para A.1(118) Annex to the GPAI Guidelines.

The cumulative amount of computation used for training includes the computation used across the activities and methods that are intended to enhance the capabilities of the model prior to deployment, such as pre-training, synthetic data generation and fine-tuning[2203]. Given the wide variety of such 'activities and methods', and their rapid evolution, it is not feasible to provide a precise and exhaustive list of what should and should not be included[2204]. Instead, the Commission considers that providers should, as a general rule, account for all compute that contributed or will contribute to the model's capabilities[2205]. In particular, any compute directly contributing to parameter updates in the model should be included[2206].

If the model is trained on synthetic data that is not publicly accessible, the forward passes used to generate the data, including discarded data, should be included in the estimation of the cumulative training compute[2207]. For example, if 100 samples were generated and only the top 10 samples were selected for training, the compute used to generate all 100 samples should be counted since the

2203 Recital 111 EU AI Act; para A.1(119) Annex to the GPAI Guidelines.

2204 Para A.1(119) Annex to the GPAI Guidelines.

2205 *Ibid.*

2206 *Ibid.*

2207 Para A.1(120) Annex to the GPAI Guidelines.

compute used to generate all 100 samples was necessary to create the selected 10[2208].

Where a model has been created by combining model weights, for example via model weight merging or model weight averaging, or through integrating pre-existing model weights, for example through weight initialisation, the training compute used to train the combined model weights should be included in the estimation of the cumulative training compute of the model[2209].

By contrast, the following are examples of compute which **need not be included** in the estimation of the cumulative training compute[2210]:

- compute used to generate synthetic data which is publicly accessible, since it may be indistinguishable from other publicly accessible data;
- compute spent on purely diagnostic processes that do not contribute to enhancing model capabilities, such as model evaluations or red-teaming;
- compute whose expenditure contributes to enhancing model capabilities only through lessons learnt by humans, such as compute spent on exploratory research projects that result in more efficient training techniques, or on experiments in synthetic data generation that fail and whose results are discarded;

[2208] *Ibid.*
[2209] Para A.1(121) Annex to the GPAI Guidelines.
[2210] Para A.1(122) Annex to the GPAI Guidelines.

- compute used to train parent model(s) used in distillation (whether or not the parent model coincides with the concerned model);
- compute used to train auxiliary model(s) such as value functions or reward models (whether or not the auxiliary model coincides with the concerned model); and
- recomputation of activations to save memory.

Providers may choose any method to estimate the relevant amount of training compute, so long as the estimated amount is, in the providers' best judgement, accurate within an overall error margin of 30% of the reported estimate[2211]. This is to account for the difficulties providers may face in obtaining precise estimates of their model's cumulative training compute, for example, when estimates are made before training of the model is complete[2212]. Providers are nevertheless expected to document the assumptions made in making their estimations, including the method of estimation, and the associated uncertainties[2213].

Providers may choose to estimate the relevant amount of training compute by tracking **graphics processing unit ('GPU') usage (hardware-based approach)** or by estimating operations directly based on

[2211] Para A.2(123) Annex to the GPAI Guidelines.
[2212] *Ibid.*
[2213] *Ibid.*

the relevant **model's architecture (architecture-based approach)**, as appropriate to what is being estimated[2214]. But regardless of the method of estimation, all operations should be counted equally, independently of floating-point precision[2215].

To estimate training compute using the **hardware-based approach**, the potential provider of a general-purpose AI model or general-purpose AI model with systemic risk should first estimate[2216]:

- the number *N* of GPUs or other hardware units used or expected to be used;
- the total duration of use *L*, achieved or expected (measured in seconds);
- the peak theoretical performance *H* of the GPUs or other hardware units used or expected to be used (measured in FLOP/second), calculated via weighted average if different types of GPUs or hardware units are used with different peak theoretical performances (where the weights are determined by the number of hardware units of each type); and
- the average percentage of GPU utilisation *U* achieved or expected to be achieved for the duration of use.

If all hardware units *N* are used for the entirety of the duration *L*, the corresponding amount of training

[2214] Para A.2(124) Annex to the GPAI Guidelines.
[2215] Para A.2(125) Annex to the GPAI Guidelines.
[2216] Para A.2.1(126) Annex to the GPAI Guidelines.

compute C (measured in FLOP) can then be calculated according to the following formula[2217]:

$$C = N \cdot L \cdot H \cdot U.$$

If different numbers of hardware units are used for different periods of time, the formula above can be applied to each period of time for which a constant number of hardware units is used (provided that the total time matches the total duration of training)[2218]. The resulting estimates can then be summed up to yield the total amount of training compute[2219].

Architecture-based approach consists in directly estimating the number of operations performed based on the relevant model's architecture[2220]. For example, essentially all general-purpose AI models or potentially general-purpose AI models today are based on neural networks that are trained through a succession of forward and backward passes[2221]. For such models, the corresponding amount of training compute C (measured in FLOP) is the product of the number of full passes (one full pass is the combination of a forward and backward pass)

[2217] Para A.2.1(127) Annex to the GPAI Guidelines.
[2218] Para A.2.1(128) Annex to the GPAI Guidelines.
[2219] *Ibid.*
[2220] Para A.2.2(130) Annex to the GPAI Guidelines.
[2221] Para A.2.2(131) Annex to the GPAI Guidelines.

made during training with the total number of operations performed in a full pass, i.e.[2222]:

$$C = \text{Number of forward passes made during training} \cdot \text{number of operations/full pass.}$$

For some dense large[2223] language models based on the transformer architecture, the amount of training compute C may be approximated by the following formula:

$$C \approx 6 \cdot P \cdot D,$$

where P refers to the total number of model parameters and D refers to the total number of training tokens used for training[2224].

The threshold that forms part of the indicative criterion for when a model is a general-purpose AI model has been informed by the estimated amount of compute used in practice to train widely used models with approximately one billion parameters[2225]. The estimated

---

[2222] *Ibid.*

[2223] A model based on a dense transformer architecture should be considered large if its number of parameters is significantly larger than one twelfth of the number of tokens in the input context. This ensures that the contribution to the training compute coming from the context-dependent compute is negligible in comparison to the contribution coming from the non-embedding compute and which equals $6PD$ (Footnote 13 para A.2.2(132) Annex to GPAI Guidelines).

[2224] Para A.2.2(132) Annex to GPAI Guidelines.

[2225] Para A.3(134) Annex to GPAI Guidelines.

compute used to train the investigated models is as follows[2226]:

Model	Billion parameters	Estimated training compute, FLOP
A (language model)	3.8	$7.5 \cdot 10^{22}$
B (image diffusion model)	1	10^{23}
C (language model)	0.6	$1.3 \cdot 10^{23}$
D (language model)	1.5	$1.6 \cdot 10^{23}$
E (language model)	1.7	$3.7 \cdot 10^{23}$
F (language model)	2.5	$1.8 \cdot 10^{23}$
G (language model)	2.6	$1.5 \cdot 10^{23}$
H (language model)	1	$6.5 \cdot 10^{23}$

The training compute values above have been obtained via the following calculations, illustrating the estimation methods[2227]:

Model A. *Architecture-based approach:* Model A is a language model with a transformer decoder architecture and 3.8 billion parameters, trained on 3.3 trillion tokens[2228]:

$C \approx 6 \cdot P \cdot D = 6 \cdot 3.8 \cdot 10^{9} \cdot 3.3 \cdot 10^{12} \approx 7.5 \cdot 10^{22}$ FLOP.

Model B. *Hardware-based approach:* Model B is a diffusion model for image generation. According to its

[2226] Para A.3(135) Annex to GPAI Guidelines.
[2227] Para A.3(136) Annex to GPAI Guidelines.
[2228] Para A.3(137) Annex to GPAI Guidelines.

model card it was trained for a total of 200,000 GPU hours on 40GB A100 GPUs[2229]. This implies a product *NL* of number of GPUs *N* and total training duration of *L* equal to NL= 200,000·3,600 seconds; assuming a peak performance of 300 TFLOP/second and GPU utilisation of 50%, the estimate yields[2230]:

$$C = N \cdot L \cdot H \cdot U \approx 10^{23} \text{ FLOP.}$$

Model C. *Architecture-based approach:* Model C is a language model with a transformer decoder architecture and 600 million parameters, trained on 36 trillion tokens; the estimate yields[2231]:

$$C \approx 6 \cdot P \cdot D = 6 \cdot 0.6 \cdot 10^{9} \cdot 36 \cdot 10^{12} \approx 1.3 \cdot 10^{23} \text{ FLOP.}$$

Model D. *Architecture-based approach:* Model D is a language model with a transformer decoder architecture and 1.54 billion parameters, trained on 18 trillion tokens; the estimate yields[2232]:

$$C \approx 6 \cdot P \cdot D = 6 \cdot 1.54 \cdot 10^{9} \cdot 18 \cdot 10^{12} \approx 1.663 \cdot 10^{23} \text{ FLOP.}$$

Model E. *Architecture-based approach:* Model E is a language model with a transformer decoder architecture

---

[2229] Para A.3(138) Annex to GPAI Guidelines.
[2230] *Ibid.*
[2231] Para A.3(139) Annex to GPAI Guidelines.
[2232] Para A.3(140) Annex to GPAI Guidelines.

and 1.7 billion parameters, trained on 36 trillion tokens; the estimate yields[2233]:

$$C \approx 6 \cdot P \cdot D = 6 \cdot 1.7 \cdot 10^{9} \cdot 36 \cdot 10^{12} \approx 3.7 \cdot 10^{23} \text{ FLOP.}$$

Model F. *Architecture-based approach:* Model F is a language model with a transformer decoder architecture and 2.5 billion parameters, trained on 12 trillion tokens; the estimate yields[2234]:

$$C \approx 6 \cdot P \cdot D = 6 \cdot 2.5 \cdot 10^{9} \cdot 12 \cdot 10^{12} \approx 1.8 \cdot 10^{23} \text{ FLOP.}$$

Model G. *Architecture-based approach:* Model G is a language model with a transformer decoder architecture and 2.6 billion parameters, trained on 61 billion tokens for 164 epochs, i.e. a total of about 10 trillion training tokens; the estimate yields[2235]:

$$C \approx 6 \cdot P \cdot D = 6 \cdot 2.6 \cdot 10^{9} \cdot 10 \cdot 10^{12} \approx 1.5 \cdot 10^{23} \text{ FLOP.}$$

Model H. *Hardware-based approach:* Model H is a language model trained for a total of 370,000 GPU hours on 80GB H100 GPUs. Assuming a peak performance of 989 TFLOP/second and GPU utilisation as previously; the estimate yields[2236]:

$$C = N \cdot L \cdot H \cdot U = 6.5 \cdot 10^{23} \text{ FLOP.}$$

[2233] Para A.3(141) Annex to GPAI Guidelines.
[2234] Para A.3(142) Annex to GPAI Guidelines.
[2235] Para A.3(143) Annex to GPAI Guidelines.
[2236] Para A.3(144) Annex to GPAI Guidelines.

CHAPTER 25. Obligations of Providers of All General-Purpose AI Models

With effect from 2 August 2025[2237], the EU AI Act imposes on all providers of general-purpose AI models a number of obligations.

The EU AI Act defines a **provider of a general-purpose AI model** as a natural or legal person, public authority, agency or other body that develops a general-purpose AI model or that has a general-purpose AI model developed and **places it on the market** under its own name or trademark, whether for payment or free of charge[2238]. The EU AI Act further defines placing on the market of a general-purpose AI model as the **first making available** of a general-purpose AI model on the EU market[2239]. And the EU AI Act defines making available on the market as the **supply** of a general-purpose AI model **for distribution or use on the EU market in the course of a commercial activity,** whether in return **for payment or free of charge**[2240]. The EU AI Act further clarifies that general-purpose AI models may be placed on the market in various ways, including through libraries, application programming interfaces (APIs), as direct download, or as physical

---

[2237] Article 113(b) EU AI Act.
[2238] Article 3 (3) EU AI Act.
[2239] Article 3 (9) EU AI Act.
[2240] Article 3 (10) EU AI Act.

copy[2241]. A person may qualify as a provider and be required to comply with the provider's obligations irrespective of whether it is established or located in the EU or in a third country[2242]. Providers established or located within a third country must appoint an authorised representative established in the EU before placing a model on the EU market[2243].

Examples:

Providers of general-purpose AI models[2244]

- A develops a general-purpose AI model and places it on the market.
- A has a general-purpose AI model developed on its behalf by B and A places that model on the market.
- A develops a general-purpose AI model and uploads it to an online repository hosted by C.
- If a collaborative or a consortium has a general-purpose AI model developed for it by different individuals or organisations and places the model on the market, then usually the coordinator of the collaborative or the consortium is the provider. Alternatively, the collaborative or the consortium

2241 Recital 97 EU AI Act; para 3.1(49) GPAI Guidelines.
2242 Article 2.1(a) EU AI Act.
2243 Article 54 EU AI Act; para 3.1(50) GPAI Guidelines.
2244 Para 3.1.1 GPAI Guidelines.

might be the provider. This must be assessed on a case-by-case basis.

Placing on the market of general-purpose AI models[2245]

- a general-purpose AI model is made available for the first time on the EU market via a software library or package;
- a general-purpose AI model is made available for the first time on the EU market via an application programming interface (API);
- a general-purpose AI model is uploaded for the first time to a public catalogue, hub, or repository for direct download on the EU market;
- a general-purpose AI model is made available for the first time on the EU market as a physical copy;
- a general-purpose AI model is made available for the first time on the market via a cloud computing service;
- a general-purpose AI model is made available for the first time on the EU market by being copied onto a customer's own infrastructure;
- a general-purpose AI model is integrated into a chatbot made available for the first time on the EU market via a web interface;

[2245] Para 3.1.2(53) GPAI Guidelines.

- a general-purpose AI model is integrated into a mobile application made available for the first time on the EU market via app stores;
- a general-purpose AI model is used for internal processes that are essential for providing a product or service to third parties or that affect the rights of natural persons in the EU.

But what if **a general-purpose AI model is integrated into an AI system**? When the provider of a general-purpose AI model integrates an own model into its own AI system that is made available on the market or put into service, the EU AI Act obligations for models should continue to apply in addition to those for AI systems[2246].

Next, an upstream actor may develop a general-purpose AI model and make it available for the first time to a downstream actor. If **the downstream actor is in the EU market**, the model would have been placed on the market and the upstream actor to be the provider of the model and have to comply with the obligations for providers of general-purpose AI models[2247]. The downstream actor integrating the model into an AI system and placing the system on the EU market or putting it into service in the EU may be the provider of the system and has to comply

[2246] Recital 97 EU AI Act; para 3.1.3(56) GPAI Guidelines.
[2247] Para 3.1.3(57) GPAI Guidelines.

with the EU AI Act's requirements and obligations for AI systems[2248].

If a general-purpose AI model is made available for the first time to a **downstream actor outside the EU market**, and the downstream actor integrates the model into an AI system which it places on the EU market or puts into service in the EU, the model should be considered to be placed on the EU market once the system into which it is integrated is placed on the EU market or put into service in the EU[2249]. The upstream actor would be the provider of the model, unless the upstream actor has excluded, clearly and unequivocally, the distribution and use of the model on the EU market, including its integration into AI systems that are intended to be placed on the EU market or put into service in the EU[2250]. If the upstream actor has done this, the downstream actor that integrates the model into a system and places the system on the EU market or puts it into service in the EU would be the provider of the model[2251].

A general-purpose AI model may be modified or fine-tuned into new models[2252]. In particular, downstream actors (distinct from the original provider and not acting on its behalf) may modify a general-purpose AI model (with or

---

[2248] *Ibid.*
[2249] Para 3.1.3(58) GPAI Guidelines.
[2250] Para 3.1.3(59) GPAI Guidelines.
[2251] Article 3(10) EU AI Act; *ibid.*
[2252] Recital 97 EU AI Act; para 3.2(60) GPAI Guidelines.

without integrating it into an AI system)[2253]. Whether it is the original provider or a downstream actor who modifies the general-purpose AI model must be assessed on a case-by-cases basis[2254]. An important factor in this assessment may be who has the control over the model's weights, for example, in case of fine-tuning via API[2255]. The EU AI Act does not specify the conditions under which downstream modifiers should be considered the providers of the modified general-purpose AI models in this scenario[2256]. The Commission deems that it is not necessary for every modification of a general-purpose AI model to lead to the downstream modifier being considered the model's provider[2257]. Instead, the Commission considers a downstream modifier to become the provider of the modified general-purpose AI model only if the modification leads to a significant change in the model's generality, capabilities, or systemic risk[2258]. An indicative criterion for when a downstream modifier is considered to be the provider of a general-purpose AI model is that the training compute used for the modification is greater than a third of the training compute of the original model[2259].

[2253] Para 3.2(60) GPAI Guidelines.
[2254] *Ibid.*
[2255] *Ibid.*
[2256] *Ibid.*
[2257] Para 3.2(61) GPAI Guidelines.
[2258] Para 3.2(62) GPAI Guidelines.
[2259] Para 3.2(63) GPAI Guidelines.

However, if the downstream modifier cannot be expected to know the value of the training compute (for example because it has not been communicated by the provider of the original model) and cannot estimate it then the threshold should be replaced as follows:

- if the original model is a general-purpose AI model with systemic risk, the threshold should be replaced with a third of the threshold for a model being presumed to have high-impact capabilities (i.e. currently 10^{25} FLOP[2260]);
- otherwise, it should be replaced with a third of the threshold for a model being presumed to be a general-purpose AI model (i.e. currently 10^{23} FLOP)[2261].

The threshold is based on the expectation that a model modified with this amount of compute will display a significant change which warrants the downstream modifier being subject to the obligations for providers or general-purpose AI models and potentially of general-purpose AI models with systemic risk:

- the change in model properties may be relevant for the Commission, national competent authorities, or downstream providers, and justifies the downstream modifier being subject to the EU AI Act's transparency obligations[2262];

[2260] Article 51(2) EU AI Act; para 3.2(64) GPAI Guidelines.
[2261] Para 3.2(64) GPAI Guidelines.
[2262] Article 53(1) (a) and (b) EU AI Act.

- a modification that meets the threshold can also be expected to have used a significant amount of data, which may be relevant for the obligations concerned with copyright policy and the public summary of the content used for training; and
- if the original model is a general-purpose AI model with systemic risk, the modified model can be expected to present significantly different systemic risk compared to the original model; in particular, the Commission deems that the original provider cannot reasonably foresee the change in systemic risk posed by such modifications in its systemic risk assessment and mitigation[2263].

The threshold is relative to the amount of compute used to train the original model because the amount of compute used to train a model is typically proportional to the number obtained by multiplying the number of its parameters with the number of its training examples[2264]. Modifications typically involve training the model on some amount of additional data[2265]. This means that more compute is required to perform a modification with a fixed amount of data on large models compared to small models[2266]. In other words, the amount of compute needed to perform a modification on a model is typically

---

[2263] Para 3.2(65) GPAI Guidelines.
[2264] Para 3.2(66) GPAI Guidelines.
[2265] *Ibid.*
[2266] *Ibid.*

proportional to the number of parameters of the model[2267]. This justifies setting a relative threshold for determining when a modification should lead to the downstream modifier becoming a provider[2268]. This approach aims to ensure equal treatment of models regardless of the number of their parameters[2269]. In particular, it should not disincentivise modifying models with fewer parameters, since although the threshold for such models is lower, modifying such models also uses less compute[2270]. Currently few modifications may meet the significant change criterion, but the number of downstream modifiers that become providers of general-purpose AI models may increase over time as the compute used to modify models increases[2271]. The criterion is thus primarily forward-looking, and in line with the risk-based approach of the EU AI Act[2272]. The Commission's approach may change in the future as technology and the market evolve[2273].

In the case of a modification or fine-tuning of a model, the obligations for providers of general-purpose AI models should be limited to that modification or fine-tuning, for example by complementing the already existing technical documentation with information on the

[2267] *Ibid.*
[2268] *Ibid.*
[2269] *Ibid.*
[2270] *Ibid.*
[2271] Para 3.2(67) GPAI Guidelines.
[2272] *Ibid.*
[2273] *Ibid.*

modifications, including new training data sources, as a means to comply with the value chain obligations of the EU AI Act, i.e. the technical documentation[2274] is limited to information on the modification, while the copyright policy[2275] and the summary of the content used for training[2276] are limited to the data used as part of the modification[2277].

If a downstream actor modifies a general-purpose AI model with systemic risk in such a way that they become the provider of the modified model, then the resulting model is presumed to have high-impact capabilities and considered to be a general-purpose AI model with systemic risk[2278]. In this case, the downstream modifier must comply with the obligations for providers of general-purpose AI models with systemic risk and notify the Commission, providing the information necessary to demonstrate that the training compute requirement has been met[2279]. The notification is discussed in detail in 23.2 in Chapter 23 of this book.

[2274] Article 53(1) (a) and (b) EU AI Act.
[2275] Article 53(1)(c) EU AI Act.
[2276] Article 53(1)(d) EU AI Act
[2277] Recital 109 EU AI Act; para 3.2.1(68) GPAI Guidelines.
[2278] Article 51(1)(a) EU AI Act; para 3.2.2(70) GPAI Guidelines.
[2279] Para 3.2.2(71) GPAI Guidelines.

25.1 Technical Documentation

The EU AI Act requires providers of general-purpose AI models (other than providers whose models are not of systemic risk and are eligible for the free and open-source licence exemption detailed in 24.10 of this Chapter 24[2280]) to draw up and keep up-to-date the technical documentation of the model, including its training and testing process and the results of its evaluation, for the purpose of providing it, upon request, to the AI Office and the national competent authorities[2281].

The technical documents must contain, as the minimum, the following information, as appropriate to the size and risk profile of the model[2282]:

- A general description of the general-purpose AI model including:

- the tasks that the model is intended to perform and the type and nature of AI systems in which it can be integrated;
- the acceptable use policies applicable;
- the date of release and methods of distribution;
- the architecture and number of parameters;
- the modality (e.g. text, image) and format of inputs and outputs; and
- the licence.

[2280] Article 53(2) EU AI Act.
[2281] Article 53(1)(a) EU AI Act.
[2282] Article 53(1)(a) and Annex XI EU AI Act.

- A detailed description of the elements of the general-purpose AI model and relevant information of the process for the development, including the following elements:

    - the technical means (e.g. instructions of use, infrastructure, tools) required for the general-purpose AI model to be integrated in AI systems;

    - the design specifications of the model and training process, including training methodologies and techniques, the key design choices including the rationale and assumptions made; what the model is designed to optimise for and the relevance of the different parameters, as applicable;

    - information on the data used for training, testing and validation, where applicable, including the type and provenance of data and curation methodologies (e.g. cleaning, filtering, etc.), the number of data points, their scope and main characteristics; how the data was obtained and selected as well as all other measures to detect the unsuitability of data sources and methods to detect identifiable biases, where applicable;

- the computational resources used to train the model (e.g. number of floating point operations), training time, and other relevant details related to the training;

- known or estimated energy consumption of the model; where the energy consumption of the model is unknown, the energy consumption may be based on information about computational resources used.

- Additional information to be provided by providers of general-purpose AI models with systemic risk:

  - A detailed description of the evaluation strategies, including evaluation results, on the basis of available public evaluation protocols and tools or otherwise of other evaluation methodologies. The evaluation strategies must include evaluation criteria, metrics and the methodology on the identification of limitations.

- Where applicable, a detailed description of the measures put in place for the purpose of conducting internal and/or external adversarial testing (e.g. red teaming), model adaptations, including alignment and fine-tuning.

- Where applicable, a detailed description of the system architecture explaining how software components build or feed into each other and integrate into the overall processing.

25.2 Information and Documentation for Providers of AI Systems Who Intend to Integrate the General-Purpose AI Model into Their AI Systems

The EU AI Act requires providers of general-purpose AI models (other than providers whose models are eligible for the free and open-source licence exemption detailed in 24.10 of this Chapter 24[2283]) to draw up, keep up-to-date and make available information and documentation to providers of AI systems who intend to integrate the general-purpose AI model into their AI systems[2284].

Without prejudice to the need to observe and protect intellectual property rights and confidential business information or trade secrets in accordance with the EU and national law, the information and documentation must:

2283 Article 53(2) EU AI Act.
2284 Article 53(1)(b) EU AI Act.

- enable providers of AI systems to have a good understanding of the capabilities and limitations of the general-purpose AI model and to comply with their EU AI Act obligations[2285]; and
- contain, as a minimum, the following elements[2286]:

- a general description of the general-purpose AI model including:
- the tasks that the model is intended to perform and the type and nature of AI systems into which it can be integrated;
- the acceptable use policies applicable;
- the date of release and methods of distribution;
- how the model interacts, or can be used to interact, with hardware or software that is not part of the model itself, where applicable;
- the versions of relevant software related to the use of the general-purpose AI model, where applicable;
- the architecture and number of parameters;

[2285] Article 53(1)(b)(i) EU AI Act.
[2286] Article 53(1)(b)(ii) and Annex XII EU AI Act.

- the modality (e.g. text, image) and format of inputs and outputs;

- the licence for the model.

- a description of the elements of the model and of the process for its development, including:

- the technical means (e.g. instructions for use, infrastructure, tools) required for the general-purpose AI model to be integrated into AI systems;

- the modality (e.g. text, image, etc.) and format of the inputs and outputs and their maximum size (e.g. context window length, etc.);

- information on the data used for training, testing and validation, where applicable, including the type and provenance of data and curation methodologies.

25.3 Copyright Policy

The EU AI Act requires providers of general-purpose AI models to put in place a policy to comply with EU law on copyright and related rights, and in particular to identify and comply with, including through state-of-the-art technologies, a reservation of rights[2287]. The free open source licence exemption does not apply to this obligation.

25.4 Training Content Summary

The EU AI Act requires providers of general-purpose AI models to draw up and make publicly available a sufficiently detailed summary about the content used for training of the general-purpose AI model, according to the template provided by the AI Office[2288]. The free open source licence exemption does not apply to this obligation.

25.5 Cooperation with the Commission

The EU AI Act requires providers of general-purpose AI models to cooperate as necessary with the Commission and the national competent authorities in the exercise of their competences and powers pursuant to the EU AI Act[2289]. The free open source licence exemption does not apply to this obligation.

[2287] Article 53(1)(c) EU AI Act and Article 4(3) of Directive (EU) 2019/790.

[2288] Article 53(1)(d) EU AI Act. The template and the explanatory notice are available here: https://digital-strategy.ec.europa.eu/en/library/explanatory-notice-and-template-public-summary-training-content-general-purpose-ai-models

[2289] Article 53(3) EU AI Act.

25.6 Compliance with Codes of Practice and Harmonised Standards

Compliance with European harmonised standards grants providers the presumption of conformity to the extent that those standards cover those obligations[2290]. Until a harmonised standard is published, the EU AI Act permits providers of general-purpose AI models to rely on codes of practice adopted under the Act to demonstrate compliance with their EU AI Act obligations[2291].

For providers of general-purpose AI models that adhere to a code of practice that is assessed as adequate, the Commission will focus its enforcement activities on monitoring their adherence to the code of practice[2292]. Providers of general-purpose AI models that sign a code of practice that is assessed as adequate will be transparent about the measures they implement to comply with the EU AI Act[2293]. They will therefore benefit from increased trust from the Commission and other stakeholders[2294].

Providers of general-purpose AI models who do not adhere to an approved code of practice or do not comply with a European harmonised standard must demonstrate alternative adequate means of compliance for assessment

---

[2290] Article 53(4) EU AI Act.
[2291] Articles 53(4) and 56 EU AI Act.
[2292] Para 5.1(94) GPAI Guidelines.
[2293] *Ibid.*
[2294] *Ibid.*

by the Commission[2295]. Such providers are expected to explain how the measures they implement ensure compliance with their obligations under the EU AI Act, for instance by carrying out a gap analysis that compares the measures they have implemented with the measures set out by a code of practice that is assessed as adequate[2296]. They may also be subject to a larger number of requests for information and requests for access to conduct model evaluations throughout the entire model lifecycle because the AI Office will have less of an understanding of how they are ensuring compliance with their obligations under the EU AI Act and will typically need more detailed information, including about modifications made to general-purpose AI models throughout their entire lifecycle[2297].

The free open source licence exemption does not apply to this obligation.

25.7 Making Incumbent General-Purpose Models Compliant

The EU AI Act requires providers of general-purpose AI models that have been placed on the market before 2 August 2025 to take the necessary steps in order to

2295 Article 53(4) EU AI Act.
2296 Para 5.1(95) GPAI Guidelines.
2297 *Ibid.*

comply with the EU AI Act obligations by 2 August 2027[2298].

25.8 Representatives of Third-Country Providers of General-Purpose AI Models

The EU AI Act requires providers established in third countries (other than providers whose models are eligible for the free and open-source licence exemption detailed in 24.10 of this Chapter 24[2299]) prior to placing a general-purpose AI model on the EU market to appoint, by a written mandate, an authorised representative established in the EU[2300] and enable the authorised representative to perform the tasks specified in the mandate[2301].

Likewise, the EU AI Act requires the authorised representatives to perform the tasks specified in the provider's mandate[2302]and provide a copy of the mandate to the AI Office upon request, in one of the official languages of the EU institutions[2303]. The mandate must empower the authorised representative to perform the following tasks[2304]:

2298 Article 111(3) EU AI Act.
2299 Article 53(2) EU AI Act.
2300 Article 54(1) EU AI Act.
2301 Article 54(2) EU AI Act.
2302 Article 54(3) EU AI Act.
2303 *Ibid.*
2304 *Ibid.*

- verify that the technical documentation has been drawn up and the provider has fulfilled all its EU AI Act obligations[2305];
- keep a copy of the technical documentation at the disposal of the AI Office and national competent authorities, for a period of 10 years after the general-purpose AI model has been placed on the market, and the contact details of the provider that appointed the authorised representative[2306];
- provide the AI Office, upon a reasoned request, with all the information and documentation to demonstrate compliance with the provider's obligations[2307];
- cooperate with the AI Office and competent authorities, upon a reasoned request, in any action they take in relation to the general-purpose AI model, including when the model is integrated into AI systems placed on the market or put into service in the EU[2308].

The mandate must also empower the authorised representative to be addressed, in addition to or instead of the provider, by the AI Office or the competent authorities, on all issues related to ensuring compliance with the EU AI Act[2309].

[2305] Article 54(3)(a) EU AI Act.
[2306] Article 54(3)(b) EU AI Act.
[2307] Article 54(3)(c) EU AI Act.
[2308] Article 54(3)(d) EU AI Act.
[2309] Article 54(4) EU AI Act.

If the authorised representative considers or has reason to consider that the provider is acting contrary to its EU AI Act obligations, it must terminate the mandate and immediately inform the AI Office about the termination of the mandate and the reasons for the termination[2310].

25.9 Codes of Practice for Providers of General-Purpose AI Models (Including Those with Systemic Risk)

The EU AI Act set the deadline of 2 May 2025 for the Codes of practice to be ready at the latest by 2 May 2025[2311]. To this end, the Act conferred on the AI Office the powers and imposed the obligations described further.

The EU AI Act requires the AI Office to:

- encourage and facilitate the drawing up of codes of practice at the EU level in order to contribute to the proper application of the EU AI Act, taking into account international approaches[2312];
- as appropriate, also encourage and facilitate the review and adaptation of the codes of practice, in particular in light of emerging standards[2313]; and

---

[2310] Article 54(5) EU AI Act.
[2311] Article 56(9) EU AI Act.
[2312] Article 56(1) EU AI Act.
[2313] Article 56(8) EU AI Act.

- assist in the assessment of available standards[2314].

The EU AI Act further requires the AI Office and the Board to:

- regularly monitor and evaluate the achievement of the objectives of the codes of practice by the participants and their contribution to the proper application of the EU AI Act[2315];
- assess whether the codes of practice cover the obligations of providers of general-purpose AI models (including those with systemic risk)[2316];
- regularly monitor and evaluate the achievement of their objectives[2317];
- publish their assessment of the adequacy of the codes of practice[2318];
- aim to ensure that the codes of practice cover at least the obligations of providers of general-purpose AI models including those with systemic risk, including the following issues[2319]:
    - the means to ensure that the technical documentation of the model, including its training and testing process and the results of its

[2314] Article 56(8) EU AI Act.
[2315] Article 56(6) EU AI Act.
[2316] Article 56(6) EU AI Act.
[2317] Article 56(6) EU AI Act.
[2318] Article 56(6) EU AI Act.
[2319] Article 56(2) EU AI Act.

evaluation[2320] and information and documentation to providers of AI systems who intend to integrate the general-purpose AI model into their AI systems[2321], are kept up to date in light of market and technological developments[2322];

- the adequate level of detail for the summary about the content used for training[2323];
- the identification of the type and nature of the systemic risks at the EU level, including their sources, where appropriate[2324];
- the measures, procedures and modalities for the assessment and management of the systemic risks at the EU level, including the documentation thereof, which shall be proportionate to the risks, take into consideration their severity and probability and take into account the specific challenges of tackling those risks in light of the possible ways in which such risks may emerge and materialise along the AI value chain[2325];

➢ aim to ensure that the codes of practice clearly set out their specific objectives and contain commitments or measures, including key performance indicators as

---

[2320] Article 53(1)(a) EU AI Act.
[2321] Article 53(1)(b) EU AI Act.
[2322] Article 56(2)(a) EU AI Act.
[2323] Article 56(2)(b) EU AI Act.
[2324] Article 56(2)(c) EU AI Act.
[2325] Article 56(2)(d) EU AI Act.

appropriate, to ensure the achievement of those objectives, and that they take due account of the needs and interests of all interested parties, including affected persons, at the EU level[2326]; and

- aim to ensure that participants to the codes of practice report regularly to the AI Office on the implementation of the commitments and the measures taken and their outcomes, including as measured against the key performance indicators as appropriate; key performance indicators and reporting commitments must reflect differences in size and capacity between various participants[2327].

The EU AI Act permits the AI Office to:

- invite all providers of general-purpose AI models and relevant national competent authorities to participate in the drawing-up of codes of practice[2328]. It also permits civil society organisations, industry, academia and other relevant stakeholders, such as downstream providers and independent experts, to support the process[2329].
- invite all providers of general-purpose AI models to adhere to the codes of practice[2330]; for providers of general-purpose AI models not presenting systemic risks this adherence may be limited to the commitments

[2326] Article 56(4) EU AI Act.
[2327] Article 56(5) EU AI Act.
[2328] Article 56(3) EU AI Act.
[2329] Article 56(3) EU AI Act.
[2330] Article 56(7) EU AI Act.

of these providers, unless they declare explicitly their interest to join the full code[2331].

The EU AI Act also permits the Commission to approve a code of practice and give it a general validity within the EU[2332]. So, on 10 July 2025 the Commission approved the Code of Practice for General-Purpose AI Models[2333] ("**GPAI CoP**"). The GPAI CoP is made up of three chapters:

- Transparency Chapter;
- Copyright Chapter; and
- Safety and Security Chapter.

Let's look at them in more detail.

25.9.1 Transparency Chapter

The Transparency Chapter provides for the commitments to:

- draw up and keep up-to-date model documentation with at least all the information specified in the Model Documentation Form provided as a part of the Code. Whilst it's tempting to include the form in this book, it may be updated from time to time, it's page size exceeds the page size of this book, and it's fillable

---

[2331] Article 56(7) EU AI Act.

[2332] Article 56(6) EU AI Act.

[2333] https://digital-strategy.ec.europa.eu/en/news/general-purpose-ai-code-practice-now-available .

version is available for download from the Commission's website here: https://digital-strategy.ec.europa.eu/en/policies/contents-code-gpai ;

- publicly disclose via their website, or via other appropriate means if they do not have a website, contact information for the AI Office and downstream providers to request access to the relevant information contained in the Model Documentation, or other necessary information. In addition, the signatories commit to provide to the AI Office the requested information in its most up-to-date form, within the period specified in the AI Office's request. Likewise, the signatories commit to provide information to downstream providers, subject to the confidentiality safeguards and insofar as such information is necessary to enable them to have a good understanding of the capabilities and limitations of the general-purpose AI model relevant for its integration into the downstream provider's AI system and to enable the downstream provider to comply with its obligations pursuant to the EU AI Act. Signatories will provide such information within a reasonable timeframe, and no later than 14 days of the request, save for exceptional circumstances. Signatories are also encouraged to consider whether the documented information can be disclosed, in whole or in part, to the public to promote public transparency.

- Signatories will ensure that the documented information is controlled for quality and integrity, retained as evidence of compliance with obligations in the EU AI Act, and protected from unintended alterations. In the context of drawing-up, updating, and controlling the quality and security of the information and records, Signatories are encouraged to follow the established protocols and technical standards.

25.9.2 Copyright Chapter

The GPAI CoP's Copyright Chapter commits the signatories to:

- draw up, keep up-to-date and implement a single-document policy to comply with EU law on copyright and related rights for all general-purpose AI models they place on the EU market; assign responsibilities within their organisation for the implementation and overseeing of this policy; and make the summary of the policy publicly available and keep it up-to-date;

- reproduce and extract only lawfully accessible copyright-protected content when crawling the World Wide Web, and to this end:
    - not to circumvent effective technological measures designed to prevent or restrict unauthorised acts in respect of works and other protected subject

matter, in particular by respecting any technological denial or restriction of access imposed by subscription models or paywalls; and

- exclude from their web-crawling websites that make available to the public content and which are, at the time of web-crawling, recognised as persistently and repeatedly infringing copyright and related rights on a commercial scale by courts or public authorities in the European Union and the European Economic Area. For the purpose of compliance with this measure, a dynamic list of hyperlinks to lists of these websites issued by the relevant EU and EEA bodies will be made publicly available on an EU website.

➢ identify and comply with, including through state-of-the-art technologies, machine-readable reservations of rights if they use web-crawlers or have such web-crawlers used on their behalf to scrape or otherwise compile data for the purpose of text and data mining and the training of their general-purpose AI models:

- employ web-crawlers that read and follow instructions expressed in accordance with the Robot Exclusion Protocol (robots.txt); and
- identify and comply with other appropriate machine-readable protocols to express rights

reservations, for example through asset-based or location-based metadata, adopted by international or European standardisation organisations, or are state-of-the-art, including technically implementable, and widely adopted by rightsholders, considering different cultural sectors, and generally agreed through an inclusive process based on bona fide discussions to be facilitated at EU level with the involvement of rightsholders, AI providers and other relevant stakeholders as a more immediate solution, while anticipating the development of standards.

- take appropriate measures to enable affected rightsholders to obtain information about the web crawlers employed, their robots.txt features and other measures that a Signatory adopts to identify and comply with rights reservations at the time of crawling by making public such information and by providing a means for affected rightsholders to be automatically notified when such information is updated (such as by syndicating a web feed).
- Signatories that also provide an online search engine or control such a provider are encouraged to take appropriate measures to ensure that their compliance with a rights reservation in the context of text and data mining activities and the training of general-purpose AI models does not directly

lead to adverse effects on the indexing of the content, domain(s) and/or URL(s), for which a rights reservation has been expressed.

- mitigate the risk that a downstream AI system, into which a general-purpose AI model is integrated, generates output that may infringe rights in works or other subject matter protected by EU law on copyright or related rights:
    - implement appropriate and proportionate technical safeguards to prevent their models from generating outputs that reproduce training content protected by EU law on copyright and related rights in an infringing manner, and
    - prohibit copyright-infringing uses of a model in their acceptable use policy, terms and conditions, or other equivalent documents, or in case of general-purpose AI models released under free and open source licenses to alert users to the prohibition of copyright infringing uses of the model in the documentation accompanying the model without prejudice to the free and open source nature of the license.

- designate a point of contact for electronic communication with affected rightsholders, provide easily accessible information about it, put a mechanism in place to allow affected rightsholders and their authorised representatives to submit, by electronic means, sufficiently precise and adequately substantiated complaints concerning the non-compliance of Signatories with their copyright commitments, and act on complaints in a diligent, non-arbitrary manner and within a reasonable time, unless a complaint is manifestly unfounded or the Signatory has already responded to an identical complaint by the same rightsholder.

25.9.3 Safety and Security Chapter

Safety and Security Chapter is **only relevant for providers of general-purpose AI models with systemic risk and not AI systems** and contains the following commitments:

- create, implement and update a state-of-the-art Safety and Security Framework, taking into account the models they are developing, making available on the market, and/or using;
- identify the systemic risks stemming from the model by following a structured process and develop systemic risk scenarios for each identified risk;
- analyse each identified systemic risk by:
    - gathering model-independent information;
    - conducting model evaluations;

- modelling the systemic risks; and
- estimating the systemic risk while
- conducting post-market monitoring.

➢ specify systemic risk acceptance criteria, determine whether the systemic risks stemming from the model are acceptable, and only proceed with the development, the making available on the market, and/or the use of the model, if the systemic risks stemming from the model are determined to be acceptable;

➢ implement appropriate safety mitigations along the entire model lifecycle;

➢ implement an adequate level of cybersecurity protection for their models and their physical infrastructure along the entire model lifecycle;

➢ report to the AI Office information about their model and their systemic risk assessment and mitigation processes and measures by creating a Safety and Security Model Report before placing a model on the market, keep the Model Report up-to-date, and notify the AI Office of their updated Model Report;

➢ define clear responsibilities for managing the systemic risks stemming from their models across all levels of the organisation allocating appropriate resources to actors who have been assigned responsibilities for managing systemic risk and promoting a healthy risk culture;

- implement appropriate processes and measures for keeping track of, documenting, and reporting to the AI Office and, as applicable, to national competent authorities, without undue delay relevant information about serious incidents along the entire model lifecycle and possible corrective measures to address them, and provide resourcing of such processes and measures appropriate for the severity of the serious incident and the degree of involvement of their model; and
- document the implementation of the GPAI CoP Safety and Security Chapter and publish summarised versions of their Framework and Model Reports.

The above is a high-level summary of the commitments in the Safety and Security Chapter. The Chapter spells out these commitments, provides specific examples, diagrams and an interpretation glossary. As this GPAI CoP Chapter is only relevant for a small number of the most advanced providers, in this book I limit the coverage of the Safety and Security Chapter to the high-level summary, by way of a "taster". The full text of the Safety and Security Chapter will need to be reviewed by a provider thoroughly prior to committing and is available for download on the Commission's website: https://digital-strategy.ec.europa.eu/en/policies/contents-code-gpai .

25.10 Free Open-Source Licence Exemption for General-Purpose AI Models Without Systemic Risk

The EU AI Act exempts providers of general-purpose AI models that are not of systemic risk and are released under a free and open-source licence that allows for the access, usage, modification, and distribution of the model, and whose parameters, including the weights, the information on the model architecture, and the information on model usage, are made publicly available[2334] from the following three obligations:

- to draw up and keep up-to-date the technical documentation (see 25.1 of this Chapter 25 for the particulars of this obligation);
- to draw up, keep up-to-date and make available information and documentation to providers of AI systems who intend to integrate the general-purpose AI model into their AI systems (see 25.2 of this Chapter 25 for the particulars of this obligation); and
- to appoint an authorised representative if the provider is established in a third country (see 25.8 of this Chapter 25 for the particulars of this obligation).

Let's explore in more detail **the conditions for the exemption** to apply.

[2334] Article 53(2) EU AI Act.

A general-purpose AI model must be released under a free and open-source licence that allows for the access, use, modification, and distribution of the model[2335]. '**Licence**' should be understood as the granting of permissions related to the model under specified terms and conditions[2336]. '**Free and open-source**' should be understood as a copyright permission to disseminate the model widely and incentivise further developments[2337]. The licence must allow the model to be openly shared and users to be able to freely access, use, modify and redistribute the model or its modified versions[2338]. If one of these rights (i.e. rights to access, use, modify, and redistribute) is missing, the licence cannot be considered free and open-source under the EU AI Act and the exemption does not apply[2339].

The Commission understands **access** as the right of anyone interested to freely obtain the model without any payment requirements or other restrictions[2340]. However, reasonable safety and security measures, such as user verification processes, may be implemented provided that

---

[2335] Articles 53(2) and 54(6) EU AI Act; para 4.2.1(76) GPAI Guidelines.

[2336] Para 4.2.1(77) GPAI Guidelines.

[2337] *Ibid.*

[2338] Recital 102 EU AI Act; para 4.2.1(78) GPAI Guidelines.

[2339] Para 4.2.1(78) GPAI Guidelines.

[2340] Para 4.2.1(79) GPAI Guidelines.

they do not unfairly discriminate against persons, for example on the basis of their country of origin[2341].

The Commission understands **usage**, in this context, to mean that the licence guarantees that the original provider will not use their intellectual property rights to restrict the use of the model, or charge for its use[2342]. The licence should allow the model to be used without any restrictions besides restrictions ensuring attribution and distribution of the model or derivatives under the same or comparable terms[2343]. These terms could include an obligation triggered when the model is distributed, requiring it to be distributed under the same (or compatible) copyright terms[2344].

The Commission understands **modification** as the right of anyone to freely make alterations to the model without any payment requirements or other restrictions[2345].

The Commission understands **distribution** as the right of those who access, use, or modify the general-purpose AI model to freely distribute it onwards, subject to limited conditions often consisting only of crediting the author(s) and retaining their copyright notice, i.e. attribution[2346]. Therefore, the recipient of the licenced

---

2341 *Ibid.*
2342 Para 4.2.1(80) GPAI Guidelines.
2343 *Ibid.*
2344 *Ibid.*
2345 Para 4.2.1(81) GPAI Guidelines.
2346 Para 4.2.1(82) GPAI Guidelines.

model should be able to modify it and redistribute the resulting derivative work under different licence terms, including closed-source proprietary terms[2347]. Examples of **restrictions that would disqualify a licence** from meeting these criteria include[2348]:

- limitations to non-commercial or research-only use (e.g. 'you may use the model solely for non-commercial, non-revenue generating, research purposes');
- prohibitions on distributing the model or its components (e.g. 'you may use the model, but you may not distribute the model');
- usage restrictions triggered by user scale thresholds (e.g. requiring additional licensing if monthly active users exceed a certain number); and (or)
- requirements to obtain separate commercial licences for specific use cases.

Aside from the rights described above, open-source licences consist of various terms and conditions[2349]. Users can use, modify, and distribute general-purpose AI models under free and open-source licences, in compliance with the terms and conditions of the licence[2350]. These can include crediting the original creators, respecting the terms of distribution, and making any modifications or improvements available under the same or comparable

---

[2347] *Ibid.*
[2348] Para 4.2.1(83) GPAI Guidelines.
[2349] Para 4.2.1(84) GPAI Guidelines.
[2350] *Ibid.*

licence terms[2351]. While the licence must generally permit use for any purpose, licensors may include specific, safety-oriented terms that reasonably restrict usage in applications or domains where such use would pose a significant risk to public safety, security, or fundamental rights[2352]. Such restrictions must be proportionate to the risks being mitigated, and based on objective, non-discriminatory criteria that do not unfairly target specific categories of users or other actors[2353].

The concept of **monetisation** also plays a crucial role in determining whether the exemptions apply to general-purpose AI models[2354]. In order for the exemptions to apply, no monetary compensation should be required in exchange for access, use, modification, and distribution of the AI model[2355]. In this context, monetisation should be understood as not only the provision of the model against a price but also other types of monetisation strategies[2356]. The Commission considers the following scenarios to be **forms of monetisation**[2357]:

- the model is provided under a dual licensing model or a comparable approach that allows free academic use but

[2351] *Ibid.*
[2352] *Ibid.*
[2353] *Ibid.*
[2354] Recital 103 EU AI Act; para 4.2.2(85) GPAI Guidelines.
[2355] Para 4.2.2(85) GPAI Guidelines.
[2356] *Ibid.*
[2357] Para 4.2.2(86) GPAI Guidelines.

requires payment for commercial usage or use over a certain scale.

- technical support and other services that are indistinguishably linked to the model itself or its security, and without which the model would not work or be accessible, provided against payment.
- users must purchase support, training, and maintenance services to access the model.
- the model is exclusively hosted by the provider on its individual hosting platform or website that requires users to pay for access, including when users can freely access the platform or website but are served with paid advertisements.

By contrast, the Commission would **not** consider the following scenarios to be forms of monetisation[2358]:

- The model is provided together with paid services that do not affect the usability or free usage of the model and that are purely optional, e.g. a business model that offers commercial services unrelated to the open-source licence.
- Paid services or support are made available alongside the model, without any purchase obligation, as long as the model's usage and free and open access are guaranteed. Such services or support could include premium versions of the model with advanced features or additional tools, update systems, extensions, or plug-

[2358] Para 4.2.2(88) GPAI Guidelines.

ins that help users work with the open-source model or extend its functionality.

The monetisation aspect is considered absent for transactions between microenterprises[2359].

For the exemption to apply, the model's parameters, including the weights, the information on the model architecture, and the information on model usage must be '**made publicly available**'[2360] in a format, and with a degree of clarity and specificity, that enables access, usage, modification, and distribution of the model[2361]. Information about the model's usage should as a minimum include information about the model's input and output modalities, capabilities, and limitations[2362]. Information about the model's usage should also include the technical means (e.g. instructions for use, infrastructure, tools) required for the model to be integrated into AI systems, which may include the appropriate configuration for the intended use cases, where applicable[2363]. This information ensures that downstream providers of AI systems, developers, and users can use the model for practical applications[2364].

[2359] Para 4.2.2(89) GPAI Guidelines.
[2360] Articles 53(2) and 54(6) EU AI Act.
[2361] Para 4.2.3(91) GPAI Guidelines.
[2362] Para 4.2.3(92) GPAI Guidelines.
[2363] *Ibid.*
[2364] *Ibid.*

CHAPTER 26. Additional Obligations of Providers of General-Purpose AI Models with Systemic Risk

With effect from 2 August 2025[2365], the EU AI Act imposes the following additional obligations on providers of general-purpose AI models with systemic risk[2366]:

- to perform model evaluation in accordance with standardised protocols and tools reflecting the state of the art, including conducting and documenting adversarial testing of the model with a view to identifying and mitigating systemic risks[2367];
- to assess and mitigate possible systemic risks at the EU level, including their sources, that may stem from the development, the placing on the market, or the use of general-purpose AI models with systemic risk[2368];
- to keep track of, document, and report, without undue delay, to the AI Office and, as appropriate, to national competent authorities, relevant information about serious incidents and possible corrective measures to address them[2369]; and

---

[2365] Article 113(b) EU AI Act.
[2366] Article 55(1) EU AI Act.
[2367] Article 55(1)(a) EU AI Act.
[2368] Article 55(1)(b) EU AI Act.
[2369] Article 55(1)(c) EU AI Act.

- to ensure an adequate level of cybersecurity protection for the general-purpose AI model with systemic risk and the physical infrastructure of the model[2370].

The EU AI Act permits providers of general-purpose AI models with systemic risk to rely on codes of practice adopted under the Act within to demonstrate compliance with their obligations until a harmonised standard is published[2371]. Compliance with European harmonised standards grants providers the presumption of conformity to the extent that those standards cover those obligations[2372]. Providers of general-purpose AI models with systemic risks who do not adhere to an approved code of practice or do not comply with a European harmonised standard must demonstrate alternative adequate means of compliance for assessment by the Commission[2373].

The EU AI Act requires any information or documentation obtained from the providers of general-purpose AI models with systemic risk, including trade secrets, to be treated in accordance with the Act's confidentiality obligations[2374].

[2370] Article 55(1)(d) EU AI Act.
[2371] Articles 55(2) and 56 EU AI Act.
[2372] Article 55(2) EU AI Act.
[2373] Article 55(2) EU AI Act.
[2374] Articles 55(3) and 78 EU AI Act.

CHAPTER 27. Enforcement of the obligations of providers of general-purpose AI models

With effect from 2 August 2025, the EU AI Act provides for the exclusive powers of the Commission to supervise and enforce the obligations of providers of general purpose AI models[2375].

In addition, without prejudice to the right to request information from the AI Office[2376], market surveillance authorities may request the Commission to exercise the enforcement powers where that is necessary and proportionate to assist with the fulfilment of their tasks under the EU AI Act[2377].

The Commission recognises that in the months following the entry into application of the obligations for providers of general-purpose AI models on 2 August 2025, providers of general-purpose AI models placed on the market *before* 2 August 2025 may face various challenges to comply with their obligations under the EU AI Act by 2 August 2027[2378]. The AI Office is therefore dedicated to supporting providers in taking the necessary steps to comply with their obligations by 2 August 2027[2379].

[2375] Articles 88(1) and 94 EU AI Act.
[2376] Article 75(3) EU AI Act.
[2377] Article 88(2) EU AI Act.
[2378] Para 5.3(110) GPAI Guidelines.
[2379] *Ibid.*

In particular, providers of general-purpose AI models placed on the market before 2 August 2025 are not required to conduct retraining or unlearning of models, where it is not possible to do this for actions performed in the past, where some of the information about the training data is not available, or where its retrieval would cause the provider disproportionate burden[2380]. Such instances must be clearly disclosed and justified in the copyright policy and in the summary of the content used for training[2381].

The Commission also recognises that in the months following the entry into application of the obligations for providers of general-purpose AI models on 2 August 2025, providers of general-purpose AI models placed on the market *after* 2 August 2025 may need time to adapt their policies and procedures to ensure they are compliant with their obligations under the EU AI Act[2382]. The AI Office is therefore dedicated to supporting providers in taking the necessary steps to comply with their obligations and invites providers to immediately and proactively contact the AI Office to ensure they are taking the right steps to ensure compliance[2383].

[2380] Para 5.3(111) GPAI Guidelines.
[2381] *Ibid.*
[2382] Para 5.3(112) GPAI Guidelines.
[2383] *Ibid.*

In particular, providers who, on 2 August 2025, have trained, are in the process of training, or are planning to train a general-purpose AI model with a view to placing it on the market after 2 August 2025, and who anticipate difficulties in complying with the obligations for providers of general-purpose AI models, especially those with systemic risk, should proactively inform the AI Office regarding how and when they will take the necessary steps to comply with their obligations[2384]. In the specific case where a provider has not placed on the market a general-purpose AI model with systemic risk before 2 August 2025, the Commission will give particular consideration to their challenging situation, in particular to allow a timely placing on the market[2385].

Furthermore, the Commission plans to take into account during enforcement that the ecosystem of external model evaluators is still developing, and that initially the methodologies used by such evaluators may be inconsistent[2386]. The AI Office will monitor the situation and, if necessary, work to set out a common approach for external model evaluators, for instance, by involving the network of evaluators and other subject-matter experts[2387].

[2384] Para 5.3(113) GPAI Guidelines.
[2385] *Ibid.*
[2386] Para 5.3(114) GPAI Guidelines.
[2387] *Ibid.*

Finally, the EU AI Act acknowledges that immediately after 2 August 2025, providers may not be able to fully implement certain measures laid down in a code of practice that is assessed as adequate or alternative adequate measures[2388]. In the first year from 2 August 2025 onwards, the Commission cannot take any enforcement actions because its enforcement powers only enter into application on 2 August 2026[2389]. This lack of enforcement does not put into question the applicability of the provider obligations from 2 August 2025 onwards[2390]. In particular, providers who, on 2 August 2025, have trained, are in the process of training, or are planning on training a general-purpose AI model with systemic risk with a view to placing the model on the market after 2 August 2025, are expected to notify the Commission without delay and in any event within two weeks after 2 August 2025 and to cooperate with the AI Office in view of ensuring full compliance[2391]. From 2 August 2026 onwards, the Commission will enforce with fines compliance with all obligations by providers of general-purpose AI models who are not fully compliant on that date[2392].

[2388] Para 5.3(115) GPAI Guidelines.
[2389] *Ibid.*
[2390] *Ibid*; Article 113(b) EU AI Act.
[2391] Para 5.3(115) GPAI Guidelines.
[2392] *Ibid.*

27.1 Enforcement by AI Office

The AI Office is tasked with supervising, investigating, enforcing, and monitoring the obligations for providers of general-purpose AI models and monitoring compliance of AI systems based on general-purpose AI models with the obligations under the EU AI Act when the providers of the model and of the system are the same[2393].

The AI Office may take the necessary actions to monitor the effective implementation and compliance with the EU AI Act by providers of general-purpose AI models, including their adherence to approved codes of practice[2394]. In doing so, the AI Office will take a collaborative, staged, and proportionate approach and encourages close informal cooperation with providers during the training of their general-purpose AI models to facilitate compliance and ensure timely market placement, in particular for providers of general-purpose AI models with systemic risk[2395]. The AI Office expects proactive reporting by providers of general-purpose AI models with systemic risk, whether as part of commitments under a code of practice or as part of alternative means of demonstrating compliance[2396]. The AI Office also expects providers to collaborate and actively

---

[2393] Articles 75(1), 88, and 89 EU AI Act; para 5.2(101) GPAI Guidelines.

[2394] Article 89(1) EU AI Act.

[2395] Para 5.2(102) GPAI Guidelines.

[2396] *Ibid.*

engage with the AI Office at the later stages of potential formal proceedings conducted in line with the AI Office's powers under the EU AI Act[2397].

As regards the obligation to keep track of, document, and report relevant information about 'serious incidents', the AI Office considers that this obligation covers serious cybersecurity breaches related to the model or its physical infrastructure, including the (self-) exfiltration of model parameters and cyberattacks[2398]. Apart from this, the AI Office considers a 'serious incident' in the context of general-purpose AI models as any incident or malfunctioning of a general-purpose AI model that directly or indirectly leads to any of the events listed in the corresponding definition of a serious incident for AI systems[2399].

In assessing compliance, including with respect to measures related to cybersecurity, accountability, and governance processes, the AI Office may take into account whether the provider has implemented relevant technical standards, in particular, if available, the harmonised standards published in the *Official Journal of the European Union*[2400].

The AI Office is tasked with monitoring whether providers of general-purpose AI models effectively comply

---

[2397] *Ibid.*
[2398] Para 5.2(103) GPAI Guidelines.
[2399] *Ibid.*
[2400] Para 5.2(104) GPAI Guidelines.

with their obligations under the EU AI Act, including adherence to codes of practice[2401]. Downstream providers have the right to lodge a complaint with the AI office alleging an infringement of the AI Act by providers of general-purpose AI models[2402]. The complaint must be duly reasoned and indicate at least:

- the point of contact of the provider of the general-purpose AI model concerned[2403];
- a description of the relevant facts, the provisions of the EU AI Act concerned, and the reason why the downstream provider considers that the provider of the general-purpose AI model concerned infringed the EU AI Act[2404]; and
- any other information that the downstream provider that sent the request considers relevant, including, where appropriate, information gathered on its own initiative[2405].

[2401] Para 5.2(105) GPAI Guidelines.
[2402] Article 89(2) EU AI Act.
[2403] Article 89(2)(a) EU AI Act.
[2404] Article 89(2)(b) EU AI Act.
[2405] Article 89(2)(c) EU AI Act.

27.2 Alerts of Systemic Risks by the Scientific Panel

The scientific panel may provide a qualified alert to the AI Office where it has reasons to suspect that a general-purpose AI model:

- poses a specific identifiable risk at the EU level[2406]; or
- meets the conditions to be classified as a general-purpose AI model with systemic risk[2407].

The alert must be duly reasoned and indicate at least:

- the point of contact of the provider of the general-purpose AI model with systemic risk concerned[2408];
- a description of the relevant facts and the reasons for the alert by the scientific panel[2409];
- any other information that the scientific panel considers to be relevant, including, where appropriate, information gathered on its own initiative[2410].

Upon receiving such alert, the Commission, through the AI Office and after having informed the Board, may exercise its powers for the purpose of assessing the

---

[2406] Article 90(1)(a) EU AI Act.
[2407] Article 90(1)(b) EU AI Act.
[2408] Article 90(3)(a) EU AI Act.
[2409] Article 90(3)(b) EU AI Act.
[2410] Article 90(3)(c) EU AI Act.

matter[2411]. The AI Office must inform the Board of any measure the Commission or the AI Office takes[2412].

27.3 Power to request documentation and information

The Commission may request the provider of the general-purpose AI model concerned to provide the documentation or any additional information that is necessary to assess the provider's compliance with the EU AI Act[2413].

Before sending the request for information, the AI Office may initiate a structured dialogue with the provider of the general-purpose AI model[2414].

Upon a duly substantiated request from the scientific panel, the Commission may issue a request for information to a provider of a general-purpose AI model, where the access to information is necessary and proportionate for the fulfilment of the tasks of the scientific panel[2415]. The request for information shall state:

- the legal basis and the purpose of the request;
- what information is required;

[2411] Article 90(2) EU AI Act.
[2412] *Ibid.*
[2413] Article 91(1) EU AI Act.
[2414] Article 91(2) EU AI Act.
[2415] Article 91(3) EU AI Act.

- the period within which the information is to be provided; and
- the fines for supplying incorrect, incomplete or misleading information[2416].

The provider of the general-purpose AI model, or its representative must provide the requested information[2417]. In the case of legal persons, companies or firms, or where the provider has no legal personality, the persons authorised to represent them by law or by their statutes must provide the requested information on behalf of the provider of the general-purpose AI model[2418]. Lawyers duly authorised to act may provide information on behalf of their clients but the clients shall remain fully responsible if the information provided is incomplete, incorrect or misleading[2419].

27.4 Power to conduct evaluations

The AI Office, after consulting the Board, may conduct evaluations of the general-purpose AI model:

- to assess compliance of the provider with obligations under the EU AI Act, where the information gathered is insufficient[2420]; or

---

[2416] Article 91(4) EU AI Act.
[2417] Article 91(5) EU AI Act.
[2418] Article 91(5) EU AI Act.
[2419] *Ibid.*
[2420] Article 92(1)(a) EU AI Act.

- to investigate systemic risks at the EU level of general-purpose AI models with systemic risk, in particular following an alert from the scientific panel[2421].

The Commission may decide to appoint independent experts to carry out evaluations on its behalf, including from the scientific panel[2422].

The Commission may request access to the general-purpose AI model concerned through APIs or further appropriate technical means and tools, including source code[2423]. The request for access must state the legal basis, the purpose and reasons of the request and set the period within which the access is to be provided, and the fines for failure to provide access[2424].

The provider of the general-purpose AI model or its representative must provide the information requested[2425]. In the case of legal persons, companies or firms, or where the provider has no legal personality, the persons authorised to represent them by law or by their statutes must provide the access requested on behalf of the provider of the general-purpose AI model[2426].

The Commission shall adopt implementing acts setting out the detailed arrangements and the conditions for

---

[2421] *Ibid.*
[2422] Article 92(2) EU AI Act.
[2423] Article 92(3) EU AI Act.
[2424] Article 92(4) EU AI Act.
[2425] Article 92(5) EU AI Act.
[2426] *Ibid.*

the evaluations, including the detailed arrangements for involving independent experts, and the procedure for their selection[2427].

Prior to requesting access to the general-purpose AI model, the AI Office may initiate a structured dialogue with the provider of the general-purpose AI model to gather more information on the internal testing of the model, internal safeguards for preventing systemic risks, and other internal procedures and measures the provider has taken to mitigate such risks[2428].

27.5 Power to request measures

Where necessary and appropriate, the Commission may request providers to:

- take appropriate measures to comply with the obligations[2429];
- implement mitigation measures, where the evaluation has given rise to serious and substantiated concern of a systemic risk at the EU level[2430]; and(or)
- restrict the making available on the market, withdraw or recall the model[2431].

Before a measure is requested, the AI Office may initiate a structured dialogue with the provider of the

---

[2427] Article 92(6) EU AI Act.
[2428] Article 92(7) EU AI Act.
[2429] Article 93(1)(a) EU AI Act.
[2430] Article 93(1)(b) EU AI Act.
[2431] Article 93(1)(c) EU AI Act.

general-purpose AI model[2432]. If, during the structured dialogue, the provider of the general-purpose AI model with systemic risk offers commitments to implement mitigation measures to address a systemic risk at the EU level, the Commission may, by its decision, make the commitments binding and declare that there are no further grounds for action[2433].

[2432] Article 93(2) EU AI Act.
[2433] Article 93(3) EU AI Act.

PART 6: AI REGULATORY SANDBOXES AND TESTING IN REAL WORLD CONDITIONS

CHAPTER 28. What are AI Regulatory Sandboxes?

An AI regulatory sandbox is a controlled framework set up by a competent authority which offers providers or prospective providers of AI systems the possibility to develop, train, validate and test, where appropriate in real-world conditions, an innovative AI system, pursuant to a sandbox plan for a limited time under regulatory supervision[2434]. A sandbox plan is a document agreed between the participating provider and the competent authority describing the objectives, conditions, timeframe, methodology and requirements for the activities carried out within the sandbox[2435].

The EU AI Act requires the EU Member States to ensure that their competent authorities establish at least one AI regulatory sandbox at national level, to be operational by 2 August 2026[2436] and that the competent authorities allocate sufficient resources to comply with this obligation effectively and in a timely manner[2437]. The sandbox may also be established jointly with the competent authorities of other EU Member States[2438], and, where appropriate,

---

[2434] Article 3 (55) EU AI Act.
[2435] Article 3 (54) EU AI Act.
[2436] Article 57(1) EU AI Act.
[2437] Article 57(4) EU AI Act.
[2438] Article 57(1) EU AI Act.

national competent authorities must cooperate with other relevant authorities and may allow for the involvement of other actors within the AI ecosystem[2439]. The obligation to establish the AI regulatory sandboxes may also be fulfilled by participating in an existing sandbox in so far as that participation provides an equivalent level of national coverage for the participating EU Member States[2440].

28.1 The Regulatory Framework for AI Regulatory Sandboxes

The EU AI Act provisions for AI regulatory sandboxes do not affect other regulatory sandboxes established under EU or national law[2441]. The EU AI Act requires EU Member States to ensure an appropriate level of cooperation between the authorities supervising those other sandboxes and the national competent authorities[2442].

The Commission may provide technical support, advice and tools for the establishment and operation of AI regulatory sandboxes[2443].

Additional AI regulatory sandboxes at regional or local level, or established jointly with the competent

---

[2439] Article 57(4) EU AI Act.
[2440] Article 57(1) EU AI Act.
[2441] Article 57(4) EU AI Act.
[2442] *Ibid.*
[2443] Article 57(1) EU AI Act.

authorities of other Member States may also be established[2444].

The European Data Protection Supervisor may also establish an AI regulatory sandbox for EU institutions, bodies, offices and agencies, and may exercise the roles and the tasks of national competent authorities[2445].

The AI regulatory sandboxes must provide for a controlled environment that fosters innovation and facilitates the development, training, testing and validation of innovative AI systems for a limited time before their being placed on the market or put into service pursuant to a specific sandbox plan agreed between the providers or prospective providers and the competent authority[2446]. The sandboxes may include supervised testing in real world conditions[2447].

Competent authorities must provide, as appropriate, guidance, supervision and support within the AI regulatory sandbox with a view to identifying risks, in particular to fundamental rights, health and safety, testing, mitigation measures, and their effectiveness in relation to the obligations and requirements of the EU AI Act and, where relevant, other EU and national law supervised within the sandbox[2448].

[2444] Article 57(2) EU AI Act.
[2445] Article 57(3) EU AI Act.
[2446] Article 57(5) EU AI Act.
[2447] *Ibid.*
[2448] Article 57(6) EU AI Act.

Competent authorities must also provide providers and prospective providers participating in the AI regulatory sandbox with guidance on regulatory expectations and how to fulfil the requirements and obligations under the EU AI Act[2449].

Upon request of the provider or prospective provider of the AI system, the competent authority must provide a written proof of the activities successfully carried out in the sandbox and an exit report detailing the activities carried out in the sandbox and the related results and learning outcomes[2450]. Providers may use this documentation to demonstrate their compliance with the EU AI Act through the conformity assessment process or relevant market surveillance activities[2451]. In this regard, the exit reports and the written proof provided by the national competent authority shall be taken positively into account by market surveillance authorities and notified bodies, with a view to accelerating conformity assessment procedures to a reasonable extent[2452].

Subject to the confidentiality requirements of the EU AI Act, and with the agreement of the provider or prospective provider, the Commission and the Board may access the exit reports and shall take them into account, as appropriate, when exercising their tasks under the EU AI

[2449] Article 57(7) EU AI Act.
[2450] *Ibid.*
[2451] *Ibid.*
[2452] *Ibid.*

Act[2453]. If both the provider or prospective provider and the national competent authority explicitly agree, the exit report may be made publicly available through the single information platform[2454].

The establishment of AI regulatory sandboxes must aim to contribute to the following objectives[2455]:

- improving legal certainty to achieve regulatory compliance with the EU AI Act or, where relevant, other applicable EU and national law[2456];
- supporting the sharing of best practices through cooperation with the authorities involved in the AI regulatory sandbox[2457];
- fostering innovation and competitiveness and facilitating the development of an AI ecosystem[2458];
- contributing to evidence-based regulatory learning[2459]; and
- facilitating and accelerating access to the EU market for AI systems, in particular when provided by SMEs, including start-ups[2460].

The EU AI Act requires national competent authorities to ensure that, to the extent the innovative AI

[2453] Article 57(8) EU AI Act.
[2454] *Ibid.*
[2455] Article 57(9) EU AI Act.
[2456] Article 57(9)(a) EU AI Act.
[2457] Article 57(9)(b) EU AI Act.
[2458] Article 57(9)(c) EU AI Act.
[2459] Article 57(9)(d) EU AI Act.
[2460] Article 57(9)(e) EU AI Act.

systems involve the processing of personal data or otherwise fall under the supervisory remit of other national authorities or competent authorities providing or supporting access to data, the national data protection authorities and those other national or competent authorities are associated with the operation of the AI regulatory sandbox and involved in the supervision of those aspects to the extent of their respective tasks and powers[2461].

The EU AI Act expressly provides that AI regulatory sandboxes shall not affect the supervisory or corrective powers of the competent authorities supervising the sandboxes, including at regional or local level[2462]. Any significant risks to health and safety and fundamental rights identified during the development and testing of such AI systems must result in an adequate mitigation[2463]. National competent authorities shall have the power to temporarily or permanently suspend the testing process, or the participation in the sandbox if no effective mitigation is possible, and inform the AI Office of such decision[2464]. National competent authorities shall exercise their supervisory powers within the limits of the relevant law, using their discretionary powers when implementing legal provisions in respect of a specific AI regulatory sandbox

---

2461 Article 57(10) EU AI Act.
2462 Article 57(11) EU AI Act.
2463 *Ibid.*
2464 *Ibid.*

project, with the objective of supporting innovation in AI in the EU[2465].

Providers and prospective providers participating in the AI regulatory sandbox shall remain liable under applicable EU and national liability law for any damage inflicted on third parties as a result of the experimentation taking place in the sandbox[2466]. However, provided that the prospective providers observe the specific plan and the terms and conditions for their participation and follow in good faith the guidance given by the national competent authority, no administrative fines shall be imposed by the authorities for these infringements[2467]. Where other competent authorities responsible for other EU and national law were actively involved in the supervision of the AI system in the sandbox and provided guidance for compliance, no administrative fines shall be imposed[2468].

The AI regulatory sandboxes shall be designed and implemented in such a way that, where relevant, they facilitate cross-border cooperation between national competent authorities[2469].

National competent authorities must coordinate their activities and cooperate within the framework of the

---

[2465] Article 57(11) EU AI Act.
[2466] Article 57(12) EU AI Act.
[2467] *Ibid.*
[2468] *Ibid.*
[2469] Article 57(13) EU AI Act.

Board[2470], must inform the AI Office and the Board of the establishment of a sandbox, and may ask them for support and guidance[2471]. The AI Office must make publicly available a list of planned and existing sandboxes and keep it up to date in order to encourage more interaction in the AI regulatory sandboxes and cross-border cooperation[2472].

The EU AI Act requires national competent authorities to submit annual reports to the AI Office and to the Board, from one year after the establishment of the AI regulatory sandbox and every year thereafter until its termination, and a final report[2473]. The reports must provide information on the progress and results of the implementation of those sandboxes, including best practices, incidents, lessons learnt and recommendations on their setup and, where relevant, on the application and possible revision of the EU AI Act, including its delegated and implementing acts, and on the application of other EU law supervised by the competent authorities within the sandbox[2474]. The national competent authorities must make those annual reports or abstracts available to the public, online[2475]. The Commission must, where appropriate, take

[2470] Article 57(14) EU AI Act.
[2471] Article 57(15) EU AI Act.
[2472] *Ibid.*
[2473] Article 57(16) EU AI Act.
[2474] *Ibid.*
[2475] *Ibid.*

the annual reports into account when exercising its tasks under the EU AI Act[2476].

The EU AI Act requires the Commission to develop a single and dedicated interface containing all relevant information related to AI regulatory sandboxes to allow stakeholders to interact with AI regulatory sandboxes and to raise enquiries with competent authorities, and to seek non-binding guidance on the conformity of innovative products, services, business models embedding AI technologies[2477]. The Commission must proactively coordinate with national competent authorities, where relevant[2478].

In order to avoid fragmentation across the EU, the Commission is required to adopt implementing acts specifying the detailed arrangements for the establishment, development, implementation, operation and supervision of the AI regulatory sandboxes, stating common principles on the following issues[2479]:

- eligibility and selection criteria for participation in the AI regulatory sandbox[2480];
- procedures for the application, participation, monitoring, exiting from and termination of the AI

[2476] Article 57(16) EU AI Act.
[2477] Articles 57(17) and 62(1)(c) EU AI Act.
[2478] Article 57(16) EU AI Act.
[2479] Articles 58(1) and 98(2) EU AI Act.
[2480] Article 58(1)(a) EU AI Act.

regulatory sandbox, including the sandbox plan and the exit report[2481]; and

- the terms and conditions applicable to the participants[2482].

These implementing acts must ensure[2483]:

- that AI regulatory sandboxes are open to any applying provider or prospective provider of an AI system who fulfils eligibility and selection criteria, which shall be transparent and fair, and that national competent authorities inform applicants of their decision within three months of the application[2484];
- that AI regulatory sandboxes allow broad and equal access and keep up with demand for participation; providers and prospective providers may also submit applications in partnerships with deployers and other relevant third parties[2485];
- that the detailed arrangements for, and conditions concerning AI regulatory sandboxes support, to the best extent possible, flexibility for national competent authorities to establish and operate their AI regulatory sandboxes[2486];
- that access to the AI regulatory sandboxes is free of charge for SMEs, including start-ups, without prejudice

---

[2481] Article 58(1)(b) EU AI Act.
[2482] Article 58(1)(c) EU AI Act.
[2483] Article 58(2) EU AI Act.
[2484] Article 58(2)(a) EU AI Act.
[2485] Article 58(2)(b) EU AI Act.
[2486] Article 58(2)(c) EU AI Act.

to exceptional costs that national competent authorities may recover in a fair and proportionate manner[2487];

- that they facilitate providers and prospective providers, by means of the learning outcomes of the AI regulatory sandboxes, in complying with conformity assessment obligations and the voluntary application of the codes of conduct[2488];
- that AI regulatory sandboxes facilitate the involvement of other relevant actors within the AI ecosystem, such as notified bodies and standardisation organisations, SMEs, including start-ups, enterprises, innovators, testing and experimentation facilities, research and experimentation labs and European Digital Innovation Hubs, centres of excellence, individual researchers, in order to allow and facilitate cooperation with the public and private sectors[2489];
- that procedures, processes and administrative requirements for application, selection, participation and exiting the AI regulatory sandbox are simple, easily intelligible, and clearly communicated in order to facilitate the participation of SMEs, including start-ups, with limited legal and administrative capacities and are streamlined across the EU, in order to avoid fragmentation and that participation in an AI regulatory

---

[2487] Article 58(2)(d) EU AI Act.
[2488] Article 58(2)(e) EU AI Act.
[2489] Article 58(2)(f) EU AI Act.

sandbox established by an EU Member State, or by the European Data Protection Supervisor is mutually and uniformly recognised and carries the same legal effects across the EU[2490];

- that participation in the AI regulatory sandbox is limited to a period that is appropriate to the complexity and scale of the project and that may be extended by the national competent authority[2491]; and
- that AI regulatory sandboxes facilitate the development of tools and infrastructure for testing, benchmarking, assessing and explaining dimensions of AI systems relevant for regulatory learning, such as accuracy, robustness and cybersecurity, as well as measures to mitigate risks to fundamental rights and society at large[2492].

Prospective providers in the AI regulatory sandboxes, in particular SMEs and start-ups, must be directed, where relevant, to pre-deployment services such as guidance on the implementation of the EU AI Act, to other value-adding services such as help with standardisation documents and certification, testing and experimentation facilities, European Digital Innovation Hubs and centres of excellence[2493].

[2490] Article 58(2)(g) EU AI Act.
[2491] Article 58(2)(h) EU AI Act.
[2492] Article 58(2)(i) EU AI Act.
[2493] Article 58(3) EU AI Act.

Where national competent authorities consider authorising testing in real world conditions supervised within the framework of an AI regulatory sandbox, they must specifically agree the terms and conditions of such testing and, in particular, the appropriate safeguards with the participants, with a view to protecting fundamental rights, health and safety[2494]. Where appropriate, they must cooperate with other national competent authorities with a view to ensuring consistent practices across the EU[2495].

28.2 Processing of Personal Data in the AI Regulatory Sandbox

In the AI regulatory sandbox, personal data lawfully collected for other purposes may be processed solely for the purpose of developing, training and testing certain AI systems in the sandbox when all of the following conditions are met[2496]:

- the AI systems must be developed for safeguarding substantial public interest by a public authority or another natural or legal person and in one or more of the following areas[2497]:
  - public safety and public health, including disease

[2494] Article 58(4) EU AI Act.
[2495] *Ibid.*
[2496] Article 59(1) EU AI Act.
[2497] Article 59(1)(a) EU AI Act.

detection, diagnosis prevention, control and treatment and improvement of health care systems[2498];

- a high level of protection and improvement of the quality of the environment, protection of biodiversity, protection against pollution, green transition measures, climate change mitigation and adaptation measures[2499];
- energy sustainability[2500];
- safety and resilience of transport systems and mobility, critical infrastructure and networks[2501]; and (or)
- efficiency and quality of public administration and public services[2502];

➢ the data processed are necessary for complying with one or more of the requirements for high-risk AI systems[2503] where those requirements cannot effectively be fulfilled by processing anonymised, synthetic or other non-personal data[2504];

2498 Article 59(1)(a)(i) EU AI Act.
2499 Article 59(1)(a)(ii) EU AI Act.
2500 Article 59(1)(a)(iii) EU AI Act.
2501 Article 59(1)(a)(iv) EU AI Act.
2502 Article 59(1)(a)(iv) EU AI Act.
2503 The requirements to high-risk AI systems are set out in Chapter III, Section 2 EU AI Act.
2504 Article 59(1)(b) EU AI Act.

- there are effective monitoring mechanisms to identify if any high risks to the rights and freedoms of the data subjects[2505], may arise during the sandbox experimentation, as well as response mechanisms to promptly mitigate those risks and, where necessary, stop the processing[2506];
- any personal data to be processed in the context of the sandbox are in a functionally separate, isolated and protected data processing environment under the control of the prospective provider and only authorised persons have access to those data[2507];
- providers can further share the originally collected data only in accordance with EU data protection law; any personal data created in the sandbox cannot be shared outside the sandbox[2508];
- any processing of personal data in the context of the sandbox neither leads to measures or decisions affecting the data subjects nor does it affect the application of their rights laid down in EU law on the protection of personal data[2509];
- any personal data processed in the context of the sandbox are protected by means of appropriate

---

[2505] The rights and freedoms of the data subjects are set out in Article 35 of Regulation (EU) 2016/679 and in Article 39 of Regulation (EU) 2018/1725.

[2506] Article 59(1)(c) EU AI Act.

[2507] Article 59(1)(d) EU AI Act.

[2508] Article 59(1)(e) EU AI Act.

[2509] Article 59(1)(f) EU AI Act.

technical and organisational measures and deleted once the participation in the sandbox has terminated or the personal data has reached the end of its retention period[2510];

- the logs of the processing of personal data in the context of the sandbox are kept for the duration of the participation in the sandbox, unless provided otherwise by EU or national law[2511];
- a complete and detailed description of the process and rationale behind the training, testing and validation of the AI system is kept together with the testing results as part of the technical documentation of high-risk AI systems[2512];
- a short summary of the AI project developed in the sandbox, its objectives and expected results is published on the website of the competent authorities; this obligation shall not cover sensitive operational data in relation to the activities of law enforcement, border control, immigration or asylum authorities[2513].

These requirements for processing of personal data are without prejudice to EU and national law which excludes processing of personal data for other purposes than those explicitly mentioned in that law, as well as to EU or national law laying down the basis for the processing of

[2510] Article 59(1)(g) EU AI Act.
[2511] Article 59(1)(h) EU AI Act.
[2512] Article 59(1)(i) and Annex IV EU AI Act.
[2513] Article 59(1)(j) EU AI Act.

personal data which is necessary for the purpose of developing, testing or training of innovative AI systems or any other legal basis, in compliance with EU law on the protection of personal data[2514].

The processing of personal data in AI regulatory sandboxes for the purposes of the prevention, investigation, detection or prosecution of criminal offences or the execution of criminal penalties, including safeguarding against and preventing threats to public security, under the control and responsibility of law enforcement authorities, must be based on a specific EU or national law and subject to the above cumulative conditions[2515].

[2514] Article 59(3) EU AI Act.
[2515] Article 59(2) EU AI Act.

CHAPTER 29. Testing of High-risk AI Systems in Real World Conditions Outside AI Regulatory Sandboxes

Providers or prospective providers of high-risk AI systems in the areas of biometrics, critical infrastructure, education and vocational training, employment, essential private and public services, law enforcement, migration, and administration of justice[2516] may test these high-risk AI systems in real world conditions outside AI regulatory sandboxes at any time before the placing on the market or the putting into service of the AI system on their own or in partnership with one or more deployers or prospective deployers[2517].

All of the requirements set out below must be met for the providers or prospective providers to conduct the testing in real world conditions.

29.1 Regulatory Compliance

The testing must comply with the requirements of the EU AI Act to testing in real world conditions, the real-world testing plan whose particulars shall be specified by

---

[2516] Article 60(1) EU AI Act. The full list of these high-risk AI systems is set out in Annex III EU AI Act.

[2517] Articles 60(1) and 60 (2) EU AI Act.

the Commission in the implementing acts[2518], and EU AI Act prohibitions for the use of high-risk AI systems[2519].

In addition, the testing must be without prejudice to EU or national law on the testing in real world conditions of high-risk AI systems related to products covered by EU harmonisation legislation[2520] and to any ethical review required by EU or national law[2521].

29.2 Approval of the Testing and of the Real-World Testing Plan

The provider or prospective provider must have drawn up a real-world testing plan and submitted it to the market surveillance authority in the EU Member State where the testing in real world conditions is to be conducted[2522].

In addition, the market surveillance authority in the EU Member State where the testing in real world conditions is to be conducted must have approved the testing in real world conditions and the real-world testing plan[2523]. Where the market surveillance authority has not provided an answer within 30 days, the testing in real world

---

[2518] The implementing acts must be adopted in accordance with the examination procedure referred to in Article 98(2) EU AI Act.

[2519] Article 60(1) EU AI Act.

[2520] The EU harmonization legislation is listed in listed in Annex I EU AI Act.

[2521] Article 60(3) EU AI Act.

[2522] Article 60(4)(a) EU AI Act.

[2523] Article 60(4)(b) EU AI Act.

conditions and the real-world testing plan shall be understood to have been approved[2524]. Where national law does not provide for a tacit approval, the testing in real world conditions shall remain subject to an authorisation[2525];

29.3 Registration of the Testing in Real World Conditions

With the exception of providers or prospective providers of high-risk AI systems in the areas of biometrics, law enforcement, migration, asylum and border control management[2526], and high-risk AI systems in the area of critical infrastructure[2527], the provider or prospective provider must register the testing in real world conditions with the following information[2528]:

- the EU-wide unique single identification number;
- the name and contact details of the provider or prospective provider and of the deployers involved in the testing in real world conditions;

[2524] Article 60(4)(b) EU AI Act.

[2525] *Ibid.*

[2526] Article 60(4) (c) and points 1, 6 and 7 of Annex III. It is unclear from the drafting of Article 60(4)(c) whether all high risk AI systems in the area of biometrics are excluded, or only those in the areas of law enforcement, migration, asylum and border control management.

[2527] Articles 60(4)(c), 71(4), and point 2 of Annex III EU AI Act.

[2528] Article 60(4)(c) and Annex IX EU AI Act.

- a brief description of the AI system, its intended purpose, and other information necessary for the identification of the system;
- a summary of the main characteristics of the plan for testing in real world conditions; and
- information on the suspension or termination of the testing in real world conditions.

The provider or prospective provider of high-risk AI systems in the areas of biometrics, law enforcement, migration, asylum and border control management[2529], must register the testing in real-world conditions in the secure non-public section of the EU database[2530], with a Union-wide unique single identification number and with the information specified in that database[2531].

The provider or prospective provider of high-risk AI systems of critical infrastructure must register the testing in real-world conditions at the national level[2532]. The EU AI Act offers no further particulars of such registration.

[2529] Article 60(4) (c) and points 1, 6 and 7 of Annex III. It is unclear from the drafting of Article 60(4)(c) whether this requirement applies to all high risk AI systems in the area of biometrics, or only to those in the areas of law enforcement, migration, asylum and border control management.

[2530] Article 49(4)(d) EU AI Act.

[2531] Article 60(4)(c) EU AI Act.

[2532] Articles 60(4)(c), 49(5) and point 2 of Annex III EU AI Act.

29.4 Provider's EU Nexus

The provider or prospective provider conducting the testing in real world conditions must be established in the EU or appointed a legal representative established in the EU[2533].

29.5 Third-Country Data Transfer

Data collected and processed for the purpose of the testing in real world conditions may be transferred to third countries only provided that appropriate and applicable safeguards under EU law are implemented[2534].

29.6 Duration of Testing in Real-World Conditions

The testing in real world conditions shall not last longer than necessary to achieve its objectives and in any case not longer than six months, which may be extended for an additional period of six months, subject to prior notification by the provider or prospective provider to the market surveillance authority, accompanied by an explanation of the need for such an extension[2535].

[2533] Article 60(4)(d) EU AI Act.
[2534] Article 60(4)(e) EU AI Act.
[2535] Article 60(4)(f) EU AI Act.

29.7 Protection of Vulnerable Persons

The subjects of the testing in real world conditions who are persons belonging to vulnerable groups due to their age or disability, must be appropriately protected[2536].

29.8 Testing in Cooperation with Deployers

Where a provider or prospective provider organises the testing in real world conditions in cooperation with one or more deployers or prospective deployers, the latter must be informed in advance of all aspects of the testing that are relevant to their decision to participate, and given the relevant instructions for use of the AI system[2537].

In addition, the provider or prospective provider and the deployer or prospective deployer must conclude an agreement specifying their roles and responsibilities with a view to ensuring compliance with the provisions for testing in real world conditions under the EU AI Act and under other applicable EU and national law[2538].

29.9 Informed Consent

The subjects of the testing in real world conditions must have given freely their informed consent prior to their participation in such testing and after having been duly

---

[2536] Article 60(4)(g) EU AI Act.

[2537] The requirements to the instructions are set out in Article 13 EU AI Act.

[2538] Article 60(4)(h) EU AI Act.

informed with concise, clear, relevant, and understandable information regarding[2539]:

- the nature and objectives of the testing in real world conditions and the possible inconvenience that may be linked to their participation[2540];
- the conditions under which the testing in real world conditions is to be conducted, including the expected duration of the subject or subjects' participation[2541];
- their rights, and the guarantees regarding their participation, in particular their right to refuse to participate in, and the right to withdraw from, testing in real world conditions at any time without any resulting detriment and without having to provide any justification[2542];
- the arrangements for requesting the reversal or the disregarding of the predictions, recommendations or decisions of the AI system[2543]; and
- the EU-wide unique single identification number of the testing in real world conditions and the contact details of the provider or its legal representative from whom further information can be obtained[2544].

[2539] Articles 60(4)(i) and 61(1) EU AI Act.
[2540] Article 61(1)(a) EU AI Act.
[2541] Article 61(1)(b) EU AI Act.
[2542] Article 61(1)(c) EU AI Act.
[2543] Article 61(1)(d) EU AI Act.
[2544] Articles Article 60(4)(c) and 61(1)(e) EU AI Act.

The informed consent must be dated and documented and a copy must be given to the subjects of testing or their legal representative[2545].

In the case of law enforcement, where the seeking of informed consent would prevent the AI system from being tested, the testing itself and the outcome of the testing in the real world conditions may not have any negative effect on the subjects, and their personal data must be deleted after the test is performed[2546]. Any subjects of the testing in real world conditions, or their legally designated representative, as appropriate, may, without any resulting detriment and without having to provide any justification, withdraw from the testing at any time by revoking their informed consent and may request the immediate and permanent deletion of their personal data[2547]. The withdrawal of the informed consent shall not affect the activities already carried out[2548].

29.10 Oversight of Testing in Real World Conditions

The testing in real world conditions must be effectively overseen by the provider or prospective provider, and by deployers or prospective deployers

[2545] Article 61(2) Eu AI Act.
[2546] Article 60(4)(i) EU AI Act.
[2547] Article 60(5) EU AI Act.
[2548] *Ibid.*

through persons who are suitably qualified in the relevant field and have the necessary capacity, training and authority to perform their tasks[2549].

29.11 Reversal of the AI System's Predictions, Recommendations and Decisions

The EU AI Act requires that predictions, recommendations or decisions of the AI system must be capable of being effectively reversed and disregarded[2550].

29.12 Reporting of Serious Incidents, Mitigation Measures, Suspension and Termination of Testing and Recall of the AI System

The provider or prospective provider must report to the national market surveillance authority any serious incident identified in the course of the testing in real world conditions and adopt immediate mitigation measures[2551].

Failing the immediate mitigation measures, the provider of prospective provider must suspend the testing in real world conditions until such mitigation takes place, or otherwise terminate it[2552].

[2549] Article 60(4)(j) EU AI Act.
[2550] Article 60(4)(k) EU AI Act.
[2551] Article 60(7) EU AI Act.
[2552] *Ibid.*

The provider or prospective provider must establish a procedure for the prompt recall of the AI system upon such termination of the testing in real world conditions[2553].

29.13 Notice of Suspension or Termination and Final Outcomes

Providers or prospective providers must notify the national market surveillance authority in the Member State where the testing in real world conditions is to be conducted of the suspension or termination of the testing in real world conditions and of the final outcomes[2554].

29.14 Liability

The provider or prospective provider shall be liable under applicable EU and national liability law for any damage caused in the course of their testing in real world conditions[2555].

[2553] Article 60(7) EU AI Act.
[2554] Article 60(8) EU AI Act.
[2555] Article 60(9) EU AI Act.

PART 7. CONFIDENTIALITY

CHAPTER 30. Confidentiality Obligations

The EU AI Act requires the Commission, market surveillance authorities and notified bodies and any other natural or legal person involved in the application of the EU AI Act to respect, in accordance with EU or national law, the confidentiality of information and data obtained in carrying out their tasks and activities in such a manner as to protect, in particular:

- the intellectual property rights and confidential business information or trade secrets of a natural or legal person, including source code, except where the alleged acquisition, use or disclosure of the trade secret took place in any of the following cases[2556]:
    - for exercising the right to freedom of expression and information, including respect for the freedom and pluralism of the media;
    - for revealing misconduct, wrongdoing or illegal activity, provided that the respondent acted for the purpose of protecting the general public interest;
    - disclosure by workers to their representatives as part of the legitimate exercise by those

---

[2556] Article 78(1)(a) EU AI Act and Article 5 of the Directive (EU) 2016/943 of the European Parliament and of the Council of 8 June 2016 on the protection of undisclosed know-how and business information (trade secrets) against their unlawful acquisition, use and disclosure (OJ L 157, 15.6.2016, p. 1).

representatives of their functions in accordance with EU or national law, provided that such disclosure was necessary for that exercise; and (or)

- for the purpose of protecting a legitimate interest recognised by EU or national law;

- the effective implementation of the EU AI Act, in particular for the purposes of inspections, investigations or audits[2557];
- public and national security interests[2558];
- the conduct of criminal or administrative proceedings[2559]; and
- information classified pursuant to EU or national law[2560].

The authorities involved in the application of the EU AI Act may request only data that is strictly necessary for the assessment of the risk posed by AI systems and for the exercise of their powers[2561]. They must put in place adequate and effective cybersecurity measures to protect the security and confidentiality of the information and data obtained, and shall delete the data collected as soon as it is no longer needed for the purpose for which it was obtained, in accordance with applicable EU or national law[2562].

2557 Article 78(1)(b) EU AI Act.
2558 Article 78(1)(c) EU AI Act.
2559 Article 78(1)(d) EU AI Act.
2560 Article 78(1)(e) EU AI Act.
2561 Article 78(2) EU AU Act.
2562 *Ibid.*

In addition, information exchanged on a confidential basis between the national competent authorities or between national competent authorities and the Commission may not be disclosed without prior consultation of the originating national competent authority and the deployer when high-risk AI systems in the area of biometrics, law enforcement, migration, asylum and border control management are used by law enforcement, border control, immigration or asylum authorities and the disclosure would jeopardise public and national security interests[2563]. This exchange of information shall not include sensitive operational data in relation to the activities of law enforcement, border control, immigration or asylum authorities[2564].

When the law enforcement, immigration or asylum authorities are providers of high-risk AI systems in the areas of biometrics, law enforcement, migration, asylum and border control management, the technical documentation of these AI systems must remain within the premises of these authorities and the authorities must ensure that the market surveillance authorities can, upon request, immediately access the documentation or obtain a copy[2565]. Only staff of the market surveillance authority

---

[2563] Article 78(3) EU AU Act.
[2564] *Ibid.*
[2565] *Ibid.*

holding the appropriate level of security clearance shall be allowed to access that documentation or any copy[2566].

The EU AI Act specifically provides that the above requirements do not affect the rights or obligations of the Commission, Member States, their relevant authorities, and notified bodies with regard to the exchange of information and the dissemination of warnings, including in the context of cross-border cooperation, nor do they affect the obligations to provide information under criminal law of the Member States[2567].

The EU AI Act further permits the Commission and Member States to exchange, where necessary and in accordance with relevant provisions of international and trade agreements, confidential information with regulatory authorities of third countries with which they have concluded bilateral or multilateral confidentiality arrangements guaranteeing an adequate level of confidentiality[2568].

[2566] *Ibid.*
[2567] Article 78(4) EU AI Act.
[2568] Article 78(5) EU AI Act.

PART 8. REMEDIES

CHAPTER 31. REMEDIES

31.1 Right to lodge a complaint with a market surveillance authority

Without prejudice to other administrative or judicial remedies, any natural or legal person having grounds to consider that there has been an infringement of the provisions of the EU AI Act may submit complaints to the relevant market surveillance authority[2569]. The complaints must be taken into account for the purpose of conducting market surveillance activities, and must be handled in line with the procedures established by the market surveillance authorities[2570].

31.2 Right to explanation of individual decision-making

Any affected person subject to a decision which is taken by the deployer on the basis of the output from a high-risk AI system in the area of:

- biometrics[2571];
- education and vocational training[2572];

[2569] Article 85 EU AI Act.
[2570] *Ibid*; Regulation (EU) 2019/1020.
[2571] Point 1 Annex III EU AI Act.
[2572] Point 3 Annex III EU AI Act.

- employment, workers' management and access to self-employment[2573];
- access to and enjoyment of essential private services and essential public services and benefits[2574];
- law enforcement[2575];
- migration, asylum and border control management[2576]; and (or)
- administration of justice and democratic processes[2577]

and which produces legal effects or similarly significantly affects that person in a way that they consider to have an adverse impact on their health, safety or fundamental rights has the right to obtain from the deployer clear and meaningful explanations of the role of the AI system in the decision-making and the main elements of the decision[2578]. But this right does not apply to the use of critical infrastructure AI systems[2579] and AI systems for which exceptions from, or restrictions to, the obligation follow from EU or national law in compliance with EU law[2580].

[2573] Point 4 Annex III EU AI Act.
[2574] Point 5 Annex III EU AI Act.
[2575] Point 6 Annex III EU AI Act.
[2576] Point 7 Annex III EU AI Act.
[2577] Point 8 Annex III EU AI Act.
[2578] Article 86(1) EU AI Act.
[2579] Article 86(1) and Point 8 Annex III EU AI Act.
[2580] Article 86(2) EU AI Act.

31.3 Reporting of infringements and protection of reporting persons

The EU AI Act provides for the EU Whistleblowing Directive to apply to the reporting of infringements of the EU AI Act and the protection of persons reporting such infringements[2581]. In particular, the Whistleblowing Directive prohibits any prohibit any form, threats or attempts of retaliation against reporting persons, including[2582]:

- suspension, lay-off, dismissal or equivalent measures;
- demotion or withholding of promotion;
- transfer of duties, change of location of place of work, reduction in wages, change in working hours;
- withholding of training;
- a negative performance assessment or employment reference;
- any disciplinary measure, reprimand or other penalty, including a financial penalty;
- coercion, intimidation, harassment or ostracism;
- discrimination, disadvantageous or unfair treatment;
- failure to convert a temporary employment contract into a permanent one, where the worker had legitimate

---

[2581] Article 87 EU AI Act; Directive (EU) 2019/1937.
[2582] Article 19 Directive (EU) 2019/1937.

expectations that he or she would be offered permanent employment;

- failure to renew, or early termination of, a temporary employment contract;
- harm, including to the person's reputation, particularly in social media, or financial loss, including loss of business and loss of income;
- blacklisting on the basis of a sector or industry-wide informal or formal agreement, which may entail that the person will not, in the future, find employment in the sector or industry;
- early termination or cancellation of a contract for goods or services;
- cancellation of a licence or permit; and (or)
- psychiatric or medical referrals.

PART 9. IMPLEMENTATION OF THE EU AI ACT

CHAPTER 32. When Does the EU AI Act Enter into Force?

The EU AI Act entered into force on 1 August 2024[2583]. It is binding and directly applicable in all EU Member States[2584]. However, the implementation of the EU AI Act spans two years, from 2 February 2025 to 2 August 2027. The reasons for the staged implementation of the EU AI Act are explained in detail in the Recitals: –

"*This Regulation should apply from 2 August 2026. However, taking into account the unacceptable risk associated with the use of AI in certain ways, the prohibitions as well as the general provisions of this Regulation should already apply from 2 February 2025. While the full effect of those prohibitions follows with the establishment of the governance and enforcement of this Regulation, anticipating the application of the prohibitions is important to take account of unacceptable risks and to have an effect on other procedures, such as in civil law. Moreover, the infrastructure related to the governance and the conformity assessment system should be operational before 2 August 2026, therefore the provisions on notified*

[2583] Article 113 EU AI Act provides for its entry into force on the twentieth day following its publication in the Official Journal of the European Union. The EU AI Act was published on 12 July 2024 (OJ L, 2024/1689, 12.7.2024).

[2584] Article 113 EU AI Act.

bodies and governance structure should apply from 2 August 2025. Given the rapid pace of technological advancements and adoption of general-purpose AI models, obligations for providers of general-purpose AI models should apply from 2 August 2025. Codes of practice should be ready by 2 May 2025 in view of enabling providers to demonstrate compliance on time. The AI Office should ensure that classification rules and procedures are up to date in light of technological developments. In addition, Member States should lay down and notify to the Commission the rules on penalties, including administrative fines, and ensure that they are properly and effectively implemented by the date of application of this Regulation. Therefore the provisions on penalties should apply from 2 August 2025." [2585]

[2585] Recital 179 EU AI Act.

CHAPTER 33. The Implementation Calendar

The detailed calendar of implementation of the EU AI Act is as follows:

Effective Date	Implemented Provisions
2 February 2025	Subject Matter Scope Definitions Provider and Deployer AI Literacy Obligations Prohibited AI Practices[2586].
2 May 2025	Codes of practice to enable providers to demonstrate compliance[2587]. However, in practice the development of the codes of practice is still in progress at the time of completing this book in February 2026.

2586 These general provisions and prohibitions are set out in Chapters I and II EU AI Act. The reason for implementing these provisions soonest is "the unacceptable risk associated with the use of AI in certain ways" (Article 113 (a) and Recital 179 EU AI Act.)

2587 Recital 179 EU AI Act.

Effective Date	Implemented Provisions
2 August 2025	The obligations and procedures of notifying bodies and conformity assessment bodies[2588]; The classification and obligations of providers of general-purpose AI models and general-purpose AI models with systemic risk, and implementation of Codes of Practice for these AI models[2589]; The governance provisions including AI Office, European AI Board, Advisory forum and scientific panel of independent experts[2590]; Penalties and fines (except fines for providers of general-purpose AI models)[2591]; Confidentiality of enforcement[2592].

[2588] Chapter III Section 4; Article 113 (b) and Recital 179 EU AI Act.

[2589] Article 113(b), Chapter V and Recital 179 EU AI Act.

[2590] Article 113(b), Chapter VII and Recital 179 EU AI Act.

[2591] Articles 101 and 113(b), Chapter XII EU AI Act.

[2592] Articles 78 and 113(b) and Recital 179 EU AI Act.

Effective Date	Implemented Provisions
2 August 2026	The governance and conformity assessment system infrastructure The remaining provisions of the EU AI Act (other than those deferred to 2 August 2027 – see below)[2593].
2 August 2027	Classification as high-risk of the AI systems placed on the market or put into service independently of the products in which they are intended to be safety components and the AI systems or the products that require a third-party conformity assessment, and the corresponding obligations[2594].

[2593] Article 113 EU AI Act.
[2594] *Ibid.*

CHAPTER 34. Implementation of the EU AI Act to Date

On 25 September 2024, the European Commission issued a press release[2595] announcing that over 100 companies signed the EU artificial intelligence (AI) Pact voluntary committing to start applying the principles of the AI Act ahead of its entry into application, with at least three core actions:

- AI governance strategy to foster the uptake of AI in the organisation and work towards future compliance with the AI Act;
- Identifying AI systems likely to be categorised as high-risk under the AI Act; and
- Promoting AI literacy and awareness among staff, ensuring ethical and responsible AI development.

In addition, more than half of the signatories committed to additional pledges, including ensuring human oversight, mitigating risks, and transparently labelling certain types of AI-generated content, such as deepfakes.

By the time of completing this book in February 2026, the Commission has published the following implementing acts:

2595 https://ec.europa.eu/commission/presscorner/detail/en/ip_24_4864.

Guidelines:

- Guidelines on Prohibited Artificial Intelligence Practices[2596];
- Guidelines on the scope of the obligations for general purpose AI models[2597]; and
- Draft guidance and reporting template on serious AI incidents[2598].

Codes of Practice:

- The General-Purpose AI Code of Practice[2599]; and
- First Draft Code of Practice on Transparency of AI-Generated Content[2600].

The Commission is also taking action to boost EU innovation in AI with several new projects, including the AI factories initiative, the deployment of Common European Data Spaces, the GenA14EU initiative, the Large AI Grand Challenge, the European AI Research Council to be set up by the EU Commission, and the Apply AI Strategy to boost new industrial uses of AI.

2596 https://digital-strategy.ec.europa.eu/en/library/commission-publishes-guidelines-prohibited-artificial-intelligence-ai-practices-defined-ai-act

2597 https://digital-strategy.ec.europa.eu/en/library/guidelines-scope-obligations-providers-general-purpose-ai-models-under-ai-act

2598 https://digital-strategy.ec.europa.eu/en/consultations/ai-act-commission-issues-draft-guidance-and-reporting-template-serious-ai-incidents-and-seeks

2599 https://digital-strategy.ec.europa.eu/en/policies/contents-code-gpai

2600 https://digital-strategy.ec.europa.eu/en/library/first-draft-code-practice-transparency-ai-generated-content

Schedule: Definitions

The EU AI Act introduces 68 defined terms. In the English text of the Act, they are not in alphabetical order. For ease of reference , I organised them alphabetically in this Chapter. In addition, some terms are defined in the EU AI Act by reference to other EU legislation. I have decrypted those terms to explain what they actually mean and annotated the source in the footnotes.

AI literacy means skills, knowledge and understanding that allow providers, deployers and affected persons, taking into account their respective rights and obligations in the context of the EU AI Act, to make an informed deployment of AI systems, as well as to gain awareness about the opportunities and risks of AI and possible harm it can cause[2601];

AI Office means the Commission's function of contributing to the implementation, monitoring and supervision of AI systems and general-purpose AI models, and AI governance[2602]; references in the EU AI Act to the AI Office shall be construed as references to the Commission[2603].

AI regulatory sandbox means a controlled framework set up by a competent authority which offers

[2601] Article 3 (56) EU AI Act.
[2602] Commission Decision of 24 January 2024.
[2603] Article 3 (47) EU AI Act.

providers or prospective providers of AI systems the possibility to develop, train, validate and test, where appropriate in real-world conditions, an innovative AI system, pursuant to a sandbox plan for a limited time under regulatory supervision[2604].

AI system means a machine-based system that is designed to operate with varying levels of autonomy and that may exhibit adaptiveness after deployment, and that, for explicit or implicit objectives, infers, from the input it receives, how to generate outputs such as predictions, content, recommendations, or decisions that can influence physical or virtual environments[2605].

Authorised representative means a natural or legal person located or established in the EU who has received and accepted a written mandate from a provider of an AI system or a general-purpose AI model to, respectively, perform and carry out on its behalf the obligations and procedures established by the EU AI Act[2606].

Biometric categorisation system means an AI system for the purpose of assigning natural persons to specific categories on the basis of their biometric data, unless it is ancillary to another commercial service and strictly necessary for objective technical reasons[2607].

[2604] Article 3 (55) EU AI Act.
[2605] Article 3 (1) EU AI Act.
[2606] Article 3 (5) EU AI Act.
[2607] Article 3 (40) EU AI Act.

Biometric data means personal data resulting from specific technical processing relating to the physical, physiological or behavioural characteristics of a natural person, such as facial images or dactyloscopic data[2608].

Biometric identification means the automated recognition of physical, physiological, behavioural, or psychological human features for the purpose of establishing the identity of a natural person by comparing biometric data of that individual to biometric data of individuals stored in a database[2609].

Biometric verification means the automated, one-to-one verification, including authentication, of the identity of natural persons by comparing their biometric data to previously provided biometric data[2610].

CE marking means a marking by which a provider indicates that an AI system is in conformity with the EU AI Act's requirements to high-risk AI systems[2611] and other applicable EU harmonisation legislation providing for its affixing[2612].

Common specification means a set of the following technical specifications[2613], providing means to

---

[2608] Article 3 (34) EU AI Act.

[2609] Article 3 (35) EU AI Act.

[2610] Article 3 (36) EU AI Act.

[2611] The definition refers to the requirements set out in Chapter III, Section 2 EU AI Act.

[2612] Article 3 (24) EU AI Act.

[2613] The EU AI Act defines technical specifications by reference to as Article 2, point (4) of Regulation (EU) No 1025/2012.

comply with certain requirements established under the EU AI Act[2614]:

(a) the characteristics required of a product including levels of quality, performance, interoperability, environmental protection, health, safety or dimensions, and including the requirements applicable to the product as regards the name under which the product is sold, terminology, symbols, testing and test methods, packaging, marking or labelling and conformity assessment procedures;

(b) production methods and processes used in respect of agricultural products[2615], products intended for human and animal consumption, and medicinal products, as well as production methods and processes relating to other products, where these have an effect on their characteristics;

(c) the characteristics required of a service including levels of quality, performance, interoperability, environmental protection, health or safety, and including the requirements applicable to the provider as regards the following information to be made available to the recipient[2616]:

-> the name of the provider, his legal status and form, the geographic address at which he is established and details enabling him to be contacted rapidly and

---

2614 Article 3 (28) EU AI Act.

2615 Agricultural products are as defined in Article 38(1) TFEU.

2616 The information to be provided to the recipient is as specified in Article 22(1) to (3) of Directive 2006/123/EC.

communicated with directly and, as the case may be, by electronic means;

-> where the provider is registered in a trade or other similar public register, the name of that register and the provider's registration number, or equivalent means of identification in that register;

-> where the activity is subject to an authorisation scheme, the particulars of the relevant competent authority or the single point of contact;

-> where the provider exercises an activity which is subject to VAT, the VAT identification number[2617];

-> in the case of the regulated professions, any professional body or similar institution with which the provider is registered, the professional title and the Member State in which that title has been granted;

-> the general conditions and clauses, if any, used by the provider;

-> the existence of contractual clauses, if any, used by the provider concerning the law applicable to the contract and/or the competent courts;

[2617] The text refers to the identification number referred to in Article 22(1) of Sixth Council Directive 77/388/EEC of 17 May 1977 on the harmonisation of the laws of the Member States relating to turnover taxes – Common system of value added tax: uniform basis of assessment, but that Directive was repealed by Council Directive 2006/112/EC of 28 November 2006 on the common system of value added tax. Neither of these documents contains the specified reference to identification number. However, it can be reasonably safely guessed from the context that the identification number is VAT registration number.

-> the existence of an after-sales guarantee, if any, not imposed by law;

->the price of the service, where a price is pre-determined by the provider for a given type of service;

->the main features of the service, if not already apparent from the context;

-> the professional liability insurance or guarantees[2618], and in particular the contact details of the insurer or guarantor and the territorial coverage.

-> where the price is not pre-determined by the provider for a given type of service, the price of the service or, if an exact price cannot be given, the method for calculating the price so that it can be checked by the recipient, or a sufficiently detailed estimate;

-> as regards the regulated professions, a reference to the professional rules applicable in the Member State of establishment and how to access them;

-> information on their multidisciplinary activities and partnerships which are directly linked to the service in question and on the measures taken to avoid conflicts of interest.

-> any codes of conduct to which the provider is subject and the address at which these codes may be

[2618] The text refers to insurance and guarantees referred to in Article 23(1) Directive 2006/123/EC of the European Parliament and of the Council of 12 December 2006 on services in the internal market.

consulted by electronic means, specifying the language version available;

-> where a provider is subject to a code of conduct, or member of a trade association or professional body which provides for recourse to a non-judicial means of dispute settlement, information how to access detailed information on the characteristics of, and conditions for, the use of non-judicial means of dispute settlement.

-> the methods and the criteria for assessing the performance of construction products, i.e. any product or kit which is produced and placed on the market for incorporation in a permanent manner in construction works or parts thereof and the performance of which has an effect on the performance of the construction works with respect to the basic requirements for construction works[2619], laying down harmonised conditions for the marketing of construction products, in relation to their essential characteristics.

Conformity assessment means the process of demonstrating whether the requirements of the EU AI Act[2620] to high-risk AI systems have been fulfilled[2621];

[2619] Construction products are defined by reference to point 1 of Article 2 of Regulation (EU) No 305/2011 of the European Parliament and of the Council of 9 March 2011.

[2620] The requirements are those set out in Chapter III, Section 2 of the EU AI Act.

[2621] Article 3 (20) EU AI Act.

Conformity assessment body means a body that performs third-party conformity assessment activities, including testing, certification and inspection[2622].

Critical infrastructure means an asset, a facility, equipment, a network or a system, or a part of an asset, a facility, equipment, a network or a system, which is necessary for the provision of an essential service[2623].

Deep fake means AI-generated or manipulated image, audio or video content that resembles existing persons, objects, places, entities or events and would falsely appear to a person to be authentic or truthful[2624].

Deployer means a natural or legal person, public authority, agency or other body using an AI system under its authority except where the AI system is used in the course of a personal non-professional activity[2625]

Distributor means a natural or legal person in the supply chain, other than the provider or the importer, that makes an AI system available on the EU market[2626];

Downstream provider means a provider of an AI system, including a general-purpose AI system, which integrates an AI model, regardless of whether the AI model is provided by themselves and vertically integrated or

---

[2622] Article 3 (21) EU AI Act.

[2623] Article 3 (62) EU AI Act; the EU AI Act defines critical infrastructure by reference to Article 2, point (4), of Directive (EU) 2022/2557.

[2624] Article 3 (60) EU AI Act.

[2625] Point (13) Preamble and Article 3 (4) EU AI Act.

[2626] Article 3 (7) EU AI Act.

provided by another entity based on contractual relations[2627].

Emotion recognition system means an AI system for the purpose of identifying or inferring emotions or intentions of natural persons on the basis of their biometric data[2628]

Floating-point operation means any mathematical operation or assignment involving floating-point numbers, which are a subset of the real numbers typically represented on computers by an integer of fixed precision scaled by an integer exponent of a fixed base[2629].

General-purpose AI model means an AI model, including where such an AI model is trained with a large amount of data using self-supervision at scale, that displays significant generality and is capable of competently performing a wide range of distinct tasks regardless of the way the model is placed on the market and that can be integrated into a variety of downstream systems or applications, except AI models that are used for research, development or prototyping activities before they are placed on the market[2630].

General-purpose AI system means an AI system which is based on a general-purpose AI model and which

---

[2627] Article 3 (68) EU AI Act.
[2628] Article 3 (39) EU AI Act.
[2629] Article 3 (67) EU AI Act.

[2630] Article 3 (63) EU AI Act.

has the capability to serve a variety of purposes, both for direct use as well as for integration in other AI systems[2631].

Harmonised standard means a European standard adopted on the basis of a request made by the Commission for the application of EU harmonisation legislation[2632].

High-impact capabilities means capabilities that match or exceed the capabilities recorded in the most advanced general-purpose AI models[2633].

Importer means a natural or legal person located or established in the EU that places on the market an AI system that bears the name or trademark of a natural or legal person established in a third country[2634].

Informed consent means a subject's freely given, specific, unambiguous and voluntary expression of his or her willingness to participate in a particular testing in real-world conditions, after having been informed of all aspects of the testing that are relevant to the subject's decision to participate[2635].

Input data means data provided to or directly acquired by an AI system on the basis of which the system produces an output[2636].

2631 Article 3 (66) EU AI Act.

2632 Article 3 (27) EU AI Act; the EU AI Act defines a harmonized standard by reference to Article 2(1), point (c), of Regulation (EU) No 1025/2012.

2633 Article 3 (64) EU AI Act.

2634 Article 3 (6) EU AI Act.

2635 Article 3 (59) EU AI Act.

2636 Article 3 (33) EU AI Act.

Instructions for use means the information provided by the provider to inform the deployer of, in particular, an AI system's intended purpose and proper use[2637].

Intended purpose means the use for which an AI system is intended by the provider, including the specific context and conditions of use, as specified in the information supplied by the provider in the instructions for use, promotional or sales materials and statements, as well as in the technical documentation[2638].

Law enforcement means activities carried out by law enforcement authorities or on their behalf for the prevention, investigation, detection or prosecution of criminal offences or the execution of criminal penalties, including safeguarding against and preventing threats to public security[2639].

Law enforcement authority means:
(a) any public authority competent for the prevention, investigation, detection or prosecution of criminal offences or the execution of criminal penalties, including the safeguarding against and the prevention of threats to public security; or

[2637] Article 3 (15) EU AI Act.
[2638] Article 3 (12) EU AI Act.
[2639] Article 3 (46) EU AI Act.

(b) any other body or entity entrusted by Member State law to exercise public authority and public powers for the purposes of the prevention, investigation, detection or prosecution of criminal offences or the execution of criminal penalties, including the safeguarding against and the prevention of threats to public security[2640].

Making available on the market means the supply of an AI system or a general-purpose AI model for distribution or use on the EU market in the course of a commercial activity, whether in return for payment or free of charge[2641].

Market surveillance authority means the national authority carrying out the activities and taking the market surveillance measures[2642].

National competent authority means a notifying authority or a market surveillance authority; as regards AI systems put into service or used by EU institutions, agencies, offices and bodies, references to national competent authorities or market surveillance authorities in the EU AI Act shall be construed as references to the European Data Protection Supervisor[2643].

Non-personal data means data other than personal data, i.e. any information relating to an identified or

---

[2640] Article 3 (45) EU AI Act.

[2641] Article 3 (10) EU AI Act.

[2642] Article 3 (26) EU AI Act; the market surveillance measures are those detailed in Regulation (EU) 2019/1020.

[2643] Article 3 (48) EU AI Act.

identifiable natural person ('data subject'); an identifiable natural person is one who can be identified, directly or indirectly, in particular by reference to an identifier such as a name, an identification number, location data, an online identifier or to one or more factors specific to the physical, physiological, genetic, mental, economic, cultural or social identity of that natural person[2644].

Notified body means a conformity assessment body notified in accordance with the EU AI Act and other relevant EU harmonisation legislation[2645].

Notifying authority means the national authority responsible for setting up and carrying out the necessary procedures for the assessment, designation and notification of conformity assessment bodies and for their monitoring[2646].

Operator means a provider, product manufacturer, deployer, authorised representative, importer or distributor[2647].

Performance of an AI system means the ability of an AI system to achieve its intended purpose[2648].

Personal data means personal data i.e. any information relating to an identified or identifiable natural

---

[2644] Article 3 (51) EU AI Act; personal data is defined by reference to Article 4, point (1), of Regulation (EU) 2016/679.
[2645] Article 3 (22) EU AI Act.
[2646] Article 3 (19) EU AI Act.
[2647] Article 3 (8) EU AI Act.
[2648] Article 3 (18) EU AI Act.

person ('data subject'); an identifiable natural person is one who can be identified, directly or indirectly, in particular by reference to an identifier such as a name, an identification number, location data, an online identifier or to one or more factors specific to the physical, physiological, genetic, mental, economic, cultural or social identity of that natural person[2649].

Placing on the market means the first making available of an AI system or a general-purpose AI model on the EU market[2650].

Post-market monitoring system means all activities carried out by providers of AI systems to collect and review experience gained from the use of AI systems they place on the market or put into service for the purpose of identifying any need to immediately apply any necessary corrective or preventive actions[2651].

Post-remote biometric identification system means a remote biometric identification system other than a real-time remote biometric identification system[2652].

Profiling means any form of automated processing of personal data consisting of the use of personal data to evaluate certain personal aspects relating to a natural person, in particular to analyse or predict aspects

---

[2649] Article 3 (50) EU AI Act; the EU AI Act defines personal data by reference to Article 4, point (1), of Regulation (EU) 2016/679.

[2650] Article 3 (9) EU AI Act.

[2651] Article 3 (25) EU AI Act.

[2652] Article 3 (43) EU AI Act.

concerning that natural person's performance at work, economic situation, health, personal preferences, interests, reliability, behaviour, location or movements[2653].

Provider means a natural or legal person, public authority, agency or other body that develops an AI system or a general-purpose AI model or that has an AI system or a general-purpose AI model developed and places it on the market or puts the AI system into service under its own name or trademark, whether for payment or free of charge[2654].

Publicly accessible space means any publicly or privately owned physical place accessible to an undetermined number of natural persons, regardless of whether certain conditions for access may apply, and regardless of the potential capacity restrictions[2655].

Putting into service means the supply of an AI system for first use directly to the deployer or for own use in the EU for its intended purpose[2656].

Real-time remote biometric identification system means a remote biometric identification system, whereby the capturing of biometric data, the comparison and the identification all occur without a significant delay,

---

[2653] Article 3 (52) EU AI Act; the EU AI Act defines profiling by reference to Article 4, point (4), of Regulation (EU) 2016/679.

[2654] Article 3 (3) EU AI Act.

[2655] Article 3 (44) EU AI Act.

[2656] Article 3 (11) EU AI Act.

comprising not only instant identification, but also limited short delays in order to avoid circumvention[2657].

Real-world testing plan means a document that describes the objectives, methodology, geographical, population and temporal scope, monitoring, organisation and conduct of testing in real-world conditions[2658].

Reasonably foreseeable misuse means the use of an AI system in a way that is not in accordance with its intended purpose, but which may result from reasonably foreseeable human behaviour or interaction with other systems, including other AI systems[2659].

Recall of an AI system means any measure aiming to achieve the return to the provider or taking out of service or disabling the use of an AI system made available to deployers[2660].

Remote biometric identification system means an AI system for the purpose of identifying natural persons, without their active involvement, typically at a distance through the comparison of a person's biometric data with the biometric data contained in a reference database[2661].

Risk means the combination of the probability of an occurrence of harm and the severity of that harm[2662].

[2657] Article 3 (42) EU AI Act.
[2658] Article 3 (53) EU AI Act.
[2659] Article 3 (13) EU AI Act.
[2660] Article 3 (16) EU AI Act.
[2661] Article 3 (41) EU AI Act.
[2662] Article 3 (2) EU AI Act.

Safety component means a component of a product or of an AI system which fulfils a safety function for that product or AI system, or the failure or malfunctioning of which endangers the health and safety of persons or property[2663].

Sandbox plan means a document agreed between the participating provider and the competent authority describing the objectives, conditions, timeframe, methodology and requirements for the activities carried out within the sandbox[2664].

Sensitive operational data means operational data related to activities of prevention, detection, investigation or prosecution of criminal offences, the disclosure of which could jeopardise the integrity of criminal proceedings[2665].

Serious incident means an incident or malfunctioning of an AI system that directly or indirectly leads to any of the following:

(a) the death of a person, or serious harm to a person's health;

(b) a serious and irreversible disruption of the management or operation of critical infrastructure;

(c) the infringement of obligations under EU law intended to protect fundamental rights;

[2663] Article 3 (14) EU AI Act.
[2664] Article 3 (54) EU AI Act.
[2665] Article 3 (38) EU AI Act.

(d) serious harm to property or the environment[2666];

Special categories of personal data means personal data revealing racial or ethnic origin, political opinions, religious or philosophical beliefs, trade union membership, genetic data, biometric data uniquely identifying a natural person, data concerning health or data concerning a natural person's sex life or sexual orientation[2667].

Subject for the purpose of real-world testing, means a natural person who participates in testing in real-world conditions[2668].

Substantial modification means a change to an AI system after its placing on the market or putting into service which is not foreseen or planned in the initial conformity assessment carried out by the provider and as a result of which the compliance of the AI system with the EU AI Act's requirements to high-risk AI systems[2669] is affected or results in a modification to the intended purpose for which the AI system has been assessed[2670].

[2666] Article 3 (49) EU AI Act.

[2667] Article 3 (37) EU AI Act; the EU AI Act defines special categories of personal data by reference to Article 9(1) of Regulation (EU) 2016/679, Article 10 of Directive (EU) 2016/680 and Article 10(1) of Regulation (EU) 2018/1725. In fact, the personal data referred to in these articles are the same, so no distinction is made in the footnote.

[2668] Article 3 (58) EU AI Act.

[2669] The requirements are those set out in Chapter III, Section 2 EU AI Act.

[2670] Article 3 (23) EU AI Act.

Systemic risk means a risk that is specific to the high-impact capabilities of general-purpose AI models, having a significant impact on the EU market due to their reach, or due to actual or reasonably foreseeable negative effects on public health, safety, public security, fundamental rights, or the society as a whole, that can be propagated at scale across the value chain[2671].

Testing data means data used for providing an independent evaluation of the AI system in order to confirm the expected performance of that system before its placing on the market or putting into service[2672].

Testing in real-world conditions means the temporary testing of an AI system for its intended purpose in real-world conditions outside a laboratory or otherwise simulated environment, with a view to gathering reliable and robust data and to assessing and verifying the conformity of the AI system with the requirements of the EU AI Act and it does not qualify as placing the AI system on the market or putting it into service within the meaning of the EU AI Act, provided that all the following conditions are fulfilled[2673]:

(a) the provider or prospective provider has drawn up a real-world testing plan and submitted it to the

---

[2671] Article 3 (65) EU AI Act.
[2672] Article 3 (32) EU AI Act.
[2673] Article 3 (57) EU AI Act.

market surveillance authority in the Member State where the testing in real world conditions is to be conducted;

(b) the market surveillance authority in the Member State where the testing in real world conditions is to be conducted has approved the testing in real world conditions and the real-world testing plan; where the market surveillance authority has not provided an answer within 30 days, the testing in real world conditions and the real-world testing plan shall be understood to have been approved; where national law does not provide for a tacit approval, the testing in real world conditions shall remain subject to an authorisation;

(c) the provider or prospective provider, with the exception of providers or prospective providers of high-risk AI systems in the areas of law enforcement, migration, asylum and border control management[2674], and high-risk AI systems in the area of critical infrastructure[2675] has registered the testing in real world conditions[2676] with a Union-wide unique single identification number and with the following information[2677]:

1. A Union-wide unique single identification number of the testing in real world conditions;

[2674] These are the high-risk AI systems referred to in points 1, 6 and 7 of Annex III EU AI Act.

[2675] These are the high-risk AI systems referred to in point 2 of Annex III EU AI Act.

[2676] The registration is addressed in Article 71(4) EU AI Act.

[2677] The EU AI Act refers to information specified in Annex IX EU AI Act.

2. The name and contact details of the provider or prospective provider and of the deployers involved in the testing in real world conditions;

3. A brief description of the AI system, its intended purpose, and other information necessary for the identification of the system;

4. A summary of the main characteristics of the plan for testing in real world conditions;

5. Information on the suspension or termination of the testing in real world conditions.

the provider or prospective provider of high-risk AI systems in the areas of law enforcement, migration, asylum and border control management[2678], has registered the testing in real-world conditions in the secure non-public section of the EU database[2679] with a Union-wide unique single identification number and with the following information:

1. The name, address and contact details of the provider[2680];

2. Where another person submits information on behalf of the provider, the name, address and contact details of that person[2681];

[2678] These are the high-risk AI systems referred to in points 1, 6 and 7 of Annex III EU AI Act.

[2679] according to Article 49(4), point (d),

[2680] Article 49(4)(a) and (b) EU AI Act.

[2681] *Ibid.*

3. The name, address and contact details of the authorised representative (for non-EU providers)[2682];

4. The AI system trade name and any additional unambiguous reference allowing the identification and traceability of the AI system[2683];

5. A description of the intended purpose of the AI system and (unless the provider assessed the system as not high-risk) of the components and functions supported through this AI system[2684];

6. The status of the AI system (on the market, or in service; no longer placed on the market/in service; recalled) [2685];

7. The Member States in which the AI system has been placed on the market, put into service or made available in the EU[2686];

8. The name, address and contact details of the deployer[2687];

9. The name, address and contact details of the person submitting information on behalf of the deployer[2688];

10. The URL of the entry of the AI system in the EU database by its provider[2689];

11. An EU-wide unique single identification number of the testing in real world conditions[2690];

12. The name and contact details of the provider or prospective provider and of the deployers involved in the testing in real world conditions[2691];

13. Information on the suspension or termination of the testing in real world conditions[2692];

[2682] *Ibid.*
[2683] *Ibid.*
[2684] *Ibid.*
[2685] *Ibid.*
[2686] *Ibid.*
[2687] Article 49(4)(c) EU AI Act.
[2688] *Ibid.*
[2689] *Ibid.*
[2690] Article 49(4)(d) EU AI Act.
[2691] *Ibid.*
[2692] *Ibid.*

the provider or prospective provider of high-risk AI systems in the area of critical infrastructure[2693] has registered the testing in real-world conditions at the national level[2694];

(d) the provider or prospective provider conducting the testing in real world conditions is established in the EU or has appointed a legal representative who is established in the EU;

(e) data collected and processed for the purpose of the testing in real world conditions shall be transferred to third countries only provided that appropriate and applicable safeguards under EU law are implemented;

(f) the testing in real world conditions does not last longer than necessary to achieve its objectives and in any case not longer than six months, which may be extended for an additional period of six months, subject to prior notification by the provider or prospective provider to the market surveillance authority, accompanied by an explanation of the need for such an extension;

(g) the subjects of the testing in real world conditions who are persons belonging to vulnerable groups due to their age or disability, are appropriately protected;

[2693] These are the high-risk AI systems referred to in point 2 of Annex III EU AI Act.

[2694] The definition refers to registration "*in accordance with Article 49(5)*" which means registration at the national level.

(h) where a provider or prospective provider organises the testing in real world conditions in cooperation with one or more deployers or prospective deployers, the latter have been informed of all aspects of the testing that are relevant to their decision to participate, and given the relevant instructions for use of the AI system containing the following information[2695]:

(a) the identity and the contact details of the provider and, for non-EU provider - of its authorised representative;

(b) the characteristics, capabilities and limitations of performance of the high-risk AI system, including:

(i) its intended purpose;

(ii) the level of accuracy, including its metrics, robustness and cybersecurity against which the high-risk AI system has been tested and validated and which can be expected, and any known and foreseeable circumstances that may have an impact on that expected level of accuracy, robustness and cybersecurity;

(iii) any known or foreseeable circumstance, related to the use of the high-risk AI system in accordance with its intended purpose or under conditions of reasonably foreseeable misuse, which may lead to risks to the health and safety or fundamental rights;

(iv) where applicable, the technical capabilities and characteristics of the high-risk AI system to provide information that is relevant to explain its output;

(v) when appropriate, its performance regarding specific persons or groups of persons on which the system is intended to be used;

(vi) when appropriate, specifications for the input data, or any other relevant information in terms of the training, validation and testing data sets used, taking into account the intended purpose of the high-risk AI system;

[2695] The EU AI Act refers to information referred to in Article 13 EU AI Act.

(vii) where applicable, information to enable deployers to interpret the output of the high-risk AI system and use it appropriately;

(c) the changes to the high-risk AI system and its performance which have been pre-determined by the provider at the moment of the initial conformity assessment, if any;

(d) the human oversight measures, including the technical measures put in place to facilitate the interpretation of the outputs of the high-risk AI systems by the deployers;

(e) the computational and hardware resources needed, the expected lifetime of the high-risk AI system and any necessary maintenance and care measures, including their frequency, to ensure the proper functioning of that AI system, including as regards software updates;

(f) where relevant, a description of the mechanisms included within the high-risk AI system that allows deployers to properly collect, store and interpret the logs;

the provider or prospective provider and the deployer or prospective deployer shall conclude an agreement specifying their roles and responsibilities with a view to ensuring compliance with the provisions for testing in real world conditions under the EU AI Act and under other applicable EU and national law;

(i) the subjects of the testing in real world conditions have given informed consent, or in the case of law enforcement, where the seeking of informed consent would prevent the AI system from being tested, the testing itself and the outcome of the testing in the real world conditions shall not have any negative effect on the subjects, and their personal data shall be deleted after the test is performed;

(j) the testing in real world conditions is effectively overseen by the provider or prospective provider, as well as by deployers or prospective deployers through persons who are suitably qualified in the relevant field and have the necessary capacity, training and authority to perform their tasks;

(k) the predictions, recommendations or decisions of the AI system can be effectively reversed and disregarded.

Training data means data used for training an AI system through fitting its learnable parameters[2696].

Validation data means data used for providing an evaluation of the trained AI system and for tuning its non-learnable parameters and its learning process in order, inter alia, to prevent underfitting or overfitting[2697].

Validation data set means a separate data set or part of the training data set, either as a fixed or variable split[2698].

[2696] Article 3 (29) EU AI Act; the EU AI Act refers to the the conditions "*laid down in Article 57 or 60*" of the EU AI Act. Article 57 does not mention any conditions. Article 60(4) lists the conditions for testing in real world conditions. As the definition refers to "or" Article 60, it would be a reasonably safe guess that the conditions laid down in it should suffice.

[2697] Article 3 (30) EU AI Act.

[2698] Article 3 (31) EU AI Act.

Widespread infringement means any act or omission contrary to EU law protecting the interest of individuals, which:

(a) has harmed or is likely to harm the collective interests of individuals residing in at least two Member States other than the Member State in which:

(i) the act or omission originated or took place;

(ii) the provider concerned, or, where applicable, its authorised representative is located or established; or

(iii) the deployer is established, when the infringement is committed by the deployer;

(b) has caused, causes or is likely to cause harm to the collective interests of individuals and has common features, including the same unlawful practice or the same interest being infringed, and is occurring concurrently, committed by the same operator, in at least three Member States[2699];

Withdrawal of an AI system means any measure aiming to prevent an AI system in the supply chain being made available on the market[2700].

[2699] Article 3 (61) EU AI Act.
[2700] Article 3 (17) EU AI Act.

About the Author

Olga Markova is a practising Solicitor (England and Wales) and holds an LL.M. in Professional Legal Practice from BPP University.

She studied EU law as part of her solicitor qualification and has over two decades of professional experience working with EU law and regulatory frameworks.

This book reflects her professional focus on the intersection of artificial intelligence and law, and is intended to support legal, compliance, and policy professionals navigating the practical application of the EU AI Act and its implementing guidance.

Further information about the author and contact details for professional or licensing enquiries are available at https://lawcis.co.uk .

www.ingramcontent.com/pod-product-compliance
Lightning Source LLC
LaVergne TN
LVHW052012200926
848481LV00005B/1470